Understanding Physical Education

UNDERSTANDING
PHYSICAL EDUCATION

Ken Green

SAGE Publications
Los Angeles • London • New Delhi • Singapore

First published 2008

SAGE Publications Ltd
1 Oliver's Yard
55 City Road
London EC1Y 1SP

SAGE Publications Inc
2455 Teller Road
Thousand Oaks, California 91320

SAGE Publications India Pvt Ltd
B 1/I 1 Mohan Cooperative Industrial Area
Mathura Road, Post Bag 7
New Delhi 110 044

SAGE Publications Asia-Pacific Pte Ltd
33 Pekin Street #02-01
Far East Square
Singapore 048763

Library of Congress Control Number: 2007931044

British Library Cataloguing in Publication data
A catalogue record for this book is available from the British Library

ISBN 978-1-4129-2112-1
ISBN 978-1-4129-2113-8 (pbk)

Typeset by Dorwyn, Wells, Somerset
Printed by Replika Press Pvt., India
Printed on paper from sustainable resources

For my parents, Betty and Stanley

Contents

Introduction		1
1	The Nature and Purposes of Physical Education	7
2	Policy and Physical Education	23
3	The 'State' of Physical Education	45
4	Extra-Curricular Physical Education	62
5	Assessment and Examinations in Physical Education	78
6	Health and Physical Education	96
7	Youth Sport and Physical Education	117
8	Gender and Physical Education	137
9	Social Class and Physical Education	154
10	Ethnicity and Physical Education	167
11	Disability, Special Educational Needs and Physical Education	187
12	Teaching Physical Education	207
Conclusion		227
References		*236*
Index		*269*

Introduction

In very many countries worldwide, young people between the ages of approximately 5 and 16 experience physical education (PE) on a reasonably regular basis. This is, then, a book about something almost everyone is familiar with and about which many people – including politicians, sportsmen and women, the media, parents and pupils, as well as physical educationalists themselves – hold deeply felt, often polarized views. Indeed, because they are students or practitioners of PE and sport, readers of this book are far more likely to be 'true believers' than sceptics in the value of PE and sport. With that in mind, it is worth establishing at the outset what the book is and is not trying to do.

The book is primarily intended for those either studying PE or training to be teachers. It is not a book about how to teach PE. Rather, it represents an attempt to understand PE by examining some of its most fundamental issues (for example, the relationship between PE, sport and health) and enduring themes (such as the nature and purposes of PE) as well as some of the more significant developments in the subject in recent years (examinations in PE, for example).

The book starts from the premise that there is a tendency for many people professionally engaged with PE to write and talk about the subject in a manner that not only takes certain beliefs for granted, but also presents them as orthodox, even factual. Such discourses often express unexamined value assumptions. Examples of research in PE carried out under the shadow of an ideological agenda are plentiful. In such cases, analyses tend to be juxtaposed with the authors' views about the way things ought to be. In order to cast a suitably critical eye over claims and counter-claims and, in so doing, arrive at a more considered, and empirically grounded, perspective on contemporary PE, the book attempts to avoid offering value judgements on the various topics under scrutiny. Indeed, one of the objectives is to recast in a new light some of the taken-for-granted assumptions about PE. Many of the chapters contribute to ongoing debate by challenging some orthodoxies and debunking a number of myths about PE.

Whatever the ideological position of the reader it would be difficult to deny that PE and school sport elicit considerable political and media attention. Physical educationalists in the UK are said to be living and working in 'exciting times' (Taplin, 2005: 3) as a consequence of substantial financial investment and political attention. The plethora of PE and sports-related initiatives introduced by governments and sporting bodies, the ongoing interest among the media, as well as the rapid expansion of sports-related programmes at university level tell us something about the topicality of PE and sport in school more generally.

Yet there are those who would argue that the growth of sport and sporting organizations has led to PE losing its coherence. For this reason it is said to have become increasingly difficult to write an introductory text for a topic (PE) that is hard to 'pin down', as its terrain develops and its borders become more contested and nebulous. Nonetheless, most commentators could readily identify a good deal of continuity in PE; for example, continued concern about the relationship between PE and health promotion and ongoing or lifelong participation in sport. There have, however, been changes alongside the undoubted continuities. Physical educationalists are now, for example, one part of a much larger network of people interested in the relationship between PE and youth sport, educational achievement and health than previously.

Some of the changes or developments witnessed in PE are short term, while others occur over a lengthy time span. Some of the changes are cyclical (for example, with each new generation of PE teachers), while some are episodic (such as the introduction of a National Curriculum for PE or the development of Specialist Sports Colleges). Still other changes are cumulative and are reflected in long-term, less obvious, transformations or trends; the academicization and sportization of PE, for example. The book attempts to identify the more significant changes and continuities, not least in order to speculate in the Conclusion on the direction in which PE might be developing.

THE SCOPE AND FOCUS OF THE BOOK

Many of the most important issues in contemporary PE involve processes beyond the gym or changing rooms, and even beyond the school gates. To begin to appreciate the assumptions upon which practices in, and beliefs about, PE are based, it is necessary to travel some distance from PE. Inevitably, the book delves into territory some of which is adjacent to PE (such as youth sport), some of which is further away (for example, public policy, ethnicity and obesity).

It is inevitable with a book of this kind that decisions are made about what and, equally importantly, what not to include. A comprehensive understanding of PE requires an appreciation of the historical emergence and development of the subject and its antecedents. I have, however, found it necessary to omit such a history from this text in order to go into greater depth in some areas (such as health-related exercise [HRE] and youth sport) that are particularly significant aspects of contemporary PE. This decision was made a good deal easier by the existence of a superlative text on the topic in the form of David Kirk's (1992) *Defining Physical Education*.

Although this book makes frequent reference to PE in primary schools, the focus is on secondary school PE, because it is here that the subject takes on the identity of a specialized subject taught by specialist teachers in specialist settings. The bulk of what is known as PE as an institution occurs in, or is significantly influenced by, secondary school PE.

Examples from England (and, to some extent, Wales and the rest of the UK) will provide many of the 'case studies' for each of the chapters. Nevertheless, it is possible to identify 'commonality in the provision for physical education within the various (European) education systems' (Fisher, 2003: 137) as well as common trends and issues in policy towards PE across Europe and worldwide. Consequently, the cross-cultural and international relevance of the various topics – such as the nature and purposes of PE, HRE, youth sport, gender, class and ethnicity, and teaching – to understanding PE in all parts of the world are, even where self-evident, highlighted by reference to international research.

TERMINOLOGY

All the chapters explore and, where necessary, define concepts central to them in order to indicate how particular terms are used. For the purposes of the book, 'PE' will be taken to refer to those physical activities and sports organized (and usually overseen) by PE teachers or their representatives during the (sometimes extended) school day and week. Very often this includes what some might prefer to call school sport, and that issue proves to be a leitmotif of the book. The term 'sport' is taken to incorporate both competitive game-contests (that is, sports such as football, hockey, basketball and badminton) and more recreationally oriented physical activities (such as swimming, aerobics and cycling) often referred to as 'lifestyle' or 'lifetime' activities. Sometimes, the phrase 'sport and physical activities' is used in order to highlight the significance of recreational or 'lifestyle' activities to the point being made.

Many countries use the term 'elementary' to refer to the junior end of the schooling spectrum; broadly speaking, ages 5 to 11. The preference in this text is for its English equivalent – namely, 'primary schools' – purely because much of the data provided in the illustrative case studies of England specifically refer to primary pupils.

THE STRUCTURE AND PERSPECTIVES OF THE BOOK

The book has a conventional and logical structure. The first few chapters cover the 'fundamentals' of PE, namely, the ostensible nature and purposes of PE, policy affecting the subject and the 'state' of contemporary PE. Thereafter, the focus is on the aforementioned enduring themes and recent developments. In some cases, the length of the chapter reflects not merely what I take to be the particular significance of the topic (for example, youth sport) but also the extensive and multidimensional nature of the relevant material (as in the case of health and PE). Of necessity, many chapters that are deserving of books in themselves appear truncated.

It is often said that PE is a field with open borders and, precisely because it is impossible to capture from a single perspective, its study tends to be a multidisciplinary and sometimes interdisciplinary undertaking. Consequently, the book incorporates pedagogical, philosophical, physiological, psychological and sociological perspectives as the subject matter requires. Nevertheless, it is underpinned, usually implicitly, by a broadly sociological perspective. In other words, it takes as read the premise that processes such as education are socially constructed and, as a consequence, are processes. For this reason PE cannot be described with any sense of finality.

ACKNOWLEDGEMENTS

The dramatic growth of robust bodies of knowledge related to PE over the past few decades has enabled the construction of a much more evidence-based and adequate portrait of PE. A text of this kind is only possible because of the body of work produced by many colleagues researching PE around the world. I hope that my reliance upon their work throughout the book will stand as some kind of testimony not only to their contributions, but also to the vibrant nature of research into PE both now and in the recent past.

In addition to the above general acknowledgement, I want to thank a number of colleagues for their constructive criticism on drafts of the various chapters. I am grateful to Mike McNamee not only for his insightful comments on Chapter 1 but also for the much needed philosophy tutorial that accompanied them. For their insightful comments on Chapter 2, my thanks go to Patrick Murphy, Daniel Bloyce and Andy Smith. I take the fact that each managed to keep their comments to below three figures as an indication that I am, in sociological terms at least, making progress! For their useful advice on Chapter 3, I owe a good deal to Ken Hardman and Joe Marshall and I am particularly grateful to my colleague Helen Odhams for her thoughtful commentary on Chapter 5. Chapter 6 bears the hallmarks of salutary advice from Ivan Waddington, Miranda Thurston and Luke Jones, and for her helpful comments on Chapter 8 I am indebted to Anne Flintoff. Similarly, the commentaries provided by Tansin Benn and Tess Kay were immensely useful in Chapter 10. Tess has been the very epitome of a 'critical friend' and I am particularly appreciative of her time and effort. For their advice on Chapter 11, I am grateful to Hayley Fitzgerald and Andy Smith. My sincere thanks are also due to Susan Capel and my colleague Steve Tones for their rich and detailed feedback on Chapter 12. I particularly want to thank John Evans, a founding father of the sociology of PE, not only for his thoughts on my concluding remarks but more especially for his continuing support. Not for the first time, nor hopefully the last, I am deeply indebted to Miranda Thurston for her comments on the whole of the manuscript. Last, but by no means least, I must thank Marianne Lagrange and Matthew Waters at Sage Publications for their support and forebearance in seeing the project through to completion.

It has been one of the features of correspondence with colleagues that their observations and criticisms have not only been pertinent and, where necessary, critical but always sympathetic and helpful. Where I appear to have ignored their advice it has not necessarily been because I have disagreed. In some instances, it has simply not been feasible to go into much greater depth or detail because of the word limit on the book. In other cases, where I have not been entirely persuaded by their observations, I fully accept that my analysis may well prove to be deficient and absolve them of any blame for my inadequacies. In all cases, I hope that colleagues will recognize where I have attempted to do their comments justice. Where there are deficiencies with the arguments contained in the book, I claim sole responsibility: *Understanding Physical Education* is a process in which I feel a little further along now than when I began!

The Nature and Purposes of Physical Education

Around the time when the National Curriculum for Physical Education (NCPE) for England and Wales was taking shape, Alderson and Crutchley (1990: 38) articulated a long-standing, and seemingly fundamental, concern for the subject-community of PE when they asked, 'But what is it that children should know of, be able to do, and appreciate about (the) activities in which they participate?' Alderson and Crutchley (1990: 38–40) observed that 'there appears to be no professional consensus regarding what being "physically educated" really means' nor 'how that state is best achieved'. They concluded that, 'in short there is, in large measure, a simple belief that involving children in a selection of physical activities will achieve valuable educational ends'.

Alderson and Crutchley need not have appeared so surprised, however, for the nature and purposes of PE have been keenly contested for more than half a century. The fact that the Qualifications and Curriculum Authority (QCA, 2005a: 1) saw fit to ask the question 'What is the purpose of physical education in the school curriculum?' more than a decade on from the introduction of the NCPE in England and Wales, illustrates the persistent and enduring uncertainty surrounding the nature and purposes of PE. This lack of philosophical and conceptual coherence is not only an issue in English-speaking countries; Naul (2003) talks of the absence of a consensus on the nature and purposes of PE across Europe. This state of confusion and uncertainty appears ironic when one considers the extensive academic literature since the 1960s on education per se and PE and sport in particular.

This chapter examines the debate surrounding what PE *is* or *should* be about – that is, its purported nature and purposes – through the eyes of those who theorize the subject, in the first instance. Recognizing that philosophers' views regarding the nature and purposes of the subject might not be shared by those who either deliver or are on the receiving end of PE, the chapter concludes with a brief portrayal of the perspectives of PE teachers and their pupils. This serves as a basis for exploration of the nature of PE, in practice rather than theory, in the remainder of the book.

THEORIZING THE NATURE AND PURPOSES OF PHYSICAL EDUCATION

Philosophical deliberations in the mainstream tradition of English-speaking philosophy typically involve arguments or statements rather than findings, and tend not to point to empirical evidence for their justifications. Rather, they tend to take the form of 'microscopic linguistic scrutiny' (McNamee, 2005: 2) involving 'a number of fine conceptual distinctions' (Kilminster, 1998: 8) intended to establish the precise meaning of concepts central to the topic under scrutiny.

The conventional starting point for educational philosophers in the liberal-analytical tradition has been to establish what is meant by the key concept of education and to draw out from this the implications for *physical education*; in other words, to reduce education to a central case and tease out the key features or criteria of that case (McNamee, 2005). What is conventionally labelled the 'Peters–Hirst' (and sometimes 'Petersian') approach to exploring the concept of education – after the two architects of liberal analytical philosophy of education in the UK, Paul Hirst and Richard Peters (1970) – starts from the premise that education has fundamentally to do with *knowledge* of a *valuable* kind. Knowledge, in turn, is said to take two general forms – propositional (or theoretical)[1] and practical. Propositional knowledge is said to be made up of two components: information and judgement (White, 2006). Practical knowledge refers to skills or abilities – what Peters, rather scathingly in the eyes of physical educationalists, viewed as the 'knack' of performing some practical activity or other. For analytical philosophers of education, however, only the former – theoretical knowledge – could be said to be educationally valuable because only it possesses the capacity to transform people's comprehension of the world around them and thus enhance their capacity to act upon it as rational, autonomous individuals – the goal par excellence of a liberal education. For Hirst (1974), anything labelled 'education' must be fundamentally about the development of theoretical or propositional knowledge. Thus, the view of educationally worthwhile knowledge as principally concerned with the development of intelligence – exercising good judgement in adapting means to ends (White, 2006) – led to the conclusion that education refers to 'the initiation of the unlearned into those intrinsically worthwhile forms of knowledge that were constitutive of rational mind' (McNamee, 2005: 2). On this 'standard', or orthodox, view what distinguishes education from other forms of socialization and training is concern with the initiation of pupils into the various (inevitably theoretical) forms of rational enquiry and associated bodies of knowledge (Carr, 1997) which, ostensibly at least, form the basis for the cultivation of individual autonomy.

This line of argument provides the foundations for an 'essentially *academic*' (Reid, 1996a: 95, emphasis in the original), curriculum model; one revolving around taxonomies of intelligence and, consequently, a number (typically seven or eight) supposedly logically distinct forms of knowledge (in the sense that they comprise differing *ways* of knowing, or methodologies, as well as differing *bodies of knowledge*). These forms of knowledge are, in turn, manifest in distinct academic subject disciplines (such as mathematics, English, science, geography, history and religious studies), among which those subjects grounded in abstract thought (such as philosophy itself) are deemed the most important and widely prized (in the sense that they point the way to or 'open up' just what human understanding consists of).

From the 1970s, the PE subject-community (and PE academics, in particular) became increasingly preoccupied with the negative connotations of the 'standard', academic conception of education and the associated purposes of schooling. Philosophers of education had 'cast a dim light' on PE (McNamee, 2005: 1) on the basis that the 'value' of the subject (whatever that was) did not reside in its contribution to the development of rational, autonomous individuals. If PE is not concerned with the acquisition and mastery of theoretical knowledge, the argument went, it is – by the very nature of education – non-academic and thus non-educational. In other words, physical activities have no educational significance in themselves and only acquire such significance when they are treated as contexts for pursuing goals and values which are truly educational and, according to the orthodox philosophy of education, these are essentially theoretical or propositional (Reid, 1996a).

As McNamee (2005) observes, the hegemony of the Peters–Hirst thesis left physical educationalists with two options: first, to acknowledge that the 'traditional' PE curriculum, in the games-dominated form it had developed, had either to 'undergo a radical change of identity and redefine itself as an academic subject in the school curriculum, or else acknowledge its incorrigibly marginal status' (Reid, 1997: 6) – in other words, to accept the non-academic and therefore non-educational (or, at best, marginal) status of PE; or, second, to argue that despite appearances, the physical activities which comprise the familiar PE curriculum might somehow be shown to have academic significance and thus educational worth (Reid, 1996a; 1996b).

To many physical educationalists it became apparent that, if the possession of academic credentials was a condition of entry to education proper, then they were (and remain) obliged to direct their subject away from 'the familiar idea of the teaching and learning of practical physical activities' (Reid, 1996a: 95) – necessarily made problematic by the conventional conceptions of knowledge and education – and towards 'academic' aspects of PE; that is, towards the *study* of sport (as illustrated by publicly recognized examinations in PE) rather than the *practice* of sport. Caught in the glare of the prevailing 'academic' view of education, physical educationalists have been constrained to distinguish between the practical performance of physical activities that typically constitute PE and the academic or theoretical knowledge which these activities are claimed to be a vehicle for. This tendency has been exacerbated by a perceived need to bolster the place of PE on the 'academic' curriculum at a time of growing competition for curriculum space. According to Reid (1996a: 102), this 'new orthodoxy' redefines PE 'in terms of the opportunities which it provides for theoretical study' and, in doing so, implicitly accepts the superiority of the kinds of knowledge that are expressed predominantly in written or verbal forms rather than by practical demonstration. The orthodoxy is said to be illustrated by several relatively recent trends: the dramatic growth of examinable PE; the proliferation of PE/Sports Science degrees; and the widespread acceptance and adoption of the academicization of PE in current curriculum and assessment policy.

Unsurprisingly, perhaps, over the past 30 years or more the PE community has attempted to extricate itself from the awkward theoretical corner that the standard 'academic' conception of education contrives and which has left the subject on the horns of the recreationalism/academic dilemma. The most popular way in which physical educationalists have tried to justify the educational worth of PE has been to point to the contribution it is said to make to other, supposedly intellectual, dimensions of education. In this manner, sport has been projected as a vehicle for (intellectual) lessons in character development, moral education, health education and aesthetic education. The fact that aesthetic activities were one of the supposed 'forms of knowledge' propagated by Hirst and other liberal philosophers of education in the 1960s allowed a number of philosophers to offer the supposed aesthetic aspects of various activities (for example, in the form of dance and movement education) as a justification for PE, if not quite for the *educational* worth of the subject. Similarly, moral education provided a suitable opportunity to suggest that one aspect of PE, competitive sports (and particularly team games), provided young people with lessons in morality (in relation to fair play, for example) as well as personal characteristics or virtues (such as self-discipline, perseverance and courage) and social characteristics (such as loyalty and civic virtues of subordination to the collective). When viewed in this light, it is unsurprising that the PE profession has long tended to parade its supposed wider social objectives publicly among its professional aims (Evans and Davies, 1986).

Whatever the merits or demerits of such approaches to justifying PE, McNamee reminds us that there are, in essence, three ways of responding to the lines of argument of the 'Peters–Hirst' kind:

1 to dispute the position in its own terms
2 to 'deny the presuppositions of those terms'
3 to 'assert or argue for a counter position' (McNamee, 2005: 4).

In the remainder of the chapter this framework is used to explore, in turn, the three most important responses to the orthodox conception of PE.

Arguing for the educational nature and worth of practical knowledge

The first of McNamee's options amounts to accepting the premise of the 'standard' conception of education – that the essence of education is theoretical knowledge – but challenging its seemingly inevitable consequence – the marginalization of PE – in short, to argue for the educational worth of practical knowledge as *knowledge* of a *valuable* kind. Andrew Reid has been one of the more recent in a long line of philosophers (see, for example, Aspin, 1976; Carr, 1979; 1997; Whitehead, 2001; 2006) who have argued the case for an alternative approach to justifying the place of PE on the curriculum. Not content with the traditional response to this dilemma – in the form of the reconciliation of the traditional content of the PE programme with the academic requirements of the orthodox view of education (via character development, for example) – Reid argues for an alternative reading of the concept of education 'broad enough to accommodate practical and physical as well as theoretical and academic pursuits' (Carr, 1997: 196). In accepting the starting point (the centrality of knowledge to education) but denying the conclusion (that *only* intellectual knowledge counts as educationally valuable) of the Peters–Hirst thesis, Reid's position represents a modification of the orthodox academic view of education by making a case for various forms of practical activity and skill as educationally significant knowledge (Carr, 1997). For Reid, practical knowledge ('knowing how') is, in its own way, every bit as sophisticated and educationally valuable as propositional knowledge ('knowing that'). Reid also dismisses the claim that practical knowledge is based on theoretical knowledge and is, in effect, reducible to theoretical knowledge (of the kinds that conventionally are studied as distinct, academic, subjects in their own right, within the field of Sports Science, such as biomechanical analysis and the psychology of motor-skill acquisition). He dismisses the notion that there is a kind of intellectual reasoning process at work which precedes actual practical performance and that the latter cannot take place without the former. For Reid (1996a), accepting this view makes redundant the felt need of many physical educationalists to search for and then highlight (or simply 'bolt on') the supposed 'academic' components of PE. The net result of

Reid's position is that it ceases to be the status of PE which is seen as problematic but, rather, the academic view of education and its preoccupation with theoretical knowledge.

Working within the analytical philosophical tradition, Parry (1998) and Carr (1997) point to a number of problems with attempts, such as Reid's, to find educational worth in the games and activities that make up the conventional PE curriculum. Many would be quite willing to accept, they argue, that there is knowledge of a kind in practical performance. Nevertheless, it is not knowledge of the *right* kind to bestow educational significance on physical activities of the kind associated with PE. Reid and others who attempt such an approach are, they argue, simply unable to show where the supposed educational significance or value of the practical knowledge expressed in practical performance lies; it neither helps illuminate other knowledge nor develops individuals' ability to think rationally or insightfully. The upshot is that Reid and others who share his point of view are unable to provide compelling grounds for the inclusion of PE practices within the school curriculum.

Still working within the analytical framework, Carr (1997) provides an escape route for those who, like Reid, appear determined to find a justification for the place of PE. Carr suggests that the solution lies in observing what he views as the crucial conceptual distinction between education and schooling. In other words, while education necessarily involves the inculcation of academic knowledge, schooling incorporates other, additional knowledge and skills, whether vocational, recreational, domestic or otherwise. In short, schools 'have a plurality of goals and purposes – only one (though a large one) of which is educational' (Carr, 1997: 203). For Carr (and Barrow, 1983, before him) talk of *education* (conceptualized in Peters's [1966], terms as initiation into worthwhile knowledge that transforms our understanding of the world around us) when one means *schooling* (initiation into activities that prepare us for adult life) and schooling when one means *education* is a confusion that bedevils much theorizing about education let alone PE. For Carr (1997), initiation into 'ways of knowing' is best viewed as the defining role of 'education', while initiation into 'valuable cultural practices' (discussed below) is the defining role of 'schooling', and it is this latter dimension that allows PE into the frame.

Much of the debate about the nature and purposes of PE (and education) has taken place against a backdrop of widespread acceptance of the fundamental tenets of the analytical philosophical approach – an approach that has been heavily criticized in a manner consistent with the second of McNamee's alternatives, namely, to challenge the starting point of the analytical conception of education.

Pointing to the socially constructed 'nature' of PE

Overlapping the development of linguistic philosophy, and its widespread application to education from the 1960s onwards, was the growth of two inter-related branches of sociology, namely, the sociologies of knowledge and of education. Together, they focused attention on the social construction not only of education per se but of knowledge itself. Educational sociologists took as their starting point not abstract (and, in their view, sterile) debates about the essence and meaning of terms such as 'education' but, rather, the ways in which school curricula and subjects could be seen to be the constructions of groups of influential people and which tended, inevitably, to reflect particular ideologically dominant values and preferences (Kirk, 1992). In this regard, curricula as a whole, as well as school subjects in particular, were said to reflect the struggles between groups of people who strove to establish their own preferred versions of their subjects, and nowhere more so than in PE.

Similarly, and with the growing criticisms of philosophical perspectives on social processes (Kilminster, 1998), a number of philosophers (see, for example, McNamee, 2005; White, 2006) have themselves pointed to the ways in which the analytical philosophical perspective – enshrined in the Peters–Hirst conception of education – was a reflection of the ideological predispositions of liberal philosophers of the time. When they claimed to be exploring PE from a neutral, value-free perspective, analytical philosophers of education conveniently overlooked the fact that the analytical approach itself rested upon a number of (ideological) assumptions and implicit value judgements. Attention was drawn to the fact that the abiding concern of philosophers such as Peters and Hirst was representing education as a vehicle for the development of intelligent, rational, self-governing and, as a corollary, 'free' individuals that reflected the dominant tradition of thought at the time – in the form of the liberal ideal of a society of autonomous individuals. This was, in short, a conception of education based on the cultural world – and a hegemonic liberal ideology – of the time rather than the value-neutral, empirical study of education that it purported to be (White, 2006). On this view, education needs to be understood for what it is in practice, namely, a normative concept, in the sense that it is shaped by a variety of 'culture-specific, historical and political factors' (McNamee, 1998: 88). 'Under the banner of ideological neutrality', McNamee (2005: 4) observes, the analytical philosophy of education 'seemed to smuggle in an awful lot of values' and, in truth, 'entailed little more than a crystallization of the kind of curriculum favoured by British grammar and public schools in the UK over the last 100 years or so'. The ideological roots of what was to count as education and appropriate curriculum content were planted firmly in theories of innate intelligence traced back to early Protestant beliefs in predestination and the power of rational thought (White, 2006). The ramifications for the structure of post-Second World War schooling in, for example, the UK – grammar[2] schools with their more academic curricula based on distinct subject disciplines for the innately intelligent and secondary schools for the rest – has had far-reaching implications for education policy, the structure of schooling and the curriculum and, eventually, PE.

The liberal-analytical philosophical tradition has directed academic reflection upon PE towards a search for supposedly timeless, essential, necessary truths; not least because philosophers have aspirations to reach such higher truths. But there is and can be no sharp line of demarcation between what is or should be inside and what is or should be outside PE (McNamee, 2005). We are bound to concur with McNamee (1998: 88) when he argues that those who look for conceptual unity are wasting their time: 'There is no meaningful essence to the concept of PE in that way.' Rather, it is necessary to 'recognise the inherent openness of the concept of physical education; pluralism in activities, pluralism in values'. While not so rootless as to be an *essentially* contested concept, there appear to be a good many equally legitimate conceptions of what counts as education. Although it makes no sense to view education as meaning whatever we want it to mean, a concept such as education (which revolves around the notion of upbringing and introducing young people to what any given society at a particular point in time views as knowledge of a valuable kind) inevitably has a wide variety of potential interpretations.

The third response to the standard or orthodox conception of education is to focus attention on the value dimension of the 'education equals knowledge of a valuable kind' equation. This is a more radical position and one which views it as unnecessary to start with a template for PE that revolves around distinguishing between superior or inferior kinds of knowledge in educational terms. Instead, this position involves arguing for a distinctly different conception of the nature and purposes of PE – a 'general model of education as initiation into sports and games as major cultural institutions' (McNamee, 2005: 5). This, as we shall see, is not only McNamee's preferred position but that of many contemporary PE academics and, implicitly at least, teachers.

Justifying sport as a 'valued[3] cultural practice'

A number of educational philosophers have argued that the starting point for debating the purposes of education and thus PE should not be the concept of education as such, precisely because there is no conceptual essence or 'nature' to education and therefore no essential criteria by which to measure it. Rather, the starting point should be the preparation of young people for adult life in their society. Then, 'what we will want to achieve in educating will be determined by what we think desirable in adult human beings' (O'Hear, 1981: 1). This is an account of education 'based on the notion of a worthwhile life' rather than identifying those activities that ostensibly inform and develop the mind, although the latter may well be an aspect of the former.

Ironically, given his position as an architect and 'high priest' of liberal analytical philosophy of education, Paul Hirst proclaimed his own 'change of mind' (Hirst, 1994) in the mid-1990s. In line with the alternative starting point signified in the notion of 'a worthwhile life', Hirst came to view education as the initiation of young people into 'valued cultural practices' (or 'valued human practices' as they are sometimes referred to) rather than initiation into 'forms of knowledge'. Formal education (in school) from this perspective involves not so much the initiation of young people into 'ways of knowing' but, rather, into those distinctive forms of activity worthwhile in life (Arnold, 1992; 1997) – valued cultural practices. From this perspective one such significant cultural practice, for very many people, in very many countries around the world, would be sport and physical activity. If education is conceived of in terms of initiation into such practices, then PE justifies its place on the curriculum as initiation into the valued cultural practice of sport:

> it is our duty ... to open up to our students the significant sporting inheritance of our cultures so that they may come to savour its joys and frustrations and know a little about that aspect of the cultures which sporting practices instantiate (for no one would seriously deny their enormous significance in modern societies). (McNamee, 2005: 7)

The evident status of sport as an established cultural institution confirms for many that sport is not only appropriate subject matter for education and for schools but also for PE. The view of sport as a valued cultural practice has found practical manifestation in recent years in the notion of 'sport education' – a conception of PE very much associated with the proselytizing of an American physical educationalist, Daryl Siedentop (1994) and one which has taken hold at the level of academe (see, for example, Kirk, 2005) if not at the level of PE practice (Penney et al., 2002). On this view, PE should be about more than simply teaching the skills and knowledge necessary for playing sport but, rather, would involve teaching pupils about the culture of sport. It would mean, in other words, initiating young people into the 'rituals, values and traditions of a sport' (Siedentop, 1994: 7) – the 'customs and conventions' (Arnold, 1997: 71) – as well as the skills and practicalities. 'Sport education', according to Siedentop (1994: 4), involves helping youngsters to 'develop as competent, literate, and enthusiastic sportspeople'.

In the next section, I try to show how even though academics may have moved on, in philosophical terms, the standard conception of PE continues to cast a lengthy shadow over the 'philosophies' of PE teachers. Before doing so, however, it is worth noting how what might be termed official 'definitions' of PE – because they are encapsulated in legislation in England and Wales, for example – express the main debates surrounding justifications for PE.

THE DEBATE CAPTURED IN OFFICIAL DEFINITIONS

Among a vast array of claims for the benefits of PE, successive NCPE have consistently displayed a tendency to conceptualize PE in terms of both sides of the philosophical debate over the nature and purposes of PE. In other words, the NCPE has tended to point up the educational nature and worth of the activities that constitute PE at the same time as identifying sport as a valued cultural practice. In claiming that PE 'educates young people *in* and *through* the use and knowledge of the body and its movement', the original NCPE for England and Wales (DES, 1991; emphasis added) grounded the justification for the subject in the development of theoretical knowledge and practical skills and in the initiation of youngsters into the practices and traditions of sport.

Similarly, the latest iteration of the NCPE (to be introduced in 2008) includes a section on the importance of physical education in which it points to many of the justificatory themes to be found in the philosophical debates surrounding the nature and purposes of PE. The notion of 'informing the mind' rather than merely 'using' it – the supposedly theoretical or propositional dimension of the standard conception – is referred to obliquely at three points: first, in the so-called underpinning knowledge, 'an understanding of the concepts that underpin success'; second, in making intellectual judgements about 'how to select and apply appropriate tactics, strategies and compositional ideas'; and, third, in contributing to pupils' personal and social development. The major alternative philosophical justification of valued cultural practices (and, by extension, sport education) is alluded to in the claim that pupils learn to 'take on different roles and responsibilities, including leadership, coaching and officiating'.

The twin ideas of developing sporting skills (in order to facilitate participation in sport as a valued cultural practice) and justifying sport as a vehicle for informing and developing the mind are also to be found in the Position Statement on Physical Education of what, until recently, was the lead body for PE in the UK (the Physical Education Association of the United Kingdom [PEA-UK][4]), which stated that PE involves both 'learning to move' and 'moving to learn' (Stewart, 2005: 33).

So much for the 'official' conceptualization of PE to be found in the NCPE for England and Wales, what do those involved at the 'sharp end' – PE teachers and their pupils – think the subject is about?

PHYSICAL EDUCATION ACCORDING TO PE TEACHERS

Coherent theoretical conceptions of PE, of the kind associated with academic 'philosophizing', are very difficult to find on the ground, that is, among PE teachers themselves. Nevertheless, it is possible to tease out a number of features of their views from various studies of PE teachers.

Mason explored the views of secondary heads of PE departments regarding differences between PE and sport and found 'broad agreement among the secondary school Heads of PE that "PE" is a wider concept than "sport"' (1995a: 3). In rehearsing the view that PE should be seen as part of 'the education of the whole child whereas "sport" is an activity undertaken to provide that education' (1995a: 3), these heads of PE echoed the widely held view – at least among academics – that PE cannot simply be reduced to sport (see, for example, Kay, 2003). The 'standard', academically oriented view of physical *education* as the acquisition of 'intellectual' knowledge – particularly in relation to personal and social development – lay just below the surface in several quotations from teachers in Mason's (1995a) study who described PE, variously, as '*educating* children *through* physical means', 'an *educational* experience whereas sport is participation in an activity'; 'more than participation … looking at the *personal and social aspects of their development*', 'not just teaching skills'; 'teach[ing] them a little bit more *about themselves, about others, the social aspects of PE, about the rights and wrongs of the way they regard other people*' (cited in Mason, 1995a: 3; emphases added).

The prevalence of such views seems to confirm the belief that the standard conception of education (and, thus, PE) is tantamount to an orthodoxy, in the sense that it is so widely accepted at all levels of the subject-community that it has become something from which it is difficult, even heretical, to dissent. There is, in effect, an in-built constraint or inertia in education in the form of teachers and academics who, having grown up with subject-disciplines, have become disciples of those subjects – with all the ideological involvement and associated vested interests that entails.

However, there are a number of studies which suggest that far from holding coherent, consistent views – revolving around conventional educational justifications for their subject – PE teachers rarely hold anything that can be called a 'philosophy'. In a relatively recent study, Green (2003) suggested that confusion and contradiction were common features of PE teachers' views. What PE teachers articulated was, in effect, a checklist of aims that typically centred upon words and phrases like 'enjoyment', 'health', 'skills' and 'character'. On a sympathetic reading one might interpret this, along with Reid (1997), as 'value pluralism' – a multiplicity of justifications for PE based on a plurality of values such as health, sports performance and character development. It seems more likely, however, that teachers do not possess the kinds of coherent, reflexive 'philosophies' that some claim. Green (2003) suggests that the 'philosophies' of PE teachers' tend to follow their practices, rather than vice versa as might conventionally be expected. In other words, PE teachers tend, in practice, to seize upon convenient, retrospective rationalizations or justifications for the things they actually *do* in the name of PE. The 'philosophies' of PE teachers in Green's (2003) study tended to incorporate several ideas or ideologies emphasizing one dimension, such as sports participation (for its own sake), among an amalgam of additional justifications, such as health or character development. Their emphasis on enjoyment of competitive sport (ironically, one of the things which appears most likely to alienate a good number of pupils from PE) suggested that PE teachers perceived their subject as somehow *different* from the rest of the curriculum.

Elsewhere, George and Kirk (1988) have demonstrated how Australian PE teachers tended to be 'anti-intellectual', to celebrate 'physicality' and to accept unquestioningly the presumed health benefits of sport and PE. Similarly, Laker (1996a: 28) claimed that 'most sports-minded people and that naturally includes most physical education teachers, have a "feeling", an intuition, that sport and physical education contribute to personal and social development'. Several studies indicate that 'vague and unexamined claims about sport's externalities' (Coalter, 2005: 191) – the benefits or 'goods' such as improved health and character development that are said to occur as a by-product of participation – continue to underpin PE teachers' claims for their subject.

It is clear that there is something of a gulf between what academics have to say about the nature and purposes of PE and PE teachers' views about what they are trying to do. In terms of the 'nature' of their subject, PE teachers 'are apt to claim that theirs is essentially a practical subject' (McNamee, 2005: 1) based upon simply *doing* sport and physical activity. It is worth noting that, despite the 'theoretical' acknowledgement of the importance of affective (broadly speaking, psychological) and cognitive (broadly speaking, intellectual) outcomes of PE (for example, in the NCPE for England and Wales [DES, 1991]), the content of the subject remains physically oriented (Laker, 1996a; 1996b). For teachers, PE is far more practically oriented, impressionistic and reactive than the kind of abstract philosophizing commonly associated with professional philosophers. This is not at all surprising. Academics can be expected to develop the kinds of abstract philosophy that attempts to bring PE into line with other elements of the curriculum by developing an 'educational' rationale for physical activity based around achieving similar goals, albeit by different means. Physical education teachers' 'philosophies', however, are an expression of their predispositions and enthusiasms blended with the constraints of their practical situations. Neither is it surprising that skill acquisition featured as one of the few overtly 'educational' goals of PE teachers' 'philosophies' in Green's (2003) study, for it is what one would expect with common-sense 'philosophies'. Nothing constrains PE teachers to think through their views in a systematic manner and identify links between the differing aspects. Consequently, they remain a 'mish-mash' characterized by preferred and ideological conceptions. On the other hand, a great deal constrains teachers to fashion their thoughts to match the 'necessities' of practice and their habitual preferences.

Physical education teachers are in something of a double bind. The insecurity of their professional status and position in relation to other competing groups makes it difficult for them to exert significant leverage within the network of groups with an interest in PE. This, in turn, makes it less likely that they will be inclined to adopt the kind of detached perspective on their subject that might enable them to be clear about their identity and status. This is because, when people are in situations of vulnerability and insecurity, they inevitably find it difficult to control their own strong feelings about events that can deeply affect their lives. Consequently, they find it hard to adopt a relatively detached perspective on the events they are caught up in, especially where they have little control over them. Ironically, as long as they cannot approach such events with greater detachment, it will be correspondingly difficult for physical educationalists to extend their understanding and control of both themselves and their situation.

Several distinguished commentators claim that real change has occurred in the ideologies and practices of PE teachers in the past 15 to 20 years (Evans, 1992; Kirk, 1992). Concern with HRE, in particular, has assumed a more prominent place in the 'philosophies' and practices of PE teachers. At the same time, 'education for leisure' and 'sport for all' (Hendry et al., 1993; Scraton, 1992), together with the promotion of active lifestyles, have become more central justifications among PE teachers. Nevertheless, sport, and especially team games, continue to be the most prominent activity area in the vast majority of curricula for boys and girls in secondary schools (see Chapter 3) and lie at the heart of many teachers' 'philosophies' of PE, albeit alongside other justificatory ideologies. In this regard, PE teachers appear to view sport as worthy of its place on the school curriculum primarily as a valued cultural practice.

While PE teachers cling to the view that their subject is in some way educationally worthwhile, their 'philosophies' tend to be an amalgam of sometimes conflicting ideological positions (regarding the relationship between sport and education, for example). As a result, although PE is presented as different from sport, for many PE teachers they appear virtually synonymous.

PHYSICAL EDUCATION ACCORDING TO THE PUPILS

Anyone who has taught PE or lectured sports science students will have abundant anecdotal evidence that young people tend not only to view PE as a radically different subject to others on the curriculum but also to see it in ways that frequently differ from the perspectives of their teachers. Although there is a dearth of empirical studies of young people's perspectives on PE and sport (Dyson, 2006) what evidence there is sends several fairly consistent messages. Pupils in secondary schools in England (Laws and Fisher, 1999) – similar to their counterparts in the USA (see Dyson, 2006) – appear to view PE as primarily about 'enjoyment' and a break from more academic subjects. Many, and older secondary school pupils in particular, equate PE with sport and competitive team games (Lake, 2001). In Thorburn and Collins's (2006) study pupils typically cited 'non-serious' or, at the very least, contrary reasons to those typically embedded in standard, educational justifications for PE, commenting upon the benefits of socializing and taking what amounted to a 'break' from other academic aspects of schooling. O'Sullivan's (2002) study of Irish 11–12-year-olds, suggested that fun/enjoyment, health and to become 'good at the activity' were primary motives for taking part in sport and physical activity in and out of school. Similarly, Macdonald et al.'s (2005: 197) study of Australian youngsters confirmed 'fun, fitness and competence' as important reasons for children to participate in sport, with fun, unsurprisingly, being the most important factor for younger children. Fisher (2003) cites Egger's (2001) study of over 1,000 Swiss pupils and Zvan's research with Slovenian children in which in both cases enjoyment, health and 'social reasons' or 'social interaction' were the top three motives for doing PE. Smith and Parr's (2007) study of 15–16-year-olds' views on the nature and purposes of PE revealed similar perceptions of PE revolving around fun, enjoyment and sociability.

What amount to non-educational justifications for PE – revolving around fun and social interaction with their peers – seem to be the major motivations for young people as far as PE and sport are concerned. Smith and Parr (2007) observed that pupils, like teachers (Green, 2003), were able and inclined to articulate some of the more philosophical justifications for PE to do with health promotion and personal development, but these were essentially rhetorical and bore little resemblance to their more deeply felt views regarding the centrality of fun and enjoyment to the nature and purposes of PE. It seems that primary- and secondary-aged pupils view PE as essentially recreational, as synonymous with sport, and do not recognize in practice the supposed educational purpose and value of PE (Jones and Cheetham, 2001). It is clear that school pupils interpret PE in more restricted, practical terms than PE teachers, policy documents or academic philosophers would want or maybe even expect. This should not be seen as surprising – there is ample evidence that young people see the main purpose of education as being to help them acquire qualifications and necessary skills for employment (Hallam and Ireson, 1999), so unless they foresee a career in sport, it is hardly remarkable that they view it in recreational, less serious terms.

CONCLUSION

This chapter has provided a brief outline of the main philosophical attempts to establish the nature and purposes of PE (the theoretical 'furniture' of the subject) before juxtaposing those with the 'philosophies' of PE teachers and the perceptions of young people. First, the debate shifted towards and then away from issues to do with the kinds of knowledge that PE is supposedly concerned with before veering in the direction of something that lies at the heart of philosophical conceptions of education – the notion of value and what constitutes educationally worthwhile knowledge.

The chapter concludes that attempts to define PE reflect a misplaced tendency to view the subject as made up of some kind of timeless essence. But there is no essence to PE in the sense of something immutable and relatively timeless that the subject is and must always be if it is to count as PE. Physical education emerged and developed over time as a consequence of the toing and froing of various competing interest groups (see Kirk, 1992). In other words, it is simply what it has become. That it appears to have an essence is entirely due to the manner in which an identifiable pattern or 'tradition' has become recognizable in the practice of PE over time. The QCA (2005a: 1) claims that 'views of PE have changed considerably over the course of the last century'. The extent of this change is, however, debatable. There have been some changes in 'philosophy' and practice but there has also been a good deal of continuity, not least in the form of the persistence of gymnastic and health-related activities, generally, and games, in particular.

In order to understand PE contemporarily it is necessary to view it as a process and to return to some of the fundamental issues that have provided the basic ideas and justifications as well as significant aspects of the language within which debates are still conducted. At the same time, it is necessary to remember that characteristic of attempts to establish the nature and purposes of PE is the manner in which much of the debate assumes what, ostensibly at least, the protagonists purport to be examining. Physical education teachers and, for that matter, academics often appear to be romantic conservatives by 'nature'. They often appear to assume that PE is a 'good' thing if only they could find out exactly why! In this vein, a leading German PE academic pointed to 'the proven benefits of physical education in the overall development of children and youth and the indispensable role of physical education in the education process' (Doll-Tepper, 2005: 41). Similarly, in the UK, the Central Council for Physical Recreation (CCPR, 2001: 1) recommends that those involved with planning PE curricula 'should recognize the unique role physical education plays in raising academic standards, promoting healthy living and in teaching pupils to manage risk as well as developing physical literacy and confidence in movement'. Such views amount to what de Swaan

(2001: 96) refers to as a 'shared illusion' brought about where ideological 'over-extensions' are 'smuggled into the analysis' (Kilminster, 1998: 91) leading advocates towards value-related, ideal-type constructs.

The remainder of this book focuses upon the debates and issues surrounding PE in practice. Inevitably, however, this will involve returning to ideologically laden questions about the nature and purposes of PE.

RECOMMENDED READING

McNamee, M. (2005) 'The nature and values of physical education', in K. Green and K. Hardman (eds), *Physical Education: Essential Issues*. London: Sage. pp.1–20.

NOTES

1 Although several authors use the terms 'intellectual' and 'theoretical' interchangeably, this chapter follows McNamee's preference for the terms 'theoretical' and 'propositional' and reserves the term 'intellectual' to refer to a subcategory of theoretical knowledge; in other words, higher-order theoretical thinking of the kind connoted in everyday uses of the term 'intellectual'.

2 Grammar schools were selective secondary schools introduced in England and Wales by the 1944 Butler Education Act. Entry was restricted to those who passed the eleven-plus examination.

3 Philosophers might observe that the term 'valuable' would be preferable to 'valued' in the phrase 'valued cultural practices' because the former suggests that there are good reasons why they should be seen as such, whereas the latter asserts it as a fact. However, proponents of this view (see, for example, Arnold, 1992; 1997) do consider it to be an empirically observable fact that cultural practices such as sport are valued. Hence, the preference for the term 'valued'.

4 The Physical Education Association of the United Kingdom (PEA-UK) recently merged with the British Association of Advisers and Lecturers in Physical Education (BAALPE) to become the Association for Physical Education (AfPE).

Policy and Physical Education

When people talk about policy towards PE, what do they actually mean by policy and what, if anything, is the significance of policy for the practice and practitioners of PE? Murphy and Waddington (1998) remind us of the need to ask several basic questions about policy:

- Are the goals of particular policies clear?
- Where policies have several goals, are they mutually compatible?
- What likely outcomes might be associated with the implementation of these policies?
- Indeed, might the achievement of one policy goal have consequences which militate against, even undermine, the achievement of yet others?

This chapter attempts to answer some of these questions as they relate to PE. Various aspects of the policy process are explored as a basis for making sense of the large number of policies currently affecting PE in the UK and internationally. Two particularly significant policies in England and Wales – the National Curriculum for Physical Education (NCPE) and the Physical Education, School Sport and Club Links (PESSCL) strategy – are examined in some detail in order to illustrate aspects of the PE policy process.

POLICY IN THEORY

Policy is a statement of intent regarding achieving, maintaining, modifying or changing something. Policies tend to begin life as issues: 'policy implies a desire to move from what is perceived to be an unsatisfactory state of affairs to a more satisfactory one' (Murphy, 1998: 104). This is why Penney and Evans (2005: 21, emphasis added) define policy as 'someone's (an individual's, institution's, local or central government's) authoritative decision about how 'things' *should* be'. The goals of policy lie somewhere on twin axes between specific/relatively simple and multidimensional/complex and short- and long-term poles.

Policy networks

It is impossible to understand developments in policy, and their effects upon practice in PE, except in relation to the various networks of individuals and groups with whom physical educationalists are unavoidably interdependent. Physical education teachers interact with each other, their teaching colleagues, their pupils and even the parents of the pupils. That is self-evident. Less obvious, however, are the people and organizations that physical educationalists are unlikely to meet face to face but who affect the context in which they work. Indeed, in increasingly differentiated and interdependent societies it is highly likely that members of networks, such as PE, will be unaware of the extent to which they are linked to other groups of people. Moreover, teachers may not entirely appreciate the many and varied ways in which their individual and collective scope for action is constrained by their interdependence with people and groups they do not have day-to-day contact with and do not know personally.

The PE policy network in England, for example, includes groups far and wide with a vested interest in young people and sport, such as government departments (the Department of Culture, Media and Sport [DCMS], Department of Health [DoH] and Department for Children, Schools and Families (DCSF)[1], for example), government quangos (especially Sport England), governing bodies of sports (such as the British Olympic Association and the Football Association) and their representatives (including the Central Council for Physical Recreation, sports development officers [SDOs] and the media).

In modern societies occupational groups such as teachers are increasingly intertwined with groups and networks far beyond the school gates. The chains of interdependence – linking PE teachers with others with an interest in their subject – have lengthened and become more complex over time. Sometimes, this has been by design. Government, for example, chose to include representatives of sport (and elite sportsmen, in particular) on the working party established in the late 1980s to develop the NCPE for England and Wales. Similarly, physical educationalists themselves often choose to become involved with groups that may have an impact, directly or indirectly, upon PE (for example, professional associations such as the Association for Physical Education in the UK [AfPE]). Elsewhere, independence is contingent. Physical education teachers often become bound up with groups beyond PE when, for example, they turn for assistance (with the day-to-day practicalities of delivering PE) to governing bodies of sport and SDOs of one type or another who are only too ready – in pursuit of their own vested interests – to extend their spheres of influence by providing materials and expertise.

Given the lengthening chains of interdependence between PE teachers and other groups of people, it is hardly surprising that PE has become an extremely 'crowded' policy arena (Houlihan, 2000) and one which gives expression to the vested interests of a large number of people and organizations. This has had two effects. First, 'individuals and organizations that may once have been regarded as outside an educational policy network (particularly sporting and sports development organizations) are now repositioned not merely within that net-work but central to it' (Penney and Evans, 2005: 25–6). Second, as the policy net-work of PE has become more extensive and complex it has become more opaque to those in its midst – the PE teachers themselves.

It is important to recognize that networks of dependencies are also net-works of expectations. In all countries, 'education systems are simultaneously blamed for economic and social problems yet paradoxically expected to solve them' (Dodds, 2006: 541). In England, for example, government has expecta-tions of PE as a vehicle for health promotion and social inclusion. Many gov-erning bodies of sport, for their part, expect PE to serve as a vehicle for the flow of talented athletes. Similarly, school governing bodies and their head teachers pursue group and personal interests when demanding that their PE departments achieve the kinds of recruitment and examination success that might give them an advantage in the educational marketplace. Such expecta-tions are typically grounded in taken-for-granted assumptions each has towards the other.

So much for the complexities of the context in which policy emerges and develops and is, eventually, implemented. The policy process itself is also more dynamic than it often appears.

The policy process

Traditionally the path from policy to practice is viewed as a relatively straight-forward one. People, with authority to do so, generate and send forth policy and those on the ground – PE teachers, for example – receive and implement it. However, this ideal-type, hierarchical and linear model of policy imple-mentation distorts a more complex, contingent and dynamic process. The tra-ditional view of policy implementation simply underestimates, among other things, the issues raised at the outset of this chapter, namely, the propensity of policy-makers to introduce policies with several, more-or-less clear goals that are neither straightforward to implement, nor entirely compatible, nor result in the outcomes anticipated.

Nor should the policy process be viewed as democratic and rational. Penney and Evans (2005: 22) stress that policy is not a routine consequence of 'mutual agreement'. Struggles over values, interests and goals develop as a consequence of the differential power relations of interdependent people and/or groups of people with vested interests who, whatever the balance of power between them, simply cannot ignore (certainly not without conse-quences) the existence, expectations and demands of others in their networks. Consequently, policy formulation and implementation is dynamic. It is 'a complex, ongoing, always contested process, in which there are struggles over values, interests and definitions' (Penney and Evans, 2005: 22) and which expresses fundamental and contested ideological views of how not only schools but also individuals and society 'are and ought to be'.

One aspect of the policy process that tends to be overlooked is the relative power of practitioners at the 'grass roots' level to amend policy in its imple-mentation and, in doing so, influence not only the outcome of current policies but also future policy-making. Thus, conventional distinctions between policy-makers and implementers and policy-making and implementation are artificial and inadequate (Penney and Evans, 2005). This begins to explain why policy – towards PE, in particular – is dynamic and complex and 'is *continually* made and remade' (Penney and Evans, 2005: 24, emphasis in the original).

Given the interdependence of those in the policy community, it is inevitable that we see both cooperation and conflict in the implementation, and in the making, of educational policy (Fitz et al., 2006). People and groups are involved in dynamic interrelationships that inevitably favour one group, or constellation of groups, over others. This is why 'the policy process rarely follows the neat, rational models of change set out in some of the ... literature' (Dopson and Waddington, 1996: 544) and the outcome of policy is frequently something that no party ideally wanted, intended or anticipated.

Policy and power

Because policy networks are networks of interdependence they always involve relations of power. This is because power is an aspect of social relations and a characteristic of a person's position within a particular network, such as a PE department or school. Physical education teachers are, therefore, inextricably bound into power relations with parents, pupils, head teachers, local educa-tion authorities, government ministers, governing bodies of sport and even the media. Power differentials between PE teachers and others upon whom they are more or less dependent, necessarily place limitations upon their rel-ative capacity to 'make a difference'. So, in order to make sense of policy development and implementation, it is necessary to view the different kinds of power relations between teachers and other parties in terms of balances of power (and power ratios) rather than zero-sum relationships (Elias, 1978; Penney and Evans, 2005).

Recognizing and appreciating the particular ties between people and groups – and the power relationships associated with these – is fundamental to understanding policy formation and implementation. Within all networks there are asymmetrical balances of power which favour some more than others: 'some have relative positions of power (a positive balance) and others have positions largely characterized by dependence (a negative balance)' (de Swann, 2001: 36). Indeed, the history of PE is a history of shifting power-balances, as illustrated in the battle for ideological ascendancy – between those (typically female PE teachers) favouring Swedish gymnastics and those (for the most part, male PE teachers) championing English public school games – within PE in the UK in the first half or the twentieth century (Kirk, 1992).

No group, however, is entirely power*less*. Even people or groups that occupy a superior power position are still dependent upon those whose power ratio is a good deal less – power is never remotely one-way (Kilminster, 1998; Murphy, 2007). So, although schools and PE teachers are necessarily constrained by policy and legislation, government is always dependent upon them because it is they who are charged with implementation. Because 'even the most carefully-picked teams evolve their own game plan' (Fitz et al., 2006: 3) – and because their attention tends inevitably to focus upon the practicalities of the process of implementation – it is 'a long way' (p. 2) from government ministers and policy-*making* to the practice of PE teaching on a wet winter's afternoon on an inner-city school playing field. There is 'slippage' (Curtner-Smith, 1999; Penney and Evans, 1999): what is actually delivered tends to be different, in one way or another, from what was originally intended. Because the *implementation* of policy is never straightforward, unplanned outcomes are an inevitable feature of the policy process. The theme of slippage between policy and implementation is returned to later on in this chapter.

Shifting power balances in PE

What fundamentally distinguishes the relatively more established from the less established groups in any policy network are 'the power resources at the disposal of one side or another' (Mennell, 1998: 124). In the case of the relationships between PE teachers and their pupils (and, to some extent, their colleagues) the resource is typically persuasive (in the form of offering inducements and withholding rewards) and occasionally coercive (in the form of punishments, such as expulsion from a group or activity). In terms of head teachers and their PE departments, it tends to be all three sources of power: economic, coercive and persuasive. In terms of the relationship between PE teachers and quangos, such as Sport England, it tends to be both economic and persuasive, with PE departments and their schools dependent upon government policy (for example, with regard to the designation of Specialist Sports College [SSC] status).

The status differentials between teachers of PE and those teaching other academic subjects provides an example of shifting power-balances, where subjects or disciplines behave like competing states 'striving to maintain clear territorial boundaries against outsiders' (Mennell, 1998: 194). The increasing use-value of examinations in PE for the standing of schools (see Chapter 5) – in the various league tables that are increasingly a feature of marketized education systems – has, for example, served as a power resource for PE teachers, making many head teachers and their colleagues more dependent upon them for examination success, thereby bolstering the status of PE within schools.

Many of the organizations involved in the PE policy network try to influence the nature and purposes of PE, be they government (the DCMS, for example), charities (Youth Sport Trust [YST]), governing bodies (the Football Association [FA]) or even teachers themselves (AfPE). One of the features of recent policy developments in PE has been the manner in which the balance of power in school sport in England and Wales has been tilting away from PE teachers and towards external agencies (such as the YST, SDOs and governing bodies of sport) as the latter have become increasingly interested in, and more directly involved with, PE. In this regard, it has been instructive to see how organizations such as the YST have managed by degrees to control certain resources (such as specialist sports equipment) which teachers (especially in primary schools) have needed or wanted.

A structural feature of networks such as PE is competitive rivalry. Just as newly emerging public schools in nineteenth-century Britain came to understand and imitate their superiors and form coalitions in order to compete for opportunities and resources, so physical educationalists today are compelled to orientate themselves towards and consider the ideas and concepts of potentially rival groups – such as sports governing bodies at the national level and SDOs and sports coaches at the local level – as the power gradient between teachers and other agencies flattens out and alliances and mergers occur. As a result, it is immensely difficult nowadays to champion one model of PE. A number of physical educationalists feel compelled to begin to identify with – and thus claim to deliver – some of the 'goods' of competing interest groups (for example, talent identification, health promotion, academic and vocational qualifications, and social inclusion).

The 'blindness' of policy

Policies are often predicated on the assumption that policy and outcome are one and the same, and that the impact of interventions will be homogenous; that is, that NCPE, for example, will have similar if not identical results in both male and female PE departments in all secondary schools in all regions of England and Wales. The assumption is that PE can be used anywhere by anybody and can be expected to achieve similar, if not identical, results. But the impact of policy is contingent and is not guaranteed, because there are so many variables, such as geographical location and, as later chapters show, the social dynamics of gender, social class and ethnicity.

Given that no group or individual will have total knowledge of any particular area or situation, the outcomes of policies are inevitably 'blind', inasmuch as policies often have unintended as well as intended outcomes or consequences. This is so because people's intended actions take place in webs of unplanned interdependencies – often with people and groups beyond PE teachers' control, such as school governing bodies or local education authorities. Developments elsewhere in education (the marketization of education and the growth of examinations in PE, for example) or even society in general (such as the 'obesity epidemic') may have consequences for PE, shaping the direction in which the subject develops. And PE teachers, like any employees, are constrained to respond – often in a piecemeal manner – to the changing landscape of their occupation.

The consequences of today's responses to pressing issues will provide the context for tomorrow's policies and practices. Nowhere is this better illustrated, perhaps, than the indirect consequences of the 1988 Education Reform Act in the UK, and the educational marketplace (Gorard et al, 2003) that ensued, for the growth of examinations in PE and the content of contemporary PE programmes for older pupils.

POLICY AND IDEOLOGY

When considering the policy process we need to keep in mind who the policy-makers and implementers are and what vested interests they represent, as well as the ways in which their interests may converge and coincide. This is because much policy towards PE and sport is often intended to bolster or sustain a particular ideological position (Murphy, 1998). Policies are unavoidably value-laden because they are constructions of people or groups of people. Different ideological positions (for example, viewing talent identification and development as a central purpose of PE) express differences in interests among the 'competing' groups. Policies involve 'struggles and contests over goals and aspirations, over whose voices should be permitted "a hearing"' (Penney and Evans, 2005: 21) as well as the status accorded to these voices. Penney and Evans (2005) utilize the concept of 'discourse' – the ways in which people communicate their, often implicit, ideological (and, therefore, value-laden) positions – to shed light upon the ideas (or ideologies) that can be hidden or visible, implicit or explicit in policy 'texts'. The 'multiple discourses' that Penney and Evans (2005: 29) suggest are contained in policy documents are, in effect, partial expressions of ideologies. These 'discourses' are veiled expressions of ideological objectives. In this manner, government White Papers can be seen to circumscribe what is acceptable – and, by extension, unacceptable – to think and do in the name of PE. Penney and Evans (2005: 32), for example, talk of 'a strong reaffirmation', through policy towards PE and sport over the last decade or more, of 'the 'taken for granted' structure and 'core content' of the PE curriculum' alongside 'a relative absence of any significant shift in thinking about PE' (p. 32). This amounts, in effect, to 'window-dressing' whereby policy-makers are more interested in being seen to be doing something rather than labouring under the belief that its implementation will achieve much (Murphy, 2007).

In order to understand the ideological positions that inform policy towards PE and sport, we need to appreciate that those involved with PE, especially teachers, tend to have strong emotional orientations to the subject. Thus, policy evokes deeply felt responses from protagonists who often connect to the prevailing occupational ideology. Indeed, to the extent that any policy (such as SSCs) gives expression to a wider social perception and chimes with at least some of the taken-for-granted assumptions of the practitioners themselves (for example, the desirability of sporting success for schools, links with sports clubs and the utilization of coaches and SDOs in PE), then it is likely to be pushing at an open door. Such situations illustrate the process by which external constraints become internalized as self-restraint by the practitioners themselves. Sometimes external constraints are not necessary because the implementers share the aims of the policy-makers (Murphy, 2007). This can be seen in a strand of the government's PESSCL strategy (DfES/DCMS, 2003) – the 'gifted and talented' scheme – the aim of which, among other things, is to profile and 'track' pupils with sporting ability.

POLICY AND PHYSICAL EDUCATION

In this section I will attempt to apply the various aspects of the policy process to PE. First, I focus on one of the most significant developments in the history of PE in England and Wales: the NCPE. The NCPE was introduced in 1992 and subsequently revised in 1995, 2000 and 2008 in order, at least in part, to take account of some of the unforeseen outcomes of the previous versions (such as the perceived disadvantages to pupils and teachers of making games a compulsory element at all key stages after 1995). I also discuss a number of salient developments in the wider political and sporting arenas, to demonstrate the processual character of PE; that is, the ways in which developments in PE are intertwined with developments in the broader policy networks. An increasingly prominent feature of the policy landscape for PE in the UK has been the emergence of a government department (DCMS) which has begun to encroach upon some of the responsibility for PE traditionally held by its 'home' department (DCSF). Until relatively recently only a few European countries (most notably, France, Germany and the Netherlands) have had government departments with responsibility for sport as an aspect of leisure. Despite the fact that few governments in the 1960s 'gave any explicit budgetary or ministerial recognition to sport', it is now 'an established feature of government [in] most economically developed countries' (Houlihan, 2005: 163).

The development of government policy implies the identification of a 'problem' in need of a collective solution that cannot simply be left to the 'professionals'. In the UK in recent years these problems are said to have been, among other things, a diminution of traditional team games and the alleged failure of PE and sport to avert the 'health/obesity crisis' or confront rising levels of juvenile delinquency. In this regard, the presence of ideological underpinnings to PE-related policy is most clearly seen in two developments. First, the shift in government policy on PE and school sport from what Coalter (2006b) has referred to as 'sport for all' to 'sport for good': 'conviction about the capacity of sport to contribute to social change has fuelled a wide range of sports based initiatives directed at diverse groups', the objectives of which 'lie beyond sports participation, to effecting change in young people's lives' (Kay, 2005: 91). Second, an increasingly ideologically driven, tendency to refer to PE as PE *and School Sport* (PESS).

The Departments for Culture, Media and Sport and Children, School and Families

The political 'home' of sport in the UK – the DCMS – is a relatively new development. The significance of the DCMS lies in the implicit recognition by government of the supposed desirability of the state being centrally involved in the provision and management of sport as a significant aspect of British culture.

The DCMS is relatively small in both financial and political terms and, as a consequence, frequently finds itself in less powerful positions, in relation to other government departments, in terms of policy development and implementation. The other major government department concerned with PE and school sport is the DCSF. In contrast to the DCMS, the DCSF is an economic and political 'big hitter'. Nevertheless, and despite its educational remit, PE has not been a priority for the DCSF and, as a consequence, the advent of the DCMS has enabled the sports lobby to adopt a more prominent and powerful role in the policy network for PE.

The state of sport in schools has been high on the agenda of the DCMS since its inception. Although largely neglected in the 1960s and 1970s in policy terms, the 1980s witnessed a change in the political importance of sport in schools and, therefore, PE (Houlihan and Green, 2006). A moral panic over the alleged precarious state of young people's health, as well as their academic attainment and behaviour, alongside the relative lack of success of elite sportsmen and sportswomen in England, led to a growth in political concern with sport in and out of school. Consequently, PE acquired a higher political profile.

Around the time that the DCMS was established, a major new player in the PE policy network in the UK came into being – the Youth Support Trust (YST).

The Youth Sport Trust and the National Junior Sports Programme

The YST was established in 1994 as a charitable organization with the self-proclaimed intention of developing and implementing PE and sport programmes for young people up to the age of 18, in both their schools and local communities. The PE profession was one of a range of agencies identified by the YST as potential partnership organizations. The YST's vehicle for the development and implementation of 'quality sports programmes' was the National Junior Sport Programme (NJSP) – launched in 1995 with the aid of £7.7 million of UK government Lottery Sports Fund money. The NJSP was expected to have a major impact on the nation's sporting chances by providing children 'with a pathway from the school playground into the international sporting arena' (Department of National Heritage [DNH], 1996). The NJSP features the so-called TOPs schemes – TOP Play (for primary schools) and TOP Sport (secondary schools) – which provide child-friendly equipment as well as training and support for teachers; especially those in primary schools where there has long been a dearth of equipment and expertise.

The extent of the penetration of the YST into PE is illustrated by the encouragement it has offered for 'suitably qualified' maintained secondary schools in England to apply for designation as SSCs,[2] which the YST has a contract with the DCSF to develop. The specialist schools programme – of which SSCs are a feature – was launched by a Conservative government in

1994 in order 'to help secondary schools to develop strengths and raise standards in a chosen specialism' (OFSTED, 2005a: 5): to act, in effect, as 'centres of excellence' for particular subjects, such as languages, technology, science and, eventually, sport. There are currently well over 2,000 specialist schools in England of which almost 400 are designated SSCs. The first SSC was established in 1997 by a newly elected Labour government. The SSCs are maintained secondary schools that receive additional funding from the government in order to: (1) increase participation and raise standards in PE and sport in a 'family' of elementary and secondary schools in their vicinity; and (2) identify and develop young sporting talent in partnership with sports clubs in their communities.

As 'the pre-eminent institutional force … behind the recent emphasis on school sport and PE' (Houlihan and Green, 2006: 85), the YST has taken the lead in championing the alleged value of school sport and PE. Consequently, it is widely regarded as having been a good deal more influential in shaping government policy towards PE and school sport than professional interest groups. This can be no accident given that the YST is a carrier of the dominant (sporting) ideological perspective favoured by government and the media. Nor is it surprising, given that the government was instrumental in setting up the YST in the first place.

The YST's TOP Play and TOP Sport projects were and are ostensibly meant to extend sporting and physical activity opportunities for youngsters. In reality, in primary schools at least, these sport-oriented programmes often provided resources which primary school teachers saw as immensely useful, not to say necessary, in delivering PE in their resource-scarce context (Thorpe, 1996). Because PE is not particularly strong in the primary sector and because the resources for sport (or some sports) provided by the TOP Play scheme were so abundant there has been ample potential for sport – and even a single sport – to dominate the PE curriculum (Thorpe, 1996). In this regard, the development and success of sporting curriculum packages for primary schools – similar to those in the UK – in Australia and New Zealand (Aussie Sport and Kiwi Sport) led to such packages becoming a kind of de facto PE programme (Alexander et al., 1996).

The establishment of a government department with responsibility for sport, alongside the emergence of the YST and the concomitant introduction of SSCs, has put in place the preconditions 'to push PE and school sport centre stage' (Houlihan and Green, 2006: 75) politically. Kirk (1992) was certainly prescient in describing the 1990s as a 'watershed' in discourse regarding the relationship between PE and school sport. Even though the various departments of state tend to seek different objectives through sport – some of which are incompatible – sport in general and school sport in particular has often been presented as 'a significant cross-departmental vehicle' (Houlihan and

Green, 2006: 77) for broader social and political objectives over the past 20 years. On such occasions, policy specifically related to PE usually reduces it to sport and redefines it in relation to broader social and political objectives. Nowhere is this better illustrated than in the development of a School Sport Alliance comprising the DCSF the DCMS, the UK National Lottery's New Opportunities Fund (NOF) and the YST.

Having said something about the 'nature' of policy, the two main governmental players and one of the more influential agencies in the PE policy arena, the next section focuses upon a number of relevant developments in policy towards PE in England and Wales in recent decades, starting with a policy that, for many, represents the most profound change of all: the NCPE.

The National Curriculum for Physical Education in England and Wales

The introduction and development of the NCPE in England and Wales in the 1990s provides a useful illustration of policy as a social process in which vested interests and deep-seated values are expressed and contested (Penney and Evans, 1999) and balances of power between the various interested parties shift. The National Curriculum for primary and secondary education in England and Wales was a product of the Education Reform Act (ERA) of 1988. The ERA established a statutory curriculum for pupils aged 5 to 16 involving four so-called 'Key Stages' at 7, 11, 14 and 16 years of age which, as the title suggests, are taken to represent distinct and significant periods in children's education. Alongside the *core* subjects of the National Curriculum – English, Mathematics, Science (and Welsh in Wales) – are *foundation* subjects, one of which is PE. All subjects consist of 'Programmes of Study' (content) and 'Attainment Targets' (in effect, learning objectives) for each Key Stage. Within the Programmes of Study for the NCPE, introduced in 1992, pupils are required to experience six areas of activity in a 'broad and balanced' curriculum (DES, 1991): athletic activities, dance, games, gymnastic activities, outdoor and adventurous activities and swimming. Attainment Targets are expressed in 'End of Key Stage Statements' about pupils' achievements. In PE, these focus upon what used to be known as 'planning, performing and evaluation'. Following adjustments in the NCPE in 2000 these 'components' have been further refined by the NCPE to be issued in 2008 to: (1) becoming physically competent in performance; (2) evaluating and improving performance; and (3) developing the ability to make informed choices about involvement in healthy, active lifestyles.

Since its inception in 1992, the NCPE – along with the National Curriculum as a whole – has been revised in 1995, 2000 and 2008. While the separate Subject Task Groups (such as the Working Party on the NCPE) charged with developing the original National Curriculum in the 1980s worked relatively independently in drawing up their own curriculum structure and attainment targets, they were inevitably influenced by their individual and collective value-orientations towards their subjects. Notable within the process of developing the original NCPE was the prestige afforded to sports people, including elite sports performers and a sports-keen public school head teacher (Talbot, 1995). The NCPE was developed with very little input from physical educationalists, who have remained on the margins of policy development through every iteration of the NCPE despite the fact that NCPE makes strong demands of teachers (Evans et al., 1993).

The National Curriculum for Physical Education 1995

The changes to NCPE brought about by the 1995 revision need to be understood in the policy context of the 1990s and the government's increasing desire to intervene in education, in general, and PE, in particular. As well as the effective lobbying of many sports governing bodies there was a background of British sporting failure at major international competitions (such as the Olympic Games and the soccer World Cup). In 1995, the then recently formed DNH published what was only the second-ever White Paper on sport in the UK, *Sport: Raising the Game*, setting out the Conservative government's intention to bring about 'a sea-change in the prospects of British sport' (DNH, 1995: 1). *Sport: Raising the Game* extolled the virtues of, and sought to retrieve a presumed decline in, competitive team sports (Roberts, 1996a). This was despite substantial evidence demonstrating that: (1) within the overwhelming majority of schools competitive sports, and team games in particular, had maintained a dominant place on the PE curriculum (Penney and Evans, 1998; Roberts, 1996a; 1996b); and (2) general trends in participation reflected increases in fitness-oriented, less competitive, individual, flexible lifestyle activities such as walking, swimming, cycling, keep fit/aerobics and weight training.

Central to the twin policy developments of *Sport: Raising the Game* and the revised NCPE was what was claimed to be a much needed 'renaissance' of sport in schools. The then Conservative Prime Minister and government sought not only to 're-establish' the centrality of sport in schools, but also to prioritize certain kinds of physical activities – team games – while marginalizing others (Penney and Evans, 1999). Having identified sport as the most significant element of the PE curriculum, *Sport: Raising the Game* pointed to an alleged need for extra sporting provision in schools and ushered in the development of awards – 'Sportsmark' and 'Sportsmark Gold' – for those secondary schools providing 'quality' PE and sports programmes in the form of provision (especially in extra-curricular PE) of opportunities for competitive sport. It also stipulated a minimum number of hours of extra-curricular PE and introduced the award of SSC status to those PE departments and schools deemed suitably sports-oriented and qualified to act as focal points for the development of sport in their communities or regions. Thus, *Sport: Raising the Game* pointed policy firmly in the direction of the assumed connection between sport in school and the development of elite sport (Houlihan, 2000; Houlihan and White, 2002).

This shift in emphasis was also reflected in the two major (and related) changes required by the revised NCPE of 1995: an emphasis upon (1) sport (and particularly the activity area of games) at all 'key stages' of schooling; and (2) 'performance' from within the triad of 'planning, performance and evaluation'.

Although the government claimed this was a dramatic shift in policy, in reality the two policy interventions of 1995 – the revised NCPE and the government White Paper, *Sport: Raising the Game* – merely reinforced a tendency inherent in PE for half a century to prioritize a 'sport and performance'-based definition of PE over other conceptions of the subject; for example, as a vehicle for health promotion. In 'positioning' and 'privileging' (Penney and Evans, 1998; 1999) a particular ideological view of the 'true' nature and purposes of PE – centring upon performance in sport and games – in public and professional debate, government policy reinforced the prevailing view among practitioners that the PE curriculum should focus upon content (in the form of activity areas). In doing so, it served to further harden the hierarchy of areas of activity long established within the subject within which games were accorded the highest status and other activities subordinated (Penney and Evans, 1999; 2005). The outcome of the 1995 revision of NCPE was a narrow curriculum experience, especially for boys. From 1995, games occupied between 50 and 70 per cent of Key Stage 3 PE, with the other three areas of activity required by the National Curriculum squeezed into the remaining time.

The National Curriculum for Physical Education 2000

The very real difficulties experienced by PE teachers in forcing the activity area of games onto 15–16-year-old young adults – coupled with the Labour government's receptiveness to the idea that a broader diet of activities for older pupils might be necessary to encourage participation in physical activity (and thereby offset the rising tide of obesity) – led to the requirement to teach the activity area of games to all age groups being rescinded in NCPE 2000 (QCA and DfEE, 1999a). The NCPE 2000 played down the emphasis on sports performance in two ways. The first was by stipulating that games become an option rather than a requirement at Key Stage 4. The second was the growing strength of the health-related exercise (HRE) lobby – as a result of increased concern with a seeming explosion of 'lifestyle diseases' such as obesity – provided the preconditions for the stipulation in NCPE 2000 that HRE be a permeating theme of all the activity areas that together made up the NCPE.

Despite the fact that the revised NCPE for 2000 loosened the grip of sport and games – especially for 14–16-year-olds at Key Stage 4 – policy statements since 2000 have reinforced the overt pro-sport ideology of successive Conservative and Labour governments since the mid-1990s and bolstered perceptions of PE as being sport in school. Consequently, the next major policy statement on sport since *Sport: Raising the Game – A Sporting Future for All* (DCMS, 2000) – ostensibly restored the encouragement of mass participation as a policy objective (Houlihan, 2002) and focused particular attention on extending the range of sporting opportunities available to youngsters after school (via extra-curricular PE) as well as creating further SSCs. The five central strands to *A Sporting Future for All* were: rebuilding sports facilities (see Chapter 3), creating further SSCs, greater support for after-school (extra-curricular) sport (see Chapter 4), creating School Sports Co-ordinators to facilitate inter-school sport and to improve the range of opportunities for competitive sport beyond the curriculum, as well as coaching support for the most talented youngsters (Houlihan, 2000). *A Sporting Future for All* confirmed school sport as central to successive governments' conceptions of PE and did not change the dominant conception of PE as synonymous with school sport. Nor did it undermine the government's commitment to integrating school sport with talent identification and elite sporting development (Houlihan, 2002.)

Government policy towards sport in general, and sport in schools in particular, has further underlined the already clear contours of PE and youth sport. Nowhere is the observation that yesterday's policy is today's policy *context* better illustrated than with the PESSCL strategy – introduced in an attempt to provide an overall coordination strategy for the many policies and strategies towards PE and school sport in England and Wales.

The Physical Education, School Sport and Club Links (PESSCL) strategy

The PESSCL strategy is intended to establish an infrastructure for PE and school sport and has four key policy outcomes which can be summarized as increased participation and increased motivation, attitudes and self-esteem on the part of pupils, and improved standards of performance, and increased numbers of qualified and active coaches, leaders and officials in schools and sports clubs/facilities (Loughborough Partnership, 2005).

At the heart of the PESSCL strategy are School Sport Partnerships. The partnerships (previously the School Sport Coordinator [SSCo]) programme is a core feature of the PESSCL strategy, with over 400 partnerships and more than 3,200 SSCos in secondary schools in 2007. School Sport Partnerships amount to 'families of schools' required to work together to develop PE and sporting opportunities for young people. All state-maintained schools in England are now part of a Partnership. Partnerships typically consist of a Partnership Development Manager – based at an SSC and who is typically an established and experienced PE teacher charged with supporting the Partnership – and up to eight secondary school SSCos – secondary school (PE) teachers released from their timetable for two days per week and responsible for developing PE and school sport in their school and their (four to eight) feeder primary schools (Easton, 2003). The SSCos are responsible for coordinating and developing intra- and inter-school sport and physical activity in general, and sporting competition and local community and club links in particular. Each primary and Special School (see Chapter 11) in the Partnership has approximately 45 primary and Special School Link Teachers who are released from teaching for 12 days each year to help improve the quantity and quality of PE in their own school.

According to the DCMS/DfES (2005), schools that have been in a Partnership for three years possessed a number of features: they offered an average of 14 different sports at primary level and 20 at secondary; provided football almost universally, closely followed by athletics and dance and gymnastics; involved over a third of pupils in competitions between schools; had links with clubs in five different sports on average at primary level and 11 at secondary; and the vast majority held a 'sports day'. The DCMS/DfES (2005) state that, according to its *School Sport Survey*, the greatest progress in participation in terms of numbers and time allocation in the Partnership schools has been in primary schools. It is necessary, however, to introduce a note of caution when considering the limited research on SSCs, not least because, in order to justify the additional monies allocated to them, they are required to demonstrate the whole-school impact of their specialism. Among other things, this involves SSCs demonstrating that the primary schools in their partnerships enable two hours or more per week of 'high quality PE and sport'. Indeed, if SSCs bear any resemblance to the much heralded City Academies, first introduced in 2002, then there is no substantial evidence, as yet, that such schools are performing any better for equivalent students than the ones they replaced (Gorard, 2005). In other words, the claim that the emergence of SSCs and partnerships between schools and between schools and sports clubs has offered increased sporting opportunities to young people as well as 'energised physical education in many schools and enthused large numbers of pupils' (Fisher, 2003: 142) is an empirical claim for which there appears to be only limited and equivocal evidence. Indeed, there is every reason to believe that many of the issues reported in the 2001 Office for Standards in Education (OFSTED) report on SSCs remain 'live'; that is, although schools with high participation rates in sport also experience lower truancy rates and better behaviour, there have been no significant improvements in academic achievements measured in terms of GCSE grades A* to C in SSCs. But it would be a mistake to assume a simple cause and effect relationship of this kind. Aspects of departmental management in SSCs that are said by OFSTED to 'need improvement', might cast doubt on the tag of 'excellence' or 'good practice' associated with the label 'specialist school' because they include some of the things – such as lesson planning, schemes of work and the evaluation of teaching – that might be considered fundamental to all schools and all PE teachers.

Nowhere, perhaps, is the influence of hitherto 'outsider' groups to PE more obvious than the PESSCL strategy (DfES/DCMS, 2003) – developed by 'multi-agency consultation' (Penney and Evans, 2005) involving interested parties beyond the government departments responsible for sport (DCMS) and education (DfES). In this regard, 'the overlap between PE and sport policy development is no longer incidental and nor are those in authority content for it now to be left to chance' (Penney and Evans, 2005: 26).

CONCLUSION

This chapter began by asking several questions about the goals of policies, including their clarity, compatibility and consequences – intended or otherwise – and concludes with an attempt to respond to each of these in turn.

Are the goals of particular policies clear?

Policies towards PE and school sport in England and Wales over the past decade or so have changed the PE terrain quite substantially. The PESSCL strategy, in particular, gives expression to the more central positioning of sporting interests in PE policy that successive governments have allowed those lobbying for sport to obtain. The pervasiveness of references to PE *and school sport* – not only in policy statements but also among the PE profession – suggests that school sport is viewed as sufficiently significant such that it is no longer realistic to talk of PE in isolation (Bloyce, 2007). Indeed, because schools are expected to provide more opportunities for sport within and beyond the curriculum as well as treat extra-curricula sport as forming a *sporting* continuum with the formal PE curriculum, references to PE and school sport may represent a stage in a process of redefining PE as *sport* education or even simply sport in schools.

The ideological pre-eminence of sport notwithstanding, the goals of government policy towards PE – rhetorically, at least – continue to be varied, and tend to include health promotion, academic attainment and social inclusion alongside the development of sport and sports performance; goals which are by no means compatible.

Where policies have several goals, are these mutually compatible?

Many of the goals of contemporary education policy are complex and, sometimes, incompatible or contradictory. As in many English-speaking countries worldwide, the direction of educational reform in the UK since the 1980s has been towards an educational market (Gorard et al., 2003) and the goal of 'individualized school improvement through competition' (Evans et al., 2005: 223). In many countries, marketization of education and schools has taken the form of a decentralization of control (for example, Local Management of Schools in England and Wales) and funding (such as Grant-Maintained Schools in England and Wales and Charter Schools in the USA). Such policies are predicated on the claimed benefits of 'specialism' and 'diversity' in school provision and 'choice' for parents, as well as the assumed ability of educational markets to deliver improvements – in terms, for example, of standards of academic attainment and proportions of the school-age population gaining suitable qualifications. More recently, however, government policy in England and Wales has shifted to include calls for 'collaboration' and 'partnership' as the main method of improving schools (Evans et al., 2005). This shift towards the, seemingly incompatible, policies of incorporating partnership alongside competition is most obvious in policy towards PE. Policies regarding SSCs, for example, require partnerships between schools and between schools and sports clubs, sport coaches and development officers as well as competition between schools for, among other things, the recruitment of talented athletes and examination success.

The potential for incompatibility between several stated aims is also seen in the manner in which policy towards PE has compounded the long-standing tension between elite sport and mass participation at the school level. The PESSCL strategy illustrates, par excellence, the impact on government policy of the well documented and publicized anxieties among governing bodies of sport about whether or not PE was and is maintaining a sufficient flow of participants. A recent evaluation of the PESSCL strategy highlights the persistent tension between the 'gifted and talented' emphasis in policy and the widely promulgated aim of increasing participation among young people.

If government and PE claims are taken at face value, one could be forgiven for thinking that sport in general, and sport in schools in particular (typically in the guise of PE), is some kind of panacea or wonder drug that, if administered in sufficient doses, would rid society of a breadth of social 'ills' ranging from the 'obesity epidemic', through deviancy to national self-esteem! Physical education teachers and academics can often be heard, along with government ministers, making grandiose claims for the efficacy of school sport and PE in helping to tackle spiralling obesity rates among children, improving Britain's sporting performance 'as well as offering young people an alternative to "hanging around on street corners"' (Baldwin and Halpin, 2004: 1). In addition to opening PE up to ridicule by making such unjustified assertions physical educationalists are offering a hostage to fortune to anyone charged with monitoring and evaluating the profession's achievement of such idealistic objectives.

What likely outcomes might be associated with the implementation of these policies?

While children's participation in sport and physical activity is not seen as exclusively the responsibility of either the PE profession or those involved with sport (for example, governing bodies of sport, sports clubs, coaches and SDOs), the values, objectives and methods of each are, nonetheless, often a source of rivalry and contestation; not least in terms of how each perceives the other's role and responsibilities. Chief among the significant differences between sports coaches and SDOs and PE teachers is their *raison d'être*. In the words of a much used aphorism in PE, 'the game is not the thing, the child is'. More than a decade ago, Capel (1996: 31–44) indirectly pointed up the potentially negative impact on the general extra-curricular involvement of PE teachers if their primary concern was to become 'identifying talent and helping talented pupils establish links with outside agencies and clubs'.

Official views of PE often portray sport as the primary focus of PE, and this view is more likely to be confirmed than challenged by physical educationalists themselves. However, greater involvement in PE by sports coaches and SDOs might have a number of unintended consequences that even those PE teachers ostensibly in favour of their involvement would not be happy with – ranging from the 'de-skilling' of PE teachers (Thorpe, 1996) through to their partial or even complete replacement.

The more the power differentials between more established (such as PE teachers) and less established (SDOs, for example) occupational groupings with an interest in PE diminish, the more the course of PE is likely to become 'indeterminate, fluid and beyond the control of any single individual or group' (Mennell, 1998: 262). The increasing support given to agencies beyond PE means that the balance of power within the subject-community of PE has become more evenly distributed in recent years and, thus, the activities of PE teachers are more constrained than they were when PE teachers had greater control of their subject. Ironically, PE teachers have probably been complicit in their own marginalization. In their search for greater occupational security and professional standing, physical educationalists – academics as well as practitioners – have tried to position themselves at the nodal point of broader, more pressing political issues – such as the 'obesity epidemic' – by seeking to forge alliances or 'advocacy coalitions' (Houlihan and Green, 2006: 84) with other more powerful government departments, such as the DoH. This is one substantial reason why PE teachers perpetuate the 'widely-held belief … that sport performs manifold welfare functions' (Heinemann, 2005: 183).

What is the significance of policy for practitioners?

In broad terms, curricula might be viewed as the meat in the sandwich between, at one end of the educational process, philosophizing upon the nature and purposes of the subject and, at the other end, the actual delivery of the curriculum by teachers. Curricula represent the 'what?' in between the 'why?' and the 'how?' But curricula are processes; they develop over time and depend for direction upon the intended and unintended outcomes of the struggles between various interested individuals and groups within, but also beyond, the immediate policy network of PE. As a result, policies are complex and sometimes contradictory and seldom straightforward in their implementation.

Policy towards PE inevitably constrains PE teachers. While the NCPE, for example, reflects the dependence of physical educationalists upon government (and, indirectly, the sports lobby), it is at the same time an example of how policy can never simply be dictated – however strongly the policy-makers believe it should be. Organizations may will the ends and even the means but they cannot guarantee either. Because the policy process involves many people at different levels and because it is a human process it is susceptible to adaptation and change in the process of being implemented by practitioners.

The limits to the state's capacity to control the practices of PE teachers is evident in the delivery of the NCPE (Curtner-Smith, 1999). Teachers tend to be portrayed as the final link in a chain between policy and practice. The image conveyed in 'ideal-type' models of policy is one of 'a transmission of policy to those whose task is to translate it, in an essentially direct manner, into practice' (Penney and Evans, 2005: 23). But teachers have certain mediating powers. Penney and Evans (2005) highlight the 'active role' of the practitioner in policy and curriculum change and what they refer to as 'slippage' in the implementation of policy: in other words, a disjuncture between the practice of teachers in classrooms and the goals or principles as outlined in particular policies or legislation. Teachers are able to find room for manouevre or slippage within the requirements of the NCPE, for example, and some areas of PE (for example, the introduction of examinations into PE) may be changeable, and quickly, on the basis of an initial intervention by a relatively small group of PE teachers. Still other areas (such as PE teachers' penchant for 'activity choice' with older pupils) might persist despite policy prescription. What PE teachers actually do in the name of PE is, it seems, often at odds with official policy. Rather than simply implementing the NCPE, research suggests that teachers have persistently modified the NCPE to make it fit with their views about PE and to make it manageable within their particular working environments (Curtner-Smith, 1999; Green, 2003). This appears to be especially true in primary schools among teachers who possess little subject-specific expertise nor often a desire to teach PE. Indeed, it is also likely that some of these processes of mediation are done in a relatively non-reflective manner (Murphy, 2007). Assumptions that a standardized NCPE leads, straightforwardly, to standardized pupil experiences and guaranteed outcomes, as well as raised standards, have been shown to be misplaced.

This chapter opened by observing that the notion of policy itself necessarily presupposes a judgement about appropriate ends; that is, policy implies a desire to move from what is perceived to be an unsatisfactory state of affairs to a more satisfactory one. This means that policy is inevitably ideological: it involves value-laden views about the way things *ought* to be. For those who do not share the analysts' ideological presuppositions this inevitably de-values analyses of policy that point to a preferred policy response.[3] It may mean that debate about policy simply involves proponents of particular positions talking past one another unless they engage at a fundamental level with the ideological presuppositions that underpin their preferred policy options.

Despite the ideological nature of policy and the potential incompatibility of various policies, it is difficult to deny that sport has become more and more prominent not only in policy towards PE but also in the justification for the practice of PE in many countries. Whether or not this represents the transformation of PE into school sport – in other words, the sportization[4] of PE – is an issue we will cover in the Conclusion. Either way, the fact that the government expresses a strong ideological commitment to sport does not mean that it will provide the resources necessary to realize its vision (Murphy, 2007) nor, indeed, realistically expects its policies to be successful!

RECOMMENDED READING

Bloyce, D. and Smith, A. (forthcoming) *Sport Development and Policy in Society*. London: Routledge.

Houlihan, B. (2003) 'Politics, power, policy and sport', in B. Houlihan (ed.), *Sport and Society: A Student Introduction*. London: Sage. pp.28–48.

NOTES

1 The DCSF replaced the former Department for Education and Skills (DfES) in June 2007.
2 The specialist schools concept is not exclusive to England and Wales. Since the beginning of the 1980s, primary schools in Berlin, for example, have been able to mark themselves out as distinct – in much the same way that British schools do – by emphasizing a particular subject (such as sport) (Pfister and Reeg, 2006). In Berlin, some pupils receive additional PE lessons through the primary years and schools choose the particular PE content of lessons.
3 I am grateful to Patrick Murphy for this point.
4 The term 'sportization' was originally coined to refer to the process by which folk games and pastimes were transformed into modern-day sports.

The 'State' of Physical Education

In very many developed and developing countries worldwide, PE is a conventional (in the sense of being generally practised), often compulsory element of primary and secondary school curricula (Hardman and Marshall, 2005). Despite the formal status of PE in many countries, it has become an orthodoxy in PE circles to advocate the view that, since the early 1970s, PE has been in a state of decline and marginalization – when measured, for example, in terms of the number and quality of facilities and suitably qualified teachers, time devoted to PE and curriculum content. The supposed downturn in the fortunes of PE is said to have occurred not only in countries in the English-speaking world such as Australia, the USA (Dollman et al., 2006) and the UK (DCMS, 2000) but in many countries worldwide (Doll-Tepper, 2005; Hardman and Marshall, 2000; 2005). The situation in the USA, where there are said to be especially 'large differences in the way in which PE is delivered and promoted' (Welk et al., 2006: 679) – between but also within states – is indicative of the differences between countries worldwide. In approximately one-third of the countries or provinces in Hardman and Marshall's (2000) worldwide survey, for example, PE provision was said to be, at best, minimal and, in some cases, non-existent. The seemingly declining *state* of PE is widely believed to reflect the diminishing *status* of the subject, particularly in primary schools.

Using several recent surveys, this chapter examines various components of PE (from facilities through to curriculum time and content) in England and Wales – while making reference to the rest of Europe and the USA – in order to explore some of the assumptions (such as that between time spent in PE lessons and young people's ongoing adherence to sport) that are often implicit in commentaries on the condition of PE. In the process, the chapter asks a number of questions about the alleged 'state' of PE, including:

- Are developments in facility provision, curriculum time and content, as well as teaching personnel indicative of a decline in the state of PE rather than merely change – some aspects of which may be 'good' while others may be 'bad'?
- To what extent do perceptions of decline reflect physical educationalists' *preferred* views regarding what constitutes (1) sufficient PE; (2) the right kinds of activities; and (3) an appropriate blend of facilities, curriculum content and teachers?

It is important to bear in mind that, whatever the statutory requirements with regard to school PE in particular regions and countries around the world, the preconditions for delivering PE in primary and secondary schools can and do differ markedly within and between developed, developing and third-world countries. Large-scale investment in PE in England in recent years, for example, stands in marked contrast to other areas of the world, including North America (Hardman, 2007). Nevertheless, England and Wales make an interesting case study for consideration of the issues surrounding the state and status of PE; not least because many of the developments and processes at issue elsewhere – in the English-speaking world and Europe especially – are being, or have been, played out there.

First, it is worth exploring the state of the facilities that 'house' PE in England and Wales before going on to examine the numbers of suitably qualified teachers, time devoted to PE and curriculum content.

THE STATE OF PE: FACILITIES

The provision of suitable and well-maintained sports facilities in schools is not only an issue in Britain (Central Council for Physical Recreation [CCPR], 2001) and Europe (Hardman and Marshall, 2005) but also worldwide (Hardman and Marshall, 2000). Teachers in both primary and secondary schools in the Sport England (2003b: 33) survey reported 'an increasing level of dissatisfaction with the adequacy of facilities available to their school' over the eight-year period between 1994 and 2002 (40 and 39 per cent of primary and secondary school teachers, respectively, in 2002 compared with 23 and 24 per cent in 1994). Primary school teachers with responsibility for PE expressed particular dissatisfaction with school halls, outdoor pitches/fields and playground areas, while specialist PE teachers in secondary schools reported reduced access to cricket nets, tennis courts and outdoor swimming pools over the same period (Sport England, 2003b).

Despite the general perception of decline among the teachers surveyed, the vast majority of secondary schools in England at the time owned or had access to outdoor pitches and sports fields (Sport England, 2003a), approximately two-thirds (64 per cent) had access to a multi-purpose sports hall (Sport England, 2000a) and 45 per cent owned or had access to an indoor swimming pool. Of 13 specific facilities surveyed, greater availability of eight was reported in 2002 compared with 1994 (Sport England, 2003a). Teachers also reported increased access to athletics facilities, school halls and playground areas over the same time span.

Secondary schools tend to possess more and a greater range of facilities than primary schools. Nonetheless, the latter appeared to have more facilities available for their use overall in 2002 than was the case in 1994 (Sport England, 2003a). This was particularly so in the form of school halls and indoor swimming pools but also of multi-purpose sports halls, 'outdoor purpose-built sports areas', synthetic athletic tracks, cricket nets and tennis courts. Amid this picture of relative improvement, half of the primary teachers in the Sport England (2003b) survey considered school hall (49 per cent) and playground area (55 per cent) provision for PE to be adequate. Indeed, the figures stood at two-thirds (65 per cent) for outdoor pitches/fields, three-quarters for indoor swimming pools (79 per cent) and 'grass/other track' (74 per cent).

Overall, the Sport England findings suggested not so much a decline in facility provision in schools as a *shift* in the *mixture* of facilities available to schools – especially secondary schools – from an emphasis on those facilities (typically, outdoor grass pitches) that support the teaching of traditional team and partner games, towards those suited to indoor-based sports and physical activities and more reliable, all-weather playing surfaces facilities such as 'astro-turf'. These trends are in line with Roberts's (1996a: 49) observation that, according to the *Community Use of Sports Facilities* (Hunter, 1995) survey, schools in England and Wales had been 'enhancing rather than reducing their sports facilities'.

The observation that, over time (especially when viewed over the course of the half-century existence of secondary PE), facilities for school sport in England have been steadily improving should not disguise the fact that provision for PE can be less than ideal and sometimes inadequate for intended use – especially in primary schools where the marginal position of PE can be made worse by unsatisfactory facilities. Where provision for PE in both primary and secondary schools is poor, both outdoor (for example, playing fields) and indoor facilities (gymnasia and sports halls) tend to be inadequately maintained (with pitches commonly being susceptible to drainage problems) and cold. Indoor facilities can also be inadequate for the numbers of pupils to be taught. Such problems with facilities and resources tend to be worse in those countries with increasingly marketized education sectors – where changes towards the localization of school management and budgetary arrangements have led many schools to redirect some of their expenditure away from expensive items such as the maintenance and upkeep of facilities and the transport used for travel to sporting fixtures and off-site activities.

In England and Wales, the sale of school playing fields has proved to be the most contentious aspect of facility provision. However, as far as public playing fields are concerned, in 959 redevelopment applications considered during 2003–04, '72 (playing) fields were created and 52 lost, out of about 44,000 pitches across 21,000 sites' (*BBC News*, 2005a: 1). Nevertheless, this did not prevent the National Playing Fields Association claiming that almost 45 per cent of England's sports pitches had been lost since 1992 and describing the situation as 'shameful' (*BBC News*, 2005b: 1). Such responses are typical of the animated manner in which those representing the major 'national' games have responded to the sale of public and school playing fields. By responding in this way, the sports lobby have clouded the issues surrounding outdoor facilities, tending to overlook the fact that they are neither powerless nor at the mercy of the planning process. Sport England is obliged to check every planning application involving a playing field (although public playing fields have to be twice as large as school fields to acquire protection) and is entitled to object if it thinks that sport will lose out – in short, playing fields can only be sold off as 'an absolute last resort'. Indeed, because the proceeds must be used to improve facilities (especially outdoor facilities), wherever possible, there has been a general improvement in facilities in terms of a closer match between participation trends among young people and the mix of indoor and outdoor facilities. For secondary schools, the sale of playing fields has tended to result in a substantial increase in the number of all-weather surfaces available to schools (Roberts, 1996a). Indeed, campaigners who continue to argue that there still need to be more outdoor rather than indoor sports spaces are flowing against rather than with trends in sports participation (see Chapter 7).

While it is undoubtedly true that effective learning and teaching may well be dependent upon the provision of suitable facilities and equipment, no clear or incontrovertible evidence can be found regarding what constitutes either a bare minimum or optimal amount or quality of provision. The significance of this is highlighted by the fact that participation in sport and physical activity among young people and adults in the UK plateaued more than a decade ago, even though the quantity and quality of public and commercial provision has ebbed and flowed. Indeed, school or dual-use (school and local government) sports centres – often considered the backbone of secondary school PE and sporting facilities – are a relatively recent phenomenon. While there are now over 2,000 sport and leisure centres in the UK, there were virtually no indoor sports facilities of this kind in the 1960s. Before the 1970s, almost the only indoor facilities in the UK were (mostly Victorian) swimming baths and dance halls. During the 1970s and 1980s, local government (some-times working in partnership with, for example, the Sports Council) set about an ambitious plan of developing sport and leisure centres in every town in the UK. Inevitably, many facilities that were new in the 1970s and 1980s now appear 'run down', dated and in need of investment. This impression is probably exacerbated by the rapid growth of attractive commercial sports and fitness centres over the past decade.

However, the kind of investment subsidy required to achieve substantial improvements in facilities is very probably unaffordable by local or central governments. Nor, for that matter, is it politically viable. Heinemann (2005: 181) observes: 'To the extent that the traditional welfare states of western industrialized countries are heading towards (funding) crises ... the sports system will also be affected by such developments and will be required to adjust and adapt.'

Before moving on to explore the 'state of PE' in terms of PE teachers, a caveat needs to be added with regard to facilities. A central contention of this chapter has been that if the situation in England and Wales in recent decades is at all indicative of developments in other western industrialized countries, then caution is called for regarding whether facilities have, in fact, deterior-ated in the manner that many physical educationalists claim. However, the situation in developing countries, even in Europe, can be markedly different.[1] Countries in Eastern Europe, for example (especially the former 'Soviet bloc' countries) have been particularly affected by political developments over the past decade or so. At the same time, however, it is important to bear in mind that many of these countries have always relied heavily on the voluntary sports club sector for (extra-curricular) sporting facilities in particular.

THE STATE OF PE: PE TEACHERS

Virtually all secondary schools in England (Sport England, 2003a), as with English-speaking countries around the world, have at least one member of staff with a specialist PE qualification. However, the same cannot be said with regard to PE specialists in primary schools. Although many primary (elemen-tary) schools in the USA do have PE specialists, in many countries (Australia and the UK, for example), PE in primary schools is taught by classroom teach-ers with limited training in PE. Indeed, only a minority of primary schools in Sport England's study had a qualified PE specialist either on a full-time (9 per cent) or part-time (22 per cent) basis: 'Instead, the vast majority of primary schools (93 percent) rely upon class teachers or other staff to teach PE' (Sport England, 2003b: 76–7). In the USA, although the government 'mandates a highly qualified (fully licensed) teacher in every classroom in core subjects' it does not do so in PE (Dodds, 2006: 542). Indeed, the No Child Left Behind policy (US Department of Education, 2002) in the USA encourages the use of highly qualified teachers for all subjects *except* PE (Collier, 2006). It comes as no surprise, therefore, to find that the marginality of PE in relation to other, more academic, school subjects often leads to a feeling of isolation among PE teachers; especially those at the primary level where there might only be one physical educationalist in any school (Stroot and Ko, 2006).

In a number of countries, increasing class sizes have been a growing concern in recent decades (Tsangaridou, 2006a) and have added to the pressure on teaching resources. In England and Wales, pupil–teacher ratios worsened in PE during the 1990s as the size of teaching groups grew as a consequence of increased pupil numbers alongside static (or, in the case of Years 10 and 11, declining) numbers of specialist PE teachers. This development added further impetus to the tendency for PE departments to make use of outside agencies for a supply of sports coaches and SDOs to aid the delivery of curricular and extra-curricular PE.

Physical education departments in England and Wales have always been inclined to make use of non-specialist teachers – especially in the delivery of activity-choice or 'option' PE for upper-school pupils and extra-curricular PE. However, this tendency has grown over the past decade, aided by the willingness of external agencies to become more involved in schools and government policy constraining schools in this direction (see Chapter 2). Specialist Sports Colleges are particularly likely to make use of specialist coaches; particularly in order to 'support … less accessible activities, such as ice-skating, horse-riding, martial arts and golf in lessons and out of school' (OFSTED, 2005a: 29). Nowhere is the trend towards broadening the range of people (or 'adults other than teachers' [AOTT] as they are known) permitted involvement in PE more evident than in primary schools. According to Sports Coach UK (2004), approximately 140,000 AOTTs (including SDOs, sports coaches, parents and other adults) were delivering sports sessions within primary schools. The trend towards increased use of AOTTs – coaches and SDOs, in particular – is reflected in the emergence of commercial companies providing sports coaches for schools. In this vein, most School Sport Partnerships in the Loughborough Partnership (2005: 29) survey 'reported an increase in the number of coaches working within the Partnership'.

The marginal position of PE in primary schools worldwide (Hunter, 2006) and the increased use of AOTTs is justified by the schools themselves in terms of the lack of PE and sporting expertise and correspondingly low levels of confidence among primary teachers regarding the teaching of the subject (see Chapter 12). This, in turn, tends to be a consequence of the lack of personal sporting expertise among would-be primary school teachers, compounded by the relatively minor part that PE plays in their training (Hunter,

2006) – many trainee primary school teachers receive little more than a day's training in PE (Caldecott et al., 2006b). Since 2003, a Coaching for Teachers scheme in England and Wales has provided opportunities for teachers and other adults involved with extra-curricular PE to gain sports governing body qualifications. The significance of the long-standing shortage of primary school teachers with sporting expertise and PE qualifications is highlighted when one considers the relatively high degree of autonomy and control teachers in primary schools worldwide tend to have over what happens in the name of PE, as well as the way in which it happens (Hunter, 2006).

Despite the seemingly bleak portrait of the numbers and availability of suitably qualified PE teachers worldwide (even in countries where PE is part of a statutory 'national' curriculum), in England and Wales the QCA (2005a) and OFSTED (2005b) feel able to point to what they perceive as an improvement in the quality of PE teaching, generally, and 'particularly' in primary schools in recent years. Despite the lack of primary teachers with sporting enthusiasm, let alone suitable training in PE, schools in England and Wales have, for a number of years, had designated curriculum leaders with responsibility for PE in their schools. This system is said to have been improved by the advent of School Sport Partnerships and the requirement for each primary school in a partnership to have a nominated Primary Link Tutor.

THE STATE OF PE: TIME

The study of time became an established dimension of PE research in the 1980s in the form of the Academic/Active Learning Time in Physical Education (ALT-PE) research. This branch of PE research focused on the proportion of PE lessons pupils actually spent 'on task'; that is, actively and appropriately engaged with purposeful, learning-related tasks (Van Der Mars, 2006). More recently, concern with time has shifted from the ways in which it is spent to the more fundamental issue of the overall amount of time available for PE.

In many ways it is the apparent reduction in time devoted to curricular PE that has precipitated the widespread claims of decline in the state and status of PE. On the basis of their international survey of the state and status of physical education, Hardman and Marshall (2005: 45) reported 'marked variations' across Europe between the amounts of PE curriculum time prescribed and actually delivered. Hardman and Marshall (2005) pointed, for example, to reductions as high as 25 per cent in curriculum time for PE in Germany since 1990 and substantial reductions in Sweden. Elsewhere, Dollman et al. (2005: 893) reported 'less time and expertise in many schools for implementing structured physical activity programmes' in Australia and a reduction in involvement in daily PE from 42 per cent of children in 1991 to 28 per cent in 2003 in the USA.

In the UK, a decline in time allocated to PE within the curriculum in England has been apparent since 1974 (Hardman and Marshall, 2000; Harris, 1994a; Sport England, 2000a) and, in particular, since 1992 (Sport England, 2000a). As in the USA, the decrease in time for every secondary year in England appears to have been particularly marked among the 14 to 16 age group (Hardman and Marshall, 2000; Harris, 1994a) with young people in this age bracket experiencing 'a slow but steady decline in the proportion receiving two hours or more PE' (Sport England, 2003a: 5). At the same time, a trend towards teaching periods of one hour's duration has added to the time pressures on PE (Hardman and Marshall, 2000; Sports Council for Wales, 1995). Despite this, the UK government's Public Service Agreement Target for school sport is 'to have increased the percentage of 5–16 year olds who spend a minimum of two hours each week on high quality PE and school sports to … 85 percent by 2008' (DCMS/DfES, 2005: 3) as a step towards the overall target of every child receiving two hours of curriculum PE each week by 2010 (Harris, 2005; QCA, 2005a).

Time for PE is a particular issue in the primary sector, with evidence of 'insufficient' curriculum time – and sometimes (for example, countries and regions of Africa) no time at all – for primary-aged pupils in particular (Hardman and Marshall, 2000). Reduced curriculum time is said to be attributable to a lack of facilities and specialist teachers and the marginal status of the subject in relation to other areas of school curricula (Hardman and Marshall, 2000). With this in mind, the Chief Inspector of Schools for England and Wales expressed concern regarding primary schools' apparent failure to devote enough time (as well as other resources) to pupils' physical development: 'In most of the primary schools, Key Stage 1 pupils usually had less PE teaching than those at Key Stage 2' (OFSTED, 2005a: 2), and both compared unfavourably with the greater amount of time allocated to PE in secondary schools.

But how far *is* government off the target of two hours in England and Wales? Despite widespread concern it appears that the apparent decline in time devoted to curriculum PE has been reversed, in England at least, with the amount of curriculum time allocated to PE having increased substantially since the end of the 1990s (DCMS/DfES, 2006; Sport England, 2003a). In 1999, 33 per cent of youngsters in Years 2–11 (that is, primary *and* secondary schooling) received two or more hours per week of PE. By 2002 this had increased to 49 per cent, a 5 per cent increase since 1994 (Sport England, 2003a). More recently, the DCMS/DfES (2006) has claimed that, according to its 2005–06 *School Sport Survey* of over 16,800 schools, 80 per cent of pupils in schools (comprising 82 per cent in primary and 78 per cent in secondary schools) participated in at least two hours of 'high quality PE and sport in a typical week'. These figures include both curricular and extra-curricular (or 'out-of-hours school sport') provision. Nonetheless, over half (61 per cent) of the more than 5 million pupils included in the DCMS/DfES (2006) study received two hours of PE entirely within the curriculum, with the greatest progress towards that threshold having been made in the primary sector. According to DCMS/DfES (2006), across all year groups in their survey, pupils spent an average of 111 minutes each week on curriculum PE – on average 110 minutes for primary schools and 112 for secondary schools; that is, eight and 10 minutes under the targets in secondary and primary schools respectively. It is particularly interesting to note that the three school years in which pupils appear to receive more than two hours' curricular PE in England are Years 7 to 9; that is, the first three years of secondary schooling. The Loughborough Partnership (2005) reported the mean curriculum time for the 22 schools in its study as just over (Years 7 and 8) or just under (Year 9) two hours for both boys and girls. At Years 10 and 11 the mean fell to one-and-a-half hours and in Years 12 and 13 (ages 16–18) it fell to less than one hour. The mean times for upper secondary Years 10 and 11 in the DCMS/DfES (2006) study were very similar, at 97 minutes and 94 minutes respectively. Whatever the picture previously, it seems that since the mid-1990s there has been an increase in the time allocated for PE in primary and secondary schools in England and Wales (QCA, 2005b; Sport England, 2003a).

At one level, the QCA's (2001) observation that time is a valuable resource is obvious. It is worth pausing for a moment, however, to ask just *why* governments, the Council of Europe, the International Council for Sports Science and Physical Education (ICSSPE) and, for that matter, PE teachers themselves consider the time allocated to PE and school sport – and the two-hour threshold, in particular – to be of such importance. Of course, the call for a minimum of two hours may well be based on perceptions of an historical norm or ideal-type. At the same time, two hours may provide a conveniently round figure as a 'line in the sand' beyond which the PE subject-community feels it cannot afford to retreat, in political terms. But that should not dissuade us from asking if there is any more to the two hours threshold than this? And, indeed, there appears to be. It is argued, for example, that insufficient time would militate against high levels of participation and achievement (QCA, 2001). But is two hours a minimum for teaching NCPE? It appears not for, as the DCMS/DfES (2005: 9) report points out, both the primary and secondary allocations of curricular PE time in England and Wales 'are above the recommended time needed to cover the PE programme of study effectively' (75 minutes per week at Key Stages 1 and 2 and 90 at Key Stage 3). In this regard, the QCA (2001) acknowledges that the overall amount of time allocated to PE is less important than the way it is distributed and used. Therefore, it is worth asking what two hours of PE each week is deemed necessary for? Might it be, for example, for skill development, health promotion or the encouragement of lifelong participation? Roberts (1996a) argued that there is no evidence to suggest that two hours is a critical threshold for either maintaining health and fitness, nurturing a liking for sport or even developing a longer-term commitment to participation. It may, however, be that the more time young people spend in physical activity the more likely they are to develop their fundamental skills: Fisher et al. (2005: 684) found that 'fundamental movement skills were significantly associated with habitual physical activity' even though 'the association between the two variables was weak'. Either way, the real significance of time allocation to PE may well lie in the potential for coverage of a range of activities. The Office for Standards in Education (2005b) comments that, in SSCs, the breadth and balance of activities are much better as a result of at least two hours a week of PE in both Key Stages 3 and 4.

Before leaving the issue of time, it is worth reflecting upon the context which provides the constraints for PE in England and Wales. The development of a statutory National Curriculum and policies aimed at improving 'citizenship' and literacy and numeracy have inevitably added further pressure to an already crowded timetable and exacerbated the pressure on curricular PE. Empirical evidence that general curriculum pressures are pushing PE and sport in primary schools, for example, into out-of-school time comes from the Loughborough Partnership's (2005) evaluation of School Sport Partnerships in England. Also, the advent of an educational market has substantially increased the pressure on non-examinable subjects (Gorard et al., 2003), thus squeezing curriculum time in particular. There are no signs of a rolling back of policies aimed at increasing the process of marketization in education and, therefore, no sign of anything other than, at best, a stabilization of the time allocated to PE. In the short to medium term, one of the more realistic avenues open to physical educationalists in England and Wales seeking an increased time allocation for PE lies in the academicization of the subject; that is, increasing the number of academic and vocational qualifications they offer through PE (see Chapter 5).

THE STATE OF PE: THE CURRICULUM

Provision: number and range of activities

Since the early 1970s, PE departments in England and Wales have focused upon increasing the range of sports available in PE (Roberts, 1995; 1996a; 1996b) and this process was reinforced with the introduction of the NCPE. In England, over 40 sports are typically tried by some young people in their school careers (Sport England, 2003a). In 2002, the average number of sports undertaken at least once in the year in school lessons for all young people in England was nine, for both boys and girls (compared with eight in 1994 and 1999) (Sport England, 2003a). More recently, the DCMS/DfES (2006) pointed to an average of 16 different sports provided by primary and secondary schools in the 16,882 schools in their *School Sport Survey*. According to Sport England (2003a), the average number of sports undertaken 'frequently' (at least 10 times in the year) by pupils in 2002 was four (unchanged since 1994). At the same time, however, there was 'a small, but notable, increase in the numbers of young people (Years 2–11) … not taking part in at least one sport regularly in lessons (from 15 percent in 1994 to 17 percent in 1999 to 18 percent in 2002)' (Sport England, 2003a: 5).

In addition to an increase in the sheer number of sports on offer in schools, there has been a substantial increase in the range of activities provided – by secondary schools in particular. According to Sport England (2003a: 16), for example, 'over the last eight years schools have focused on increasing the range of sports that young people take part in, rather than the frequency in which they participate'. The most widely available sports and physical activities for the 5 million-plus pupils in the DCMS/DfES (2006) survey were football (98 per cent), dance (96 per cent), gymnastics (95 per cent), athletics (92 per cent), cricket (89 per cent) and rounders (87 per cent). These, according to DCMS/DfES (2006: 17), 'have consistently been the most widely available sports' over all three of their surveys. In their study of School Sport Partnerships, the Loughborough Partnership (2005) also reported increases in the range of activities provided, at both primary and secondary school levels, alongside an expansion of 'new' activities. They pointed to more than 150 partnerships offering traditional sports (such as athletics, gymnastics, hockey, netball, rounders, rugby and soccer) and over 100 offering 'newer' activities (such as orienteering, fitness, table tennis, dance, basketball and badminton), with many tens of schools offering activities such as volleyball, cycling, boccia, canoeing, softball, sailing and martial arts. Indeed, 'the expansion of choice went well beyond the conventional school range and included sports and activities such as archery, bowls, kabbadi, triathlon, goalball, cheerleading, handball, circus skills and new age curling' (Loughborough Partnership, 2005: 25). This expansion was also reflected in the DCMS/DfES (2006) survey which revealed increases in the provision of fitness, orienteering, cycling, canoeing, golf and archery among other activities. Despite the breadth of curricula, the provision of teaching resources for (some) sports by external sporting agencies such as the YST (see Chapter 2) has, in recent years, begun to exert a substantial influence on the content of primary PE in particular, such that there is potential for particular sports to dominate the primary school PE curriculum.

Despite the provision of an increased number and range of activities in PE, the content of PE curricula can still appear irrelevant to some pupils' needs – especially girls' (Ennis, 1999) (see Chapter 8). Girls' levels of participation decline in many sports during the secondary years, particularly in volleyball, hockey, rugby, cross country, swimming and baseball (Sport England, 2003a). Nevertheless, in England, girls' participation at both primary and secondary levels has grown substantially over the past decade or more in rounders, tennis, football, cricket, basketball and dance (Sport England, 2003a). The breadth of activities reflects the fact that 'the types of sports that girls participate in, during lessons, has changed over the last eight years and to a greater extent than boys' (Sport England, 2003a: 12).

In terms of regularity and reliability of provision, as well as breadth and depth of coverage, the PE curriculum in primary schools has never been especially strong. The relatively minor place that PE occupies in the primary curriculum has compounded the uncertainty and confusion among teachers regarding what counts as PE in primary schools, who is responsible for its delivery and the extent to which it should be allocated seemingly precious time from other, supposedly more fundamental, aspects of primary education (Hunter, 2006). It is, perhaps, unsurprising, therefore, that research in the USA suggests that 'recess' – 'break time' in the UK – is often used to supplement PE (Hunter, 2006) and this suggests that PE is treated more like 'play' than an introduction to particular sporting activities.

Provision: the state of sport

Roberts (1996a: 49) points to the spectre raised by the British government's White Paper, *Sport: Raising the Game*, that schools had been 'neglecting Britain's traditional team games where national success has a purchase in popular culture'. Nevertheless, Roberts's analysis of the 1994 Sport England survey (Mason, 1995a) led him to comment that 'team games and other competitive sports were alive and well in England's schools' in the mid-1990s. 'Neither PE teachers nor their colleagues', he observed, 'had turned against Britain's traditional team sports and nearly all pupils were playing team games at school during every year in their school lives'. 'The situation', Roberts (1996a: 50) concluded 'was not that team games had been dropped, but rather that they had been joined by other activities in broader sports curricula than the traditional games regime'. As indicated earlier in this chapter, subsequent surveys (see Sport England, 2003a) have confirmed that this remains the case.

Although the curriculum diet has changed over the years, PE curricula in many countries reflect a good deal of continuity (as well as undeniable changes in the form of a broadening and diversity of activities) in the shape of a continued emphasis on competitive team sports. In secondary PE, in England, the top eight sports participated in frequently in secondary PE lessons in England in 2002 – athletics (36 per cent), gymnastics (32 per cent), tennis (31 per cent), rounders (29 per cent), hockey (27 per cent), netball (26 per cent), football (25 per cent), badminton (21 per cent) – reflected the persistence of a sport and traditional games core to the PE curriculum (Sport England, 2003b).

In the mid-1990s, Roberts (1996a: 50) reported that 'most pupils were competing at sport regularly both in and out of lessons'. More recently, the DCMS/DfES (2006: 2) found that, in the nearly 17,000 primary and secondary schools in their 2005–06 *School Sport Survey*, competitive sports such as football and athletics remained popular 'with almost all schools offering them' (DCMS/DfES, 2006: 15). The vast majority of schools, for example, offered football, athletics, cricket, netball, hockey, rugby and tennis. In addition, 71 per cent of pupils (79 per cent primary, 62 per cent secondary) were involved in *intra*-school competitive sport at some stage during the academic year 2005–06 and 39 per cent (46 per cent primary, 32 per cent secondary) were involved in *inter*-school competitive sport (DCMS/DfES, 2006) with the peak year for both intra- (86 per cent) and inter-school (58 per cent) involvement being Year 6 – the final year of primary school. Similarly, the Loughborough Partnership (2005: 27) reported 'marked increases in representative participation at almost all levels of competition' in their sample of 22 schools in the School Sport Partnership programme. The year-on-year consistency of this kind of data reflects the continuing orthodoxy of PE curricula and the continued pre-eminence of sport.

One of the key strategic aims of the PESSCL strategy and School Sport Partnerships in England and Wales has been the development of links and 'out-of-school hours' programmes with local sports clubs, national governing bodies, coaches and SDOs. In this regard, the DCMS/DfES (2006: 18) survey pointed to football, cricket, rugby union, dance and athletics as 'the most common club link sports'. The Loughborough Partnership (2005: 30) reported that 'the greatest success' in developing links between schools and sports clubs in its survey had been with those sports that have 'the most extensive coaching and sports development networks such as football, tennis and rugby' (see Chapter 2). Once again, the links between school and sports clubs appear to be at a peak in the upper primary school years (ages 7 to 10). Interestingly, the growth in representative participation at almost all levels of competition in the schools in the Loughborough Partnership's (2005: 27) evaluation included increases particularly among girls.

Trost (2006) identifies a number of surveys which demonstrate that in the USA, PE curricula in middle and high schools continue to consist primarily of competitive team sports such as baseball/softball, basketball, soccer and volleyball: 'as early as the 3rd and 4th grades, the focus of school physical education had shifted from movement education and fitness to competitive team sports such as soccer and basketball' (p. 182). As a result, Trost (2006: 181) observes, PE programmes 'have primarily served the interests of athletically gifted children at the expense of less athletic children'. Indeed, Collier (2006) notes that some state (or 'public') schools in the USA are replacing PE with inter-scholastic sport (and even marching band practices). It is worth bearing in mind, however, that the trend that Collier points to in the USA might not be such a new phenomenon: inter-scholastic sport has dominated the PE curriculum, especially in senior high schools for more than 30 years (Hardman, 2007).

So, surveys in the UK and abroad send a clear message: far from being threatened by the broadening of curricular diets, competitive sports, in general, and so-called 'traditional' team games, in particular, remain at the heart of PE, especially in secondary schools.

CONCLUSION

According to teachers in the Sport England surveys, secondary schools have experienced a decline in 'accessibility and adequacy' of facilities between 1994 and 2002. This perceived decline was, however, more marked in relation to particular facilities – cricket nets, outdoor swimming pools and tennis courts, for example. For some facilities this may reflect raised expectations on the part of teachers with regard to health and safety requirements and the diminishing appeal to pupils of activities such as cricket and outdoor swimming. Physical education teachers' perceptions may reflect not only real, observable changes in the condition of their once new facilities but also 'higher expectations over levels and standards of facilities in economically developed countries' (Hardman and Marshall, 2005: 54). Either way, teachers are doubtless sincere when they suggest that insufficient and inappropriate facilities (Tsangaridou, 2006a) significantly impact upon their teaching particularly in primary schools. Nevertheless, while provision for PE can be less than ideal, when viewed over the course of the half a century or more of secondary schooling and the century-long history of PE and physical training, it is difficult to deny that facilities for school sport have improved in many developed countries in a manner similar to the UK.

The findings in England suggest not so much a decline in facility provision as a shift in the mixture of facilities available to PE departments – from an emphasis on facilities that support the teaching of traditional team games and towards indoor-based sports and activities and more reliable, all-weather playing surface facilities. The growth of indoor provision, in particular, has been one of the main reasons for the evident broadening of school-age youngsters' sporting experiences to incorporate activities such as basketball and badminton.

The irony of the moral panic surrounding the sale of playing fields and the bemoaning of the supposedly attendant downgrading of traditional sport in English schools is that the UK government's emphasis upon outdoor (rather than indoor) playing facilities and the club-based traditional sports associated with them, reflects a misreading of both participation trends among young people and the practices of the schools accused of selling pitches. Roberts's (1996a: 52) interpretation of the available data for sport among young people in England in the mid-1990s remains applicable more than a decade on: 'the provision of sports centres which are available for everyone appears to have obliterated the "Wolfenden gap" and reduced the sport give-up rate from its former chronic level in the immediate post-school years'. Whether young people continue to play sport in their leisure time and after leaving school will probably have more to do with the availability of indoor facilities and all-weather surfaces than grass pitches, outdoor swimming pools and cricket nets.

The average allocation of time to curricular PE in England and Wales each week is much closer to the two hours threshold than is often claimed. This has become especially so in England recently (DCMS/DfES, 2006).

Putting to one side the reliance of some recent studies on impressionistic data (for example, the views of those most deeply involved, such as the PE teachers themselves), the resources provided by the government in England and Wales (to School Sport Partnerships, for example) and the emphasis these schools are able to give PE may simply be unlocking latent interest among those on the margins of commitment to sport for a generation of youngsters for whom 'sport is cool' (Sport England, 2003a; 2003b). After all, in 2002, the motivation to participate in sport was the highest it had been for almost a decade, according to Sport England (2003a), with fewer young people being 'put off' sport. A more recent study of the attitudes to sports and physical activities, both in and out of school, among 800 11–16-year-olds – as part of the BSkyB and the Youth Sport Trust's Living for Sport project – concluded that PE was the favourite subject of almost two-thirds (62 per cent) of pupils (Sportsteacher, 2005a).

Before offering a final commentary on the state of PE, it is important to recognize that the latest, yet to be published, research may well indicate a stabilization in PE provision rather than a continuing decline (despite persistent examples of cutbacks in time allocation). The 'mixed messages' likely to come from this research may well confirm the desirability for a portrayal of the state of PE based upon a continuum from positive through stability to negative, with a tendency towards the first two – at least as far as policies are concerned. The issue of policy rhetoric and the reality of practice persists, however (Hardman, 2007).

According to Penney (2006: 565), 'the past decade and a half has been a time of unprecedented externally driven curriculum "change" in education and physical education specifically'. It is also true to say that there is evidently a great deal of continuity in many countries between curricula of the past 30 years or so and those of the present. Although PE curricula have broadened, they continue to be dominated by sport and, in particular, team games. Because schools continue to place emphasis within PE upon conventional sports – especially through links with external sports clubs and coaches – they may not reach a broader swathe of pupils. Indeed, School Sport Partnerships, for example, may be providing more opportunities for those already predisposed towards sport.

These observations are not necessarily criticisms. Nevertheless, they do indicate the need for more circumspection on the part of those who may feel constrained to advocate government policy towards school sport. There can be no doubt that in marketized education systems, characterized by ever more crowded primary and secondary curricula, seemingly non-serious subjects such as PE are likely to be viewed by governments and schools as expendable in favour of more academic and examinable subjects. The 'increasing competition for space in the Australian school curriculum' (Dollman et al., 2005: 893) with 'less time and expertise in many schools for implementing structured physical activity programmes' is symptomatic of the pressures physical educationalists in very many countries worldwide are experiencing. In this respect, addressing what many see as the 'serious concerns about the current situation and the future of physical education' (Doll-Tepper, 2005: 41) and the 'global crisis of physical education' (Doll-Tepper, 2005: 43) has become a central policy objective of many PE bodies. Nevertheless, concern with the state of PE may have more to do with the age-old preoccupation among physical educationalists: the marginal status or esteem of their subject.

This chapter began by asking a number of questions about the supposed 'state' of PE. Using data on PE from England and Wales, in particular, it has been suggested that a less ideological, less emotive, perspective on the 'state' of PE reveals a different, more complex, picture to the taken-for-granted one of decline or crisis. First, it is important to keep in mind that the surveys upon which claims are made regarding decline, stabilization and so on are just that, surveys. In other words, they are based on *perceptions* of decline or change and not, for the most part, on audits of, for example, facility provision. In addition, use of relative terms, such as 'decline' indicate a judgement made against some, often unspecified, time in the past which might not hold up to scrutiny when viewed over a longer period. The range (and, sometimes, the sheer number) of facilities, activities and 'teachers' available to PE, for example, has grown quite substantially. Whether this is a good or bad thing (or both good and bad) depends on what one views as the proper aims and purposes of PE; what constitutes *enough* PE, the *right kinds of facilities and activities* and the most appropriate *people* to 'teach' PE.

RECOMMENDED READING

Hardman, K. and Marshall, J. (2005) 'Physical education in schools in European context: charter principles, promises and implementation realities', in K. Green and K. Hardman (eds), *Physical Education: Essential Issues*. London: Sage. pp.39–64.

NOTES

1 I am grateful to Ken Hardman (2007) for reminding me of this point.
2 11th and 12th grades in the USA represent the final two years of high school.

Extra-Curricular Physical Education

This chapter provides a broad outline of the state of extra-curricular PE – challenging a number of common-sense assumptions in the process – before attempting a brief explanation of why this supposedly fundamental aspect of PE remains relatively conventional in both content and form, especially at secondary school level. Finally, some of the more important issues surrounding extra-curricular PE are explored in the conclusion.

There may be a general lack of empirical information, internationally, regarding extra-curricular PE (De Martelaer and Theebom, 2006), but this is not so in the UK where a number of large-scale national surveys (see, for example, Sport England, 2003a; 2003b; Sports Council for Wales, 2003a; 2006) and medium- (see Smith, A., 2006) and small-scale (see Daley, 2002) studies have explored the topic in recent years. These studies form the evidence-base for the chapter.

Extra-curricular PE can be defined, based on Penney and Harris (1997), as the organization and provision by (PE) teachers of activities beyond the formal PE curriculum – typically after school and at lunch times but also, in some schools, before the school day begins or at weekends. In this form, extra-curricular PE is more common in English-speaking countries such as the UK, Australia and New Zealand. In North America, extra-curricular provision tends to take the form of after-school sports clubs oriented towards inter-scholastic sporting competition (rather than an extension of the PE curriculum), organized and delivered by school coaches rather than PE teachers (Curtner-Smith et al., 2007). Elsewhere, and in mainland Europe in particular, it is conventional for voluntary sports clubs to be the sole or main providers of sporting opportunities for young people after school. Nevertheless, even in central Europe, there is evidence of a merging of these different types of after-school or extra-curricular provision. In Flanders, for example, 'sports academies' provide multi-sport programmes after school without young people having to be members of sports clubs (De Martelaer and Theebom, 2006). Despite differences in format, extra-curricular PE in Britain is not as different, in qualitative terms, from its counterparts in the USA and Europe as it might seem at first glance. Traditionally, extra-curricular PE in secondary schools in England and Wales has been 'almost exclusively oriented towards competitive team games' (Daley, 2002: 44) and sport.

The sporting orientation of extra-curricular PE in the UK has not prevented government, media and the sports lobby repeatedly expressing their dissatisfaction with the alleged demise of sport in schools, in general, and extra-curricular PE provision, in particular. Against a backdrop of claims of deterioration, the next section explores the state of extra-curricular PE in Britain in terms of levels and forms of provision and participation.

THE STATE OF EXTRA-CURRICULAR PE

Provision of extra-curricular PE

In marked contrast to the portrayal of extra-curricular PE in official and semi-official government publications, the picture emerging from much research in England and Wales is one of extra-curricular provision as 'a strong and developing area of PE in state schools' (Penney and Harris, 1997: 42). In 1997, Penney and Harris (1997: 42) noted that 'almost without exception' secondary schools in England were 'providing activities after school and at lunch-times and many also ... at weekends'. By the end of the 1990s, Bass and Cale (1999: 45) felt able to claim that extra-curricular sporting activities continued to 'thrive in many schools' in England while, at the turn of the millennium, Daley (2002) suggested that most secondary schools in her study were offering extra-curricular opportunities. Similarly, Sport England (2003b) observed that all 63 secondary schools in their 2002 survey of *Young People and Sport in England* had provided extra-curricular sports and physical activities for their pupils. According to Sport England (2003a), between 1994 and 2002, opportunities for extra-curricular PE improved significantly and there was a steady climb in the percentage of secondary schools in England reporting an increase in the number of sports offered to pupils. In 2002, 89 per cent of schools reported that the number of sports provided in extra-curricular PE had either stayed the same (34 per cent) or increased (55 per cent) over the previous three years (Sport England, 2003b). This, it was suggested, reflected the increasing levels of participation in after-school sport in general (see Chapter 7) reported by young people (Sport England, 2003a).

In terms of *time* allocated to extra-curricular PE, the average per week in schools surveyed by the QCA (QCA, 2001) was just under 3 hours each week in primary schools (2 hours 24 minutes per year group at Key Stage 1 and 3 hours at Key Stage 2) and over 7 hours at secondary level (8 hours 18 minutes per year group at Key Stage 3 and 7 hours at Key Stage 4). The Sports Council for Wales (SCW, 2002) reported that the overall time devoted by teaching staff to extra-curricular activities each week in Wales had increased since 1997–98 to an average of approximately 30 hours per school. This amounted to an average of over 20 hours of extra-curricular PE each week in primary schools and between 30 and 35 hours in secondary schools (QCA, 2001; SCW, 2002; 2006).

Levels of participation in extra-curricular PE

Despite the seemingly widespread provision of extra-curricular PE in secondary schools in England and Wales, estimates of actual rates of participation among pupils tend to vary. In the mid-1990s, for example, Mason (1995b: 61) observed that although 'virtually all schools' in the 1994 Sport England survey 'provided at least some extra-curricular activity' most of this activity was undertaken 'by very small proportions of pupils'. Sport England's (2003b) 2002 survey reported 41 per cent of young people of secondary school age participating at least once in the previous 12 months in extra-curricular PE. Although this figure was down 8 per cent from 49 per cent in 1999, it remained almost identical to the 42 per cent participating in 1994. Thus, three-fifths (59 per cent) of secondary-aged pupils in Sport England's most recent survey had taken no part in extra-curricular PE in the previous year. More optimistic estimates of participation rates for extra-curricular PE can, nevertheless, be found. The SCW, for example, reported that in Wales, in 2004, 80 per cent of primary-aged children and 71 per cent of secondary-aged youngsters had taken part in extra-curricular PE in 2004 (SCW, 2006): only slightly higher than the SCW found in their earlier (1995 and 2001) studies.

It is, perhaps, when we turn to look at weekly, or more frequent, participation that we get a more telling picture of the state of extra-curricular PE in the UK. In terms of frequent participation (usually weekly) in extra-curricular PE, half of the heads of PE departments in Cale's (2000) study of 50 secondary schools in central England expressed the view that 'between 5 percent and 30 percent of pupils regularly took part in the extra-curricular activities their departments offered' (p. 75). The upper-end of this broad estimate is in line with findings from recent Sport England (2003b) and SCW (2003a and b; 2006) surveys. In England, 34 per cent of secondary-aged pupils reported taking part in extra-curricular PE at least once per week in 2002, 23 per cent on two or more days per week and 15 per cent on three or more days. In Wales, over half (58 per cent) of primary and just under half (42 per cent) of secondary pupils reported weekly or more frequent participation (SCW, 2006). The 42 per cent of secondary age pupils taking part at least once a week comprised 17 per cent once a week, 17 per cent two to three times a week, and 8 per cent three times a week or more.

If, as the available research evidence suggests, somewhere between one-third (at secondary level) and one-half (at primary level) of school-age youngsters in the UK take part in extra-curricular PE on a weekly basis, then around half to two-thirds of youngsters are doing very little on a regular basis and about one-quarter are doing none at all. In this regard, Daley (2002) suggests that the numbers of pupils taking part in extra-curricular PE have always been relatively low and continue to be so despite an upward trend through the 1990s. 'Most pupils', she observes, 'are given the opportunity to participate in physical activities outside of formal physical education lessons, but ... many choose not to do so' (Daley, 2002: 38) – or not on a regular basis.

This is particularly so at either end of the school-age continuum; that is, in the early years of primary and the later years of secondary schooling. Analyses of participation rates by year group in England and Wales reveal that participation in extra-curricular PE tends to peak in or around the final year of primary schooling – with virtually three-quarters (72 per cent) taking part frequently in Wales, in 2004, for example. Participation declined sharply, however, to approximately half (51 per cent) of pupils in the first year of secondary school (Year 7) in Wales. Thereafter, frequent (weekly or more often) participation in extra-curricular PE in both England and Wales displays a tendency to drop as pupils move from lower through to upper school; that is, from Years 7–9 to Years 10–11. Participation once a week or more in Wales, for example, declined steadily across the secondary age range from 51 per cent for Year 7 pupils (11–12-year-olds) through to 38 per cent for Year 11 pupils (15–16-year-olds). In the upper secondary years (ages 14–16) it remained fairly stable in Wales at just over a third taking part on a weekly basis (SCW, 2006). Corresponding figures for England indicated a drop from approximately 43 per cent for Years 7–9 to 35 per cent for Years 10–11 (Sport England, 2003b). According to Sport England (2003a: 64) this pattern of participation across the year groupings has 'remained fairly consistent year-on-year' since 1994.

Whatever the 'true' figure for levels of participation in extra-curricular PE it is probably the case, as Littlefield et al. (2003: 219) observe of Scotland, that the figures 'hide large differences between schools and regions'. This is certainly the case in Wales, where the SCW (2001: 4) reported 'considerable variations' among young people 'in the range and nature of (extra-curricular) activities undertaken across Wales and between local authorities'.

Interestingly, Braddock et al. (2005) observed similarly wide variations in access to and involvement in inter-scholastic sports and teams between boys and girls in many states in the USA; a situation which they suggest is associated, in part, with state educational expenditure and the racial composition of the student body. While the significance of 'race' or ethnicity and sex for PE generally will be explored in greater depth in later chapters, their impact upon extra-curricular PE merits more detail here.

Sex and extra-curricular PE Sex differences in participation in extra-curricular PE appear negligible during the primary years (Sport England, 2003a; SCW, 2006). In Wales, in 2002, 59 per cent of primary school boys and 57 per cent of girls took part in extra-curricular PE on a regular (at least weekly) basis. However, participation declines sharply during the early years of the secondary phase, particularly among girls, and more steadily thereafter. Although the sex gap is wider at secondary level – average levels of at least weekly participation among secondary-aged boys and girls in Wales were 45 per cent and 40 per cent – it has evidently narrowed over time, even though the general age-related decline in participation continues to be more marked among girls than boys and widens substantially in Years 10 and 11. In England, in 2002, 41 per cent of girls in Years 7–9 took part in extra-curricular PE; a figure which declined relatively little to 35 per cent in Years 10 and 11. Interestingly, this figure of 35 per cent was only 1 per cent below that of boys (36 per cent) at the same stage (Sport England, 2003b). However, whereas boys' participation remains in the 40–49 per cent range through Key Stages 1–3 (that is, from primary through to secondary schooling) – only dropping to 36 per cent at Key Stage 4 – with girls the pattern is far more changeable, moving from 28 per cent at Key Stage 1 to a substantial high of 55 per cent at Key Stage 2 (upper primary school) then steadily declining through 41 per cent at Key Stage 3 (Years 7–9: the lower secondary years) to 35 per cent at Key Stage 4 (upper secondary school).

In terms of frequency of participation among boys and girls of secondary age, Daley's (2002: 42) study found that 'boys were involved in extra-curricular activities on more occasions and for longer periods of time each week than girls'. However, the 2002 Sport England (2003b) survey suggests that the 'frequency' gap between the sexes is closer than one might expect, with the figures for participation only widening substantially at five days or more per week (7 per cent for boys compared with 2 per cent for girls). The figures for one day or more per week were 36 per cent for boys compared with 32 per cent for girls. Indeed, according to the Sport England (2003a) study, the percentage of girls spending between one and five hours each week on extra-curricular sport rose from 44 per cent in 1994 to 48 per cent in 2002. Despite these trends, Flintoff and Scraton (2001) suggest that there remains a gap between curricular and extra-curricular PE programmes and young women's active leisure lifestyles out of school (see Chapter 8). Most of the Australian young women in Wright's (1996, cited in Flintoff and Scraton, 2001:5) study were physically active out of school and concluded that, in general, 'more women than ever before are taking part in physical activity in out of school contexts'.

Ethnicity and extra-curricular PE Ethnicity can have a substantial impact upon participation in extra-curricular PE, especially as youngsters get older. While the participation of some minority ethnic groups in leisure sport generally and extra-curricular PE in particular, such as Chinese British, tend not to be constrained by their ethnicity, that of groups such as South Asian Muslims tend to be so. Muslim youngsters (and girls in particular) are especially unlikely to engage with extra-curricular PE for a variety of reasons: ranging from interference with academic progress or domestic responsibilities through to the requirements of Islam. Chapter 10 explores these themes in greater detail.

Disability and extra-curricular PE Relatively few disabled youngsters take part in extra-curricular PE. Sport England (2001b) reports that only 14 per cent (made up of similar proportions of boys and girls but twice as many secondary than primary-aged pupils) of young people with a disability reported taking part in extra-curricular PE, in their 2000 survey – compared with 45 per cent of the general population of young people surveyed in 1999 – and only 6 per cent claimed to have taken part once a week. Conversely, 86 per cent of youngsters with a disability did not take part in any extra-curricular sport in 2000 compared with 55 per cent of young people as a whole.

This relatively low engagement tends to be explained in terms of the conventional competitive, sport and team-game oriented character of extra-curricular PE. However, there are strong similarities between the top five activities undertaken by youngsters with a disability and the general school population. Activities such as football and netball are popular among disabled youngsters as are activities such as climbing and abseiling that are particularly popular in special schools.

The difficulties young people with a disability experience in accessing extra-curricular PE are made worse where they attend a school (particularly special schools) geographically removed from the immediate vicinity of their home. Burgess (2007: 42) reports that over half the pupils in her study of wheelchair-users were less likely to participate in extra-curricular sporting activities because accessible transport was unavailable, and 'because more adult help was needed and classroom assistants were not employed after school'.

Types of sports on offer in extra-curricular PE

A common feature of research into extra-curricular PE in the 1990s has been the identification of a strong sporting (and team-game) orientation or 'bias' (Penney and Harris, 1997) amid burgeoning extra-curricular provision. Despite the apparent vitality of extra-curricular PE when measured in terms of the *quantity* of provision and, albeit to a lesser extent, levels of participation, concern had been expressed regarding the *quality* or nature of that provision (see, for example, Bass and Cale, 1999; Penney and Harris, 1997). Such concerns have to do with the *types* of activities on offer – what Penney and Evans (1998) term the 'privileged' position of school sport within PE – and for whom they are intended rather than how *much* extra-curricular PE is available.

The title of Penney and Harris's (1997) paper (*Extra-curricular physical education: more of the same for the more able?*) indicated that their concern was not, so much, with the amount of extra-curricular PE on offer nor, for that matter, the commitment of PE teachers in England to it; for both of these were and remain demonstrably non-issues. Rather, their specific interest was with the 'content, organization and delivery' of extra-curricular PE (Penney and Harris, 1997: 41). Penney and Harris (1997) were concerned, in particular, with the manner in which extra-curricular PE was 'dominated by traditional team games', typically had 'a competitive focus' and was highly 'gendered' (p. 43). Accordingly, they argued that this 'particular focus' resulted in extra-curricular PE *'offering limited opportunities to only a minority of pupils'* (p. 43; emphasis in the original). Competitive sport, Penney and Harris (1997: 44) argued, had tended to gain disproportionately in the time devoted to it in extra-curricular PE in comparison to recreational sporting activities. Schools in Wales, it was noted, were running more representative teams in a wider range of sports in the mid-1990s than ever before (SCW, 1995). Sport England's (2003a) findings also suggested that involvement in sporting competition in extra-curricular PE in England had continued to rise since 1994. With regard to the continuing imbalance in extra-curricular PE in favour of sport, Penney and Harris (1997) argued that, in the process of becoming ever more performance oriented, extra-curricular PE had become increasingly biased towards, thereby favouring, the minority of pupils with sporting ability at the expense of the majority of ostensibly less able pupils. In the first decade of the twenty-first century the bulk of extra-curricular PE in Great Britain continues to be devoted to coached and competitive sport (Littlefield et al., 2003; SCW, 1995; 2003; 2006; Sport England, 2003a and b; 2003b).

Extra-curricular PE continues to be characterized by a large amount of continuity. Sport England (2003a: 63) points to 'a level of consistency in the types of extra-curricular sports that schools are offering young people'. In

Scotland, Littlefield et al. (2003) report that, whereas games are offered by over 80 per cent of secondary schools, individual sports are only offered by just over 40 per cent. Sport and team games remain very much at the heart of extra-curricular provision. The only non-sports in the top 14 extra-curricular PE activities in secondary schools in England in 2002 were gymnastics (including trampolining), dance, cross-country, swimming and climbing and other outdoor pursuits. In England, the top seven (with 5 per cent or more 11–16-year-olds involved) activities provided in extra-curricular PE in 2002 in secondary schools were almost the same as in 1994 and were, indeed, sports (and team games in particular): that is, football, athletics, netball, rounders, hockey, rugby and cricket (Sport England, 2003a). These were closely followed by a range of sports and physical activities in the form of tennis, basketball, gym, dance, cross-country, climbing and swimming. Sport England (2003b) observed that while, overall in 2002, young people engaged in a wide range of sports, there were only four sports that had been participated in by more than 5 per cent of all pupils and these were not merely sports, they were, for the most part, team games: football (15 per cent), netball (7 per cent), athletics (6 per cent) and cricket (5 per cent).

The distinguishing features of primary and secondary school extra-curricular PE in England were also found in Wales in 2004. The top five extra-curricular activities undertaken by primary (football, rugby, baseball/rounders, cricket and athletics) and secondary (football, rugby, athletics, cricket and basketball) school boys in Wales were sports – again, team games in particular – with the only 'lifestyle' or recreational activities being swimming and dance at primary level and swimming at secondary level (SCW, 2006). Among girls, the top five extra-curricular activities in primary (football, netball, baseball/rounders, dance and athletics) and secondary (netball, hockey, athletics, dance and football) schools were also sports (and predominantly team games), with the only lifestyle activities being the same as for boys – swimming and dance. The only difference in lifestyle activities between the sexes was the inclusion of dance among girls at secondary level. The big difference between boys and girls occurred at secondary level, where girls' 'traditional' team games came to the fore. While football dominates primary-aged boys' extra-curricular PE, with two-thirds taking part over the course of 2004 (more than twice as many as all other activities except rugby), both football and rugby dominate secondary boys' extra-curricular PE and these, too, are more than twice as popular as the rest.

It is particularly interesting to note the consistent patterns (over Sport England's three data collection points of 1994, 1999 and 2002) in participation trends in particular types of activity as young people move from primary to secondary schooling. The activities that show a marked increase in participation rates in extra-curricular PE are mostly those traditionally associated with the expanded provision for, and greater focus upon, sport at secondary level (for example, rugby, hockey, rounders and basketball). However, a notable omission from that list is football which repeatedly experiences a drop-off in participation as youngsters move from primary to secondary school (Sport England, 2003a). Other activities that experience a decline in participation as youngsters move to secondary school include netball, gymnastics, dance, cross-country and, interestingly, given the lack of pools in primary schools, swimming.

Some extra-curricular activities (most notably football) are offered to girls as well as boys. In Wales, the SCW identifies what it refers to as 'positive trends' in the extra-curricular provision for girls 'of traditionally male-domi-nated sports such as football and rugby' and 'the likelihood of schools having at least some girls' teams in these sports' (SCW, 2002: 4), despite the percent-age of schools offering such activities on a regular basis remaining low. Similarly, 'the increase in football as an extra-curricular sport' in England 'is common to both boys and girls' (Sport England, 2003a: 63). In England, in 2002, football was the most popular extra-curricular sport for secondary-age youngsters. Interestingly, football was the joint-second most popular extra-curricular PE activity for girls (aged 5–16) behind netball (Sport England, 2003a). For 13–14-year-old Year 9 pupils in the NWDA (2005) survey, as well as being the most popular extra-curricular activity (28 per cent), football was also the most popular activity for both sexes (41 per cent of boys and 15 per cent of girls) and the same appears to be true in primary schools in England (Waring et al., 2007) and Wales (SCW, 2006).

Despite these trends, overall the types of extra-curricular PE partici-pated in by boys and girls remain pretty consistent as does the tendency for sex differences in extra-curricular participation in specific activities to be more pronounced at secondary level. Netball remains the most popular extra-curricular activity among secondary girls in England, with football first choice for boys. Boys and girls in primary schools in Wales shared similar par-ticipation rates for the majority of extra-curricular activities: girls were more likely to participate in dance and netball while boys were more likely to par-ticipate in football and rugby. Participation rates for all other activities tended to be similar (SCW, 2006).

It is in secondary schools where the biggest sex differences in the types of activities undertaken in extra-curricular PE are to be found in England and Wales. Boys tend to be offered a wider range of activities than girls and most schools offer activities such as rugby and netball exclusively to boys and girls, respectively. Nevertheless, there is a real and potentially significant change occurring as well as continuity in the types of activities undertaken in extra-curricular PE. For example, while netball assumes top spot among secondary girls, football is by far the fastest growing girls' extra-curricular sport at secondary level. Similarly, basketball and dance are two of the fastest growing activities among primary school boys, with basketball experiencing the largest increase in extra-curricular participation among secondary boys. It is evident that as well as the growth in provision and participation in extra-curricular PE over the past decade or more there has been a marked broadening and diversification in the variety of sports and physical activities on offer. Sport England (2003a: 63) noted that in 2002, young people in England 'were taking part in a wide variety (over 45 sports) of extra-curricular sport'. At the same time frequent involvement in extra-curricular sport had increased slightly since 1999 from 4.2 to 4.6 sports per young person (Sport England, 2003a). The increase in the number of sports on offer is said to be a major factor in the apparent 'increase in the number of pupils taking part' (Sport England, 2003b: 117) in extra-curricular PE.

Despite the broadening of programmes to incorporate more recreational sporting forms and lifestyle activities in many schools – not only in the UK but elsewhere in Europe, such as Flanders (De Martelaer and Theebom, 2006) – extra-curricular PE continues to have a competitive sport orientation. In the USA, the focus on competitive sport is taken to a logical conclusion as extra-curricular sport is delivered by coaches and/or teachers hired primarily as coaches. Unsurprisingly, 'the goals of American school sport are not particularly educational' (Curtner-Smith et al., 2007: 133) because coaches 'are generally more concerned with providing entertainment for the local community, sending their players on to a "higher level", and (using their teams) as a means of increasing school funds and as a vehicle for promoting school and community cohesiveness, spirit, and pride'. For these reasons, in the USA, extra-curricular sport tends to be viewed by many as more important than school PE. Whether focused on the development of 'gifted and talented' youngsters or simply inter-school sporting competition, studies in England and Wales tend to corroborate Curtner-Smith et al.'s (2007) finding from the USA that in extra-curricular PE, or after-school sport, teachers tend to focus 'almost exclusively on teaching skills and strategies' (p. 138). In countries such as Greece, where extra-curricular PE revolves almost exclusively around competitive sports, this is believed to be a major reason for what are seen to be relatively low levels of pupil engagement (Dagkas and Benn, 2006).

. However, while a 'sporting bias' in extra-curricular PE may be a major reason why more youngsters do not take part, it is not the sole reason. In addition to the family and religious constraints facing some minority ethnic youngsters and the transport problems confronting many youngsters with a disability, others have commitments that make attendance at extra-curricular PE difficult. Many of the boys in Bramham's (2003) study of 22 15-year-old boys in four inner-city schools, for example, held 'substantial evening and week-end part-time jobs' and were, therefore, reluctant to become involved with extra-curricular PE and enter into commitments towards school sport. Similarly, many reported having to reduce involvement in school sports and out-of-school active lifestyles because of the growing demands of public examinations in the form of GCSEs.

In the light of the alleged 'sporting bias' and the growth of coached and competitive sport, one aspect of extra-curricular PE provision is worthy of particular mention: the increasing involvement of outside agencies (Hardman and Marshall, 2000) and 'adults other than teachers' (AOTT).

OUTSIDE AGENCIES AND EXTRA-CURRICULAR PE

The growth in provision of extra-curricular sports in England and Wales is only partly attributable, it seems, to greater levels of involvement among existing and new teaching staff, even though there may have been an increase in the involvement of non-teaching staff in the delivery of extra-curricular activity (SCW, 2002). Where growth in extra-curricular PE provision has occurred, the main reason appears to be increased involvement of sports coaches, SDOs and sports organizations generally, as well as AOTT (see Chapter 3). In their most recent survey, Sport England (2003b) point out that two-thirds (68 per cent) of secondary schools 'have called on other organisations to help teach or lead sports out of school time' (p. 111). This has been the case with team games and football in particular.

It may be that 'increased workloads' and 'fewer staff helping or willing to take clubs' (Sport England, 2003b: 114) – cited by a small number of PE teachers as the main reasons for what they anticipate will be a future decline in the number of activities on offer in extra-curricular PE – will lead to increased opportunities for the utilization of coaches and SDOs in extra-curricular PE. The development of extra-curricular PE in the primary sector in England and Wales has been aided by the funds of £1 million from the UK government in 2005 for the YST programme of after-school sports clubs – aimed at improving the basic skills said to underpin sporting participation – with the intention of establishing over 800 such clubs.

SCHOOL SPORT PARTNERSHIPS AND EXTRA-CURRICULAR PE

Any review of the state of extra-curricular PE in England must make mention of School Sport Partnerships (SSPs), one of the more significant developments in PE in England in recent years. The partnerships' aim of building bridges between school- and club-based sport via extra-curricular PE resembles the growing cooperation between sports clubs and schools in Flanders in the development of 'sports academies' (De Martelaer and Theebom, 2006). Despite the fact that the Loughborough Partnership (2005) found it difficult to disentangle out-of-school-hours clubs run and hosted by schools or clubs exclusively or in partnerships, they claim that 'the net effect' of partnerships between schools, groups of schools and local sports clubs 'has been to increase significantly the participation opportunities for pupils' (p. 31): data collected from 22 SSPs demonstrated an increase of more than 50 per cent in extra-curricular sport since schools (primary and secondary) joined the programme. The recent DCMS/DfES (2005) and Loughborough Partnership (2005: 30) surveys both point to 'a substantial increase in the range of activities available for pupils out of school hours' in partnerships. Eleven activities were reported as being available in more than three-quarters of schools with specialist school sports coordinators. 'Nearly all' the SSCs were described as providing a good or very good range of opportunities before, during and after school alongside 'good use of coaches to support provision' and 'links with local sports clubs' (OFSTED, 2005a: 15). The sports and activities offered reflected the blend of 'traditional' sports (athletics, football, netball) and 'newer' sports, such as basketball, as well as 'lifestyle activities', such as fitness and skateboarding, to be found in all secondary schools. The generally positive portrayal of the impact of partnerships between schools and sports clubs warrants a cautionary note, however, inasmuch as the growth of provision in extra-curricular PE is a general trend among primary and secondary schools and not simply one found in partnerships. There are grounds for thinking that SSPs are, indeed, having some impact on extra-curricular PE. Small and Nash (2005: 94) claim that School Sport and Active Primary School Coordinators have been central in 'raising the profile of extra-curricular sport' in primary and secondary schools. Small and Nash's study leads them to conclude that, in one Scottish town, the impact of primary school coordinators has led not only to improved sporting provision but also to improved participation levels among children.

Before concluding with an exploration of some of the salient issues surrounding extra-curricular provision, the next section offers a tentative explanation for the shape and character of what many within and beyond secondary school PE in England and Wales consider to be a barometer of the health and well-being of PE and school sport.

EXPLAINING EXTRA-CURRICULAR PE

Despite sometimes feeling their professional (and, often, personal) lives to be dominated, sometimes blighted, by it, many secondary PE teachers appear to view extra-curricular PE as the 'high point' of their PE teaching lives (Green, 2003). When the immediate, day-to-day constraints of managing and delivering curricular PE recede – that is, during extra-curricular PE – then teachers' preferred views of their subject come to life. It is in extra-curricular PE that the extent of many PE teachers' commitment to competitive sport and, in particular, traditional team games is most visible. How might we explain this? In large measure it is explainable in terms of PE teachers' individual and collective predispositions. For very many PE teachers, sport (and especially traditional team games) is an important aspect of their lives: they often have strong emotional ties to sport and it forms a significant dimension of their individual identities (Green, 2000a). For many, teaching PE represents an opportunity for them to continue their association with sport – an area of life in which they have had extensive and positive experiences: it appears a 'natural' progression from enjoying, and being successful at, sport while at school themselves. Male PE teachers, especially, tend also to be a self-replicating group and experiences gained in teacher training (see Chapter 12) – especially the process of being mentored by experienced PE teachers during 'teaching practice' – result in a tendency, among new and established teachers alike, towards conservatism which manifests itself in the passing on of skill-oriented and sport-dominated (extra-)curricular programmes. The sporting ideologies and practices embedded in the normative behaviour of PE teachers, are reinforced by such things as the expectations of their fellow PE teachers, the traditions of PE and of their schools, government policy (such as the PESSCL strategy) and the use of extra-curricular sport as a marketing device in the increasingly competitive educational marketplace.

CONCLUSION

Despite widespread concerns regarding the supposed decline in extra-curricular PE – blamed in England and Wales on the combined effects of an industrial dispute on the part of teachers in the mid-1980s (and subsequent changes in teaching contracts), a new breed of 'liberal-minded', politically left-leaning PE teachers, the sale of school playing fields and an increasingly crowded National Curriculum – opportunities for extra-curricular PE in secondary schools in England and Wales have grown over the past decade with corresponding increases in the percentage of all young people involved.

Nevertheless, more than half of secondary-aged youngsters may seldom, if ever, engage with extra-curricular PE provision with, at best, around 15–20 per cent taking part three times or more each week. While there can be little doubt that levels of participation in extra-curricular PE are lower than physical educationalists would want, the question remains: are they lower than one might reasonably expect? If so, 'low' in what terms: absolutely or relatively? The 50 per cent reported by Daley (2002) might be considered high if one were to view sport and physical activity as having limited appeal as a leisure activity. It is interesting to note that Daley (2002: 43) herself recognizes that while 'many pupils do not participate in extra-curricular sport and physical activities, the same appears to be true for other types of non-physical activities (for example, music and arts clubs) where pupils also reported low participation rates'. In short, participation levels can only be considered low by those whose higher expectations are based upon more optimistic views of the potential appeal of extra-curricular PE.

When viewed over time, it is evident that extra-curricular PE has not only grown in terms of provision and participation, but has also broadened and diversified. Nevertheless, it retains a quite conventional, not to say conservative, character and, being largely independent of developments such as the NCPE, it remains a relatively autonomous dimension of PE. It is conventional in remaining dominated by sport and team games and a performance orientation. It remains conservative in the sense that when PE teachers have a greater degree of freedom to choose what they do, both male and female PE teachers tend to opt for sport and games. Perhaps unsurprisingly, therefore, extra-curricular PE tends to express traditional forms of gender-stereotyping. Indeed, it is evident that more gender differentiation is to be found in extra-curricular PE than curricular PE and this is true in terms of rates of participation as well as provision. Grounds for optimism about the potential for further growth in extra-curricular PE lie in two areas. First, in the form of increased participation in some sports and physical activities among young people in their leisure time beyond school. Second, when compared with the relatively higher levels of participation in the final years of primary schooling and, to a slightly lesser extent the first year of secondary schooling (see SCW, 2006), there may well be latent potential for improvement in the relatively lower participation rates among older pupils.

One of 'the main reasons' for the 'past', as well as what PE teachers perceive to be the likely 'future' increases in provision of, and participation in, extra-curricular PE is, according to Sport England (2003b), 'increased involvement from coaches, specialists and sport organisations' (p. 112). Unsurprisingly, perhaps, it is anticipated that increased involvement from external agencies will 'act as a catalyst' (p. 115) for the expected increase in participation in extra-curricular PE. Whatever the scale or form of involvement of coaches and SDOs, there may be a number of unintended consequences of involving AOTT in extra-curricular PE. First, although PE teachers appear very receptive to the involvement of coaches, SDOs and outside agencies, generally, in extra-curricular PE, to do so implies that there is no need for a specialist teaching qualification in order to be involved in PE.

This might, in turn, be seen as undermining claims for the kinds of specialist professional knowledge and status which has been something of a preoccupation for PE teachers in recent years. Second, as purveyors of specialized sporting knowledge to extra-curricular PE, coaches and SDOs will inevitably acquire positions of relative power in relation to PE teachers for as long as the latter feel they need the expertise of the former. Thus, an unintended consequence of developing links with and involving outside agencies may well be a weakening of the status and power of PE teachers in relation to the provision of extra-curricular PE and, ultimately, PE itself.

A particularly significant issue in relation to extra-curricular PE has to do with the issue of whether it can provide the 'fundamental link' (De Martelaer and Theebom, 2006; Penney and Harris, 1997) between curricular PE and young people's involvement in sport in their spare time that many expect of it. Put another way, can extra-curricular PE do anything to bridge the 'clear disparity' (Sport England, 2003b: 6) between what young people are experiencing in curricular PE and what they are choosing to do out of school in a manner that will enhance and reinforce their ongoing involvement in sport and physical activity? While Sport England (2003a; 2003b) and the SCW (2002; 2003a and b; 2006) data bears out Roberts's (1996a) claim that schools have been extending and enhancing rather than cutting back on their provision of sports in extra-curricular (as well as curricular) PE, nevertheless, provision continues to be largely focused around competitive sports in general and team games especially, making Penney and Harris's (1997) description of extra-curricular PE as 'more of the same for the more able' as pertinent now as it was a decade ago. Despite this, Sport England (2003a: 6) suggest that 'extra-curricular sport has done much to increase young people's participation in sport'. The substantial increase in young people's participation in sport and physical activity over the past decade or more is largely attributable to the popularity of recreational physical activities (for example, health and fitness gym work, swimming, cycling, badminton, tennis, ice-skating and skateboarding) and smaller increases in team sports (such as football, among girls especially, and basketball). In short, young people's leisure participation is typically characterized by a blend of 'lifestyle activities' and more competitive, less recreational performance-oriented team games and sports. Extra-curricular PE is only likely to form a bridge between school PE and young people's future leisure lives if emphasis is given to developing extra-curricular provision in the direction of their preferred participation forms and styles. There is evidently room for improvement in three broad areas:

1 A better 'match' in the *aims* and *purposes* of extra-curricular PE – towards an emphasis upon the intrinsic pleasure of sport and physical activities rather than preoccupation with levels of performance and achievement.

2 A better 'match' in *format* – between the more recreational, informal manner in which many young people (and, for that matter, adults) prefer to take part and the way in which extra-curricular PE is provided.

3 A better 'match' in *activities* – between those offered in extra-curricular PE and those that 'track' into young people's leisure.

Despite the optimism brought on by recent increases in both provision and participation, as things stand there may (in theory at least) be considerable room for improvement in all three.

RECOMMENDED READING

Penney, D. and Harris, J. (1997) 'Extra-curricular physical education: more of the same for the more able', *Sport, Education and Society*, 2(1): 41–54.

Sport England (2003b) *Young People and Sport in England, 2002: A Survey of Young People and PE Teachers*. London: Sport England.

Assessment and Examinations in Physical Education

This chapter briefly explores the increasingly complex area of assessment in PE before focusing on examinations in PE/Sport. More specifically, the chapter traces the rapid growth of GCSE and A level PE in England and Wales, and explores some of the more important issues surrounding the topic before attempting to make sense of its popularity among physical educationalists. The chapter concludes by reflecting upon the impact of the rise of examinable PE on the supposed nature and purposes of the subject.

ASSESSMENT IN PHYSICAL EDUCATION

In general terms, assessment involves the collection of information in order to establish whether, and to what extent, something has been attained or achieved. In education, assessment tends to be used as a 'catch-all' term to refer to the processes by which teachers establish or make a judgement about the nature and extent of their pupils' learning when compared against certain criteria; in other words, what a pupil can do and how well he or she can do it (Carroll, 1994). Assessment is conventionally considered to take two broad forms: summative (often formal) assessment of students' work (examinations[1] or essays, for example) against external criteria (such as those set by examination boards or inherent in national curricula) and formative (often informal) assessment of the ongoing performances of pupils aimed at helping improve pupils' learning and, in the process, their longer-term performances in summative assessments.

In terms of teachers' judgements regarding their pupils' attainment, behaviour and effort, assessment has long been a feature of schooling. For many years assessment took the form of end-of-term or end-of-year reports on pupils' achievements (in effect, summative assessments) in PE. These tended to concentrate on their skill levels and commitment, and became apocryphal in their effects on young people's perceptions of themselves as 'sporty' or otherwise. In recent years, assessment has become not only more prominent in the day-to-day practice of PE teachers around the world (Hay, 2006) but also more elaborate and complex.

According to its advocates, appropriate and regular assessment can make a substantial contribution to raising student achievement through higher standards and greater accountability (Dodds, 2006). The increased emphasis on assessing the extent and nature of pupils' learning has manifested itself in demands upon teachers to incorporate various forms of assessment at all levels of their work, from units or programmes through to lessons themselves. This, in turn, has led to a substantial growth in record-keeping – monitoring and assessing pupils' achievements.

Greater focus on formative assessment as an educational tool is reflected, in England and Wales for example, in OFSTED's (2003) (the government's advisory and inspectorate agency) view that assessment should not be confined to a sedentary, plenary activity; that is, it should not simply be viewed in the traditional, retrospective end of activity or module (or end of term or year) summary report focusing upon achievement. Rather, information garnered through assessment should be used by teachers 'to intervene and provide specific feedback to guide pupils towards improvement' (OFSTED, 2003: 1) in PE. It should be viewed as formative – what is increasingly referred to as 'assessment for learning'. In this regard, assessment is intended to be 'ongoing': 'to check pupils' progress' (OFSTED, 2003: 1) and help them improve in individual lessons, during the school year and throughout school life.

In England and Wales, its use as a policy tool to effect broader political goals is reflected in the inspectorate's view that a major function of assessment is 'to determine (pupils') attainment against national curriculum levels' (OFSTED, 2003: 5), through end-of-unit assessments. Thus, the term 'assessment' is most commonly used by teachers in reference to the grades (1 to 8) applied to pupil attainment in National Curriculum subjects, such as PE. The use of such grades, at all levels of the curriculum, enables government and non-governmental agencies to identify issues related to national levels of pupil attainment. The QCA (QCA, 2005: 1), for example, has pointed to 'a rise in the number of pupils achieving level 5+ in Key Stage 3 teacher assessments' in PE. At the same time, however, the QCA made use of the grades to observe that fewer pupils were achieving the top levels of 7+ in PE than in most other school subjects in England and Wales.

Unsurprisingly, perhaps, OFSTED is clear in its view that 'effective assessment' is as 'integral to teaching and learning' in PE as it is said to be in other subjects on the curriculum. Assessment is said to enable teachers to reflect on the content and delivery of the PE curriculum. According to OFSTED (2003: 2): 'The very best (PE) departments use assessment information as a means of reflecting upon curriculum planning and programme design.' At the level of the individual pupil, the assumption is that 'work is differentiated to cater for the more able or the less able pupils' and that all pupils are then set individually oriented tasks to enable them to develop. In this manner, teachers are required to 'concentrate on the needs of individual pupils rather than simply completing the lesson' (OFSTED, 2003: 1). So, assessment is not simply viewed as a process for teachers alone. Teachers are expected to provide their pupils with 'well-structured opportunities to develop their (own) observation and evaluation skills' (OFSTED, 2003: 4) in each key stage; in other words, to enable pupils to provide their own formative feedback by self-assessment of their current levels of performance and self-diagnosis of the improvements they would need to make in order to reach the next level of performance.

When commenting upon PE departments' effective use of assessment, OFSTED seldom explains what it means by judgements such as 'the very best departments' or 'the most effective departments' or 'the best lessons'. The OFSTED reports in general, and on assessment in particular, read like an attempt to constrain PE teachers towards what, in official terms, is deemed 'good practice' or 'high-quality PE' (see Chapter 12).

It is difficult to avoid the impression that if teachers were doing everything suggested by OFSTED reports they would have time for little other than assessment. Greenwell (2005: 35) notes the frustrations among PE teachers with the administrative demands associated with assessment paperwork. Similarly, teachers in Green's (2003) study expressed the view that in making such demands, OFSTED rarely engages with the day-to-day realities of PE teaching. Interestingly, it is their 'everyday' knowledge of their pupils that encourages teachers to believe that they can 'see' whether or not they are learning and that making spot judgements rather than relying upon what teachers believe they know of pupils over time is inherently problematic. There is a clear link between teachers' expectations of their pupils in PE and those pupils' achievements. Although this may be indicative of a self-fulfilling tendency, it seems more likely to reflect teachers' genuine knowledge of their pupils' capabilities (Hay, 2006). Many PE teachers also consider testing – and training in assessment – to be unnecessary (Tsangaridou, 2006a), especially where the criteria of public examinations (at Key Stage 4 in England and Wales, for example) enable PE teachers to feel more secure in their judgements. Nevertheless, even with nationally recognized, public examinations, there are evidently problems associated with establishing consistency of judgement between teachers, across sporting activities and in the interpretation of criteria.

Regardless of whether or not assessment is a suitable vehicle for encouraging pupil learning and 'driving up' standards of attainment in schools, the growth of assessment in education can also be viewed as a means of ensuring teacher accountability and monitoring and evaluating teachers' performances in delivering prescribed curricula (Broadfoot and Black, 2004) – in England and Wales, the NCPE – while ensuring that pupils do, indeed, make the kinds of progress that governments pledge to bring about. Put another way, while assessment is presented as a carrot to pupils it is, at the same time, a stick with which governments can 'beat' teachers; especially when comparisons can be made between schools, even teachers, via standardized, large-scale tests (Hay, 2006). Whether foreseen and anticipated or not, it is likely that the increasing significance of assessment in education, generally, and PE, in particular, will reinforce the well-established tendency among teachers to rely upon formal, command-style teaching strategies. An additional consequence of the increased importance of assessment may well be the alienation of those less able pupils who, although on the margins of 'recruitment' to PE and sport, remain 'biddable' with a less extrinsically oriented approach (Hay, 2006).

The irony of the continued emphasis on formative feedback is emphasized when one reflects upon the rapid growth in PE of formal public examinations. Formal, nationally recognized, public examinations emerged as a prominent aspect of the education system in the UK in the second half of the nineteenth century (Brook, 1993) and examinations remain the main means of assessing attainment in the National Curriculum for England and Wales. As well as the growth of assessment in PE there has been a steady increase in the range of PE and sport-related qualifications available in schools in England and Wales over the past 20 years or so. These include a vast array of academic and vocationally related qualifications and awards. The result has been a substantial rise in the number of pupils (and particularly older pupils aged 14–16 years) taking accredited courses – including 'leadership' awards such as Junior Sports Leaders Award (JSLA) and the Duke of Edinburgh Award, as well as national governing body awards – such that schools appear to be placing increasing emphasis upon enabling young people to gain nationally recognized sporting awards (Stidder and Hayes, 2006). Nevertheless, two particular public examinations – the General Certificate of Secondary Education (GCSE) and Advanced (A)-level – remain at the heart of the expanding portfolio of educational qualifications in England and Wales.

Against this backdrop, arguably the most dramatic development in secondary PE in England and Wales over the past 30 years has been the growth of GCSE and A level examinations. Some would argue that this growth is indicative of not only a 'new orthodoxy' (Reid, 1996a) among physical educationalists regarding the nature and purposes of PE, but also the 'future direction' of the subject (Stidder and Wallis, 2003). It is for these reasons that the remainder of this chapter focuses on GCSE and A-level examinations in PE.

EXAMINATIONS IN PE

The growth and development of examinations in PE

Carroll (1994; 1998a) has charted the emergence and proliferation of examinations in PE in England and Wales from a period of innovation in the early 1970s, via successive phases of consolidation in the mid to late 1970s and rapid and sustained growth in the 1980s, to a widespread expansion and acceptance of GCSE and A-level PE/Sport and Sports Studies during the 1990s. In recent years the substantial growth in examinable PE – in terms of both pupil examinees and school exam centres – has continued apace (see Table 5.1). Entries in GCSE PE, which more than doubled in the five-year period up to 1997, totalled approximately 140,000 in 2006 – up by over a third from three years previously. A-level PE/Sport has expanded even more swiftly: from 35 candidates at its inception in 1985 to over 11,000 by 1998 and nearly 22,000 in 2006. These figures represent a 300 per cent growth in GCSE PE between 1990 and 2006 and a 3,000 per cent growth for A-level PE/Sport over the same period.

Table 5.1 *Total entries for GCSE and A-level PE/Sport in England 1990–2006*

	GCSE PE	A-level PE/Sport
1990	34,529	639
1992	42,026	2,600[1]
1994	50,400[1]	6,000[1]
1996	80,645	9,732
1998	84,200[1]	12,027
1999	94,100[1]	13,030
2003	110,900[1]	18,931[2]
2006[4]	140,555[3]	21,834[2,3]

First published in K. Green (2001) 'Examinations in physical education: a sociological perspective on a "new methodology"', *British Journal of Sociology of Education*, 22(1): 51–74. Website: www.informaworld.com

[1] These figures have been rounded up or down by either the authors listed below or the DfEE/DfES.

[2] For comparative purposes this figure does not include Advanced Subsidiary-(AS) level entries.

[3] Figures taken from www.jcq.org.uk.

Sources: Based on Carroll, 1998a; DfEE, 2003a; 2003b; DfES, 2004a; 2004b; Joint Council for Qualifications, 2006; MacKreth, 1998.

The emergence and rapid growth of GCSE and A-level PE/Sport has, as one might expect, thrown up a number of more or less significant issues.

Issues in examinable PE

Issues, by definition, are 'live' or current. Some issues related to examinable PE, such as a lack of appropriate resources (for example, in the form of suitable textbooks) for theory work (Carroll, 1991), appear to have been sufficiently resolved for reference to them – in the PE professional literature, for example – to have dissipated if not quite disappeared. Other issues, however, persist, particularly those to do with the gendered nature of the subject, standards of attainment, the practicalities of teaching examinable PE, the impact of examinations on curricular PE and the implications for conventional PE of the ostensible academicization of the subject. This section explores each of these issues.

Gender, social class and examinable PE Despite its dramatic growth, examinable PE remains heavily gendered. This is evident in the significantly greater popularity among boys than girls of GCSE and A-level PE/Sport, at a ratio approaching two to one. Although year-on-year growth has been similar for both boys and girls (up by 8.8 per cent from 2005 for boys and 7.9 per cent for girls), in 2006 13,640 boys sat A-level (12,532 in 2005) compared with 8,194 (7,594) girls. In 2006, 99,614 boys sat (full-course) GCSE PE in England compared with 53,212 girls.

In terms of gender 'bias', it is interesting to contrast PE with other subjects. Of the 805,698 A-level students in England and Wales in 2006, just over half (54 per cent) were females and just under half (46 per cent) males (Joint Council for Qualifications, 2006). The vast majority of subjects were sat by either roughly equivalent numbers of males and females (for example, Chemistry, Geography, History, Music, and General Studies) or a balance of two-thirds females/one-third males (for example, Biology, English, French and other languages, Religious Studies, Expressive Arts and Drama). Along with Business Studies, Mathematics and Technology, PE/Sport was sat by two-thirds males. A small minority were more heavily gendered; including Home Economics and Computing – virtually 90 per cent female and male pupils respectively. These figures may tell us something about lingering gender stereotypes regarding supposedly suitable boys' and girls' activities: business, numbers, technology and sport for boys, and 'caring' or domestic activities for girls.

The sex differences in enrolment in GCSE and A-level PE/Sport examinations may reflect a difference in appeal and this, in turn, may in part be attributable to the gendered nature of PE in general (see Chapter 8) and the examinable form of the subject in particular. The latter ranges from 'gender bias' in textbooks (Stidder, 2001a) to the ways in which physical characteristics (especially strength and size) tend to be 'embedded' in the practical aspects of any assessment where 'physical performance is central to the assessment programme' (MacDonald and Brooker, 1999: 185). This is often exacerbated where PE teachers have a substantial say in the sports to be assessed, resulting in the marginalization or rejection of 'aesthetic' activities on the basis that 'boys in particular would reject the subject if an aesthetic activity were to be included' MacDonald and Brooker (1999: 186). The gender bias in enrolment to GCSE PE/Sport also tends to be exacerbated by the increased provision and popularity of GCSE Dance – a subject dominated by girls and often located within the same timetable slot as GCSE PE, thereby preventing girls from doing both even if they were inclined to (Odhams, 2007).

Sex is evidently a powerful variable in educational terms. The relationship between the socio-economic background of pupils and examination results is, however, stronger and the scale of difference between the top and bottom performing pupils dwarfs the difference between boys and girls (Gorard et al., 2003). This is particularly so at GCSE level in England and Wales (Connolly, 2006). The impact of gender on examinable PE in particular, however, suggests that it is the configuration of class and gender that is most significant as a determinant of participation and performance in GCSE and A-level PE/Sport.

Standards of attainment Concern with standards of attainment has been a leitmotif of the British examination system for more than a decade, particularly in relation to what is often referred to as the 'gold standard' of the English and Welsh education systems – A-level. The term 'grade inflation' is used to refer to the increasing proportion of students gaining high grades in public examinations (and GCSE and A-levels in particular) and is usually taken to be a negative development that results in the devaluing of the currency of public examinations. Over time, more students are being awarded the top grades in GCSE and A-levels and, in 2006, almost all A-level candidates passed, with approximately 23 per cent getting the top, A, grade. Despite the fact that only about 4 per cent of the total year cohort achieved three or more A grades in 2006, more students get A grades in GCSE and A-levels today than a quarter of a century ago. This is, in part, explainable in terms of the quotas for the number of grades awarded at each level that were in existence then but no longer. Nevertheless, detractors continue to claim that the GCSE and A-level syllabuses, generally, are less challenging than those of 20 years ago – not least because of the system of dividing the qualification into modules that feature a large element of ongoing coursework rather than unseen examinations. The 'atomized' nature of modular exam syllabuses – together with the reliance upon coursework and tests which can be re-submitted and retaken and the alleged tendency of teachers to teach to the examination – are said to be major reasons why success has now become easier to achieve in the British examination system.

Despite this, and despite the fact that more pupils are gaining GCSE and A-level qualifications in PE/Sport, standards of attainment (especially in the theoretical aspects of programmes) remain a 'cause for concern' for OFSTED. However, concern with 'standards' has been a persistent theme throughout the relatively brief history of examinable PE. In 1991, Carroll (1991: 144) commented upon the need for PE teachers 'to become more familiar with the theoretical content [and] depth required' in examinable PE. Despite subsequent claims of 'a much closer relationship of theory to practical participation' (McConachie-Smith, 1996) the reality, according to OFSTED, remains quite different. The continuing 'gap between achievement in the theoretical and practical aspects of the course' (OFSTED, 2002: 2) and the perceived need to raise achievement in GCSE theory – highlighted in their subject reports for PE – remain live issues with OFSTED. It is interesting that, despite its claims that 'the good standards of attainment in GCSE (PE) highlight the improvements made in recent years', OFSTED also observes that there has been no substantial increase in the proportion of candidates gaining higher grades. In 2006, the proportion of A-level candidates gaining grades A and A–C had increased by approximately 1 per cent from 2005 (to 13.7 per cent in the case of the former and to 59.9 per cent in the case of the latter).

Table 5.2 *Comparison of A-level grades in England in selected subjects in 2006 (percentages of pupils)*

	A	A–C
Art & Design	29.6	77.5
Biological Sciences	24.4	66.3
Business Studies	16.7	70.6
Chemistry	31.3	74.2
English	21.9	74.6
French	34.7	81.6
Geography	25.6	77.0
History	24.6	75.6
Mathematics	43.5	79.9
Music	17.8	65.7
PE/Sport	**13.7**	**59.9**
Religious Studies	26.5	80.2

Source: Based on Joint Council for Qualifications, 2006

Table 5.3 *Comparison of GCSE (full course) grades in England in selected subjects in 2006 (percentages of pupils)*

	A/A*	*A*–C*
Art	21.7	71.2
Business Studies	15.5	60.0
English	51.4	61.6
French	22.3	64.1
Geography	24.3	65.8
History	28.4	66.1
Mathematics	13.1	54.3
PE	**19.5**	**60.5**
Religious Studies	30.1	70.2
Science: Biology	44.6	88.3
Science: Chemistry	46.0	90.1

Source: Based on Joint Council for Qualifications, 2006

Once again, it is interesting to compare PE with other subjects (see Tables 5.2 and 5.3). Across all A-level subjects, 24 per cent of students were awarded an A grade in 2006. However, PE/Sport was one of a number of noteworthy outliers. Alongside General Studies, Media and Information and Communication Technology (ICT), A-level PE/Sport achieved one of the lowest proportions of A grades at 14 per cent. Although the QCA (2005: 1) points to 'an increase in the number of pupils achieving A★ to C grades in (GCSE) PE', from approximately 54 per cent in 2000 to 61 per cent in 2005, it is forced to concede that there are still fewer pupils achieving the top (A★ and A) grades in PE than in other subjects with similar numbers of candidates.

Despite the fact that approximately twice as many boys as girls enrol for GCSE and A-level PE/Sport, girls continue to outperform boys in terms of attainment. Although they make up just over a third of students taking PE/Sport at A-level, girls are more likely to achieve grades A–C (69 per cent of girls compared with 55 per cent of boys) and twice as likely to achieve grade A as boys (20 per cent versus 10 per cent). The gender dimension is, however, not confined to PE/Sport. In many other subjects where boys predominate in numerical terms – such as Business Studies, Economics, Mathematics, Physics, Technology and Computing – girls still outperform them. The fact that one of the subjects (ICT) – characterized by one of the lowest proportions of A grades (14 per cent) at GCSE – is another of those disproportionately overpopulated by males points towards a significant aspect of the explanation, namely, the underachievement of boys in the education system as a whole.

Teaching examinable PE Salter (2005: 23) observes that PE teachers identify a number of problems with teaching the theoretical component of examinable PE: including 'boring' theory lessons involving 'too much writing' that 'puts the kids off' (not least because lessons often follow textbooks very closely to ensure that the requisite content is 'covered' by getting pupils 'to sit down, shut up and get on with the writing'). Teachers' enduring concerns with the standards of achievement in the theoretical elements of GCSE PE begins to explain a move among the PE profession to 'redress the balance of theory and practical' within A-level PE/Sport, 'which is now effectively 80 percent theory and 20 percent practical' and, as a consequence, makes A-level PE/Sport 'somewhat off-putting to ... practically oriented students' (Green, 2002: 34).

Problems with teaching the theoretical components of examinable PE are compounded, unintentionally, in the training of PE teachers. Although more teacher trainees are gaining experience of teaching the theoretical components of examinable PE, there remains an unwillingness on the part of schools to provide teaching experiences for trainees where examination classes are concerned: 'the understandable reluctance among teachers to allow trainees to teach their examination classes' (Stidder and Hayes, 2006: 323) leads to trainees observing rather than teaching these classes, resulting in a lack of confidence on the part of trainees to teach examinable PE.

The impact of examinations on curricular PE An additional issue associated with the increasing popularity of nationally recognized, public examinations in PE is the relationship between examinable PE and 'core' or curriculum PE. Physical education teachers in England have reported that the bureaucracy associated with providing examinable PE places extra burdens on PE departments in a variety of ways(Green, 2001). These range from detracting from extra-curricular PE provision to placing added pressure on the budgets of PE departments compelled to allocate scarce resources to such things as textbooks and videos that might otherwise have been spent on sports equipment, for example. Some of the boys in Bramham's (2003: 66) study of 15-year-old boys in four inner-city schools reported having to 'cut back on school sports and out-of-school active lifestyles because of the academic demands of GCSE'.

Of greater significance, perhaps, is the evidence to suggest that in some schools the time allocated to GCSE PE replaces part (sometimes all) of curriculum PE, so, non-examination or 'core' PE programmes are, in effect, competing for timetable space with other forms of PE, including examinable PE (Stidder and Wallis, 2003). In many schools, nevertheless, time is allocated to GCSE PE in addition to the average time assigned to NCPE at Key Stage 4; that is, between one and two hours per week. This has not prevented critics

from claiming, however, that while GCSE PE may protect and even supplement PE time for 15–16-year-olds, much of this time is spent on theory rather
than 'in actual sports participation' (SCW, 2002: 16). Taken together, these
developments are said by some to reflect a marked trend towards examinable
PE becoming separated from, rather than integral to, curricular PE – becoming a different subject, an *academic* subject (Reid, 1996a; 1996b).

Similarly, the increasing segregation of academic and vocational routes
through secondary education across Europe (Furlong and Cartmel, 2007) also
points to the possibility of segregation between GCSE and A-level PE/Sport
and vocational sporting qualifications, or even between both forms of qualification, in PE and other, seemingly more academic, subjects. This is because
vocational qualifications (and, to some extent, GCSE PE) are taken up disproportionately by working-class youngsters in the lower attainment bands.
Set against this, the relative success of A-level PE suggests the possibility of
an 'academic' variant of the subject becoming established alongside the more
vocationally oriented qualifications available through PE.

The academicization of PE When placed alongside the significant growth of
examinable PE, several developments suggest that a process of academicization has gathered pace within school PE over the past few decades (Reid,
1996a, 1996b). These developments include the proliferation of PE/Sports
Science programmes at degree level (Carroll, 1998a) and the widespread
acceptance and adoption of 'academic' justifications for PE in curriculum and
assessment documentation and policy.

Academicization is probably best defined in terms of an increasing
emphasis upon the theoretical study of physical activity and sport, in both
absolute and relative terms (that is, in relation to, and sometimes at the
expense of, practical activities). According to Reid (1996a), a consequence of
the broad acceptance of the 'standard' liberal educational view of PE (see
Chapter 1) has been repeated calls for a greater emphasis upon 'theory'
within the subject, at the expense of unreflective practice or 'playing'. In
effect, this 'new orthodoxy' redefines PE, according to Reid (1996a: 102), 'in
terms of the opportunities which it provides for theoretical study'. In so
doing, he argues, it implicitly accepts the superiority of the kinds of
knowledge that are expressed predominantly in written or verbal forms
rather than by practical demonstration. The rapid growth of examinations,
coupled with their continued expansion (Carroll, 1998a; Green, 2001;
MacKreth, 1998), appears to lend weight to the claim that the 'standard'
academic view of education – which has flourished at all levels of education
since the 1960s (see Chapter 1) – is in the process of further marginalizing
any vestige of a practical justification for PE and is, indeed, an expression of
a 'new orthodoxy' at the level of PE teaching: in other words, a sea change in

teachers' 'philosophies'[2] (Green, 2000b) towards an acceptance (at a practical as well as a conceptual level) of a theoretical or intellectual core at the heart of PE. In this vein, PE appears to have joined other school subjects on the academic 'treadmill' (Dore, 1997) and is becoming more, rather than less, like other (academic) subjects and, correspondingly, less like conventional or 'traditional' PE.

Having traced the rapid growth of examinable PE and explored some of the more important issues surrounding the topic, the rest of this chapter attempts to make sense of the seeming academicization of PE. It outlines the justifications for examinations in PE before exploring how the development might best be explained, as well as what, if anything, it tells us about shifts in physical educationalists' views of their subject.

Explaining the growth and development of examinable PE

The case for examinable PE (see, for example, Carroll, 1994; Stidder and Wallis, 2003), as presented by physical educationalists (as either academics or teachers) over the years, can broadly be divided into two parts: the surface-level or rhetorical justifications and the deep-lying motivations or reasons. On the surface, the case for examinable PE revolves around three different types of justification:

1   Providing opportunities for those 'practically minded' *pupils* with ability in and/or enthusiasm for PE and sport (who may also be less academically 'able'), to study an area to their liking and one that enables them to obtain a qualification that may, in turn, have vocational 'spin-offs'. This justification is often presented in terms of the promotion of equal opportunities.
2   Providing opportunities for *schools* to (a) attract students keen to pursue an increasingly popular examination subject – thereby improving their positions in performance-related 'league tables', gaining better OFSTED reports and strengthening applications for SSC[3] status; while (b) motivating and thereby endearing (or so it is claimed) less able pupils to their schools.
3   In the process, it is said, *PE teachers* and *PE departments* are able to improve their academic and professional standing or status while, at the same time, establishing the alleged centrality of the physical as well as the intellectual to the process of education.

Set alongside this mixture of idealistic and pragmatic justifications, PE teachers have a tendency to offer more immediate and prosaic justifications for favouring examinable PE. These include, 'a break from the teaching in the

gym' and on the playing fields, 'a chance to teach something more intellectu-
ally demanding and interesting', 'an alternative source of income' (from
examining) and, most pertinently, a necessary step towards career enhancement (Green, 2001). In the case of the latter, one of the more compelling constraints on PE teachers has to do with the career benefits they, and
particularly those relatively new to the profession, identify as accruing from
being involved with examinable PE. Teachers in Green's (2001) study, for
example, perceived an increasingly direct association between teaching examinable PE and employment opportunities – to the extent that they considered
their career prospects would be significantly hampered by not being involved
in teaching GCSE or A-level PE.

Rather than simply representing 'a growing acceptance of the value of
examinations in physical education' (Carroll, 1991: 141), the dramatic growth
and normalization of examinable PE may best be explained as the outcome of
a combination of several interrelated processes. The next section explores in
more detail the circumstances and processes that together, it is argued, have
created a context which has facilitated the rise of examinable PE.

Making sense of examinable PE

The academicization of PE A process of academicization has been apparent
in PE for over a quarter of a century. In this respect, developments in examinable PE in secondary schools can be seen to reflect developments in tertiary
institutions, one dimension of which has been the emergence of PE and
Sports Science degrees that have come to form the main career route (when
supplemented with a postgraduate teaching qualification) into PE for would-
be teachers of the subject (MacDonald et al., 1999). A consequence of this
development has been an increase in the proportion of secondary PE teachers
who have a strong attachment to examinable PE (many of them, after all, will
have benefited from it) and an attendant commitment to the supposed value
of theoretical knowledge and examinations in PE. They have, in effect, been
socialized into the academic PE ethos.

One additional aspect of occupational socialization which serves to further encourage or constrain teachers towards examinable PE, is what might be
referred to as workplace socialization; that is, the manner in which the culture
of the (secondary school PE) workplace has become internalized by teachers
– especially their perceptions of necessary, pragmatic responses to the constraints of their everyday work situations. Among these constraints are the
expectations of significant others within and beyond the school setting (such
as head teachers, heads of department, parents and OFSTED) regarding the
desirability of examinable PE.

An additional constraint towards the academicization of PE has been the explicit support for examinable PE in national and school OFSTED reports. Shaw et al. (2003: 70) observe that 'students' examination performance is commonly taken to be an important measure of a school', not least by governments and OFSTED. Comments from teachers in Green's (2001) study suggested that OFSTED inspectors were keen to encourage teachers to extend examinable PE. When placed alongside OFSTED inspectors' informal comments to teachers themselves, the formal observations in OFSTED school reports can be seen as tangible evidence of their keenness to support the academicization of PE and to encourage such a development where it is lacking.

The professionalization of PE The processes of academicization and occupational socialization overlap and are intimately related to another significant process within PE, that of professionalization: that is, the process by which an occupational group seeks recognition as a distinct, suitably qualified group, entitled to a high degree of control (and self-regulation) over its work. Concern with professional status has developed in relation to the perceived threat of 'marginalisation' of the subject and the 'broad problems of legitimation' (Yates et al., 1997: 436) faced by physical educationalists at all levels over many years. For numerous commentators since the 1970s, deep-seated and persistent concern among physical educationalists about their professional standing within education has manifested itself in many teachers and academics becoming increasingly concerned with the academic credentials of PE. Such feelings of professional susceptibility have been exacerbated in England and Wales by the arrival of a national curriculum and the identification, therein, of core and foundational subjects.

Against a backdrop of low status for PE and its practitioners within and beyond the world of education, it is somewhat unsurprising to find physical educationalists (teachers as well as academics) enthusiastically embracing examinations in an attempt 'to bring about the redefinition and re-evaluation' (Eggleston, 1990: 63) of their marginalized, poorly esteemed subject. As Eggleston (1990: 62) says of professional subject associations in general, the recent history of PE associations in the UK appears to reflect a 'struggle to redefine the subject ... as one that is examinable at school, college or university' level.

All told, the dramatic growth of examinable PE is best viewed against the 'backdrop of subject marginality' (Alexander et al., 1996: 23) not only in the UK but also worldwide[4] (Hardman, 1998). Thus, the quest for educational status is deeply implicated in the rise to prominence of examinable PE. Physical education teachers have, in effect, used examinations to mimic higher status, more powerful subjects than their own. It is, perhaps, telling that there is a very real sense among PE teachers that the more demanding the theoretical aspect of the work, the greater the status attached to the subject in the eyes of their colleagues and pupils (Green, 2001).

The marketization of education In many countries in recent decades, neo-liberal educational policies have found expression in the development of increasingly regulated/deregulated educational markets (see Chapter 2). Australia, Canada, Germany, Japan and the UK, for instance, have witnessed a blurring of the distinction between public or state and private education. Market-based reforms of the state schooling system in the UK over the past two decades, for example, have been justified on the basis of the benefits in 'driving-up' educational standards and the dissemination of good practice that greater degrees of inter-school competition (within local schooling 'markets') are claimed to bring.

In England and Wales, heightened pressures towards competition between schools increasingly able to control their own income and expenditure – not least by competing for potential pupils as if vying for a market share – have reinforced the academicization of PE. Head teachers, school governing bodies and physical educationalists themselves have become acutely aware of the financial implications of examinable PE. Head teachers are particularly appreciative of its recruitment potential as the development of GCSE and then A-level examinations in PE have enabled schools to keep and recruit more pupils and, in particular, financially lucrative sixth-formers (Green, 2001). The publication of school performance tables (based on public examination results) and the introduction of tiered examination papers (Fitz et al., 2006) has exacerbated the tendencies of schools to seek to maximize their chances of obtaining high levels of examination passes in the top grades. Consequently, head teachers and PE teachers have also identified the scope for practically oriented pupils to achieve hitherto unexpected examination success in PE, with the associated benefits for school status and profile that can result (Green, 2001). The constraints towards the academicization of PE in recent decades have, in many respects, reflected the increasing pressures on schools, their governing bodies and head teachers – evident since the introduction of market principles to the education system (Gorard et al., 2003) – to seek any available market advantage in order to survive, let alone flourish.

The evident appeal of examinable PE to pupils, teachers, head teachers and the inspection service alike has not gone unnoticed by examination boards that have been quick to bring a variety of PE syllabi to the examination table. Syllabi have been generated by examination boards that were once controlled in the main by universities (Fitz et al., 2006) but are nowadays almost entirely commercial enterprises. Largely at the request of schools, examination boards have introduced larger elements of course work to 16+ examinations generally (Fitz et al., 2006) and PE, in particular.

CONCLUSION

It is difficult to deny that the emphasis upon assessment of the intellectual dimensions of ostensibly practical PE activities, and the continued success of examinations in PE, tells us something about what may be coming to count as worthwhile knowledge and valid realization of that knowledge (Bernstein, 1975) in PE; namely, that the standard or orthodox conception of education as essentially academic continues to occupy the ideological high ground, even in the world of PE.

However, rather than simply representing a change in PE practice resulting from a shift in teachers' views of their subject towards a more academic conception of PE, the rapid growth of examinations in PE may be better understood, in part, as representing teachers' pragmatic responses to a perceived threat and a clear opportunity. The threat came in the form of the 'Cinderella status' of PE and the clear implications of the persistent 'cognitive imperialism' (McNamee, 1998; 2005) of the intellectual and, thus, academic conception of education associated with educational theorizing from the 1960s onwards. Opportunity came with the advent of an educational market in the UK. Examinable PE has become a power resource in the PE subject-community, which many PE teachers and academics have been quick to appreciate and exploit. Whereas the growth of assessment is largely attributable to political interventions, the growth of examinations in PE – in the form of GCSE and A-level – has, it is argued, resulted from a configuration of circumstances, prominent among which is PE teachers' desire for increased professional status and the marketization of education generally, as well as the practical day-to-day benefits examinable PE is perceived as having.

Nevertheless, examinable PE has by no means been an unmitigated success in terms of status and credibility. There have been unintended and seemingly unforeseen consequences. The struggle for professional status and security has shaped, and continues to shape, the 'Catch-22' situation PE teachers find themselves in – damned if they do examinable PE, damned if they do not. Also, the seemingly inexorable growth of examinable PE camouflages a strong element of resistance: the dominance of examinable PE is by no means complete. There are evidently many PE teachers who feel themselves 'demeaned' by 'the hierarchical dominance, or positioning, of propositional over performative knowledge' (McNamee, 2005: 8). Some teachers in Green's (2001) study reported that not only was examinable PE undesirable but that there were no internal pressures in their schools for such a development. It seems that head teachers in academically successful schools are less likely to encourage – or even, at times, allow – the development of examinable PE. Head teachers in such schools can clearly afford to concentrate on 'proper' academic subjects without risking penalizing themselves in terms of recruitment or academic results. Perhaps unsurprisingly, most of the schools resisting the development of examinations in PE were relatively academically successful schools, located in economically advantaged catchment areas.

In the early 1990s, Fitzclarence and Tinning (1990) suggested that three themes remained unresolved and problematic despite the apparent popularity of examinable PE among pupils and teachers alike; these were the nature of essential or worthwhile knowledge in PE, the educational status of PE as a school subject, and the place of physical activity within an examinable 'academic' subject. In 2008, while the juggernaut that is examinable PE rolls on, these issues endure.

RECOMMENDED READING

Carroll, B. (1998a) 'The emergence and growth of examinations in physical education', in K. Green and K. Hardman (eds), *Physical Education: A Reader*. Aachen: Meyer and Meyer Verlag. pp. 314–32.

NOTES

1 While, as here, the term 'examination' is more conventionally used to refer to physically and temporally segregated assessment activities, throughout the remainder of this chapter it is used in a more generic sense to refer to publicly recognized assessments in PE/sport – specifically, the more academic forms of assessment (such as GCSE and A level) rather than other forms of externally accredited vocationally oriented courses in PE (such as City and Guilds, BTEC and GNVQ) and national governing body and sports leader awards.

2 The term 'philosophies' indicates the everyday views of PE teachers upon the nature and purposes of their subject.

3 There is anecdotal evidence to suggest that a number of SSCs have adopted GCSE PE as a compulsory subject for *all* pupils, alongside 'core' PE. This is said to have occurred at the request of school management . and the YST as a means of raising not only the profile of PE as an academic subject but also schools' status as SSCs in terms of achieving one of the avowed objectives of the SSC programme.

4 The trend towards the academicization of PE in the UK is also evident in other countries. MacDonald et al. (1999: 38), for example, observe in relation to Australia that, 'in the school sector, perhaps the most significant development in recent years has been the emergence and consolidation of examinable … physical education'.

Health and Physical Education

In the world of PE and sport there are probably few ideas which are as widely and uncritically accepted as that linking sport and exercise with good health (Waddington, 2000). It is widely assumed that PE not only *can* but *should* play a central role in the promotion of health among young people. Telama et al. (2005: 115), for example, describe health promotion as 'the main goal of physical education in many countries'. Policies promoting physical activity in schools as a suitable means of combating the supposed obesity/health crisis – of which *Healthy People 2010* (US Department of Health and Human Services, 2000) in the USA and the UK's *Choosing Health* (Department of Health, 2004) are prime examples – are widespread. In Australia and New Zealand, the titles of the learning area or subject – 'Health and Physical Education' and 'Health and Physical Well-being' – express the assumed centrality of health to PE. In England and Wales the requirement for PE teachers to develop pupils' knowledge and understanding of the impact of exercise on health, as well as the skills and predispositions necessary to carry it out, is built into the National Curriculum for Physical Education (NCPE) (QCA, 2006).

This chapter examines the supposed relationship between PE and health. First the chapter outlines the scale and nature of the health problems said to be associated with inactivity, as well as the ostensible role of sport and PE in combating these. It then explores other key contributors to health, before pointing to some of the limitations of sport and PE as vehicles for health promotion.

THE SCALE AND NATURE OF THE 'PROBLEM'

It is widely accepted that the major public health problems of developed and developing societies are increasingly degenerative, rather than infectious, dis-

eases of the kind associated with changes over time in lifestyles. The most per-
nicious of these is thought to be the 'tide of obesity' which is said to be 'sweep-
ing' across the developed world in particular and which shows no sign of
halting. In the USA, the number of obese adults has doubled since the mid-
1970s so that by the turn of the twenty-first century more than 60 per cent of
American adults were classified as overweight or obese (Bouchard, 2000). In
the UK, it is estimated that by 2010 75 per cent of the population will be overweight, resulting in more than 30,000 deaths each year from weight-related
illnesses (National Audit Office, 2001). The rapidity with which this 'pan-
demic of fat' (World Health Organization [WHO], 2002) is becoming truly
'global' is illustrated by the revelation that China – a country which, until
recently, was seen as having one of the leanest populations – is 'fast catching
up with the West' with approximately one-fifth of the 1 billion overweight or
obese people in the world living in China (Wu, 2006: 362).

The prevalence of obesity among the young also appears to be increasing
rapidly, particularly in the economically developed countries of the western
world. In the USA, for example, Cohen et al. (2005: 154) point to 'the tripling
of overweight young people (ages 16–19) over the last 30 years'. Schenker (2005)
estimates that 10 per cent of primary-aged youngsters in the UK are overweight
and a further 2 per cent obese – a 100 per cent increase in both categories in the
past decade. Elsewhere, Welk et al. (2006) point out the prevalence of obesity
among Australian, Canadian, Chinese and Spanish youth. It seems that at
current rates of increase, '"adult" percentages of overweight children will be
reached within 30 years' (Dollman, Norton and Norton, 2005: 895).

The *consequences* of being overweight and being inactive are said to be
clear for all to see. Obese people are likely to experience a wide range of
chronic diseases, ranging from mild ailments such as breathlessness and vari-
cose veins, at one extreme, through greater risk of osteoporosis, to serious,
life-threatening conditions such as coronary heart disease, hypertension and
diabetes, as well as some forms of cancer (American College of Sports
Medicine, 2000; Bouchard, 2004) at the other. Although the clinical manifestations of diseases associated with overweight and obesity do not become
apparent until mid-adulthood they are thought to have their origins in childhood and adolescence.

If the *scale* and *consequences* of the problem appear self-evident so, too,
does the *nature* of the problem: namely, the rapid decline of physical activity
in people's lives in less than a generation. The WHO estimates that well over
60 per cent of the world population (and young people in particular) is
simply not active enough to benefit their health (Puska, 2004). In the UK,
Europe and North America, 'significant numbers of children lead relatively
sedentary lives and rarely experience sustained periods of moderate or
vigorous physical activity during the weekdays or weekends' (Winsley and

Armstrong, 2005: 72) sufficient to enhance their health status and there have been no appreciable changes (among youth) in recent years (Welk et al., 2006). Adolescence and youth appear to be characterized by high levels of inactivity and, to make matters worse, children's levels of physical activity (in terms of energy expenditure) decrease with age. Low and diminishing levels of physical activity are especially marked in females and older children, and the activity levels of both groups deteriorate as they move through the secondary school years.

Although guidelines on what constitutes sufficient and appropriate frequency and intensity of exercise for health benefits differ between countries and organizations (Bissex et al., 2005), many western countries now have national physical activity recommendations or guidelines for children and adolescents (Marshall et al., 2002) and guidelines for the delivery of health-related exercise (HRE) through PE (Harris, 2005). Current activity guidelines reflect a paradigm shift in the mid-1990s whereby the health benefits of moderate forms of physical activity rather than vigorous intensity are recommended (Welk et al., 2006). Guidelines tend to recommend that children and young people take part in moderate to vigorous physical activity (MVPA) for at least 30 minutes but preferably for an hour on most, if not all, days of the week (Harris, 2005; Winsley and Armstrong, 2005).

For many commentators the issue is not simply that levels of *activity* have decreased, young people's *fitness* (and their aerobic fitness, in particular) appears in 'perilous decline' (Rowland, 2003) – especially among 15-year-olds and older girls – diminishing worldwide by 'about 1% a year' over the past quarter of a century as a consequence of the 'reduced exposure of current children to fitness enhancing physical activity' (Dollman et al., 2005: 895).

With less physically active lifestyles, there has been a rise of so-called 'obesogenic environments' (Catford, 2003) over the course of several decades. Cultural and economic changes have resulted in an environment that facilitates obesity by normalizing sedentary lifestyles. These changes range from a rise in the number of less physically active occupations, the growth of labour-saving devices, increased use of cars, television and computers through to increases in 'low intensity leisure activities' (Dollman et al., 2005: 892), such as watching television and reading, to changing patterns of family eating and an increase in snacking.

Psychological health

Although the focus of attention in relation to health remains on the degenerative diseases associated with overweight and obesity, there is a growing body of evidence to suggest that mental ill health is the coming disease of the twenty-first century, especially in the developed world. The WHO predicts that 'depression will be the second most debilitating illness in the world by 2020, following CHD' (Fox, 2003: 8). It seems that the psychological health of young people, in particular, is deteriorating, especially among women (Bynner et al., 2002). Young people are exhibiting a growing range of disorders ranging from anxiety and depression through eating disorders, self-harm and obsessive compulsive behaviour, to psychosis.

In the same way that the fostering of active lifestyles from early in life is viewed as critical in combating so-called hypokinetic, under-exercising or 'lifestyle' diseases', psychological benefits are also thought to accrue from regular involvement in sport and physical activity (Biddle, 2006). In a twenty-first-century variation on the nineteenth-century public school justification for games – *mens sana in corpore sano* (a healthy mind in a health body) – there is a growing body of evidence supporting claims for the role of exercise in promoting individual psychological and social health and well-being.[1] More specifically, Biddle (2003) highlights the evidence linking physical activity to specific aspects of psychological well-being and, most notably, anxiety and stress, depression, mood and emotion, self-perceptions and esteem and psychological dysfunction.

However, while physical benefits such as fitness appear relatively straightforward to plan for – as well as observe and measure – psychosocial outcomes are more difficult to anticipate. Nevertheless, the recipe for 'positive psychosocial outcomes' seems readily identifiable and more likely to accrue from environments that are primarily concerned with self-improvement and the mastery of particular sporting or physical activity tasks for the intrinsic pleasure they bring (Biddle, 2006). In addition, it seems that physical and psychological health is often interrelated: psychological health can benefit from positive physical self-perceptions and these can be enhanced through developing positive perceptions of sporting competence and physical fitness and attractiveness (Biddle, 2006). Childhood obesity, on the other hand, is 'associated with poor psychological well-being and social problems' (Stevinson, 2003: 12).

In the light of the prevailing view that one of the most important determinants of health is how physically active people are, the concerted effort to utilize sport and physical activity – often through the medium of PE – as a vehicle for health promotion is to be expected.

PHYSICAL EDUCATION AS THE SETTING AND SPORT AND PHYSICAL ACTIVITY AS THE SOLUTION

On the face of it there are a number of reasons for viewing sport and physical activity in schools, and thus PE, as a vehicle for the promotion of health and fitness among young people. Roberts and Brodie's (1992) study, *Inner-City*

Sport, suggests that sport confers health benefits which are not only experienced by 'ordinary' participants but are also evident across all socio-demographic groups (male/female; young/old; employed/unemployed; rich/poor). These benefits have the added bonus of acting in addition to other favourable lifestyle practices such as healthy diets. Also, being physically active produces precisely the same health-related benefits from physical activity for children and adolescents as for adults (Boreham and Riddoch, 2001): it reduces body fatness and aids the management of obesity, lowers high blood pressure, increases bone mineral density and enhances psychological well-being (Winsley and Armstrong, 2005).

It is typically assumed that PE provides an appropriate setting for health promotion through physical activity and exercise in several ways. First, PE is expected to provide opportunities for pupils to engage in appropriate levels of physical activity during school time. More important, however, is the assumed role of PE in preparing children for a lifetime of regular physical activity by passing on the requisite knowledge and skills, as well as the attitudes, thought to sustain an ongoing commitment to health-promoting exercise. Since the early 1980s, the main vehicle for health promotion in PE in many English-speaking countries has been health-related exercise – or health-related fitness (HRF) as it is sometimes known.

Health-related exercise

Conventional definitions of health define it as 'the maximisation of physical and socio-psychological well-being' (Roberts and Brodie, 1992: 96) rather than merely the absence of disease. Similarly, HRE is said to involve physical activity associated with health enhancement as well as disease prevention (Harris, 2005) and tends to be defined as 'an attempt to effect an understanding and awareness of the health benefits of an active lifestyle, which aims to bring about a series of rational decisions, made autonomously by the individual, to engage in various forms of physical activity' (McNamee, 1988: 83). This conception of HRE and PE as a vehicle for health promotion rests upon a widely accepted assumption that increasing people's knowledge and understanding is likely to lead to changes in their attitudes and, subsequently, and more importantly, their health-related behaviours. Put another way, they will abandon the things that are bad for their health and take up those that are good. The NCPE in England and Wales points to the alleged role of PE in promoting 'positive attitudes towards active and healthy lifestyles' by helping pupils to make appropriate choices about how to get involved in sport and physical activity (QCA, 2005a: 1). I return to this claim below.

Despite the seemingly self-evident arguments regarding the significance of physical activity for health and the alleged role of PE in health promotion, there are a number of substantial caveats in relation to claims about the contribution of PE and sport to health and the role of PE in health promotion, beginning with the reality of HRE.

HRE in practice Over its 30 years or more history, what has become known as HRE has more usually been referred to as 'health-related *fitness*' among many alternative terms. Increasingly, during the 1990s, academics stated their preference for the term 'exercise' over 'fitness' on the basis that the latter placed undue emphasis upon the relationship between health and fitness rather than health and physical activity and, in so doing, encouraged teachers and pupils to focus upon strenuous and intense physical activity in PE lessons in pursuit of high fitness scores.

Despite the shift in terminology away from health-related *fitness* and towards *exercise* in the theoretical literature, not much appears to have changed on the ground. Health-related exercise in PE continues to be dominated by an emphasis on fitness – more specifically, fitness as it relates to sports performance (Harris, 2005) – rather than exercise as a vehicle for health promotion. Critics point to the prevalence of simplistic, inaccurate and potentially damaging practices in PE lessons based upon 'narrow interpretations of HRE' (Harris, 2005: 85) formed around 'relatively limited knowledge and understanding' (Harris, 2005: 80) on the part of teachers of the relationship between health and PE. Despite the existence of 'good practice' guidelines for HRE in primary and secondary schools in England and Wales, Harris (2005: 85) highlights the continuing existence of undesirable practices in the form of 'forced fitness regimes … inactive PE lessons involving excessive theory or teacher talk; dull, uninspiring drills, or an overemphasis on issues related to health and hygiene'. Physical education teachers tend to focus upon a limited range of 'health' topics such as safety issues and warm-ups and stretching and some aspects of the effects of exercise on health outcomes (Harris, 2005).

Such restricted interpretations are also reflected in gender-specific forms of HRE based on sex-stereotypical assumptions about appropriateness for boys and girls (Harris and Penney, 2000) with boys' HRE focusing upon strength and endurance work and fitness-testing rather than suppleness, preferring to utilize activities such as cross-country running and weight-training. Unsurprisingly, perhaps, young people tend to dislike and misunderstand the nature and purposes of fitness activities and testing which are said to be fruitless and counter-productive (Harris and Cale, 2006). Indeed, PE teachers' tendency to rely upon aerobics, circuit- and weight-training and cross-country running as the core activities alongside fitness-testing merely serves to alienate many young people (Harris, 2005).

Whether or not the differing connotations of health-related exercise rather than health-related fitness are fully understood by practitioners and/or have simply not yet filtered down to school level adequately is an open question. Nevertheless, the likelihood that PE teachers would (1) focus their practice on a simple equation linking health to fitness (something which academics tended to do in the 1980s) and (2) emphasize its theoretical dimension (in much the same way they have done with GCSE and A-level examinations in PE) was, perhaps, the foreseeable consequence of utilizing health promotion as a convenient vehicle for bolstering the status and educational credibility of PE via academic lessons in health promotion. Neither should it be surprising – given what we know about the relationship between teachers' 'philosophies' and their practices (Green, 2003) – to find that while information about HRE has a positive impact on PE teachers' knowledge, planning and delivery of HRE, it is 'less successful in changing teachers' philosophies and teaching methods' (Harris, 2005: 82). What amounts to widespread continuity and small degrees of change in the practice of HRE in PE has been described by Harris (2005) in Sparkes's (1989) terms as 'innovation without change'. At the more fundamental level of day-to-day practice, whether or not health promotion is universally accepted as the *raison d'être* for PE, teachers – like government and its agencies – continue to view sport and especially team games as the main focus for PE and the primary vehicle for HRE and health promotion (Green, 2003). The teaching of HRE in PE in secondary schools continues to be characterized by 'much confusion and considerable variation in practice' (Harris, 2005: 79). It seems that many – from policy-makers through to pupils – continue to view exercise as synonymous with fitness and sports performance, and fitness as being 'tuned up to maximum performance' (Roberts and Brodie, 1992: 96).

OTHER KEY CONTRIBUTORS TO HEALTH

It would be over-simplistic and misleading to think that lack of exercise is the major threat to the immediate health and well-being of young people. Riddoch and Boreham (1995: 88) have pointed out that 'the primary morbidities of children and youth are unwanted pregnancy, substance abuse, physical and sexual abuse and anxiety disorders ... [while] the primary cause of death in this age group is violence (accidents, homicide and suicide)'.

Over the longer term, other aspects of individual lifestyles – such as diet, alcohol and tobacco and, other forms of exercise – can be more influential in determining an individual's health status than levels of sporting and physical activity (Roberts and Brodie, 1992). In short, other features of young people's lifestyles deserve to command more attention in health terms than participation in sport and physical activity.

Diet

Although weight-gain on the part of young people may, in part, be a consequence of decreasing energy expenditure, there is a good deal of evidence that 'at least part of the problem may lie with increasing energy consumption' (Dollman et al., 2005: 892). It seems that 'small imbalances in excess energy of only a few kilojoules per day may result in significant body fat increases in a few years even in the face of constant physical activity patterns' (Dollman et al., 2005: 893). And this may well be what has happened in practice. The diet side of 'the "too much food, too little exercise" equation' (All Party Parliamentary Group [APPG], 2005: 3) has changed over recent decades in favour of the former with the abundance of and ease of access to a wide variety of 'snack' (otherwise known in pejorative terms as 'junk') foods in affluent societies, such that people eat more calories than they need before they feel satiated or 'full'.

But the health problems associated with contemporary diets are a consequence of the nature of the food as well as the amount. Diets in the developed world rely heavily on processed, calorific foodstuffs with a high sugar and salt content, and modern foods, especially fast foods, tend to be energy-dense. Also, increasing proportions of energy intake in the west are taken from animal sources (Lang, 2006). Morgan Spurlock's (2004) infamous 'experiment' in eating three McDonald's meals each day for a month provides compelling, if anecdotal, evidence of the impact of fast-food diets on the prevalence of obesity in the USA. More scientifically, a 15-year study in the UK, reported in the *Lancet*, established a link between fast food and 'soaring' levels of obesity and type-II diabetes across affluent nations (Boseley, 2004). Pidd (2004: 4) noted that 2.5 million Britains make use of one of the 1,235 McDonalds fast-food outlets in the UK every day. In Thomas et al.'s (2005: 181) study, almost 90 per cent of Welsh schoolchildren 'consumed diets containing more than 30 percent total fat, while 93 percent exceeded the [WHO's criterion threshold of] 10 percent saturated fat cut-off point'. Similarly, Renton (2006) claims that the sugar intake of Scottish children – one in three of whom are overweight – doubled in the two decades leading up to 2006.

The clustering of unhealthy behaviours among young people is well established. In addition to changes in diet, consumption of alcohol has increased dramatically in recent decades among both adults and young people (Roberts, 2006). Despite the fact that most youngsters of secondary school age do not drink and those who do tend to drink moderate amounts (Schools Health Education Unit, 2006) (and, for the most part, at home with the knowledge of their parents), there has been a significant growth in the numbers of young people in England consuming high levels of alcohol. And it is not only teenagers from affluent homes but young women from the middle-classes, in particular, who are drinking more. Quite apart from the direct threat to life that alcohol can present, in broader more indirect health terms most alcoholic drinks (including the increasingly popular 'alco-pops') are as calorific as high-sugar soft drinks.

Despite the fact that young people and adults are less active overall, they are tending to consume more energy-dense foods and more alcohol. Wu (2006: 362) puts China's recent epidemic of overweight and obesity down to 'changes to the traditional diet, reduced levels of physical activity, and increased sedentary lifestyles'. Because exercise alone has a small impact on levels of body fat, 'the most efficient way to lose excess body fat is through a multidisciplinary approach comprising diet, exercise and behavioural change interventions' (Winsley and Armstrong, 2005: 67).

But this is not the whole story. One crucial component to weight gain is the steady decline in the prevalence of other forms of exercise in day-to-day living in modern societies.

Other forms of exercise

Young people's sports participation has risen over the past 30 years (see Chapter 7) but in general terms their lifestyles are more inactive and their fitness may well be declining. So, what are young people doing with the rest of their time? If young people's health and health-related fitness have declined in recent decades this must owe more to their diets or their more frequent use of private transport or something other than a flight from sport. What has changed is the rest of life beyond sport and, in particular, according to Dollman et al. (2005: 895), 'the rise and rise' in popularity of television watching and high-technology entertainment as well as eating and sleeping.

It seems that young people spend 'considerable portions of their leisure time being sedentary' (Marshall et al., 2002: 413). Approximately two-thirds of 11–13-year-olds in North America and Europe watch television, for example, for more than two hours a day (Marshall et al., 2002). Indeed, watching television is now the industrialized world's main pastime, accounting for more time than any single activity except work and sleep. Sigman (2007: 12) points to research which suggests that 11–15-year-olds spend 55 per cent of their waking lives watching television; that is, 53 hours a week or seven and a half hours a day. The average 6-year-old will have already watched television 'for more than one full year of their lives' and by the age of 75, the average Briton will have spent more than 12 years of 24-hour days watching television' (Sigman, 2007: 12). However, it seems that television viewing may have 'stagnated' (Wray, 2006) as Internet usage booms across Europe with people 'surfing the net' for over 11 hours a week on average. Daily usage of the Internet is particularly high among the 16–24-year age group.

These changes are thrown into sharp relief through comparisons across generations, subgroups and cultures. Fisher (2002) found that while young people (8–19 years of age) in the UK were the most likely to play sport, those over 65 were more physically active generally because young people were more sedentary overall. Under-20-year-old boys were more active than girls, but in all other age groups women were more active than men.

All this suggests that inactivity and obesity are best viewed not so much as the consequence of an *ir*rational response to a rational message, but as 'normal' responses to living in environments that make inactivity the norm. Among young and old alike, sedentary behaviours and lifestyles have become normalized. Marshall et al.'s (2002) study of teenagers in the USA and the UK suggested that sedentary behaviours can and do coexist with physical activity, and that some of the most active children in sporting terms are also among the most sedentary overall (Kirk, 2002a). Indeed, sedentary behaviours such as watching television are more likely to replace other sedentary behaviours, such as reading, than sport and physical activity (Marshall et al., 2002). Such claims are, however, disputed. Sigman (2007) points to studies in Mexico, New Zealand and China which suggest a strong relationship between the amount of television viewing and increases in the prevalence of obesity. He points to a variety of studies that pinpoint television as a factor in a number of health issues such as sleeping difficulties, attention deficit hyperactivity disorder and raised blood cholesterol levels. Sigman (2007: 16) concludes that '[W]atching television, irrespective of the content, is increasingly associated with unfavourable biological and cognitive changes'.

This might be interpreted as suggesting that the personality structures (or habituses) of young westerners, in particular, may be in the process of changing over time towards the normalization of two trends that may appear paradoxical but are, in fact, two sides of the same coin; that is, youngsters with busy leisure lives who – while involved in sport – are, nevertheless, more sedentary overall and more likely to be overweight than ever before.

Other lifestyle factors – themselves strongly correlated with social class position – exert more pervasive and often stronger effects on health and fitness (Roberts and Brodie, 1992) than sports participation. The contributions to health and fitness of various lifestyle practices seem to be additive (Roberts and Brodie, 1992). In this regard, the 'best recipe' for staying free of physical illness seems to be healthy diets and low or nil alcohol consumption. When added to not smoking, these same lifestyle variables, 'made the best combination for impacting directly and positively on cardiovascular health'. General exercise, together with high overall levels of participation in energetic and non-energetic sport, and – perhaps surprisingly – unhealthy diets, 'were the lifestyle practices associated with low stress scores' (Roberts and Brodie, 1992: 111–12). Roberts and Brodie

(1992) also noted a tendency for the same individuals to be involved in all lifestyle practices shown to be health-promoting. Those who were playing the most sport in their study were more likely than other individuals to improve their health, to be drinking moderately rather than heavily, and to have either given up tobacco or never to have smoked. Thus, participation in sport and physical activity has been associated with a number of complementary health and lifestyle behaviours related to diet as well as tobacco and alcohol consumption (Boreham and Riddoch, 2001; Koska, 2005). Not only are physically active girls more likely to have healthy habits but they are also more inclined to follow health recommendations and to consider the future health-related consequences of their actions (Koska, 2005).[2]

Sports participation is not only more likely to be adopted but tends, in concert with other everyday lifestyle practices, to make the greatest difference to the health of the socio-economic groups that are health privileged to begin with (Roberts and Brodie, 1992): the middle-classes.

The significance of social class and other social dynamics for health

However much physical educationalists might want to believe in the health-promoting capacity of PE, the main determinant of inequalities in health remains socio-economic deprivation (Wanless, 2004). Sport and physical activity are extremely unlikely to 'render these influences dormant' (Shilling, 2005: 38), negate or override them.

The significance of social class for health status and sports participation lies in the effects of poverty in the past rather than the present. Even though income fluctuates over the life-course the effects of poverty endure, not least in terms of restricted opportunities to develop skills and interests. Physical activity levels themselves vary according to socio-economic status and it is those people who have the requisite financial resources, spare time and cultural capital who are most likely to treat their bodies as 'projects' to be moulded in line with their preferred images of themselves (Shilling, 2005). '[T]he most effective way, possibly the only effective way, of improving the notoriously poor relative health of lower socio-economic groups will be to reduce their economic deprivations' (Roberts and Brodie, 1992: 111–12). Evans and Davies (2006a: 117) put the argument more pithily: 'Want health and longevity? Forget health education, fitness regimes and expensive diets; just avoid being working class'!

The significance of social class for health status is frequently compounded by other social dynamics. Lower levels of physical activity tend to be observed not only among lower socio-economic groups but also among women and ethnic minorities. A five-year longitudinal study of almost 6,000 11–12-year-olds from a variety of ethnic groups in London revealed that vigorous physical activity decreased while hours spent in sedentary behaviour increased between the ages of 11–12 and 15–16 years, with a larger decline in physical activity in girls than in boys. Asian pupils were substantially less physically active than their white counterparts, with Asian girls, in particular, exhibiting faster increases in sedentary behaviour between ages 12–13 and 15–16 years than white girls. Sedentary behaviours were higher among black students generally and black girls engaged in less physical activity than white girls. Students from lower socio-economic neighbourhoods reported higher levels of sedentary behaviour while girls from lower socio-economic groups (but not boys) were less physically active than those from more affluent backgrounds (Brodersen et al., 2007). In both the UK and the USA, obesity is far more prevalent among ethnic minorities, especially African Americans and African Caribbeans, than other ethnic groups (Brodersen et al., 2007; Harrison and Belcher, 2006). In the USA, African-American children are, according to Harrison and Belcher (2006), not only far more likely to be overweight and obese than children in other ethnic groups, but are prone to much higher rates of increase. If physical activity in youth is a predictor of later adiposity, the finding from Brodersen et al. (2007) that ethnic and class-related differences are largely established by age 11–12 years is particularly important.

THE LIMITS TO SCIENCE

Research into the relationship between sport and HRE has grown in line with the professional interests of a growing band of sports scientists (and physiologists in particular), concerned with demonstrating that regular sport makes people fitter and, by inference, healthier. Nevertheless, in recent years a number of authors (see, for example, Evans and Davies, 2006a; Gard and Wright, 2005) have pointed to what they take to be the limitations of 'scientific' claims regarding the relationship between health (and particularly overweight and obesity) and exercise. There are two distinct concerns expressed in these arguments: first, with the science itself and, second, with what are perceived as the ideological underpinnings to that science.

With regard to the science of HRE, critics flag up the problems associated with measurement of overweight/obesity and levels of fitness. It has become increasingly apparent that satisfactory measures of overweight and obesity (and the definitions that are based upon them) are difficult to establish. The most frequently used measure of overweight/obesity, the body-mass index (BMI), is recognized as a good deal less than exact. Body-mass index is not only imprecise, it is also an inappropriate measure because the health-related 'problem' with overweight and obesity lies in the fact that it is adipose tissue or fat lying wrapped around the heart and vital organs (and especially the abdomen in men) and streaked through muscles that is the biggest threat to health (Welk et al., 2006). It is this 'internal fat' that sends out the chemical signals which eventually lead to insulin resistance, diabetes and heart conditions, even in especially slim people who do not exercise. It seems, then, that those jokingly referred to as TOFIs (thin on the outside, fat on the inside) are as susceptible to fat infiltration of the liver, for example, as overweight and obese people. This is especially significant in relation to the health of young people, among whom much excess fat surrounds the internal organs rather than simply being subcutaneous. Hence, waist circumference and waist:hip ratio are considered to be more strongly correlated with cardio-vascular risk and, therefore, more informative measures of obesity (Wu, 2006). This is especially so with children and young people, 'due to the changes that occur in the ratio of velocity of weight gain to height gain in normal growth' (Schenker, 2005: 10). However, critics often overlook the fact that, because BMI has been the most commonly used measure over a period of time, it does enable trends to be identified.

In relation to the issue of measurement, Rich et al. (2005) are typical of those questioning the assumption that there is a significant health problem associated with being overweight. Rich et al. (2005) argue that 'whilst there may be health risks for those individuals at the extreme ends of the weight continuum', the relationships between weight, diet, physical activity and health are far more complex and uncertain than is currently being suggested. They point to studies which suggest that individuals who are 'overweight' but who are physically active, may well be healthier than their thinner counter-parts who are not physically active. In other words, size, shape and weight might not be the straightforward health issue it is widely assumed to be. Such criticisms do tend, however, to overlook the fact that the best predictor of future weight is current weight: fat children are demonstrably more likely to become fat adults.

One of the more substantial limitations of conventional scientific (health-related) exercise measurements is whether it is possible to gather meaningful data on the fitness status of young people. Dollman et al. (2005: 892) argue that there are 'serious methodological limitations and inconsistencies … inherent in physical activity measurement', not least because people's 'ability to meet the complex demands of recall is limited' and, consequently, there is 'considerable random error associated with self-reported physical activity, upon which representative surveys are largely based'. It is also apparent that young people's performances in fitness tests are commonly affected by motivation (Harris and Cale, 2006). Fitness-testing of children is often presented as an important step in educating young people about their health status. However, because it frequently reinforces the notion of exercise as competitive and unpleasant, fitness-testing has been shown to be inimical to many children's perceptions of HRE and PE. Consequently, it may be counterproductive to the promotion of active lifestyles in children and young people (Harris and Cale, 2006).

Measurement issues compound the commonplace misconception that fitness in children and young people is primarily a function of their levels of physical activity (or, more specifically, physical exertion) as well as the assumed corollary that those who are fit must thereby be the most active (Armstrong and Welsman, 1997). Such assumptions reflect a widespread misunderstanding involving the conflation of two independent variables: physical fitness and physical activity (Winsley and Armstrong, 2005). Fitness levels do not necessarily reflect, and cannot be read off, from levels of physical activity. Despite the widespread claims that young people's fitness is in decline, there is limited evidence that young people's aerobic fitness – as defined by both endurance and maximal aerobic power (Harris and Cale, 2006) – is either 'low or deteriorating from generation to generation' (Winsley and Armstrong, 2005: 76). In short, it may be inaccurate and misleading to think that, as a consequence of their relative inactivity, children and young people are necessarily unfit. There is, it seems, only a weak relationship between their aerobic fitness and physical activity levels. Indeed, children and adolescents appear to be the fittest section of the population (Armstrong and McManus, 1994). This is because there is a significant genetic contribution to children's fitness which manifests itself during maturation. Indeed, 'when aerobic fitness is expressed relative to body size, children's aerobic fitness is at least as good as that of most adults' and 'has changed very little' since the 1930s (Winsley and Armstrong, 2005: 75). In addition to disputes regarding scientifically valid means of measuring fatness and fitness, uncertainty surrounds exactly what constitutes enough physical activity – in terms of frequency, intensity and duration – to maximize the health benefits. Consequently, 'there is no consensus on the optimal level of physical fitness for young people' (Harris and Cale, 2006: 219) in health terms.

Despite evidence for the existence of a strong relationship between physical activity and fitness and health in adults, there is not yet conclusive empirical evidence that physical activity and fitness during childhood have a major impact on future health status. Nevertheless, high levels of physical fitness during adolescence and young adulthood appear to be related to a healthy risk-factor profile in later life. What can be said unequivocally, is that physical fitness and physical activity have a positive influence on young people's psychological health (Harris and Cale, 2006).

It seems, then, that what PE teachers in particular consider one of the key functions of PE in health terms – the testing and enhancement of fitness

– is redundant. All this begins to explain why, among academics if not practitioners, there has been a steady shift in emphasis over the past decade or so from a focus on health-related *fitness* to health-related *exercise* and other lifestyle behaviours (Harris and Cale, 2006); that is, away from an emphasis on increasing youngsters' levels and intensity of physical activity (in order to alleviate or offset the health problems said to be associated with increasingly sedentary lifestyles) and towards encouraging predispositions for active lifestyles.

Not only are the science of obesity and the supposed health-related benefits of sport under attack, so too are the taken-for-granted assumptions that form the basis of most people's thinking about overweight and obesity. Gard and Wright (2005: 3) describe the 'science' of obesity as based on a 'pot-pourri' of science, morality and ideological assumptions which become regurgitated by the media in the form of 'popular science' and subsequently embedded in the public consciousness. Among other things, they challenge the idea that overweight and obesity necessarily cause ill-health and that modern western lifestyles and technologies, by creating the conditions for overeating and sedentariness, cause obesity. Gard and Wright (2005) also highlight the gender dimension to claims surrounding obesity. They observe that expectations regarding women's bodies have changed over time and reflect attitudes towards women and demands upon women to model their bodies and appearance on stereotypical norms which result in stigma and anxiety for women.

Other critics focus upon the ways in which people communicate the 'facts' about HRE. The discourse of HRE, they argue, frequently involves an over-simplistic view of individual freedom.

THE LIMITS TO INDIVIDUALISM

If one takes conventional definitions of HRE as read, then health is largely, if not entirely, an individual matter. From the starting assumption of individual responsibility, it is entirely appropriate that PE emphasizes 'the *controllability* of such behaviour and the personal *responsibility* element of activity' (Biddle, 1989: 64; emphases in the original). For a significant number of dissenters, however, the focus on individual responsibility reflects the prevalence of an enduring 'ideology of healthism' in PE. Healthism is defined as an ideology (a set of beliefs that are a mixture of myth and reality or, more pithily, fact and fiction – an amalgam of what there is good reason to believe combined with what people prefer to believe) in which (young) people are 'largely responsible for their own health and making healthy choices' (Rich et al., 2004: 178). Young people not only *can* but *should* make the necessary lifestyle choices to improve their health. Individuals are assumed to have a moral responsibility not only to regard being unhealthy or sick as undesirable but also as something they can and should overcome by their best efforts. A corollary of the presumption of individualism built into the ideology of healthism is the moral condemnation of those who fail to adopt active, healthy lifestyles.

A central criticism of the ideology of healthism is that it 'reduces the complex causes or aetiology of diseases to simple behaviour or lifestyle factors' (Colquhoun, 1991: 9) – that is, to the ways in which people lead their lives – and ignores social, economic and cultural factors, including governmental policies and the economic and political power and social influence of the food, alcohol and tobacco industries. By exaggerating the role of individual 'choice' in such a multidimensional and complex matter as health, physical educationalists are said to peddle a profoundly misguided myth, individualizing both the problem (simplistically interpreted as 'lifestyle' diseases 'caused' by under-exercising) and the remedy. Not only does healthism 'heap responsibility' (Evans and Davies, 2006c) on teachers as well as pupils, it also implicitly apportions blame when unrealistic expectations regarding what each might achieve are not attained. The messages about exercise, fitness and health are, after all, messages 'about self-discipline, control and willpower' (Tinning, 1991: 40) as young people are portrayed as responsible for the construction of their own healthy, active lifestyles. In playing up 'the pseudo-sovereignty' (Frew and McGillivray, 2005: 173) of the individual, the neo-liberal individualistic ideologies that lie at the heart of healthism reduce complex social processes to the individual level and explain them purely in psychological terms.

Rich et al. (2005) and Evans and Davies (2006a), among others, point out the potentially damaging effect on children of schools employing strategies such as pressing children to monitor their own diets, body shapes and levels of physical activity. Not only might measures such as height and weight reveal little or nothing about young people's state of health, but the costs may outweigh the benefits. Conventional definitions and measurements of overweight and obesity, and the crude strategies recommended to combat the 'problem', may result in a number of unhealthy and unnecessary responses by young people encouraged to believe that they must be thin in order to be healthy (Evans and Davies, 2006a). The well-meaning actions of teachers and health experts may only further stigmatize children and even constrain girls and young women towards eating disorders, such as anorexia nervosa and bulimia nervosa (Rich et al., 2005).

The ideology of healthism falls into the trap of perceiving as a private problem something that is better understood as a public issue. There is far more to health than lifestyle variables. This brings us to the limitations of education and sport – the backbone of PE curricula – in health promotion.

THE LIMITS TO EDUCATION

The model underpinning the HRE perspective is traditionally associated with health education; that is, a blind faith in the idea that making information available to individuals enables them to make better informed choices about their lifestyles (McDonald and Scott-Samuel, 2004). On this view, the role of PE is to develop in youngsters the requisite knowledge, attitudes and skills to develop healthy lifestyles. In effect, PE teachers 'skill' young people for 'responsible' health 'careers'. Yet, it is readily apparent that passing on knowledge about the associated risks of inactivity – as well as what needs to be done to rectify matters and why – frequently does not lead to changes in behaviour. Nevertheless, physical educationalists remain committed to the belief that inculcating knowledge about HRE will lead to changes in attitudes and subsequently behaviours.

THE LIMITS TO SPORT

There are two fundamental problems with the case for sport in health promotion. First, the abundant reservations about just what difference sports participation can actually make to health; and, second, the often ignored health 'costs' of sport. In terms of the contribution of sport and physical activity to health, it is apparent that in order to improve normal day-to-day health (in terms of lowering body fat, lowering cholesterol and improving physiological functioning generally) people need to raise their heart rate by exercising regularly throughout the life-course. This is the problem of persistence: for benefits to be lifelong it is necessary to be a lifelong participant. The same is true in relation to healthy diets and limiting tobacco and alcohol consumption.

As Chapter 7 shows, getting young people to participate in sport is not an issue. However, getting them to participate *often enough* and at *sufficient intensity* to improve their health is. Despite the high participation rates in sport and physical activity recorded among children and young people in Wales, for example, it appears that levels of energetic physical activity remain 'below what might be desired': 'Only 24% of secondary pupils and 41% of primary school pupils are physically active for 60 minutes on at least five days of the week' (SCW, 2006: 6). Most young people simply do not do sport regularly enough to improve their health. In addition, the very nature of much sport is such that levels of physical activity are inevitably sporadic and intermittent.

Not only do people tend not to do enough physical activity to benefit their health, they tend not to do it in the right way. While the health-related arguments in favour of regular, rhythmic and moderate exercise may be persuasive, the health-promoting case for energetic and competitive sport, and its beneficial health-related effects, deserves only qualified support. Waddington et al. (1997: 169) point to the fallacy of assuming that sport and physical activity are *necessarily* beneficial to health:

> [O]ne cannot assume that the health benefits associated with moderate exercise will simply be duplicated – still less can one assume that they will be increased – by exercise which is more frequent, of longer duration and of greater intensity, for exercise of this kind … may generate health 'costs' in terms of additional stresses or injuries, for example those associated with overuse.

In general, it is reasonable to suggest that in the case of rhythmic, non-competitive exercise, where bodily movements are to a large extent under the control of the individual participant, the health benefits substantially outweigh the health costs. However, 'as we move from non-competitive exercise to competitive sport, and as we move from non-contact to contact sport, so the health costs, in the form of injuries, begin to mount' (Waddington et al., 1997: 178). While the kinds of specific training associated with competitive sport do not necessarily lead to generalized health benefits, they do make sports players more susceptible to sports injury. Whyte (2006: 14) suggests that the commonly held belief that 'if a little is good a lot must be better' is mistaken. 'Sports participation', he observes, 'is associated with injuries that have both acute and chronic implications for health and well-being. Exercise can result in injury to all systems associated with an acute or chronic insult' (Whyte, 2006: 14). Forty years ago, sports injuries comprised 1–2 per cent of all injuries presented in the emergency rooms of hospitals whereas nowadays 'about 10% of all hospital-admitted injuries are sustained in sports' (Whyte, 2006: 14). And this only represents the most severe tip of the injury iceberg. Whyte (2006) points to the prevalence of arthritis, urinary incontinence, gastro-intestinal disturbance, amenorrhea and perturbations in the immune system and deaths associated with asthma as some of the many health problems associated with sport. As if to compound the potential health 'costs' of sports participation, some would argue that participation in sport might, itself, be viewed as a kind of drug; not least because it elicits withdrawal symptoms from those who feel themselves to be 'addicted' to it (Dunning and Waddington, 2003; Koska, 2005) – harmless as this form of addiction may well turn out to be.

THE LIMITS TO PHYSICAL EDUCATION

Physical education is expected to impact on health in two ways: first, in terms of increasing levels of activity and HRE within the school day and, second, by increasing young people's adherence to sport and exercise in a manner that will lead to lifelong participation. The latter is addressed in Chapter 7. With regard to the former, PE represents only '2 per cent of a young person's waking time and, therefore, cannot in itself satisfy the physical activity needs of young people or address activity shortfalls' (Harris, 2005: 79). Various studies examining the amount of physical activity performed during PE classes in the USA 'have consistently shown that students spend a limited amount of time engaged in moderate to vigorous physical activity' (Trost, 2006: 172). Studies in the USA suggest approximately one-third of lesson time for third-graders is taken up in MVPA (Trost, 2006). In the UK, primary-aged children were moderately or vigorously active for less than 20 per cent of PE lessons and large sections of primary school PE lessons are spent relatively static while developing skills (Waring et al., 2007). The relatively low levels of MVPA characteristic of PE lessons are insufficient to meet the recommendations for health-promoting levels of physical activity (Harris, 2005; Wallhead and Buckworth, 2004). Schools cannot realistically be expected to ensure that young people experience a sufficient volume of physical activity to fulfil current HRE guidelines.

An additional limitation to PE is the inherent shortcomings of an aspirant profession. For some observers, physical educationalists have deliberately appropriated the discourse of health: telling young people what to believe about health, what they need to do about their health, and then presenting themselves as best able to provide that service. Thus, physical educationalists are replicating the kinds of claims made by medical and non-medical groups to be experts in the field of health. In promoting PE as a vehicle par excellence for health promotion – by donning a paramedical cloak and claiming to be particularly well placed to treat a problem by virtue of their specialist, professional knowledge – physical educationalists (academics and teachers alike) stand accused of an opportunistic attempt to revive a flagging profession by establishing its relevance and, consequently, its legitimacy by association with a more established profession: medical science (Johns, 2005).

CONCLUSION

It is difficult to dissent from Roberts and Brodie's (1992: 139–40) sceptical reply to the health case for sport. First, sport does not impact on all health factors (self-assessment and strength it may, but not cardiovascular health or illness freedom). Second, sport does not eliminate or even reduce health inequalities associated with age, sex and socio-economic status, and may even increase them. Finally, not only is it the case that gains in aerobic fitness are lost if the new level of physical activity is lost (Winsley and Armstrong, 2005), it is unlikely that many adults can or will participate in enough sport and physical exercise to achieve more than improvements in feeling better – given that 'frequency and continuity' of activity appear to be 'the features of energetic sport participation with health effects' (Roberts and Brodie, 1992: 99). To these might be added the fact that, far from being an irreconcilable paradox, co-occurring increases in sports participation and obesity among young people appear to be the reality.

It seems that the widespread assumption that health and fitness are largely dependent on the quantity and quality of school PE programmes exaggerates not only the role of exercise in health but also the control of the individual in lifestyle construction and the potential for PE to countervail wider social processes. It appears necessary to conclude along with Parry (1988: 108) that 'sport *may* assist a healthy life-style, but it *may not*' (emphases in the original). Far more important to health status are social class and related lifestyle factors. Sport and physical activity are useful in health promotion *with*, but not as a substitute for, other healthy lifestyle practices (Roberts and Brodie, 1992). Although it has the merit, in public health terms, of being relatively cheap (and much cheaper than addressing the underlying socio-economic causes of ill health) the exercise intervention can only have a marginal effect. Despite this scepticism towards the role of PE in health promotion, it is important to acknowledge that active lifestyles play a crucial role in helping people to feel better and happier with their lives. That said, while sport and physical activity can make people feel better, so do many other active forms of leisure.

RECOMMENDED READING

Kirk, D. (1992) *Defining Physical Education: The Social Construction of a School Subject in Post-War Britain*. Basingstoke: Falmer Press.

Roberts, K. and Brodie, D. (1992) *Inner-City Sport: Who Plays and What are the Benefits?* Culemborg: Giordano Bruno.

Waddington, I., Malcolm, D. and Green, K. (1997) 'Sport, health and physical education: a reconsideration', *European Physical Education Review*, 3(2): 165–82.

NOTES

1 See Bloodworth and McNamee (2007) for an example of the widespread critique of subjective interpretations of health and well-being. In short,

pleasures associated with exercise induced well-being may mask activities that are harmful. Conversely, it is quite possible that sport could be good for someone whether they liked it or not or recognized and acknowledged it or not. In other words, well-being amounts to more than merely 'felt pleasure'.

2 It is worth bearing in mind, however, that the evidence regarding the relationship between sport and drinking and drug use is ambivalent.

Youth Sport and Physical Education

There are two underlying assumptions to be found in many commentaries on youth sport. The first is that levels of sports participation among young people are a 'problem'. In England and Wales, for example, the DCMS/DfES's (2005: 3) *School Sport Survey* points to an assumed need for 'further effort ... to engage the youngest pupils ... and those reaching the end of the secondary phase of education' in sport both within and beyond school. Even academics appear to accept that there are problems with levels of sports participation among the young and ask 'why current efforts are not working?' (Flintoff et al., 2005: vi) and 'why ... the PE profession [is] not more successful in terms of fostering lifelong activity in young people?' (Harris, 2005: 90). Questions such as these implicitly incorporate the second assumption; namely, that PE *can*, and *should*, have a powerful influence on promoting lifelong participation in sport, despite the fact that there remains a dearth of research demonstrating the critical role that PE is assumed to play in the promotion of physical activity among young people (Wallhead and Buckworth, 2004).

This chapter examines these two assumptions. First, it pinpoints the actual trends in participation on the basis of the available empirical evidence.

YOUTH SPORT

Despite the fact that the measures in studies of sports participation may be 'somewhat conservative' and provide 'little evidence about the intensity and quality of the activity' (Coalter, 1999: 25), the available data reveal some pretty straightforward patterns. First is a clear trend, since the 1970s, towards increased participation among young people and adults not only in Britain but across Europe and worldwide.

Although there has been a plateauing of levels of participation among

adults in the UK through the 1990s, and even a slight decline in overall participation levels among young people, when viewed over half a century participation rates can be seen to have grown substantially. Despite the fact that there
remains a significant minority of young people doing little or nothing in participatory terms, more young people in the UK are doing more sport (especially
in a recreational form) than ever before. Indeed, according to Sport England
(2003a: 58), in 2002, there were 'fewer youngsters spending less than one hour,
or no time, in a week doing sport and exercise than was the case in 1994'. At the
same time, 80 per cent of secondary age youngsters spent more than one hour a
week on sport and exercise[1] outside PE lessons (during term time) and 40 per
cent spent as much as five hours or more (Sport England, 2003a; 2003b). The
Sport England national surveys paint a more optimistic picture of sport participation rates among UK youth over the past decade than that portrayed in popular and political rhetoric. Other studies underline this impression. Ninety per
cent of pupils in the BSkyB and the YST's 'Living for Sport' project, for example, 'were active in some way outside of school' (Sportsteacher, 2005b: 9). The
YST study found that young people between the ages of 11 and 16 years did over
four hours of physical activity on average out of school, 'with 28 percent undertaking more than five hours' activity a week' (2005b: 9). Alongside an increase
in levels of participation, there appears to have been a marked decline in the
drop-out rate during late adolescence with young people much more likely to
continue participating in sport and physical activities after completing their
full-time education (Roberts, 1996a).

This trend towards increased participation in sport among young people,
as well as adults, in recent decades is evident in many countries. In Spain,
Puig (1996) observed how sport participation among Spanish youth was
higher in the mid-1990s than it was among previous generations, while in
Germany, Brettschneider and Sack (1996: 140) observed how, over the previous 30 years or so, the number of young people who participated in sport had
'increased enormously, to a point at which sport (had) a top position among
the favourite leisure-time activities of adolescents'. Similarly, in the
Netherlands levels of participation in sport among young people have 'grown
extensively and since 1960 explosively' (Buisman and Lucassen, 1996: 158). In
a more recent review of participation, De Knop and DeMartelaer (2001: 40)
noted that Dutch youth continued to 'participate in large numbers' and in
Flanders, sports participation rates among high school boys and girls over the
past three decades are reported to have increased (Scheerder et al., 2005a;
2005b), with more than 85 per cent of this group 'actively involved in leisure-
time sports' by the end of the 1990s (Scheerder et al., 2005a: 325).

In their cross-national study of Belgium, Estonia, Finland, Germany,
Hungary and the Czech Republic, Telama et al. (2002: 140) observed that
'physical activities and sports (continue to) belong to the most popular

[leisure] activities of young people'. The data drawn from Telama et al.'s European studies were based primarily upon the results of a cross-sectional study which explored the leisure-time sports participation – in what the authors call 'organised competitive sport' and 'recreational sport' – of a sample of 6,479 12- and 15-year-olds (3,270 males, 3,209 females) from six European countries (Telama et al., 2002). Telama et al.'s (2005) study corroborates the findings of many of the earlier studies in various European countries.

Participation appears to be particularly well established among young people in Scandinavian countries. In Norway, Sisjord and Skirstad (1996: 173) pointed towards the 'tremendous increase in the number of young people taking part in organized sport' in the 1970s and 1980s and noted how sport was 'still the most popular (leisure) activity among youths' (1996: 175) in participatory terms. Koska (2005: 295) has recently described Finland as 'one of the most active nations … probably the most active', in terms of both sports participation and energy expenditure. Nevertheless, it is not simply in Europe that sports participation is well established among young people. In Australia, for example, playing sport remains the most preferred activity of male and female 12- to 15-year-olds (Dollman et al., 2006). As Dollman et al. (2005: 896) observe, 'The media driven characterisation of today's youth as slothful and lazy by choice is not supported by the data'.

In addition to the general increase in participation rates there has been a *broadening* and *diversification* in the kinds of sports undertaken both by adults and young people (Coalter, 2004; Roberts, 1996a; Telama et al., 2005). Telama et al.'s (2002: 141) data indicated 'many more physical activities and sports mentioned both as recreational and competitive sports than those in which young people participated, say, 20 years ago'. A particular feature of this trend has been a shift towards so-called 'lifestyle activities' (Coalter, 1996): activities that are characterized as being non-competitive or less competitive (than traditional sports), more recreational in nature, flexible, individual or small-group activities, often with a health and fitness orientation. The relative predominance of lifestyle activities over more competitive performance-oriented sports was apparent in the participatory profiles of young people in the six European countries featured in Telama et al.'s (2002) study. Among the 15-year-olds, for example, cycling was the most popular activity for young males in Belgium (35 per cent), Estonia (30 per cent) and Finland (27 per cent) and the second most popular activity behind soccer for those in Germany (32 per cent). The evident popularity of cycling was not confined to males, however, for 31 per cent of young women in Belgium and 46 per cent in Germany as well as 43 per cent of Finns and 25 per cent of Estonians also cycled (Telama et al., 2002). While jogging was the second most popular lifestyle activity among 15-year-old males in Estonia (29 per cent) and Finland (26 per cent) and was favoured by a relatively high number of Belgians (18 per cent), it was also popular among a significantly higher proportion of females in Estonia (44 per cent) and Finland (58 per cent). Another popular lifestyle activity – swimming – also featured prominently in the participatory profiles of young males and females in Estonia (23 per cent and 38 per cent respectively), Germany (21 per cent/43 per cent) and Belgium (8 per cent/24 per cent) (Telama et al., 2002).

Elsewhere, Dollman et al. (2005) suggest that, according to several large cross-sectional surveys of Australian youngsters, the participation rates of children in 'organized sport' at schools and/or community groups has decreased substantially over the past two decades. The implication seems to be that participation in traditional team sports has fallen in direct proportion to increased engagement with less structured, more recreational lifestyle activities. But the picture is not as straightforward as it seems. As with their counterparts in the UK, it appears that sport and team games as well as lifestyle activities have become an integral feature of young people's participation both inside and outside of school in many European countries (De Knop and De Martelaer, 2001; Scheerder et al., 2005a; Telama et al., 2005). In Denmark, France, Germany, Great Britain, Italy and Spain, 'a large and rapidly growing proportion of the population is engaging somewhat informally in sport, in other words, independently from membership of a club' (Heinemann, 2005: 181–2). It seems that rather than simply replacing traditional sporting styles, 'new styles of physical activities have been added to the sports scene' (Scheerder et al., 2005a: 337). Telama et al.'s (1994: 68) observation regarding Finland in the mid-1990s – where 'the most popular types of sports [or, rather, physical activities] among adolescents [were] ... cycling, swimming, walking and running' (Telama et al., 1994: 68) *as well as* other more competitive, performance-oriented team sports such as soccer and basketball – is equally applicable to many youngsters across Europe.

Despite the fact that only a small minority play competitive sports in their adult lives (Kirk, 2002a), the substantial shift towards lifestyle activities cannot be taken to indicate that sport – especially competitive games – is in terminal decline among young people. The trends in PE and leisure-time sport among youth reflect a broadening and diversification of participation rather than a wholesale rejection of sport. According to Sport England (2003b), for example, in 2002 52 per cent of young people aged between 11 and 16 years participated in team games 'frequently' (10 times or more) in their out-of-school (leisure) time, with 36 per cent playing racket games. Thus, it is not only football (32 per cent), and other 'traditional' games – such as tennis (26 per cent) and cricket (13 per cent) – that maintain degrees of popularity among secondary age youngsters in their leisure time. 'Newer' team sports, such as basketball (15 per cent) as well as partner sports such as badminton (12 per cent) and table tennis (11 per cent), also feature alongside more potentially recreational, less or non-competitive lifestyle activities, such as swimming (37 per cent), cycling (37 per cent), rollerblading and skateboarding (18 per cent), running (15 per cent) and tenpin bowling (13 per cent) (Sport England, 2003a).

Although some team games, such as football and cricket, have become less popular in participatory terms in England since the early 1990s – especially among secondary school pupils – this has not been so for other 'traditional' team games, such as netball and hockey. Neither does it apply to secondary girls, among whom football has experienced a marked growth of interest in recent years (Sport England, 2003a). Football played by girls is illustrative of a trend towards greater involvement by girls and young women in traditionally male-dominated activities (the frequent participation of girls in team sports increased by 5 per cent between 1994 and 2002). In England, levels of girls' frequent participation in football in PE lessons, for example, virtually doubled among primary and secondary aged pupils in the period between 1994 (7 per cent) and 2002 (13 per cent), while levels of participation in football as an extra-curricular activity among girls more than doubled (from 3 to 7 per cent) between 1994 and 2002 (Sport England, 2003a). Indeed, in 2002, 18 per cent of school-aged girls participated in football out of lessons on a frequent basis. While young people's levels of participation in football have fallen to their 1994 level – and some other team games, such as cricket, continue to lose their appeal among boys – many games remain as popular as they were nearly a decade earlier in England (Sport England, 2003a). Similarly, participation in sports clubs among young people in England was stable between 1994 (42 per cent) and 2002 (43 per cent) (Sport England, 2003a).

Increases in participation in games that might be deemed lifestyle or recreational activities, such as tenpin bowling, and those that are more stereotypically sporting in orientation, such as basketball, reflect the complexity of the youth sports participation scene. Even though lifestyle activities have become an increasingly prominent feature of the participation profiles of youth and adults, it is evident that a number of sports, such as golf, badminton and martial arts, are not only popular among secondary-age youngsters (Sport England, 2003a) in their leisure time but also track into youth and through to adulthood for significant numbers of people (UK Sport/Sport England, 2001). On the basis of national and regional surveys (see, for example, Greater Manchester Sports Partnership, 2001; Sport Cheshire, 2002; Sport England, 2003a; 2003b), it seems that sport, as well as lifestyle activities, have become integral to many young people's leisure lifestyles. 'Ball sports', for example, remain among the favourite activities of many young people as they are to7- to 8-year-olds in Australia (Macdonald et al., 2005). It is clear that the more individualistic, recreational and flexible activities dominate many young people's sporting and physical activity participatory profiles – especially in their leisure. Not only have have they 'experienced substantial increases in participation' (Coalter, 2004: 79) among young people, lifestyle activities are also 'among those with the most regular participants' (2004: 80). While the evident shift, in participatory terms, towards more individualistic, recreational and lifestyle activities may not signal the end of sport in its more competitive, institutionalized forms, it may signal a 'redrawing of the traditional boundaries and meaning of sport' (Coalter, 1999: 37).

As well as increases in participation in lifestyle or recreational pursuits, and a broadening of the range of activities in which young people are engaged, there is another feature of their patterns of participation, *diversity*, in the form of an increase in the number of different sports and physical activities young people do frequently in England, for example, both in school (four on average) and out of school (five on average) (Sport England, 2003a). Such increases in the average number of sports undertaken will be seen as particularly significant later in the chapter in relation to the 'wide sporting repertoires' (Roberts and Brodie, 1992) that appear to form the foundation for lifelong participation.

It is clear, from the findings of a variety of studies across Europe, that participation in sport has assumed a significant place in the leisure and educational experiences of young people in the later decades of the twentieth century and the early years of the twenty-first century. Overall, involvement in sport among young people is sufficiently commonplace for us to refer to the 'sportization' of young people's lives (Brettschneider, 1992; Telama et al., 2005).

So, how might we explain the increased rates of participation in sport and the changing patterns in their participation exhibited by young people and adults in recent decades? According to Roberts (1996a; 1996b), in the UK the changes can be explained in a coming together of several interrelated processes:

- the broadening and diversification of the diet of activities available in school PE
- the compatibility of changing patterns of participation with the broader trends in young people's preferred leisure styles (Brettschneider, 1992; Coakley and White, 1999; Roberts, 1996b; 1999) – associated with what Roberts (1996b) has referred to as 'youth's new condition'
- the dramatic growth of indoor facilities.

The next section discusses further some of these developments.

The significance of multi-activity PE programmes

The continued dominance of PE programmes by sport and particularly team games cannot be justified in terms of trends in participation among young people, or adults. This should not be taken to suggest, however, that sport-based PE, or multi-activity PE programmes, are devoid of merit in relation to the goal of lifelong participation. The increases in levels of participation witnessed in recent years appears due mainly to the wide sporting repertoires that young people have developed. These repertoires or portfolios have their roots in the multi-activity and, to a lesser extent, sport-based programmes increasingly prevalent in PE in England and Wales since the 1970s. While MacPhail et al. (2003: 68) may be broadly correct in claiming that 'young people are telling us that they do not support programmes dominated by these traditional activities', it seems that young people want these traditional activities supplemented by other activities in broader curricula, rather than simply expunged. Sport and team games continue to hold a place in both the preferences and participatory repertoires of many young people. Indeed, in relation to the promotion of life-long participation there appears to be a strong case for retaining multi-activity programmes. Roberts et al.'s (2001: 171–2) observation on leisure education is equally applicable to multi-activity PE programmes; that is to say,

> [it] will not merely help but is likely to be crucial in so far as it can give everyone a broad base of interests and skills, and encourage them to be discriminating, so that they can pick their own mixes from the opportunities that are available, thereby using leisure to construct or express individual identities while becoming integrated into their particular social milieu.

Fisher (2003: 145) points to studies in Denmark, Germany and Switzerland which indicated not only that 'pupils like a range of experience' or 'rich curriculum' but that, in Germany specifically, so-called 'traditional sports' remained popular in PE.

The widespread adoption by schools of Sport for All policies and a broadening of PE curricula was associated with a steady broadening of the sports interests of young people both within the PE curriculum and beyond school (Houlihan, 1991; Roberts, 1996a). The traditional games-based curricula were significantly modified by teachers, not least in terms of the provision of what OFSTED (1998) refer to as 'activity choice' for older teenagers as part of the trend towards 'education for [post-school] leisure' (Scraton, 1992: 73). In this regard, the significance of 'activity choice' and 'lifestyle activities' for engaging older pupils should not be underestimated. Bramham's (2003) study of 22 15-year-old boys in four inner-city schools concluded that boys valued the opportunities to choose activities at Key Stage 4 and, sometimes, where choice was not satisfactory, this led to pupils not bringing their PE kit. Bramham also found that the minority of boys with little commitment to PE tended to 'favour indoor, individualized activities such as trampolining, badminton and volleyball' (2003: 67). Unsurprisingly, in the light of trends towards lifestyle activities, dissatisfaction among some pupils occurred where the choices they were offered 'were structured in such a way to make outdoor games compulsory' (Bramham, 2003: 66).

Rather than being characterized by 'clear disparity between the activities children are likely to experience at school and the activities adults are likely to participate in' (Kirk, 2002a: 4), participation in sport has become part of current youth cultures in part because teachers, via the provision of multi-activity PE programmes, have facilitated the development of wide sporting repertoires among young people by introducing them to a broad range of sports as well as lifestyle activities.

In more democratized, individialized and informalized societies, PE teachers will be bound to respond, knowingly or otherwise, to developments in youth cultures. Nevertheless, the normalization of sport within youth cultures is not attributable solely to the actions of PE teachers – the process of broadening the PE curriculum from the 1970s onwards was not simply an example of a far-sighted PE profession recognizing broader social trends on the horizon and preparing their charges to meet them. Rather, teachers were responding to the changing lifestyles of young people as well as the more immediate and pressing concerns associated with the raising of the minimum school leaving age to 16 in 1972 in Britain. Nevertheless, in preparing young people for what they view as positive uses of their leisure, PE teachers have in effect prepared young people for the kinds of 'choice biographies' (du Bois-Reymond, 1995, cited in Roberts, 1996b) well suited to their new circumstances and more individualized leisure lifestyles.

Youth's new condition

Since the 1970s the western world has witnessed the emergence and development of what has become known as the 'new condition of youth' (Roberts, 2006) – a process characterized by several features. These include:

- a prolongation of the life stage of youth as the typical ages at which young people cross thresholds into work, parenthood and the like have risen over the past 30 years or so
- young people's biographies and youth as a life-stage have become more individualized as a consequence of their more varied experiences in post-compulsory education, in the work place, in leisure and in the social networks to be found in all these places
- young people's futures have become more uncertain, not least because of the pace of economic and social change
- as a corollary of their uncertain futures, all the steps that young people might take have a more pronounced sense of risk attached to them than previously. The changing youth labour market has led to more young people spending longer in education
- 'young people's dependence upon their family has been prolonged' (Roberts, 2006: 131) (Hendry et al., 2002; Iacovou and Berthoud, 2001; Roberts, 2006; Schizzerotto and Lucchini, 2002; Wallace and Kovatcheva, 1998).

As a consequence of these 'changes in the social context' and the 'meaning of childhood and youth' (Wyn et al., 2002: 23) there have been substantial changes in recent decades in young people's day-to-day and week-to-week leisure styles (Roberts, 2006). The result of these developments is that the leisure 'tastes and styles' of youth have fragmented (Hendry et al., 2002: 1). For several decades, the trend has been towards every young person 'having a particular combination of leisure interests and activities, and a unique leisure career' with individuals developing 'personal stocks of leisure skills and interests' (Roberts, 1999: 43) in the construction of 'their own leisure biographies' (Zeijl et al., 2001: 380).

Against this backdrop, there are three striking features of young people's leisure lives: first, the importance they assign to gaining and demonstrating their independence (Coakley and White, 1999); second, the important part leisure plays in their routes to independence (Bynner et al., 2002; Roberts, 2006); and, finally, the significance of friends (Smith, A., 2006; Sport England, 2006). Young people use leisure to engage in 'activities that would prepare them for adulthood or enable them to do adult things' (Coakley and White, 1999: 80). In this manner, sport acts as a key site for young people to decide for themselves *what* they will do and *how* they will do it, as well as *who* they will do it with. And friends are central to the process of independence. Friends take pride of place among young people's leisure lives, and other leisure activities tend to be subordinated to this priority: 'simply being with their friends is extremely important to most young people' (Roberts, 1999: 118). It is during youth and adolescence, in particular, that the meaning of what youngsters do lies mainly in what it means to significant others around them – young people want to become independent in socially acceptable ways. According to De Knop et al. (1996a), it has been a trend across Western Europe for young people's own age group to become more significant as agents of socialization than their parents. Social networks such as friendship groups are especially likely to affect the degree of exercise in which people engage (Fisher, 2002) and, as young people get older, friends tend to become more significant influences upon their tastes and practices. O'Donovan (2003: 1) notes how the 'social involvement' goals of young people 'influence their participation in PE', not least because their 'first agenda is to socialize and have fun'.

Individualization and the increasing significance of friends has led to corresponding changes in the ways in which young people participate in sport. During youth, Roberts (1999: 118) observes, 'there is a gradual trend away from spending leisure in organized and supervised [settings] … towards spending time with groups of friends in unsupervised situations, then, later on, towards using commercial facilities'. Hence the increased appeal of informal, casual, recreational activities. As 'leisure activities have become more informal' (De Knop et al., 1996a: 9) – that is, less organized – across Europe so, too, has participation in sport. Unsurprisingly, the process of individualization has had inevitable repercussions for team sports and sports clubs, Europe-wide (De Knop et al., 1996b). It is interesting to reflect upon the kinds of provision available for youth sport, not least because some systems appear more effective in keeping young people in sport. While in countries such as Finland 'young people participate more in unorganized physical activity than in organized sport' (Telama et al., 2005: 128), 'the traditional style characterized by participation in a formal organizational context (e.g. sports club, extracurricular school sports), remains very popular ... among young people of school age' (Scheerder et al., 2005a: 337) not only in Flanders but in a number of countries, Europe-wide. Indeed, a good deal of young people's participation in sport in many European countries (such as Belgium) continues to be of the organized variety. The number of sports undertaken in a club setting is growing in Flanders, for example, according to Scheerder et al. (2005a; 2005b). Neither is organized and club-based sport disappearing from the youth map in the UK. While over half (55 per cent) of primary and secondary pupils visited leisure centres on a weekly basis or more frequently, three-quarters of primary- (78 per cent) and secondary-aged (73 per cent) youngsters in Wales took part in sport organized by clubs independent of schools at some stage during 2004 (SCW, 2006) and almost two-thirds (62 per cent) of primary and over half (53 per cent) of secondary pupils in Wales took part in sports club-based activity on a weekly or more frequent basis. The SCW (2006) study reflects a virtual doubling of sports club memberships among secondary-aged pupils in Wales over the decade 1994 to 2004 (38 per cent to 73 per cent) and a 50 per cent increase (58 per cent to 78 per cent) among primary-aged pupils since 1998.

Even though club-based sport retains a place in the sporting profiles of many youngsters and adults and may be experiencing a renaissance if developments in Flanders and Wales are anything to go by, it is evident that sports clubs are far less important in terms of fostering mass participation than has conventionally been thought. Across Western Europe, 'after the age of 14 there is a clear drop-off of membership in sports clubs' (De Knop et al., 1996a: 9). The trend towards lifestyle activities among young people and adults across Western Europe is particularly significant because these kinds of involvement are typically provided by public or commercial venues rather than by the sports clubs associated with central European countries and even the most successful sporting countries in the western world: Australia and the USA. A particular feature of the increased participation evident among young people in the UK is an observable pattern within the high retention rate among post-compulsory schooling (the 16-plus) age groups; that is, while participation (particularly casual participation) in outdoor, competitive and performance-oriented sport begins to tail off among 16–21-year-olds, participation in facility-based, more recreationally oriented indoor sport does not follow the same pattern. Indeed, as Roberts (1996a: 52) observed in the mid-1990s in relation to England, 'As many 18–21 as 11–15 year olds were going to sport and leisure centres'. It is playing sport elsewhere (such as outdoor games pitches) that appears to decline with age. As with adults generally, there has been a marked movement to indoor sport among young people (Sport England/UK Sport, 2001): the age group, it is worth noting, that tends matter-of-factly to be associated with heavy involvement in outdoor, team-based sport.

The significance of facilities

The increases in participation (among young people and adults) charted through the 1970s and into the 1980s occurred in tandem with a dramatic growth in indoor facilities. Local government reorganization in England and Wales in the early 1970s brought a substantial growth of sport and leisure centres over the following two decades. The rapid increases in the supply of largely public sector facilities for sport and leisure centre provision created the preconditions not only for the higher participation rates of young people in sport, but also changes in the nature of participation and, in particular, the shift towards individualized activities and increased concern with fitness and physical appearance (Coalter, 1999).

Because new sports facilities tend to be used primarily by established participants, they do not automatically increase participation. To do so the facilities need to be local to those who might be enticed to engage with sport, and the growth of relatively accessible, cheap and new sporting facilities (including pools, badminton and squash courts) at secondary schools – often in the form of dual-use facilities – probably played a part in the boosting of participation among youth and adults alike. According to Roberts (1996a: 52), in the UK: 'The provision of sports centres which are available for everyone appears to have obliterated the "Wolfenden gap"[2] and reduced the sport give-up rate from its former chronic level in the immediate post-school years.' Roberts (1996a: 52) continues, 'whether young people continue to play sport after leaving school may well be strongly related to whether they are using community facilities'. Ironically, however, UK government policy continues to place great emphasis upon the alleged importance of links between schools and sports clubs but attaches little importance to facilities despite the fact that sports clubs are far less important in fostering mass participation. The 'straightforward and attractive way', to borrow from government policy (DNH, 1995), to continue playing is not through sports clubs, but through continued use of local sport and leisure centres as well as the growing numbers of commercial facilities.

There is every reason to believe that drop-out from sport and physically active recreation occurs because participation is less convenient during adult lives (Roberts and Brodie, 1992), and the best way to change this would be to make sport more compatible with people's lifestyles. This would involve more facilities but the cost would be prohibitive. However, while facilities might be a necessary condition for participation in some of the newer lifestyle activities, they are not sufficient. Membership of private health and fitness clubs, for example, has sky-rocketed in recent years but overall rates of participation in the activities provided by these gyms has not risen.

Unsurprisingly, young people's early experiences are likely to have profound implications for their subsequent patterns of participation in sport. The particular significance of youth for lifelong participation in sport is its likely impact on leisure tendencies in later life. Indeed, by the age of 16 very many young people have already begun to adopt some of the adult leisure practices that will become features of their adult leisure lifestyles (Roberts, 1999). Thereafter, young people's 'leisure lifestyles tend to become focused around a smaller number of retained pastimes' (Roberts and Brodie, 1992: 39). With the significance of past behaviours for future participation in mind, the next section explores further the relationship between young people's involvement in sport and the likelihood of lifelong participation.

LIFELONG PARTICIPATION

Despite the overall trend towards increased participation over the past 30 years, the fact is that age has a deleterious effect on sports participation. In general, participation declines with age and this decline becomes more marked after the age of 45 (Sport England/UK Sport, 2001). When compared with other uses of leisure, loyalty rates in sport are not good. Lessons from studies of adherence to sport through the life-course are pretty clear: it is much easier to keep people in sport – that is, to stop them dropping out in the first place – than to bring them back. The supposed leisure renaissance often said to accompany the later life-stages simply does not occur in practice. Indeed, adults become more rather than less conservative in their leisure tendencies and use the 'relative freedom' of leisure as they get older to continue with their established routines. The tendency is for people to reduce what they did before rather than to increase it as they get older (Roberts, 2006). So what encourages those who remain in sport to do so?

Motivation and adherence

Research on motivation towards sport focuses, in particular, on 'goal orientations' – the personal meaning that individuals attach to the achievements that are said to sustain motivation. Goal orientations tend, at a simplistic level, to be divided into two categories: task oriented and ego oriented (Salvara et al., 2006). Whereas ego-oriented dispositions involve the individual being predisposed towards a concern for performance outcomes and comparison with others, task-oriented outlooks focus upon learning and improving. Much research on motivation concludes that intrinsic rewards (or intrinsically-motivated experiences) are a more powerful motivator of behaviour, especially over the long term, than extrinsic rewards. A learning environment or climate which emphasizes the mastery of skills and techniques is strongly positively correlated with psychological outcomes such as satisfaction and enjoyment. By contrast, environments that focus on demonstrating high levels of ability and success in competition can be as demotivating for many youngsters in PE and sport (Salvara et al., 2006) as in education more generally (Meece et al., 2006).

Enjoyment is a central dimension of intrinsic motivation. From their study of the impact of goals, beliefs and self-determination in girls' PE in Singapore, Wang and Liu (2007: 159) concluded that 'when (female) students were more self-determined or intrinsically-motivated, they enjoyed their PE experience more'. Although what constitutes pleasure or enjoyment is not easy to establish, there is every reason to think that 'optimal experiences', if not simply enjoyment, revolve around striking a balance in any activity between the participant's skill-levels and the challenge she or he faces – what Csíkozentmihalyi (1990) refers to as 'flow'. In a number of studies on youth sport 'fun and enjoyment emerge as the major motive for participation' (Goudas and Biddle, 1993: 145): '[P]eople are more likely to engage in an activity, repeat a particular behaviour, or perform an activity well when they *enjoy* what they are doing' (Graef et al., 1983: 155, emphasis in the original). It appears that most adherents to sport participate not for extrinsic reasons (such as health promotion) but for the sheer pleasure of playing or, at least, reasons to do with the intrinsic nature of the activity itself (and the pursuit of 'flow'-like experiences) rather than any externalities that might accrue – in effect, they learn the satisfactions to be had from doing sport and want to repeat them.

Unsurprisingly, *competence* is intimately related to enjoyment. Indeed, some argue that competence is the best predictor of participation (Biddle, 2006). If people (and especially young people) feel that their skill levels and all-round competence in an activity are good enough or improving, they will be likely to enjoy that activity and continue participating. Many studies offer support for the idea that promoting perceived competence is a significant factor in encouraging adherence to particular sports (Telama et al., 2005). Wallhead and Buckworth's (2004: 286) research in the USA explores the correlates of youth physical activity and concludes not only that 'perceived competence is a powerful psychological correlate of youth physical activity' but that 'if physical educators are able to increase students' perceived competence and subsequent enjoyment of their experiences in physical education, these affective outcomes … will transfer into motivation to adopt a physically active lifestyle out of school' (2004: 295). An approach to content and teaching styles that focuses upon 'trying' and improvement towards mastering skills and activities (rather than focusing on competition and identifying winners), while allowing pupils sufficient time to learn skills, appears more likely to encourage both competence and enjoyment in PE and sport. Girls, it appears, are more likely to approach PE with a task orientation and boys with an ego orientation (attributable to their socialization into masculine norms of achievement). This may begin to explain why boys are less influenced by different teaching styles than girls (Salvara et al., 2006).

While enjoyment and competence might be viewed as necessary conditions for participation for many people, by themselves they are very often insufficient for lifelong participation. An additional and crucial dimension of becoming 'locked-in' to sport and physical activity appears to be possession of what Roberts and Brodie (1992) refer to as 'wide sporting repertoires' and others label skill or activity 'portfolios' (SCW, 2000) or 'sports literacy' (DCMS/Strategy Unit, 2002). In their study of men and women who had become 'committed' to sport as adults, Roberts and Brodie (1992) found that virtually all those who play regularly between the ages of 16 and 30 become 'locked-in' to sport and are frequently 'established on continuous sports careers which … are unlikely to be disrupted for many more years' (1992: 37). Of particular note is what Roberts and Brodie identified as the chief characteristics of the committed minority who become 'locked-in': that is, they had been 'active in several (usually three or more) games (or activities) throughout their sports careers' (1992: 37). In other words, they tended to possess wide sporting repertoires (Roberts and Brodie, 1992). It was not so much the sheer amount as the number of different sports that young people learned to play that appeared crucial in determining whether people would remain sports active into adulthood. The point about wide sporting repertoires was that 'whatever their reasons for dropping out of particular sports, where the individuals played several games, their entire sports careers were less vulnerable' (Roberts and Brodie, 1992: 44).

Herein lies the significance of the relationship between the diversity of young people's participation in sport and the potential for lifelong participation. Changes in youth experiences, transitions and leisure lifestyles are significant in sport and activity terms because it is clear that childhood and youth are the life-stages where the foundations for long-term uses of leisure are laid. During their teenage years, young people 'typically dabble and experiment with a wide range of leisure interests, many of which are soon dropped' (Roberts and Brodie, 1992: 39). While young people are the age group most receptive to 'doing new things' their leisure interests are characterized by changeability; they are, according to Roberts (1997: 3), 'the section of the population with highest levels and most diverse patterns of cultural consumption'. So, instability is an attendant feature of young people's leisure lifestyles (Iacovou and Berthoud, 2001; Roberts, 1999; Schizzerotto and Lucchini, 2002). However, the tendency towards changeability and instability does not necessarily mean a tendency towards disengagement: teenagers do not just lapse from sport, they move to other activities in their relatively busy leisure lives – something they enjoy more. As the UK government has acknowledged, 'Most young people stop [sport] because of interest in other activities' (DCMS/Strategy Unit, 2002: 96).

Unsurprisingly, while as a group they have the highest participation rates 'across out-of-home leisure in general' (Roberts, 1999: 114), and sport in particular, young people also have the highest drop-out rates. This high level of initial involvement is one of the main reasons for the perception of high drop-out rate – in sporting terms – from youth to young adulthood.

In terms of facilitating wide sporting repertoires on the part of their charges, it seems that what matters is not so much what PE teachers might anticipate young people doing as adults, or even what they do now. Whether youngsters experience precisely the same activities at school as those they appear likely to engage in as adults does not appear to be crucial. What seems to matter more is to provide young people with a repertoire or portfolio of sports and physical activities. Some of these will endure; others will be replaced, supplemented or dropped as their lives unfold. The forms of activity in which young people find pleasurable excitement change in the course of their development.

Breadth of content, however, does not appear to be enough on its own. Nor, for that matter, is a pedagogical approach that prioritizes enjoyment of the task and the development of a basic level of competence. As significant as these things are, young people need also to experience a degree of self-determination. Hence the significance of pupil choice. Along with competence and enjoyment, opportunity and choice appear to be significant variables for participation (Wallhead and Buckworth, 2004). Motivation is enhanced when students are given a choice in the content and style of PE lessons. Increases in participation are a consequence of the fact that the mode of delivery has coincided with the age group's preferred leisure styles and the process of individualization more generally. Hence, the importance – in the promotion of involvement in sport and physical activities – of preparing young people for 'choice biographies' (du Bois-Reymond, 1995, cited in Roberts, 1996b); that is, of enabling young people to do the *things* they choose with the *people* they choose, *when, where* and *how* they choose.

Beyond enjoyment and competence, another dimension to motivation is the assumed impact of role models in providing an initial impetus towards sports participation and improvement. Role models, especially in the form of elite sporting stars, are often portrayed as highly significant in shaping young people's inclination towards sport. However, the impact of role models on young people's participation is often misunderstood and, consequently, over-stated. Vescio et al. (2005) demonstrate how young people have difficulty identifying with sporting stars who appear several steps removed from them – elite sportsmen and women are simply unlikely to be viewed by young people as meaningful role models. The significance of role models appears to lie in their relationship with, and proximity to, children and young people, rather than their status. Young people are far more likely to be influenced by people closer to them – people who were, or are, similar to them; most notably, their peers. The 'aspirational model' of 'efficacy expectancy' – focusing attention on friends, and family, for example – is a much better model than the elite model (Coalter, 2006a). Hence the potential impact on participation of friends and peer groups, and, for that matter, family members and the limited significance for many young people of their PE teachers. Unsurprisingly, there is substantial evidence that families as well as friends are major players in sports socialization (Sage, 1980). Parents (see Chapter 9) provide the earliest opportunities and experiences, financial and emotional support (Stroot, 2002) and, with older siblings, provide early models of sporting practices: 'If the parents are not actively involved, nor intentionally provide sporting experiences for the child, the chance that the child will be exposed to the sporting world at an early age is limited' (Stroot, 2002: 131).

CONCLUSION

In the UK, the avowed goal of government policy towards sport is 'to increase and widen' the base of participation in sport (Rowe, 2005: 2). In pursuit of this goal Sport England is in search of an evidence-based model for behaviour change: 'This aim will not be achieved', Rowe (2005: 2) suggests, 'unless we have a more sophisticated understanding of the motivations and barriers to taking part in sport and the likely interventions that will achieve behaviour change'. Foster et al. (2005: 4) agree, 'little is known', they suggest, 'about how children and adults start, stop or maintain sport throughout their lives'.

This chapter, however, has argued that a good deal is, in fact, known about the pre-conditions for adherence to sport and physically active recreation. Some of this 'evidence base' has become apparent from the substantial growth in participation in many countries in the developed world and research into this (see, for example, Coalter, 1996; Roberts and Brodie, 1992). In terms of the recipe for lifelong participation, it should come as no surprise to find that the foundations for sports careers are laid in childhood (Roberts and Brodie, 1992) and that later-life involvement in any leisure activity depends largely on the 'skills and interests that individuals carry with them from earlier life stages' (Roberts, 1999: 140). The message is loud and clear – improving the participation rates and levels of adults is not simply a problem of introducing young people to sport – they already do a lot of sport both in and out of school. The problem is the likelihood that people will drop out of sport and physically active recreational pursuits at key periods of transition in their lives; for example, when they leave education and start work and when they form serious relationships. It is simply less convenient to play sport at times in people's lives when they are constrained by a variety of contextual pressures or are developing alternative interests. But the difficulties or barriers to participation are not insuperable. If people can survive these key transitions then they may well be 'locked-in' to sport for a long time. The wider the sporting repertoire people carry with them the more likely their sports careers are to survive the transition to adult roles.

Contrary to the common-sense views of government, media and other interested parties, in many developed countries sports participation has become part of current youth cultures. Roberts's comment on participation in the mid-1990s applies equally a decade later; that is, 'The past Golden Age when the mass of young people were heavily involved in physically active recreation is pure myth ... young people in Britain are playing more sport than at any time in living memory' (1996a: 52). The levels of sport participation among young people recorded in recent UK (see, for example, Sport England, 2003a) and Western European (see, for example, Scheerder et al., 2005a; Telama et al., 2005) studies are substantially above the levels variously reported on in the 1960s and 1970s. At that time, most girls did no out-of-school sport and most boys did no leisure-time sport except football. The norm then was for most people to be lost to sport, probably for ever, at the end of their school careers (Roberts, 1996a).

Despite the current 'golden age', it is quite possible that the current levels of participation have stabilized at an optimal level (Coalter, 2006b). If so, the issue facing advocates becomes one of retaining those already in, rather than chasing new recruits. Whatever the recipe for encouraging participation, it is necessary to recognize that patterns of participation 'may reflect broader social, economic, cultural and educational factors which are largely beyond the direct influence of sports policy makers' (Coalter, 1999: 25). The significance of peer and friendship groups to young people is a case in point. As they get older – especially as they approach school-leaving age – young people's leisure focuses increasingly around their peers and casual pursuits (Hendry, 1986; Smith, A., 2006). 'The most popular activities for the mid-adolescent years', Hendry (1986: 53) observes, tend to be socially oriented pursuits, 'and few of these activities could be directly related to school influences'. It is also important to appreciate that the plural nature of the influences upon leisure patterns in general, and physical exercise in particular, means it is almost impossible for any single policy to have other than a marginal influence on public leisure behaviour (Roberts, 1999).

Nevertheless, for 'true believers' (Lapchick, 1989: 17) in the benefits of sports participation there are undoubtedly grounds for optimism if policy-makers and PE take on board lessons to be learned about the centrality of enjoyment, competence and sporting repertoires. While there is every reason to believe that sport and physical activity can appeal to people, such popularity is contingent upon physical activity being presented appropriately, and particularly so with young people. In order to move with the prevailing grain of young people's leisure lifestyles – particularly their preferences for individual or small group, non-competitive, flexible (so-called, lifestyle) activities – there needs to be a shift in emphasis in several respects:

- There needs to be a further shift towards those lifestyle activities and more 'recreational' versions of 'traditional' sports that appear more likely to involve intrinsically motivating activity experiences that generate feelings of enjoyment and satisfaction.
- Such programmes must allow young people to sample a large number of activities while allowing individuals to concentrate gradually on a handful which they see themselves as more likely to engage in regularly – in order that they can begin to 'tailor their own sporting activities to their individual lifestyles' (Roberts, 1996b: 112–13).
- These activities should have the potential to bind individuals into group settings – such as dancing, swimming, badminton – for we know that satisfying leisure experiences typically involve being with other people in a manner that generates social commitments (Roberts, 1999).
- Many PE activities come in 'blocks' of a finite duration, typically between six and 10 weeks. This may simply not be of sufficient longevity to enable a habitual pattern of exercise to develop – they may be insufficient to allow individuals to feel 'locked into' participation by the routinization of the behaviour, the development of skills and the generation of social networks.

In answer to the question 'How do children and adults start, stop or maintain sport throughout their lives?', ongoing participation is best conceptualized not so much in terms of what Moran (2004) describes as motivation to 'initiate' and to 'adhere' to activity but rather as a desire to repeat satisfying experiences. In other words, becoming motivated is not necessarily a precursor to engagement with sport but may, rather, be a *consequence* of positive engagement and the resultant satisfaction associated with involvement. It also seems that perceived competence and attitudes to physical activity can be altered significantly by lesson content and teaching styles (Wallhead and Buckworth, 2004). Salvara et al. (2006: 66) conclude that 'the teaching style used by the teacher to deliver PE experiences is likely to have a considerable impact upon the motivational orientation of the pupils' and if the teaching style emphasizes mastery of tasks and improvement it is more likely to motivate pupils.

Continuation in sport is more likely to result from habit and enjoyment and being built into a social network, and the more likely 'role models' among teenagers are friends. However, it is necessary to add a caveat: 'Since', as Collins and Kay (2003: 244) put it, 'leisure activities are inherently those of choice and the choice is ever-widening, non-participation may, for many leisure activities, be the norm'.

In the mid-1990s, Evans and Davies (1986) commented that if the success of PE in general and extra-curricular PE in particular, is measured in terms of equipping pupils with not only the skills and knowledge but the desire to participate in sport beyond the school context – that is, in their leisure – then the PE profession has clearly failed in its mission. A decade later Sandford and Rich (2006) felt compelled to ask 'why young people disengage with PE and engage with other physical cultures'. The answer is that they do not. Or, at least, according to the available data, significant numbers continue to take part in sport in their leisure time and many do not 'switch-off' in terms of motivation and enjoyment. Young people's leisure lives have many dimensions expressing different interests and habits. Consequently, youth cultures are diverse, consisting of a number of elements, prominent among which are music, the media, peers, consumption and sport. The increased spending power of young people has enabled them to increasingly partake of commercial as well as public and voluntary leisure provision. Although it may be fair to say that the 'traditional' PE curriculum continues to alienate many young people (Macdonald, 2006) it does not automatically lead to a flight from sport and physical activity any more than music lessons lead to a flight from music among young people.

RECOMMENDED READING

Coalter, F. (2004) 'Future sports or future challenges to sport?' in Sport England (ed.), *Driving Up Participation: The Challenge for Sport*. London: Sport England. pp.79–86.

Green, K., Smith, A. and Roberts, K. (2005) 'Young people and lifelong participation in sport and physical activity: a sociological perspective on contemporary physical education programmes in England and Wales', *Leisure Studies*, 24(1): 27–43.

NOTES

1 While Sport England tends to use the phrase 'sport and exercise' to incorporate health- and fitness-oriented and recreational activities as well as conventinal sports, the rest of this chapter uses sport and physical activity as umbrella terms, as indicated in the Introduction.

2 The phrase, the 'Wolfenden gap' was coined following the Wolfenden Committee's (Central Council for Physical Recreation, 1960) identification of a 'gap' between the opportunities available to young people at school and the limited access to sporting opportunities available to young adults thereafter and the associated 'drop-out' from sport among young people on leaving school.

Gender and Physical Education

Sex differences might be the same everywhere but they are associated with a range of different experiences in all walks of life, from politics and business to family and leisure. Nowhere is this more evident than in sport, where differences are wider than in any other area of young people's leisure. While in many countries, these differences have lessened over recent decades – as young people have taken up more and newer sports, many of which are played by both sexes – differences remain.

Indeed, despite the fact that the NCPE in England and Wales is supposed to embody principles of equal opportunity and equity, PE remains the most sex-differentiated and stereotyped subject on the school curriculum – particularly at secondary level – when measured in terms of organization, content and delivery. Although PE purports to be a single subject it contains, in practice, two distinct sex (or, rather, gender) subcultures. This is not surprising given that PE is built on a history of sex segregation: distinct male and female traditions expressed in quasi-separate departments, teaching differing activities to sex-specific teaching groups and holding, by degrees, differing perceptions regarding suitable content and teaching methods. Contemporary PE reflects the customs and practices of the relatively distinct female and male traditions: from the nineteenth-century foundations of girls' PE – based upon callisthenics and Swedish gymnastics and exercises complemented by swimming and a limited range of female-appropriate games (such as netball, hockey and lacrosse) – to male PE teachers' predilection for the public school games of the nineteenth century which formed the blueprint for the subject for successive generations of male teachers following the introduction of state secondary education in the UK after the Second World War (Fletcher, 1984; Kirk, 1992).

Consequently, PE continues to be underpinned by gendered ideologies in a manner succinctly expressed by Talbot (1993: 74): 'While teachers of physical education may claim that they espouse equality of opportunity for all children, their teaching behaviours and practices reveal entrenched sex-stereotyping, based on common-sense notions of what is suitable for girls and boys.'

Against this backdrop, this chapter examines the significance of sex and gender for our understanding of PE. More specifically, it explores a number of key themes or issues, including:

- the similarities and differences between boys' and girls' involvement in PE and sport
- gender-related issues associated with contemporary PE
- the socialization of boys and girls into or away from sport.

While the relationship between other social dynamics such as social class and ethnicity and PE are dealt with elsewhere in the book, their significance for gender is briefly considered towards the end of this chapter. First, it is necessary to say something about the terms 'sex' and 'gender' and the relationship between them.

SEX AND GENDER

Sex is generally considered a straightforwardly biological term indicating distinct, genetically inherited, anatomical and physiological characteritics. Gender, on the other hand, is a more complex concept which refers to learned masculine and feminine behaviours. It is a common mistake to use the term 'sex' when what is actually being referred to are normative, learned behaviours regarding 'appropriate' sex-specific behaviours – in other words, 'gender' – and to talk of gender when distinguishing between the sexes. Sex is, of course, an aspect of gender. Nevertheless, it is crucial to recognize that the latter cannot simply be 'read off' from the former – the one does not lead inexorably to the other. Masculinity and femininity are neither natural nor immutable (Humberstone, 2002: 59); that it sometimes appears that way is testimony to the effectiveness of socialization processes. It is also important to bear in mind that the 'bi-polar' (Flintoff and Scraton, 2006) distinction between masculinity and femininity represents a false dichotomy. Gender is a dynamic and fluid category. Rather than constituting rigid and unchanging characteristics, masculinity and femininity are more adequately viewed as poles on a continuum with each individual expressing both masculine and feminine attributes to varying degrees.

PARTICIPATION IN PE AND SPORT

An abundance of research over the past three decades has greatly enhanced our understanding of girls' and women's lives, generally, and their involvement in leisure, sport and PE, in particular (see, for example, Flintoff and Scraton, 2001; Green et al., 1990; Hargreaves, 1994; O'Donovan and Kay, 2006; Scraton, 1992). One of the central claims has been that girls' and young women's involvement in PE and sport are not merely different and unequal but in some ways inappropriate, even deficient – in terms of the range and accessibility of particular activities and with regard to their lived experiences of sport and PE. Allied to this, girls' experiences of PE and sport are believed to reinforce, rather than challenge, gender stereotypes and act as an additional barrier to participation. The fact that the vast bulk of research into the relationship between gender and PE continues to focus upon girls merely confirms the experiences of females as an enduring issue for many teachers and academics.

Despite such concerns, the picture emerging from research into patterns of participation in sport can often appear complex and contradictory. On the one hand, it has been amply demonstrated in England (see, for example, Sport England, 2003a; 2003b), the USA (see, for example, Wallhead and Buckworth, 2004) and Europe (see, for example, Pfister and Reeg, 2006) that girls' and young women's participation in sport continues to decline sharply during adolescence. This decline appears most marked in the upper secondary school years and is much greater for girls than for boys of the same age. Reporting on the national project, *Girls in Sport*, O'Donovan and Kay (2005; 2006) highlighted the persistence of relatively low levels of participation in sport among girls and their associated reluctance towards physical activity. Sport England's (2003a) typology of young people in relation to sport identified four main types: 'sporty types' (those who enjoy sport: 25 per cent of 5–16-year-olds); those with 'untapped potential' (who like sport: 37 per cent); the 'unadventurous' (who do not mind sport: 14 per cent) and 'reluctant participants' (who actively dislike sport: 24 per cent). It was noticeable that young females were disproportionately over-represented among those with 'untapped potential' while 11–14-year-old and 13–16-year-old females were to be found in relatively high numbers among the 'unadventurous' and 'reluctant participants' respectively. Indeed, secondary-aged girls were especially prevalent within the 'couch potatoes' – a subcategory of the 'reluctant' group – who disliked sport intensely.

On the other hand – and despite the fact that reports of a growth of participation among girls and young women may be over-exaggerated – a good deal of research into girls' and young women's participation patterns reveals not only a trend towards substantially greater participation in sport, but also in PE itself (in terms of numbers participating, frequency of participation and time spent on activities) than is often believed to be the case. The young women in Flintoff and Scraton's (2001) research, for example, were active both within and beyond school PE; albeit often in non-traditional PE and sporting activities. Similarly, large-scale data-sets from Sport England's (2003a; 2003b) studies, *Young People and Sport*, confirm trends towards greater involvement of young women in sport in England. In 2002, young males and females were participating equally in sport during school lessons according to the Sport England survey (2003b). At the same time, the mean number of sports played in lessons hardly differed between males and females in either primary or secondary schools. Nor were there any sex differences in the proportions playing no sports 10 times or more in school lessons or, at the other end of the continuum, playing seven or more sports this frequently (Sport England, 2003b). Overall, in PE lessons in England, girls were playing as much sport, and almost as many sports, as boys.

The sexes were not always playing the same sports in school. In secondary schools, girls were more likely to do dance, aerobics and swimming, for example, while boys were more likely to participate in contact sport and games such as soccer and rugby. Nonetheless, girls as well as boys were being offered a wide range of activities, including those played mainly by girls (for example, netball and aerobics) and others played by both sexes (for example, basketball and badminton). Indeed, in primary schools most of the main sports (that is, those reported by the largest percentages) were played by roughly equal numbers of both sexes. This applied in particular to gymnastics, swimming, athletics and rounders, with football being the only major sport in which one sex (boys) predominated.

Alongside growing involvement in recreational activities such as aerobics and swimming, young women's participation in traditionally male sports such as football and rugby appears to be increasing substantially. Sport England's (2003a) surveys indicated that, in 2002, primary- and secondary-aged girls were 'significantly more likely' (2003a: 52) to play two particular games (football and netball), as well as swim and dance, out of lessons than they were in 1994. They were also more likely to play golf, tenpin bowling, basketball, tennis and badminton: a mix of competitive sports (especially games) and recreational activities. Similarly, swimming, running/jogging, dance and football were the most popular participatory activities among the 11–15-year-old girls in a SportScotland study (Biddle et al., 2005). While PE may not have been interrupting the reproduction of gender differences, very many sports and physical activities were, nevertheless, being played by substantial proportions of both sexes, even in secondary schools (Sport England, 2003b).

It is beyond school PE lessons where sex differences in sports participation are at their most stark. In Germany, Pfister and Reeg's (2006) study found boys to be more involved in physically active recreation and more frequent members of sports clubs than girls: 'the kinds of leisure activities the children choose and the intensity with which they take part in them display noticeable gender-specific differences' (2006: 7). In extra-curricular PE and leisure-sport in England, boys tend to play more sports, for more hours per day and are more likely to participate in the largest number of different sports regularly (Sport England, 2003b). Although these differences exist among both primary and secondary school pupils they are widest at the secondary level. Nevertheless, there has been a significant increase in the percentage of girls taking part in extra-curricular PE (from 36 per cent to 41 per cent) between 1994 and 2002 according to Sport England (2003a) (see Chapter 4). Similarly, Flintoff and Scraton (2001: 13) noted that the majority of young women in their study 'were physically active out of school in some way' and Biddle et al. (2005) reported around half (51 per cent) of the 10–15-year-old girls surveyed by SportScotland classified as highly active in participatory terms (compared with 19 per cent as moderately active and 29 per cent as low active). Indeed, Fisher's (2002: 15) use of time diaries with young people in the UK suggests that 'younger women and men have similar total exercise profiles'.

Despite the growing involvement in leisure sport of girls and young women, much of this growth is likely to be attributable to increases among a particular group – primary school girls – and in particular activities: football and games (Sport England, 2003a, 2003b). The SportScotland study noted that levels of activity among girls were highest at age 11 with approximately 12.5 hours of sport per week.

All things considered, girls do not appear, in Leaman's (1984) terms, to be simply sitting on the sidelines and watching the boys play (Roberts, 1996a) in either PE or leisure sport. This may have applied a quarter of a century ago but in the first decade of the new millenium the situation is different. While it is clear that boys and girls continue to do a number of different things in the name of PE and sport it is not clear that the differences between them in terms of time and range are large or significant. Despite observations that two decades ago (see, for example, Scraton, 1992) girls were 'eased out of sport not so much because they (were) unable to enjoy the activities themselves than by the surrounding masculine culture that conflicts with girls' preferred feminine identities' (Roberts, 1999: 98), girls and young women are, it appears, no longer slaves to femininity. Nowadays, girls are almost as likely as boys to construct busy leisure and sporting lives (Roberts, 2006). Many young women, as Roberts (1999: 103) observes, have 'broken out of the bedroom culture' and are, for example, as likely as young men to use indoor sports facilities. Indeed, girls appear increasingly likely to challenge and resist masculine dominance (Flintoff and Scraton, 2001): Cockburn and Clarke's (2002: 658) findings suggested 'that there are teenage girls and young women who not infrequently refuse the choices forced upon them by enthusiastically taking part in sport – both in PE and in other physical activity'.

In Norway, there is evidence that the growth of more informal, recreational activities – 'deliberately organized and delivered in ways which are different from the ways in which conventional sport is organized' (Skille and Waddington, 2006: 266) and are less intensive, less physically demanding, and less competitive and formal as well as more flexible – has played a substantial part in breaking down barriers to participation among young, working-class women in particular. Despite the evident appeal to girls and young women of 'lifestyle' or 'lifetime' activities, it seems that young women are not necessarily disadvantaged by multi-activity, sport-based programmes to the extent we may be inclined to think. Flintoff and Scraton (2001: 14) observed that young women's out-of-school physical activity lifestyles included 'some of the more traditional "female" sports and activities, such as netball, hockey, keep fit, dance, swimming and aerobics' as well as 'other, less traditional activities, such as kick-boxing and weight training' albeit usually 'in female-only settings'. The Sport England 2002 survey revealed, in turn, that 'girls are now more likely to try football, tenpin bowling, basketball, gymnastics and athletics out-of-lessons than they were in 1994' (Sport England, 2003a: 41). More recently, the *Girls in Sport* study found that 'high levels of latent demand were evident, with most girls expressing a desire to be more active' (O'Donovan and Kay, 2005: 29–30). All this research suggests that the times are, indeed, changing in relation to girls' and young women's involvement with sport.

However, even if their participation in PE is similar overall to that of boys (mainly because of the obligatory nature of schooling), girls' involvement in leisure sport remains lower than boys'. Roberts (1996a) challenges what he perceives as the tendency to lay at least part of the blame for girls' relative lack of interest and involvement in leisure sport on a gendered PE culture. The main reason for the girls' lower participation outside lessons, Roberts (1996a: 56) argues, seems to be simply that they like sport less. He suggests that the sexes bring the different attitudes they have acquired in their younger lives into school with the result that girls are likely to resent, and boys more likely to enjoy, the similar amounts of sport in which they are required to participate. Out of school, he adds, girls have the option of playing less and that, in practice, is what tends to happen.

How, then, might we explain the changes in participation, such as they are? First, there have been changes in the social circumstances of many women. Legislation can, of course, be one precondition for greater gender equity. Wallhead and Buckworth (2004), for example, point to various claims that the passage of *Title IX* legislation in the USA, in 1972, substantially improved the opportunities for girls to participate in school-related physical activities and led to a threefold increase in the number taking part in interscholastic sports in the USA. Nevertheless, legislation towards greater formal equality tends to reflect changed conditions in society generally. Diminishing gender-based employment and lifestyle differences (Coalter, 1999) and evident changes in the balance of power between the sexes in an equalizing direction (Dunning, 1999; Mennell, 1998) have resulted in the lifestyles of men and women converging. So, the gap between men and women in behaviours such as smoking, drinking, fast driving, dangerous sports and violence (Gabe et al., 2004) has been reduced or reversed, and the sex differences in sports participation have become more modest than before (Fox and Rickards, 2004; Sport England, 2003a). Over time, most aspects of leisure have become, or appear to be becoming, genderless (Roberts, 2006) – in broad participatory terms, at least. In short, the preconditions for greater involvement of young women in sport appear to be in place and substantial changes in leisure and sports participation are occurring alongside the undoubted continuities.

Bearing in mind the contrasting views on the significance of the gendered PE culture and the different attitudes boys and girls acquire in their younger lives, the next section of this chapter explores, in more detail, young people's experiences of PE and school sport, and their socialization into norms of femininity and masculinity.

GIRLS' AND BOYS' EXPERIENCES OF PE AND SCHOOL SPORT

The findings from a recent study of 10–15-year-old girls in Scotland neatly encapsulates several of the most salient issues in the relationship between gender, PE and sport of the kind commented upon in numerous studies over more than two decades. Biddle et al. (2005) found that when girls were reluctant to participate in sport many factors were present, including an aversion to team and competitive games, problems associated with mixed-sex environments, a lack of self-confidence (typically coupled with a negative body image) and poor quality changing and showering facilities, as well as perceptions of sport as 'uncool'. Some of these issues demand more detailed analysis.

The nature of provision for PE

When it comes to designing PE curricula, teachers tend to possess quite clear and conventional ideas regarding young people's (gendered) predispositions and abilities and the kinds of activities viewed as appropriate for boys and girls. Despite developments in recent decades towards broader and more varied PE diets (see Chapters 3 and 7), boys and girls continue to be confronted by curricula dominated by competitive, physically vigorous, games; that is, 'traditional' PE. This inevitably is viewed as limiting the opportunities for girls in particular to move beyond the confines of 'acceptable' physicality (Flintoff and Scraton, 2006). A striking feature of the *Girls in Sport* project was that many of the initiatives focused upon changing girls' impressions of sport while comparatively few focused upon changing the actual content of the curriculum (O'Donovan and Kay, 2005). Nonetheless, there is ample evidence in the USA (Wallhead and Buckworth, 2004) and England (Flintoff and Scraton, 2001), for example, of a mismatch between those activities available to girls at school and those they find enjoyable and are more likely to engage in beyond school. Neither do the sports that girls have available to them in PE resemble those participated in by adult women. Despite some girls' evident willingness to take part in conventional sports and team games (and especially traditional boys' games such as football), many secondary-age girls and young women favour 'lifestyle' or 'lifetime' activities (such as dance and swimming) and even individual games over traditional team games (Williams et al., 2000). It is perhaps unsurprising, then, that girls' perceptions of incompetence and boredom are often related to what they perceive as a lack of choice in activities and that this, in turn, increases the likelihood that girls will not engage positively with PE and sport.

The development of the NCPE in 1992 in England and Wales held forth the promise of a significant contribution to the dissipation of gender segregation in PE. However, and despite rhetorical claims about equal opportunities, the NCPE has been something of a double-edged sword. On the one hand, the NCPE protects and bolsters the traditional female games, such as netball and hockey, that Scraton (1993) speculated might be in danger of dying with the emergence of co-educational PE in the 1980s. On the other hand, by identifying 'activity areas' – among which games has continued to feature very prominently – the NCPE has, in effect, hardened the well-established hierarchy of activity areas in PE within which girls and boys are offered 'different and stereotypically "appropriate" activities' (Penney and Evans, 1997: 87). Indeed, the 'flexibility' available to PE teachers – within the statutory requirements for NCPE – appears to have indirectly facilitated the continued provision of sex-differentiated curricula (Waddington et al., 1998).

It is not only differences in activities that characterize boys' and girls' PE, it is also differences in teaching styles (see Chapter 12). Dominant forms of masculinity and femininity are said to be developed and reinforced not only through competitive, team sports (YST, 2000) but also through conventional teaching styles (Hargreaves, 1994). Female PE teachers, it seems, are more likely to use informal and reciprocal styles, males more likely to employ formal, command approaches. These tendencies are facilitated by the inclusion of particular activities in girls' (dance and educational gymnastics, for example) and boys' (Olympic gymnastics and HRE) PE that lend themselves to the preferred styles of female and male PE teachers.

Self-image

Physical education is a very public and visible arena for both boys and girls, and offers numerous opportunities to conform to, or even contradict, accepted stereotypes of masculine and feminine behaviour (Clarke, 2006). The activities and processes that constitute PE are said to 'school' boys and girls into gender-appropriate (that is, feminine or masculine) ways of behaving. Among boys, successful participation and performance in traditionally male sports in PE lessons (team games, for example) provides boys with 'an apprenticeship in orthodox masculinity' (Pronger, 1990, cited in Clarke, 2006: 726). School sport does not, however, provide the same avenue to orthodox femininity for girls. Because stereotypical perceptions of appropriate and inappropriate sports and activities for girls influence whether (and in which) young people choose to participate as well as how they are viewed by others (Alley and Hicks, 2005), PE reinforces the construction of heterosexual femininity (Flintoff and Scraton, 2006). In this manner, PE provides a powerful illustration of the workings of the informal or hidden curriculum as played out in unscrutinized interactions in changing rooms, on playing fields and in gymnasia and swimming pools.

Girls' relationship with sport and exercise is frequently intimately related to their perceptions of their own bodies and their 'look'. Indeed, concerns about their body shape were the main reasons for the participation of young girls in sport in England and Wales, according to Rowe (2005). Nevertheless, a leitmotif of the abundant research on girls' experiences is the recognition that PE has a tendency to alienate girls from sport and frequently, in the process, exacerbates any unease they may feel with their bodies. Unlike many boys, girls appear to need more frequent and supportive extrinsic judgements from their teachers (Wallhead and Buckworth, 2004) as well as their parents – a situation that is not helped by the continued predominance among adults of stereoptypical gender ideologies 'concerning expectations of women's physicality, their sexuality and their role as mothers and carers' (Scraton, 1993: 143). Male and female PE teachers often reinforce and reproduce gender stereotypes (Scraton, 1993) and many girls' feelings of bodily awkwardness are often exacerbated by the frequently stereotypical perceptions of, and associated attitudes towards, girls by their parents, teachers and friends.

Many of the traditional and stereotypical sports and rituals in PE contradict many girls' conceptions of an appropriate and desirable female and feminine 'appearance' and, consequently, cause conflict for girls (Cockburn and Clarke, 2002; Gorely et al., 2003). Furthermore, many of the activities – and the 'traditional' behaviours associated with them (for example, the demonstration of physical vigour and the associated likelihood of getting sweaty and dirty) – are performed in public, not just in front of other girls and their teachers, but often in front of boys and their teachers.

The issue of weight, 'shared peer norms for thinness' (Dohnt and Tiggerman, 2005: 103) and having a desirable figure are especially significant for many young women (Cox et al., 2005). Consequently, the problems of performing outside can be intensified when girls feel they are over- (or under-) weight (Cockburn and Clarke, 2002). Research has shown how the 'childish' clothing requirement constraints and showering routines usually required when taking part in PE and school sport (Flintoff and Scraton, 2001; Scraton, 1993), exacerbate young women's preoccupation with their bodies and frequently result in feelings of shame and embarrassment. Girls' feelings of awkwardness are further exacerbated by the presence of boys – in the form of co-educational PE, for example – where girls 'run the gauntlet of persistent comment on their physical appearance and sexuality' and their responses tend either to be to attempt 'to disguise their bodies by dressing in loose clothing or to opt out of the activity' (Scraton, 1993: 145). This is typical of the unintended consequences of activities often viewed as potentially liberating for girls.

The potential for PE not only to highlight girls' self-consciousness (O'Donovan and Kay, 2005) but to impact negatively on girls' self-esteem appears to be exacerbated during early adolescence (Cockburn and Clarke, 2002). It is during the particularly sensitive years of adolescence, when young women are developing physically and sexually, that ideologies of women as sex objects and mothers become all important (Scraton, 1993). Indeed, it is suggested that many of the more popular activities among women, such as aerobics and dance, merely serve to sexualize the female body in conformity with male stereotypes. In the process, these activities further divide young women from each other in terms of those who are fat and those who are fit and attractive (Harris, 2005).

Embarrassment is viewed by teenage girls as a very real likelihood and a substantial cost of participating in PE (Cockburn and Clarke, 2002). However, in contrast to the young women who 'never' participate in sport (see later) those in Cox et al.'s (2005) study who 'always' participated reported very low levels of self-consciousness and claimed to rarely get embarrassed when participating in sport. Deeply involved in sport, they appeared not to care what other people might think of them. Nevertheless, it remains the case that girls who resist gender stereotypes – especially during adolescence – run the very real risk of 'alienation from the people around them and those most important to them' such as friends and family (Cockburn and Clarke, 2002: 659).

At either end of the continuum of engagement with PE are girls who either 'hate' or 'love' PE. Many, however, lie somewhere between the two – they are biddable but not at any cost to their self-esteem. Consequently, many girls find themselves in a 'no-win' situation: damned if they do sport and damned if they do not. 'It is highly unlikely that girls can achieve being both physically active *and* [heterosexually] desirable, so they are often obliged to choose *between* these images. The result is a paradox, a double standard to which teenage girls and young women are subjected ... and most girls compromise' (Cockburn and Clarke, 2002: 665, emphasis in the original). It is perhaps, unsurprising, then, that many girls appear to feel constrained to appear disinterested in PE and sport.

In recent years, gender-related research has broadened to encompass the significance of gender for boys' experiences of PE and sport and, in particular, the socialization of boys into PE and sport (see, for example, Gard, 2006). Whitson (1990: 19) articulates a commonplace view that sport acts as 'one of the central sites in the social production of masculinity' and that the kinds of sports conventionally prioritized in PE are ones that 'naturalize' the idea that masculinity involves aggressiveness and a desire to compete with and overcome others. In other words, via many of the activities that constitute PE, and the ways in which they are taught, the physical and psychological attributes of sport are often implicitly if not explicitly presented as the physical and psychological attributes of being, or becoming, a 'man'. An incidental expression of this dominant ideology of masculinity is the prevalence of the view among boys that activities such as dance are not only pointless but 'gay' (homosexual) or 'unmasculine'.

Dissatisfaction with one's body is not, then, solely the preserve of girls. Physical education and sport are arenas in which the demanding nature of living up to masculine norms for boys (Martino and Pallotta-Chiarolli, 2003; Wright, 1999), as well as feminine norms for girls, are thrown into sharp relief. Young men's anxieties regarding their masculinity are reflected in their concern for physical strength and muscularity – around a quarter or more of the 15–16-year-old boys in A. Smith's (2006) study reported partcipating regularly in their spare time in gym/weight-training activities. In this regard, boys have to negotiate individual ways through the demands of masculinity (Bramham, 2003) in a manner reminiscent of girls' attempts to compromise between sporting and heterosexual images. It seems that there are established and outsider groups within as well as between the sexes.

Mixed or co-educational PE

One of the more deliberate ways in which physical educationalists have sought to effect changes in gender relationships and gender stereotypes has been through the introduction of what became known as co-educational PE. In many PE lessons in primary schools (5–11 years) and some (for example, dance and gymnastic) in the first three years of secondary schooling (11–14 years), it has been commonplace to introduce both sexes to some compulsory 'core' activities in co-educational or mixed-sex classes. As a result of the *Title IX* legislation, many PE classes in the USA are required to be taught to mixed-sex groupings (even though some 'contact' sports such as basketball, football, ice hockey and rugby can be segregated for competition). In a number of European countries, such as Greece and Norway, similar and sometimes the same activities are taught to mixed-sex groups throughout the duration of compulsory schooling and often by male teachers.

As the name implies, the growth of what was referred to as co-educational PE at secondary-school level in the USA and UK from the 1970s and 1980s was ostensibly aimed at reducing gender inequalities on the grounds that 'traditional sex segregation' in PE lessons 'does little to create gender understanding between boys and girls' (Humberstone, 2002: 66). Nevertheless, teachers often had more pragmatic and less egalitarian reasons for teaching boys and girls together, such as their own sporting expertise and preferences and staff shortages (Green and Scraton, 1998). In reality, it seems, co-educational PE amounted to little more than mixed-sex teaching groups. While mixed-sex grouping ostensibly enabled boys as well as girls to access a wider variety activities in the PE curriculum, it resulted in a number of unanticipated consequences. The lessons typically became oriented towards, and as a result dominated by, boys, who received more attention and had more contact with the teacher (who tended to be distracted by their behaviours [Evans, 1989]), talked more, and were far more 'visible' in class (Scraton, 1993). The fact that many of the activities chosen for mixed-sex lessons were traditionally male activities meant that, in practice, equal access to PE often meant equal access for all pupils to boys' PE (Scraton, 1993). This was exacerbated by boys' domination of those activities, notably team games, in which they had more experience. Interestingly, pupils' shared experiences of mixed-sex PE – the norm in primary schools – appears to do little to diminish the power of traditional ideas about gender in secondary PE or to change the expectations and experiences of pupils or, for that matter, PE teachers (Green and Scraton, 1998). This may be in part due to the fact that beyond PE lessons at break times, boys continue to monopolize playground spaces at the primary level (Williams, 1989), typically to play football (Skelton, 2000) and games.

It appears that where PE classes are not controlled effectively by teachers, a dominance hierarchy tends to develop with males at the apex (Skille and Waddington, 2006). This results in gender inequalities and male-dominance of 'open' sporting settings whereby girls' behaviours are constrained by boys' competitiveness and aggression, especially in sport-based PE (Azzarito and Solomon, 2005; Wright, 1999). Traditional divisions along gender lines are almost always retained in games, where boys have a tendency to discriminate against girls and dominate possession. In such situations, girls tend to either give up or acquiese (Skille and Waddington, 2006). Mixed-sex grouping has also resulted in girls losing out in terms of teachers feeling unable to address specifically female issues (for example, in relation to health and hygiene) (Evans, 1989).

Girls in the USA who saw themselves as not being good at sport have tended to favour same-sex instruction and teachers in Germany, the UK and the USA have tended to perceive co-educational classes as less applicable as pupils get older (Lirgg, 2006). In the UK, female teachers have, themselves, favoured a return to sex-segregated classes for many activities. Consequently, in many secondary schools (and especially in Years 9 and above), boys and girls continue to be taught separately and differently.

Motivation and competence

Girls, it seems, are more likely to participate if their primary motivation is intrinsic; that is, the activity is viewed as being enjoyable in its own right, emphasizing fun and enjoyment. Biddle et al. (2005) found that girls whose main motivation was intrinsic were less likely to feel self-conscious about taking part than those for whom changing their body image was the main motivation. Nevertheless, approximately a third of girls in the SportScotland study reported not liking to see how they looked when they were exercising. Similarly, competence and voluntariness are key dimensions to sports participation for girls. Girls are more likely to participate if they feel competent enough to do so. Biddle et al.'s (2005) study of 10–15-year-old girls in Scotland found that perceived competence was 'particularly influential' in the withdrawal of girls from sport. In addition, when girls felt that they were 'forced' to participate this impacted negatively on their overall participation (Biddle et al., 2005). Also, opportunities for 'social interaction with friends' (Rowe, 2005: 4) is an especially important consideration for girls.

Underpinning gender-related issues in PE is the more fundamental dimension of the manner in which boys and girls are socialized into norms of masculinity and femininity and the consequences of such experiences for their attitudes towards, and involvement in, PE and sport.

SOCIALIZATION INTO NORMS OF FEMININITY AND MASCULINITY

Physical education and sport are processes through which, formally and informally, young people are likely to learn gendered identities or, rather, have their developing views of themselves as masculine or feminine reinforced or challenged. Through PE and sport, particular, often stereotypical, views of what are considered appropriate behaviours and sporting practices for boys and girls are normalized in the sense of becoming widely accepted and taken for granted. To the extent that young people have their views of themselves shaped by their early experiences, PE and sport – because they tend to evoke emotional responses – are especially likely to act as subconscious vehicles for messages about appropriate gender-related behaviours and (sporting) practices.

Gender socialization refers to the ways in which boys and girls are introduced to what are seen as male- and female-appropriate behaviours and practices, including those activities that might be seen as forming the initial preparation for later engagement with, and adherence to, sport. Research in paediatric exercise and fitness by Armstrong (1991) and colleagues (Armstrong and Welsman, 1997), points up the significance of parental behaviours in encouraging differential rates and frequencies of exercise among boys and girls. Commonplace sex-stereotyped assumptions regarding exercise and sport manifest themselves in boys receiving more parental reinforcement towards exercise than girls. Similarly, parents are likely to elicit more gross-motor behaviour at a young age from their sons than their daughters: 'Girls are still being given dolls and prams and are instructed to be neat and tidy. Boys are still being sent to play with footballs and soldiers and are excused if they are rough and dirty' (Roberts, 2006: 120). Boys continue to be given greater encouragement to engage in sport by parents and teachers and, consequently, tend to play more sports than girls (Balding, 2001; SCW, 2001, 2003a; Sport England, 2003b) and this tendency increases as young people grow older. This is hardly surprising in light of the research that demonstrates the central position of not only family (Biddle et al., 2005) but fathers, in particular, in their children's leisure and sporting socialization (Harrington, 2006). 'Men', it seems, 'are typically more likely to spend time with their children in playful activities than routine caring tasks' (Kay, 2006: 126) and 'fathers are more likely than mothers to have or claim expertise in sport' (2006: 127). For these reasons, it is far more likely that fathers will be the ones to get involved in this aspect of children's socialization.

Boys' activities also appear to be advantaged. Boys' games tend to be of longer duration and incorporate a higher ceiling of skill than those of girls. In addition, the types of game normally adopted by boys can be played in more simple versions at younger ages, becoming more challenging with age as higher levels of skill and strategy are incorporated (Armstrong, 1991). In contrast, the kinds of games that girls tend to favour 'seem to be less challenging with increasing age because the ceiling of skill was achieved at an earlier age' (Armstrong, 1991: 9–10). To compound the constraints on their physical activity experiences, teenage boys appear to enjoy a greater 'right to roam' while girls – for safety reasons – are discouraged from doing so and, as a result, their freedom tends to be curtailed.

Gendered practices and experiences such as these form the basis of boys' and girls' common-sense assumptions regarding what constitute appropriate activities for them to engage in. Consequently, the 'gender order' comes to appear quite normal, even 'natural', to those involved and 'common-sense assumptions about what it means "to be a girl" or "to be a boy"' (Scraton, 1992: 9) remain widespread. A study of 357 secondary-school students in Norway indicated that boys rated appearance of strength, competence in sport and masculinity as particularly important, whereas girls were more concerned with looking good and being feminine (Klomsten et al., 2005). This, the authors suggested, resulted in more boys participating in traditionally male sports and girls in traditionally female sports. Nevertheless, the dramatic growth in popularity (not only in Scandinavian countries but worldwide) of girls' and women's football in recent years, points to the socially constructed character of gender. In other words, such developments in women's patterns of sporting participation underline the processual and, therefore, changeable character of gendered identities. Cox et al.'s (2005) study suggested that young women aged 15–19 years who, as they put it, 'always' participate in sport – and often increased participation as they got older – reported regular participation in and positive experiences of sport from an early age. Interestingly, some young women in the 'never' participate group also reported positive experiences of sport from an early age. It was the move to secondary school – where sport was seen as more competitive – that was associated with sport becoming less enjoyable among this group.

While young people as a whole are experiencing a broader diet of sports and physical activities in PE at school than previous generations, they nevertheless continue to be introduced to various sports and physical activities according to their sex. There remains a great deal of continuity alongside the evident change in the sporting experiences of girls and young women.

GENDER AND SOCIAL DYNAMICS

To fully appreciate the similarities and dissimilarities within and between girls and boys in terms of their participation in and experiences of PE and sport, we must appreciate that they are not homogenous groups (Penney and Evans, 2002). Leisure and sporting opportunities continue to be 'structured and unequally distributed' (Roberts, 2005: 2) by sex, class and ethnicity both in isolation and in configuration (see Chapters 9 and 10). Seefeld et al. (2002: 146) observe that 'women, especially ethnic minorities and those in the lower socio-economic strata, have routinely recorded lower rates of adherence than men in structured activity programmes'.

Trends towards greater participation in PE and sport among girls and young women are mediated by social class, in particular. It is more likely to be the daughters (and, for that matter, the sons) of middle-class families that will not only be encouraged to do sport by their parents but will be introduced to a variety of sports and activities when young. It is in the middle classes where sex differences are evidently narrowing and so it is middle-class girls and young women whose lives are more likely to resemble the working, leisure and sporting lives of males. Little has changed among the 20 per cent or so, predominantly working-class girls, who will become teenage mothers and whose lives are very likely to be impoverished in every sense of the term.

CONCLUSION

Times are changing as far as girls' and young women's participation in PE and sport are concerned. Participation has risen steadily in recent decades and this is correlated with, if not straightfowardly attributable to, changes in the PE curriculum. There is, in effect, some convergence between boys' and girls' experiences of PE and sport and it appears that if girls can be recruited into sport their participation levels can be similar to those of boys.

Nevertheless, PE remains gendered in terms of organization, content and delivery. Although the number and breadth of activities made available to girls and young women in PE has increased over time – during the past two decades in particular – provision and expectations continue to be constrained by assumptions about femininity in relation to masculinity (Flintoff and Scraton, 2006). As a result, gender differences are not being obliterated either in terms of the nature of PE provision or the lessons to be learned through PE regarding gender-appropriate behaviours. The tendency for PE to reinforce more than challenge hierarchical relations between the sexes remains. Experiences of marginalization and alienation in PE are not the sole prerogative of girls, however. Boys also experience marginalization (Wright, 1999) if they are lacking in sporting skills and/or are not deemed by their peers sufficiently competitive or masculine. Consequently, many boys as well as girls disengage from PE and sport during their childhood and adolescence.

However, the available evidence does not straightforwardly suggest that schools bear a major responsibility for girls' lower or differing rates of out-of-school participation, because 'schools may sometimes be unable to counter-vail against wider socialising influences even if they wish to do so' (Roberts, 1996a: 56). It seems that the wider lives of children and young people are more significant than school PE in shaping their leisure and sporting participation. Indeed, the available quantitative or 'hard' evidence 'does not, in itself, suggest that either sex is clearly the more advantaged' (Roberts, 2006: 98) in sporting terms. In other words, differences are not necessarily disadvantages and non-participation in an activity does not necessarily amount to exclusion, disadavantage or inequality (Coalter et al., 2000; Roberts, 2006): there may well be distinctive strengths rather than simply deficiencies in girls' and young women's leisure (Roberts, 2006). Young men and women may actively choose not to take part in a sporting or leisure activity because they are not attracted by it or find no satisfaction or achievement in it (Collins, with Kay, 2003). In the sense that these are 'barriers' to participation, they are barriers of boredom or perceived lack of ability. Exclusion only occurs if and when young men and women want to take part but cannot. This, however, sidesteps the issue of young people's predispositions towards PE and sport, and the manner in which their 'tastes' and 'choices' act as barriers, and that these pre-dispositions, in turn, reflect young people's gendered socialization. This is not the same as saying that they would find the activities they are not inclined to do as enjoyable as those that they are doing. And this would be the point for critics of the persistence of gender differences in PE; namely, that despite similar levels and forms of PE and sports participation, it tells us little about girls' experiences of PE and the likely consequences of these for the place of physical activity and sport in the adult leisure lives of young women. Nor, for that matter, does it tell us the extent to which young women's participation levels could be further enhanced by a curriculum and teaching styles more suited to girls' developing tastes and experiences.

Despite the impression that many young women continue to dislike PE and that girls' levels of participation continue to be viewed as problematic, more young women than ever before are taking part in PE, leisure sport and physical activity. Flintoff and Scraton (2005) are typical of commentators who take the view that many young women express a desire to be active in sport, despite, she adds, rather than because of school PE. O'Donovan and Kay's (2005: 30) research led them to conclude that there remains 'considerable potential for PE to elicit a much more favourable response from young women' and that a substantial transformation of girls' PE would be required if this latent potential were to be realized.

RECOMMENDED READING

Flintoff, A. and Scraton, S. (2006) 'Girls and physical education', in D. Kirk, D. Macdonald and M. O'Sullivan (eds), *The Handbook of Physical Education*. London: Sage. pp.767–83.

Penney, D. and Evans, J. (2002) 'Talking gender', in D. Penney (ed.), *Gender and Physical Education: Contemporary Issues and Future Directions*. London: Routledge. pp.13–23.

Social Class and Physical Education

A great deal is known about the relationship between social class and education and, to a lesser extent, about social class, leisure and sport. Very little, however, is known about the relationship between social class and PE. This chapter teases out the significance of social class for understanding PE. In the process it shows how 'the class divisions that arise in economic life are liable to spill over' (Roberts, 2001: 21) into other areas of young people's lives that have implications for PE, such as their leisure lifestyles, sporting abilities and dispositions.

Social class has proved to be related to virtually all areas of life so it is no surprise to find that it is related to leisure, in general, and sports participation, in particular. However, within leisure there are exceptions (watching television, for example) and other uses of leisure where the predictive power of class is relatively weak (for example, gambling) (Roberts, 2001). This also applies to certain sports such as angling and football. Might it, then, be possible, via PE, to weaken the link across the whole of sport? Indeed, can we expect PE to have a positive impact upon the likely involvement of young people from all social class backgrounds in sport beyond school and into adult life? Before exploring the significance of social class for sport and PE in greater detail we need to look at social class as a concept.

DEFINING SOCIAL CLASS

In academic as well as popular thinking, attempts to define social class tend to have an economic base. In other words, 'All concepts of class group together people with similar ways of making their livings, that is, in similar occupations' (Roberts, 2001: 21). Because the concept of class revolves around market situation – in terms of labour market experiences and education – and

154

life-chances, as well as occupation, the term 'socio-economic' status is often used as a synonym (Gabe et al., 2004; Roberts, 2001).

Social class also has a cultural as well as an economic dimension. It is evident, for example, that leisure and sports participation cannot be reduced to questions of control over economic resources – class-based patterns of participation often reflect more than merely differences in disposable income. People have at their disposal social, cultural and physical, as well as economic, resources and this begins to explain why, even though they may have sufficient money to play sports such as golf or squash, some choose not to, preferring soccer, martial arts and the like instead.

THE SOCIAL AND CULTURAL DIMENSIONS OF CLASS

The social dimension of class (often referred to as 'social capital') consists of social relationships in which people 'invest'. The relationships that constitute social capital are often conceptualized as having two dimensions or forms: bonding (in effect the ties and relationships between [similar] people) and bridging (the links between groups of people) capital (Putnam, 2000). People can draw upon the ties and links they have (their social capital) with, for example, circles of friends or colleagues as and when they need to, and this is especially useful in sporting and leisure contexts.

The cultural dimension of class (or 'cultural capital'), on the other hand, consists of the skills, knowledge, beliefs, predispositions and values people acquire in their particular social milieu (Bourdieu, 1984; Roberts, 2001) and serves as a kind of cultural coinage or currency (Field, 2003). Cultural capital is typically a product of early socialization experiences and conditioning in particular social networks and specific class-based lifestyles (Kew, 1997: 150). Cultural capital, as an aspect of social class, becomes part of people's habituses (Bourdieu, 1984; Elias, 1994). In other words, it becomes literally and metaphorically embodied in their dispositions, skills and abilities. Shared experiences, leading to shared dispositions and outlooks, constitute group or class habitus (Elias, 1994). This is why structural factors, such as neighbourhood residence, remain influential in shaping the identities and predispositions of some groups of young people (Shildrick, 2006) and especially those from the working classes.

An individual's habitus, predispositions or 'assumed world' are said to be a reflection of their class-related 'horizon of possibilities' (Lane, 2000: 194, cited in Blackshaw and Long, 2005: 251). The possibilities of those from lower socio-economic groups tend to be constrained by limited social networks which typically lead to 'a poverty of expectation' (Blackshaw and Long, 2005: 251). Put another way, '[A]t all subsequent life stages, and in all spheres of life, the cultural capital that individuals bring to their situations affects their opportunities' (Roberts, 2001: 218).

Cultural capital is 'built up gradually' (Roberts, 2001: 218) and, in the same way that economic resources can be passed down the generations, so can social and cultural resources; hence, the claims for the significance of families in intergenerational transmission of cultural capital (Gunn, 2005) and the observation that the form it takes changes over time. While it is something that we all possess, the crucial differences lie not so much in the amounts of cultural capital each of us possesses but in the types and how valuable these prove to be (Roberts, 2001) – in sporting terms, for example.

Notions of cultural and social dimensions of class help us to appreciate that while economic resources lie at the heart of social class, social and cultural relations and resources help create and reproduce differences and inequalities: money is not the sole reason for the less well-off having 'a narrower range of tastes and activities' (Roberts, 2001: 86), in sporting terms in particular. Kew (1997) suggests that some sports – probably those such as polo and sailing and, to a lesser extent, fencing, golf, skiing and sub-aqua – remain socially exclusive whether or not they continue to be cost exclusive. Wilson (2002: 5) observes that findings from the General Social Survey in the USA suggest that 'those who are richest in cultural capital and those who are richest in economic capital are most likely to be involved in sports generally' and that 'these tendencies are independent of one another'. Wilson (2002: 5) adds that whereas economic capital has no bearing on involvement in what he refers to as 'prole' or working-class sports, 'those richest in cultural capital are least likely to be involved' in such sports.

Taking part in sport not only benefits from social and cultural capital – knowing relevant people and possessing relevant knowledge and skills; that is, *who* you know as well as *what* you know – it actually *requires* it: sports participation 'requires confidence, skills, knowledge, ability – [and] a group of supportive friends and companions, including some who share the same desire to take part' (Collins, 2003: 69).

THE PHYSICAL DIMENSIONS OF CLASS

The bodily or physical manifestations of social class position are typically referred to as 'physical capital' (McDonald, 2003; Shilling, 1998). It may be better, however, to view physical capital as an aspect of cultural capital, that is, a dimension of *what* people know – in terms of their physical skills and abilities as well as their physical condition and health. The physical dimensions of behaviour are said to reflect an individual's social class (Evans, 2004; Kirk, 2004; Shilling, 1998, 2005) and, consequently, their 'orientation to the world' (Kirk, 2004: 52): 'different patterns of socialization result in class-based orientations' (Shilling, 2005: 38) towards the body, for example.

According to McDonald (2003: 171), the body is pivotal 'in understanding the relationship between, class, sport and PE'; in other words, 'How we manage our bodies in terms of diet and exercise, how we carry our bodies in terms of posture and deportment, how we present our bodies in terms of clothing, and how we use our bodies in social and physical activities, carry significant social and class meanings' (2003: 170). In effect, people's physical skills, experiences and even condition have a significant influence on their predispositions towards new or familiar activities and help shape their tastes in sport. The ways in which young boys and girls from different social classes hold particular views of what sports and physical activities it is 'cool' – that is, socially appropriate or normative – to be involved in as well as how they want their bodies to look, are an expression of the cultural dimensions of social class and are reinforced not only by their peers but also by the activities of PE and the expectations of PE teachers.

Particular social class locations make it more or less likely that involvement in differing kinds of sport (such as skiing or weight-lifting, rugby union or rugby league) will lead to young people acquiring particular forms of physical capital (skills and physical attributes, for example) that have symbolic value and kudos and can prove to be valuable social, cultural and even economic resources. It is argued that young people's bodies have been, and continue to be, socially constructed in the sense that the programmes of sports and/or physical activities (from military drill in the nineteenth century through team games to 'body management' activities such as aerobics and HRE in the twenty-first century) that they experience at their various class-differentiated (Gorard et al., 2003) schools leads to young people developing particular skills and particular views of their bodies which serve to reinforce social class positions and orientations. The point is that social class does not just impact on 'choice and preferences' (Evans, 2004: 102) in sport, it also has a substantial impact upon individuals' physical capabilities: in other words, their skills and abilities. Consequently, the distinctive sporting practices that characterize working- and middle-class people 'are not arbitrary or accidental' (McDonald, 2003: 170) but arise out of their class-related physical capacities and related dispositions (or habitus).

The physical dimension of social class also incorporates physical condition and health. As long as 'socio-economic status remains positively related to health' (Roberts and Brodie, 1992: 117), physical capital will have implications for health generally and HRE in particular. 'Poorer households in poorer communities', for example, 'are less likely to have access to healthy, affordable food and suitable recreational facilities' (Royal College of Physicians et al., 2004: 21). Middle-class children have healthier diets and become generally stronger and healthier than working-class youngsters. In terms of health-related exercise, it is apparent that physical activity is associated with social class and, in particular, income and educational attainment. In all age groups, 'people of higher socio-economic status take part in more physical activity' (Wanless, 2004: 99). Low educational attainment is particularly associated with higher levels of inactivity and, as if to compound their more sedentary lifestyles, the children of working-class families tend to lack safe places to play or exercise (Royal College of Physicians et al., 2004). Also, overweight and obesity is a condition 'exacerbated by low socio-economic status' (2004: 21). It is clear that economic deprivation is strongly correlated with relatively poor physical condition and overall health (Roberts and Brodie, 1992; Townsend et al., 1988). Indeed, although active involvement in sport can make a difference to individual's health it 'will not eradicate or necessarily even lessen' the inequalities associated with social class (Roberts and Brodie, 1992: 119).

From this consideration of the economic, social, cultural and physical dimensions of social class, and the development of class-related habitus, the next section deals with the relationship between social class and education.

SOCIAL CLASS AND EDUCATION

The relationship between social class and education is firmly and incontrovertibly established. Despite a 'general rise in children's and young people's educational attainments' (Roberts, 2001: 107) since the 1970s, young people from higher socio-economic classes 'tend to have "better" educational life chances in terms of examination results and full-time further education' (Meighan, with Siraj-Blatchford, 2003: 346). Middle- and working-class children also tend to have differing experiences of school – not only with regard to academic success but also in terms of the development of self-esteem and social and cultural capital – and these place them at greater or lesser advantage in leisure terms, generally, and in sporting terms, in particular.

Education is significant in terms of the development of an attachment to sport among young people. This is because a variety of leisure and sporting benefits of being middle-class are associated with education. Levels of educational experience and attainment appear to be 'the most important component of social class for influencing participation/non-participation' (Kew, 1997: 147). Furlong et al. (1990: 222) found that 'young people who were in education tended to have the most active and varied leisure experiences', while Collins with Kay (2003: 248) point to research across Europe demonstrating social class gradients in sports participation and associated evidence that 'people with a higher level of final education were less likely to drop out of sport, having been more likely to take it up in the first place'. In short, the longer a young person stays in full-time education the higher their rate of participation in sport is likely to be (Coalter et al., 1995; Roberts, 1995, 1996a) and the more likely she or he is to become 'locked in' to sport on a regular basis in their adult lives (Roberts and Brodie, 1992). The reason education appears to be the most important component of social class in sporting terms is 'because those who remain in full time education after the statutory leaving age are more likely to have the free time and more likely to be provided with the opportunity for free participation in a wide range of sports' (Coalter et al., 1995: 70). In this respect, Collins (2003: 71) highlights 'the combined advantage enjoyed by full-time students who have access to facilities and clubs which are often subsidised and who come disproportionately from social groups ABC1'.

SOCIAL CLASS AND SPORT

In any discussion of the impact of particular social dynamics, such as class, on involvement with sport it is important to recognize the clear trend towards increased participation in sport among young people and adults in Western Europe since the 1980s (De Knop et al., 1996a; Scheerder et al., 2005c). In the UK, as with Western Europe generally, all occupational groups have experienced increases in sports participation. The greatest increases, however, have been among the lower middle- and working-class groupings (Coalter, 1999). Nonetheless, a large body of research provides 'compelling evidence' of the continued salience of social class 'in structuring sport, if not determining a person's choice, preferences and opportunities in sport in the UK and elsewhere' (Evans, 2004: 102). For example, the further down the social classification system an individual is located the greater is the probability that their participation in sport will decline markedly beyond adolescence (Flintoff et al., 2005).

Social class and adults' participation in sport

Various sociological studies demonstrate that active involvement in sport among adults is correlated with social class (see, for example, Coakley, 2004; Collins, 2003; Kew, 1997; Scheerder et al., 2005a) and, as a consequence, the higher the social class, the greater the rate of participation and overall involvement (Coakley, 2004; Donnelly, 1996; DCMS/Strategy Unit, 2002; SCW, 2002; Wilson, 2002). In charting the rise in sports participation in Flanders between 1969 and 1999, Scheerder et al. (2005a) noted how the gap in participation between the social classes had not diminished substantially. In England, while participation rates for male and female unskilled manual workers at the turn of the twenty-first century were 34 per cent and 19 per cent respectively, at the other end of the socio-economic scale the figures were 61 per cent and 67 per cent for male and female professional workers (DCMS/Strategy Unit, 2002). In North America, Gruneau (2006: 560) observes that 'systematic socioeconomic differences' are 'still clearly evident in Canadian amateur sport'. Overall, people from economically disadvantaged groups are the least likely to be in sport to begin with and are more likely to reduce participation. Indeed, lower class groups play fewer sports and, as a consequence, their sports careers are 'slightly more vulnerable' (Roberts and Brodie, 1992: 58) to drop out.

However, it is not only rates of participation but also forms of participation and numbers of sports participated in that social class impacts upon. Scheerder et al. (2005a; 2005b) observe that in Belgium sports such as golf, fencing, sailing, skiing, squash and tennis are more common among the middle and upper classes, while boxing, angling, weight-lifting and karate, for example, are more popular among lower socio-economic groupings. Stroot (2002) points out that, in 1999, according to the US Census Bureau, twice as many people with what might be termed middle-class incomes participated, for example, in swimming, cycling, basketball and aerobics than those from the lowest income bracket. While activities such as golf and sailing/motor boating tend to be, almost exclusively, the domain of the middle-classes, working-class adults in the USA appear more likely to engage in activities such as hunting and firearms sports than the middles classes (Stroot, 2002).

It is not merely, however, *what* people (in terms of specific sports) and *how much* they do it but, also, *where* they play sport is influenced by social class. The middle and upper classes are more likely to play sport in voluntary or commercial sporting and physical activity venues, while the lower or working classes are more likely to inhabit local authority-run centres and to be more frequent participants in hall and pitch sports (Coalter, 1999). Similarly, in Germany, membership of sports clubs is closely related to social status with middle-class workers far more likely to be members of sports clubs (Pfister and Reeg, 2006). In Wales, the SCW (2002) reports socio-economic groups A and B to be more than twice as likely to participate than group E in outdoor and indoor games and activities.

Social class and young people's participation in sport in and out of school

Increases in participation in recent decades have been especially noticeable among young people. The majority are taking part in sport reasonably regularly, both in and out of school, across Western Europe, and particularly in the northern Western European countries. While age and gender differences in youth sport are reasonably well documented, the impact of social class on youth sports participation is less well understood (Scheerder et al., 2005b). Nonetheless, the British government's recent strategy document, *Game Plan* (DCMS/Strategy Unit, 2002: 13), observed that young, white males are those most likely to take part in sport. To age, ethnicity and gender we need to add, social class, however, and specifically *middle* class. In Norway, for example, 'adolescents from middle class homes with above average income and highly educated parents, and who attend an academic secondary school, are more likely to participate in sport than their peers from working class families with lower incomes and less well educated parents' and are more likely to remain involved in sport throughout their teenage years (Skille and Waddington, 2006: 252).

In contrast to this picture, however, the SCW's study of young people of secondary school age (11–16 years) – using free school meals as a proxy measure of pupils from the lowest social classes – led them to conclude that socio-economic status 'had only a minimal impact upon the likelihood and level of sports participation' (SCW, 2003a: 4) among school-age youngsters in Wales in 2001. This, they suggested, was the case with curricular and extra-curricular PE and whether rates of participation were either occasional (at least once) or regular (more than 10 times over the year) (SCW, 2003b). Nevertheless, another SCW study found that, in terms of young people's involvement in sport in their leisure time (in the form of either extra-curricular PE and/or spare time sports clubs), the mean number of activities undertaken – by those who did participate – was marginally lower for those receiving free school meals and thus, by extension, working class (SCW, 2001). Similarly, Sport England's (2003b) 2002 study also concluded that social class remained a significant variable in sports participation among young people. They found, for example, that 'pupils living in the top 20 percent of deprived areas in England [were] less likely to have taken part in extra-curricular sport[1] (37 percent versus 44 percent of young people who did not live in the top 20 deprived areas)' (Sport England, 2003b: 104).

It is important to note that while social class impacts upon the likely involvement of young people in sport in the first place, its impact upon committed participants is minimal and largely restricted to kinds and amounts of involvement (Roberts and Brodie, 1992). In this respect, as with leisure participation generally, the main social class differences among sports participants is not so much whether they do sport or not but, rather, the particular sports they do and the general 'styles' of participation; including who individuals choose to play with, the clubs they belong to and the facilities they use (Roberts and Brodie, 1992). Skille and Waddington (2006) describe how the

Norwegian Sports City Programme, established in 1992, demonstrates that middle-class young people are far more likely than their working-class counterparts to take part in both conventional sports and 'alternative', lifestyle activities. Working-class boys and girls on the programme were far more likely than their middle-class equivalents to take part in alternative sports only.

The sporting benefits of being young and middle class Primary socialization, especially via the family, is particularly important for sports participation (Bourdieu, 1984). Even recreational engagement in play before more formal engagement with sport, can be crucial. Parents are, of course, significant mediators of social and cultural, as well as economic, capital for sports participation among the young. In their study of Flanders youth over three decades, Scheerder et al. (2005b: 12) noted that 'participation is more frequent for high school boys and girls whose parents (both) actively participate in sports activities' and these youngsters tend to be involved to a higher degree in leisure-time sports than those whose parents do not participate. In this sense, sports participation is socially inherited. In their study of lower primary school children in Australia, Macdonald et al. (2004) found evidence to confirm the commonplace observation that children from single-parent families and families in lower socio-economic groups do not receive the amounts and kinds of support for involvement in sport that their middle-class counterparts do.

Middle-class parents often go to great lengths to ensure that their off-spring enjoy a breadth of abilities and advantages: the middle classes 'invest heavily in the cultivation of the physical capital of their off-spring from a very early age' (Evans, 2004: 101). In doing so, they not only 'inculcate "the right" attitudes, values, motivations, predispositions, representations but also the right physical capital in terms of skills, techniques and understanding' (Evans, 2004: 101). And the sporting benefits of being middle class are not simply related to the 'here and now' of participation. As implied by the notions of social and cultural dimensions of class, the benefits tend to be enduring, particularly in terms of ongoing participation in sport throughout the life-course. Middle-class parents, Roberts and Brodie (1992) suggest, are not only more likely to possess the material resources, or economic capital, to enable their offspring to engage in sport; they are also more likely to be in a position to transfer their social and cultural capital by virtue of being already actively involved themselves and inclined to pass their 'love of sport' on to their children. Hence, young people on middle-class life-courses are the most likely to be introduced to a wider range of sports and to continue to participate at times in their lives when their participation is most vulnerable to disruption (Roberts and Brodie, 1992).

It is apparent, then, that although income and wealth are likely to be the most important mediating variables in some of the sporting activities that it predicts – such as skiing, ocean yachting and even golf – class is also related to people's predispositions; for example, the importance they attach to sport. Thus, being a more prominent feature of middle-class leisure lifestyles, sport is more likely to be a feature of the abilities, experiences and predispositions of middle-class youngsters.

SOCIAL CLASS AND PHYSICAL EDUCATION

What, then, are the implications of an understanding of the relationships between social class, education, leisure and sport for PE? First, in terms of education, middle-class youngsters are more likely to display the characteristics of 'ideal pupils' and, in being compliant in the education process (Meighan, with Siraj-Blatchford, 2003), are more likely to acquiesce in the process of PE. Added to this, sport, like valuing academic success, is a more prominent feature of middle-class lifestyles and, therefore, is more likely to be a cultural resource that middle-class young people bring to school and to PE lessons in particular. In other words, they are more likely to have the skills, abilities and experiences necessary to be involved with and successful in the sports and physical activities characteristic of school PE. In this respect, young people on middle-class life courses are the most likely to be introduced to a wider range of sports by their parents, including those from the range of activity areas (such as swimming, dance, outdoor and adventurous activities) that they are obliged to engage with in PE lessons. In particular, middle-class youngsters are more likely to be comfortable with the typical activities that constitute 'traditional' curricular and extra-curricular PE: team-based games. This is particularly true for middle-class, white, boys. In this manner, secondary-school PE probably serves to 'identify and endorse' (Evans, 2004: 99) the sporting and physical abilities that the parents of middle-class youngsters have invested in differentially. Young people with the experiences, abilities and tastes acquired 'by virtue of' their social class 'may be more or less "able" and willing' (Evans, 2004: 101) to take part in various sports: male PE teachers in deprived neighbourhoods, for example, can frequently be heard to bemoan the fact that all the boys typically want to do is play football (Green, 2003).

SOCIAL CLASS, GENDER AND ETHNICITY AND SPORT AND PHYSICAL EDUCATION

There are two overall points to be made regarding the relationship between class, gender and ethnicity. First, although social class is important this is not necessarily at the expense of other social dynamics, such as gender and ethnicity. Second, there are interactive effects; class-related inequalities are frequently 'compounded by other social characteristics' (Evans, 2004: 102) and, in particular, gender and ethnicity. These interactive effects can be seen, for example, in black males' prominence in football, boxing and track athletics. Thus, the significance of social class is compounded by the ways in which it adds to the likelihood of variation in participation, and more so in some sports than others; for example, swimming, golf, keep-fit and cycling (Coalter, 1996). Put another way, young people's sporting and leisure involvement continues to be subject to the social dynamics of social class, gender and ethnicity, both in isolation and in configuration and the scale of class variation differs substantially depending upon not only age and sex, but also differing kinds of sport activity (Roberts, 1995).

Despite this, Roberts (1999) notes how, over the past decade or so, we have witnessed a blurring of class, gender and, to some extent, ethnic differences in sports participation. Although participation continues to be related to age, sex and social class (Farrell and Shields, 2002), 'it is no longer true that all or nearly all participants are young, male and middle-class' (Roberts, 1996a: 54). While young people (especially young males) on middle-class life trajectories continue to have higher levels of participation than working-class youngsters, the main social class differences are no longer in whether young people play any sport, but how much, how many sports and how often.

CONCLUSION

Class cultures and divisions are evidently surviving the surrounding economic and political changes of recent decades (Roberts, 2001). There has, nevertheless, been a democratization of many aspects of leisure over time, including participation in sport. This is not the same, however, as equality; the middle-classes not only continue to do a wider variety, they also do more of most sporting and physical activities. This inevitably gives the sons (especially) and daughters of the middle-classes a head start in curricular and extra-curricular PE and further reinforces the already greater social and cultural benefits of being middle-class.

This chapter opened by asking the question 'Might it, then, be possible, via PE, to weaken the link across the whole of sport?' and make good the deficiencies in the quantity and quality of working-class children's sports participation. At first sight, the evidence looks promising; not least because, as indicated, among compulsory school-age children the relationship between class and sport participation is rather weak. Nevertheless, there is no escaping the realization that the class–sport relationship strengthens as young people grow up, for a number of reasons. First, the differential stay-on rates in education: 'middle-class children have benefitted academically much more than working class counterparts from the expansion of school and university over the past 20 years' (Evans, 2004: 102). Second, middle-class social and cultural capital gives middle-class youth greater 'staying power'; in effect, they are more likely to develop the kind of wide sporting repertoires that appear to 'lock' people into sport as they move into adulthood (Roberts and Brodie, 1992). In addition, although the relationship between class and sports participation can appear weak while youngsters are at school, class differences tend to be reinforced by the process of PE. In this regard, middle-class youth tend to possess broader experiences of sport and tend also to be 'better' at sport (judged by the origins of elite sports players). They have greater physical/cultural capital. Finally, in monetary terms, it remains the case that 'economic inequalities lead inexorably to inequalities in leisure' (Roberts, 2001: 171) and the middle classes, young and old, can afford more money to do the sports and physical activities (such as attend health and fitness gyms and join sports clubs) that cost money.

So, can PE do anything to supplement, even extend, the physical and cultural resources of working-class youngsters in a manner that might increase the likelihood of their continued involvement in sport beyond school and into adult life? It may be that exposure to the various activity areas that characterize PE curricula can enable youngsters from working-class backgrounds to acquire the broader repertoire of skills and interests that characterize young middle-class males in particular. In doing so, PE has the potential to build upon the evident interest in sport among young people (Roberts, 1996a; Smith, A., 2006; Sport England, 2003a). While young people of school age consider 'sport to be cool' and a prominent aspect of their leisure lives (Sport England, 2003a; 2003b), an opportunity clearly exists. And although class is a significant variable in terms of participation, once people are 'in' sport, the influence of social class changes and becomes less prominent (Coalter, 1999; Roberts and Brodie, 1992). However, it is extremely difficult for schools, let alone particular subjects such as PE, to overcome the disadvantages associated with being working-class.

RECOMMENDED READING

Evans, J. and Davies, B. (2006b) 'Social class and physical education', in D. Kirk, D. Macdonald and M. O'Sullivan (eds), *The Handbook of Physical Education*. London: Sage. pp.796–808.

Roberts, K. and Brodie, D. (1992) *Inner-City Sport: Who Plays and What Are the Benefits?* Culemborg: Giordano Bruno.

NOTE

1 The Sport England surveys of young people between 1994 and 2002 refer to 'out of lessons' sport and physical activities, a category which includes participation during extra-curricular PE (Sport England, 2003b).

Ethnicity and Physical Education

10

This chapter explores three broad aspects of the relationship between ethnicity and PE: first, the involvement of ethnic minority youngsters in PE and sport; second, the difficulties PE teachers have encountered in engaging with such youngsters; and third, whether differences in engagement are merely expressions of differing perspectives on PE and sport among the various ethnic groups or whether, in one form or another, they are better understood as expressions of racism – manifest in the attitudes and practices of individual teachers and pupils and in the social structure and organization of institutions such as schools and sports facilities.

Coverage of the relationship between ethnicity and PE is inevitably uneven. In part, this is an expression of the differential attention paid to particular ethnic groups by those researching PE and sport since the 1980s. Early research imitated the broader sociological interest in the experiences of African-Americans and African-Caribbeans and, in particular, their disproportionate over-representation in top-level sport in the USA and the UK (see, for example, Cashmore, 1982). This research examined the 'push–pull' effects of the stereotypical assumptions held by PE teachers and coaches, as well as 'black' youngsters themselves, regarding the supposedly 'natural' sporting abilities and aptitudes of the latter (see, for example, Jarvie, 1991). The over-representation (or 'stacking') of 'black' youngsters in – and degrees of enthusiasm or reluctance towards – some sports rather than others were viewed as creating particular problems for physical educationalists. Nevertheless, the attitudes and behaviours of African-Caribbean and African-American youngsters, although problematic, were never seen as representing a fundamental challenge to the nature and purposes of conventional sport-based PE programmes. The situation regarding the growing numbers (in absolute and relative terms) of South Asian youngsters of school age in the UK and Europe, however, has been different. Hence, the sustained academic and professional interest in the relationship between these groups and PE. Consequently, while some of the issues addressed in this chapter can be viewed as aspects of broader issues (such as the general significance of religion for participation in PE and sport) and are applicable to ethnic minorities not only in the UK but also internationally, other issues are quite specific to particular ethnic groups.

Before examining the relationship between ethnicity and PE in greater detail, it is necessary to clarify what is meant by the terms 'race' and 'ethnicity', and to identify the central features of the latter.

RACE AND ETHNICITY

Despite the continued widespread use of the term 'race' in the world of sport, this chapter takes as axiomatic the view that the concept of 'race' has no scientific validity – based, as it is, upon superficial, observable, physical differences such as skin colour, facial features and hair texture (Harrison and Belcher, 2006; Trowler with Riley, 1984). Populations cannot be meaningfully subdivided on this basis, not least because geographical boundaries have become less fixed over time as human societies have experienced widespread and massive movements of populations – leading to the growth of 'mixed race' populations. In short, the lines of demarcation between supposed races are, at best, 'profoundly blurred' (Harrison and Belcher, 2006: 741) and, at worst, drawn arbitrarily and ideologically.

'Ethnicity' is a far more useful concept with which to make sense of differences in relatively distinct cultures or ways of life. The term 'ethnicity' draws attention to cultural traditions and heritage (Coakley, 2004). More specifically it focuses upon membership of, and identification with, social groups or collectivities on the basis of country of origin, ancestry and history, family, language, religion and culture and the shared values, beliefs, customs and traditions and lifestyles these generate (Gabe et al., 2004; Kay, 2005; Verma and Darby, 1994). Belonging to a particular ethnic group is, then, best viewed in terms of shared social experiences rather than shared genetic material. The concept of ethnicity helps make sense of the processes by which particular ethnic groups learn to identify themselves as specifically 'black' or Muslim, for example.

While the term 'ethnicity' can legitimately be used to refer to broad ethnic similarities – in, for example, region of origin, religious affiliation and language – it is often (mis)used as an umbrella term to incorporate people whose origins, ways of life and belief systems are quite different. In the USA, for example, 'Hispanic' is used as a generic term to group together all people whose ethnic roots can be traced to Spanish-speaking countries, even though the term applies to such large and diverse groups as Mexican-Americans, Puerto Ricans and Cubans. Similarly, in the UK and elsewhere, 'South Asian' is typically taken to refer to people from Bangladesh, India and Pakistan, who have as many dissimilarities – not least in terms of religious beliefs – as they do similarities. In the UK, use of the term 'ethnic minorities' as a catch-all reference to South Asians, in particular, has tended to lead to 'many bogus assumptions' about 'South Asian people as a single homogenous mass, and about "South Asian culture" as an all-embracing explanation for all the lifestyle characteristics of South Asian people in Britain' (Fleming, 1994: 160). Although Pakistani and Bangladeshi groups are almost entirely Muslim and tend to be more conservative and traditional in cultural terms than Indians (who are more likely to be Sikh, Hindu and other religious groupings), in reality South Asia is a heterogeneous socio-political region constituted of diverse groups of people with frequently dissimilar lifestyles and by no means uniform cultures (Fleming, 1994; Verma and Darby, 1994).

Not only is ethnicity itself less rigid and more dynamic and fluid than categories such as Hispanic or South Asian might be taken to imply, so too is the ethnic character of particular countries and regions. While ethnicity tends to be used as a static and rigidly defined term, it is more adequately employed in relational terms to refer to the culture of particular groups at particular points in time and in particular places. Used in this manner, ethnicity indicates the manner in which the religious, language and family dimensions of particular ethnic cultures develop as a consequence of the economic and social interdependencies between ethnic groups within a 'host' country.

Diversity and integration among ethnic groups

Debates about 'race' and ethnicity tend to be characterized by exaggerated, often erroneous, claims – especially during periods of increasing social polarization such as that currently characterizing relationships between 'Muslims and non-Muslims, Islam and the West' (Benn and Dagkas, 2006: 184) in the UK and the USA. Ironically, this polarization is occurring at a time when very many western countries are, like the UK, 'more culturally diverse than ever before' (Kay, 2005: 97). Britain, for example, is said to be becoming 'a 'mosaic' society' in which complexity and diversity are the rule' (Diamond, 2007: 91). The introduction for the first time of the category of 'mixed race' in the 2001 UK Census reflected the growing complexity of the western world in which increasing levels of migration are a significant development. In the UK, the Asian/British-Asian ethnic grouping constituted half of the non-white population in the UK in 2001, while Black/Black-British made up 25 per cent and mixed race accounted for nearly 15 per cent of the ethnic minority population and 1.2 per cent (680,000) of the overall population. While mixed race is a very small proportion of the non-white population of the UK (which stood at over 4.6 million and approximately 9 per cent of the total in 2001) overall, it is the fastest growing ethnic minority group (Smith, L., 2006).

Compounding this complexity is the fact that minority ethnic groups also differ in terms of whether they were born in the host country or migrated there, their migration histories and their social class, economic, educational and religious profiles (Platt, 2005). The bulk of the growth of Britain's established minority ethnic groups since the 1970s has been 'through reproduction rather than primary immigration' (Platt, 2005: 699). Just under half (46 per cent) of Muslims living in the UK in 2001 had been born there. Unsurprisingly, diversity becomes more marked within the second and successive generations of minority ethnic groups. Overall, many developed countries are experiencing 'a condition of super-diversity' (Vertovec, 2007: 94) exacerbated by immigration from a broader range of countries. In Western Europe, increasing numbers of immigrants have come from Eastern Europe. Alongside the relatively well-established African-Caribbean and Asian communities living in the UK, for example, are newer, smaller groups including Romanians, Poles, Kurds, Iraqis, Algerians among the 40 national or ethnic groups, each comprising over 10,000 people, in London alone (Vertovec, 2007).

During the relatively large-scale immigration in the decades following the Second World War – as various industries actively sought labour from the Caribbean and India, as well as Europe, in the period of post-war reconstruction (Platt, 2005) – it was commonplace to depict host societies, such as the UK, as culturally homogeneous and immigrants, correspondingly, as 'bearers of an "alien" (and potentially "disruptive") culture' (Elliott, 1996, cited in Kay, 2005: 93). This gave rise to what became known as the 'host-immigrant thesis': the belief that 'in the long term the immigrant population would relinquish their own values and adopt those of the host' (Kay, 2005: 93), assimilating the dominant culture(s) by adopting the patterns of behaviour and ways of life of the dominant groups (Fleming, 1994). This was naively optimistic, not to say ethnocentric. Rather than assimilating to host countries, many migrants have tended to remain closely tied to the cultures of their countries of origin and only partly integrated into the host society (Nagel, 2006). In this regard, policies aimed at creating a single, 'common' culture in either the UK or the USA, for example, were bound to fail, because immigrant groups did not consider that 'belonging' required cultural conformity (Nagel, 2006). The fact that the majority of every religious group in the 2001 UK Census identified themselves as British, English, Scottish or Welsh, with approximately three-quarters of Hindus, Muslims and Sikhs giving one of these British identities, appears to substantiate this view. It seems that, in practice, 'outsider' minority populations have managed to preserve many of their own traditions in one form or another by drawing upon the cultural capital of their ethnic communities in order to establish and maintain their identity in western contexts.

Despite the heterogeneity and relative cultural distinctiveness of minority ethnic groups, cultural identities are inevitably dynamic and unstable. The interplay of interdependent 'host' and 'immigrant' cultures has, inevitably, led to some changes in both dominant and minority ethnic ways of life. As a result, far from becoming culturally homogeneous, Britain, like very many countries, is becoming ever more culturally diverse. Hence the possibility, even probability, that the diverse range of minority groups can differ more markedly from each other than from the larger white population (Kay, 2007).

In terms of the religious dimension to ethnic groupings in the UK, the 2001 Census shows that while the British population is more culturally diverse than ever before, White Christians remain the largest single group by far. In Great Britain, 40 million people (nearly seven in 10) described their ethnicity as White and their religion as Christian; this included majorities of Black people and those from mixed-race or mixed-ethnic backgrounds. Among 'other faiths', the largest groups were Pakistani Muslims and Indian Hindus followed by Indian Sikhs, Bangladeshi Muslims and White Jews. Some faith communities were concentrated in particular ethnic groups – the vast majority of Sikhs, for example, were Indian – while others were more widely dispersed. Muslims remain the second largest religious group in Britain (Sport England, 2000b) at almost 3 per cent of the population (somewhere between 1.5 million-strong [Burke, 2006] and 2 million [Benn, 1996a]).

Muslim groups are similarly prominent elsewhere in Europe, making up approximately 9 per cent of France (5–6 million), almost 4 per cent of Germany (3 million) and approximately 2, 3 and 5 per cent of Norway (80,000), Sweden (300,000) and Denmark (270,000) respectively. Overall, Muslims make up approximately 4 per cent of Europe's population. The Muslim populations of the UK, in particular, and the West, in general, are growing rapidly. The growth of Muslim communities in the West is hardly surprising given that Islam is the fastest growing religion in the world and that diaspora communities of Muslims are growing in many western countries (Dagkas and Benn, 2006). The majority of the increasing ethnic minority population in the UK 'is Asian of Islamic heritage with their origins in Pakistan or Bangladesh' (Benn and Dagkas, 2006: 184). Indeed, 95 per cent of British Muslims are of Asian origin and approximately a half (750,000) of specifically Pakistani origin. One consequence of this rapid growth is that those issues in PE that tend to be correlated to the religious dimension of ethnicity are likely to become more prevalent across Europe and, indeed, anywhere where Islam is growing.

Along with the evident cultural diversity of western societies such as the UK and the USA, one of the most striking features of the 2001 UK Census is the youthful make-up of minority ethnic groups. While they constitute approximately 8 per cent of the population as a whole, ethnic groups make up roughly 12 per cent of young people. Alongside rising numbers of youngsters of South Asian heritage (Benn and Dagkas, 2006), the 2001 UK Census revealed more than 50 per cent of the rapidly growing 'mixed race' category to be under 16 years of age, making it the fastest growing ethnic minority group in Britain. In the USA, the national census reveals a decreasing proportion of the population as 'white' (down to approximately two-thirds from three-quarters) with Latinos the fastest growing minority group. Overall, ethnic minorities constitute an increasingly significant proportion of the state school population not only in the USA (Harrison and Belcher, 2006) and the UK but in many western countries.

Kay (2005: 107) notes how 'the power of tradition, and the pressure for change' is reflected in the multiple and diverse identities of contemporary British-born youngsters of South Asian heritage. In this regard, Warikoo (2005) found that Indo-Caribbean young men and women in London and New York drew from multiple influences on their identities and, in the case of boys, often chose to distance themselves from an Indian identity. The particular mixes of social identities experienced, for example, by young South Asian Muslim men and women inevitably result in 'cultures of hybridity' (Dagkas and Benn, 2006: 22).

Two of the most significant aspects of ethnicity are religion and family, and it is worth saying a little more about these.

KEY DIMENSIONS OF ETHNICITY

Religion

The popular view is that religion and culture tend to be conflated (Kay, 2005: 95), because for peoples with strong religious attachment the two can be so strongly intertwined. Where religion does not have a substantial impact upon the ways of life of particular groups (in the case of African-Caribbean, British and Chinese Christians, for example) this tends to be because religiosity – the degree to which people regard themselves as religious – is relatively weak or the religion itself (Christianity, for example) does not strongly circumscribe many aspects of people's lifestyles, including leisure and sport.

While there may be room for manouevre and accommodation between culture and religion, this is less likely to occur in the case of Muslims for whom there is usually little or no separation of religious and secular activities.

In such cases, religiosity impacts upon whole swathes of everyday life. Muslim religiosity impacts, for example, upon the way youngsters in particular are constrained by their families to retain cultural distinctiveness by being 'visibly Muslim'; that is, by adopting and adhering strictly to Islamic dress codes (Benn and Dagkas, 2006).

In case one were inclined to conclude that the requirements of Islam are antithetical to the practice of PE and sport, it is worth dwelling upon the ambiguities that surround Islam in relation to participation in sport and exercise and the 'complex and contradictory influences' (Kay, 2005: 100) which South Asian Muslim girls and young women, in particular, are subject to. According to Benn (1996a: 9), 'There is much support for physical activity in Islam; for example, care of the body, and exercise and promotion of healthy lifestyles are important for males and females, conditional upon Islamic requirements for modesty[1] being respected by young people after puberty, including adapted dress and single-sex activities.' Muslims are not even forbidden by Islam to participate in sport as such (Benn, 1996a; Kay, 2005). Indeed, the women in Kay's (2005: 104) study embraced sport 'enthusiastically' and, for the most part, family members supported their involvement, with the proviso that participation conformed to norms regarding acceptable behaviour for young Muslim women. Similarly, many female Muslim students in Dagkas and Benn's study (2006: 34) viewed PE 'as an enjoyable subject, where they had fun'. Overall, while exercise and sport are condoned, in principle, by Islam, they are 'severely restricted by cultural restrictions on women' in particular (Kay, 2005: 110). In practical terms, constraints on participation 'arise from the circumstances in which girls and women can participate, for unless they are concealed from the male gaze, girls participating in sport will infringe the religious requirement and cultural expectation of modesty in females' (Kay, 2005: 104). Dance, for example, 'is viewed very differently by many Muslim and Hindu people because of the religious traditions surrounding the activity in Hinduism and perceptions of dance as a sexually provocative activity among some people from the Muslim community' (Benn and Dagkas, 2006: 182). Walseth's (2006: 91) study of young Norwegian Muslim women found that 'young women, and not men, are sometimes sanctioned and sometimes even harassed by members of their ethnic group, for participating in sport'. Pressures towards conformity are, on the one hand, a matter of religious constraint and, on the other, social respectability and the family acts as a 'conduit for both' (Kay, 2005: 105).

One of the most pressing concerns among Asian families has to do with the likelihood that PE and sports facilities might not be suitable for Muslim girls because as they fail to provide sufficient privacy or female-only sessions. To be suitable, sporting facilities must have female-only access, sports programmes need to be run by female instructors, and the usual dress codes associated with PE and sport need to be changed or relaxed (Lowrey and Kay, 2005).

Family

Along with religion, the centrality of the family and family life in the subcultures of minority ethnic groups should not be overlooked or underestimated. Nevertheless, family life reflects a good deal of change alongside evident continuities. Berthoud (2000) talks of three main patterns of diversity in family formation on a continuum from 'old-fashioned values' through to 'modern individualism', with Caribbeans ahead of the trend and South Asians – especially Pakistanis and Bangladeshis – behind it.

Although the significance of the family has as much to do with the cultural traditions of particular regions as with religious doctrine, family is, nevertheless, a particularly central institution among Muslims, in particular, as well as South Asians in general. Families can exert tremendous influence over their members (Lowrey and Kay, 2005). The interests of the family have a tendency to override concern for individual freedoms and the prominence of the family in the lives of Muslims has especially profound consequences for the young and for women (Kay, 2005). Therefore, the lives of young Muslims in Kay's (2005: 110) research tended to be more localized, much more home based and involved a good deal less contact with friends as well as more time spent in the company of immediate family, than youngsters from other ethnic groups. This persistent feature of South Asian cultures, in general, is frequently compounded by family perceptions of their young people as the next generation of owners and an important human resource for family businesses (Lowrey and Kay, 2005). Although based on small-scale, in-depth research with a particular group of women, the findings from Lowrey and Kay's study supported those of Verma and Darby's (1994) research of more than a decade earlier. Nonetheless, it is important to bear in mind that there is enormous diversity in how families interpret Islam (Kay, 2007) (see, for example, Walseth and Fasting, 2003), and religiosity has significant ramifications for young people's relative autonomy and that of girls and young women in particular.

In the light of the concerns over the past decade or more with Muslim girls' tendency to disengage from PE, it is worth dwelling upon the particularity of young Muslim women.

Muslim girls and young women The gendered structure and 'privileged position of males as the family's defining members' (Kay, 2005: 96) is a feature of South Asian families in the UK. Different forms and degrees of freedom tend to be made available to young Muslim men and women by their families, depending on levels of religiosity. When compared with non-Muslim youth, young Muslim women in more traditional Islamic families, following a more traditional interpretation of Islam (Kay, 2007), are more likely to spend a high proportion of time in the home and seldom travel very far from it, and almost never independently (Kay, 2005). The roles ascribed to females in more traditional families (especially Muslim families of South Asian origin) continue to constrain women, in particular, especially 'the sense of surveillance' (Kay, 2005) that young women can experience. South Asian females, generally, tend to have less time that they could call their own and are under greater constraints in their use of it, tending to be relied upon to perform 'a range of family, social and domestic responsibilities' (Verma and Darby, 1994: 116) far more than males.

Religion and family – in isolation but especially when combined – have a crucial impact on daily life for South Asians, but especially for Muslims of Pakistani and Bangladeshi origin. The relative lack of involvement in sport and PE among South Asian girls in particular is best explained in terms of the constraints and conflicts of religious orthodoxies and family values (Flintoff and Scraton, 2006). Religion, whichever one, is 'likely to be more important to females than males' (Verma and Darby, 1994: 96), while parents and family are likely to affect behaviour from all ethnic groups. Nevertheless, whatever the impact of religion and family, it is invariably males who possess greater amounts of freedom.

Despite the significance of religion and family in enabling continuity of ethnic traditions, it is inevitable that the character of South Asian family life will develop as a consequence of being located in dominant cultures that differ in some significant respects to its own. Indeed, South Asian (especially Muslim) family life appears to be changing in Britain, in part because of the increasing numbers of young women in these families who are achieving educational qualifications (Kay, 2005) – with all that entails in terms of movement away from traditional family values among all minority ethnic groups and especially among younger generations. Kay (2005) highlights a number of changes in the lives of the growing number of young women who are staying longer in education and obtaining educational qualifications. Developments in family life and educational experiences appear to be placing young South Asian Muslims 'in the vanguard of changing South Asian ethnic identities in Britain' (Kay, 2005: 99). The young women in Lowrey and Kay's (2005) study appeared to be fusing the Islamic traditions of their ethnic origins 'with elements of the majority culture' and this was reflected in a 'combination of small indications of movement towards more liberal lifestyles counterbalanced by ... Islamic teachings' (Kay, 2005: 111). Young Pakistani and Bangladeshi women educated in the UK (and the western world) have acquired host language and qualifications not available to their parents and 'most have been exposed to Western cultural values as well as the traditional Muslim values of their parents and families' (Kay, 2005: 99). In this regard, a potentially profound shift in the life patterns of minority ethnic women from South Asian Muslim communities may well be taking place. Nonetheless, religion and family, currently remain central to the construction of young Muslim women's identities in particular. Indeed, recent research (Mirza et al., 2007) suggests that the younger generations appear to be adhering more strongly to Islamic values than the older generations, in the form of a growing (and politicized) religiosity. Kay (2007) suggests that this may be indicative of a strengthening independent Muslim identity rather than a greater level of assimilation.

The following sections explore the relationship between ethnicity and PE and sport.

ETHNICITY AND PHYSICAL EDUCATION

Claims about the relationship between ethnicity and PE are very similar to those for sport, because sport lies at the heart of conventional PE programmes. Prominent among these claims has been the belief that sport serves as a model of the extent to which 'racial equality' can be attained in society. On this view, (school) sport operates as a social 'glue', facilitating the integration of ethnic minorities into dominant (typically white) cultures while providing a valuable avenue for upward mobility for some – and for African-Americans and African-Caribbeans in particular.

Despite the intuitive plausibility of such an egalitarian ideology, various studies have demonstrated that PE and sport frequently reinforce, rather than dissipate, pervasive racial stereotypes regarding the 'natural' sporting abilities of some ethnic minorities, and 'black' youngsters in particular (see Coakley, 2004). Indeed, far from breaking down barriers and encouraging tolerance between cultures, PE and sport often serve to 'maintain and fortify ethnic boundaries' (Fleming, 1991: 36). Sport acts as a vehicle for legitimizing violence (Fleming, 1991) and racist provocation and taunting (Johnson, 2000) towards young Muslims, in particular, and South Asian ethnic groups, in general, as their apparent physical and sporting deficiencies and alienation are interpreted as confirming their general social inferiority. In addition, the marginalization of African-American and African-Caribbean youngsters in education, and their tendency to disengage with the academic elements of schooling, is often exacerbated by PE. Physical education teachers and sports coaches, and the youngsters themselves, view sport as one area of school life where they can experience success and avoid the kinds of failure they typically experience in other areas of the curriculum. Consequently, PE teachers have tended to channel African-American and African-Caribbean youngsters towards sport per se and some sports in particular (and even particular positions within those sports – usually those that place a premium on speed and power). In doing so, teachers and coaches stand accused of perpetuating stereotypical myths of the 'black sportsman', while at the same time depressing academic attainment and motivation and encouraging 'black' youngsters towards narrow – and ultimately fruitless – career routes (Carroll, 1998b; Cashmore, 1990; Coakley, 2004; Jarvie, 1991).

The disproportionate numbers of African-Caribbeans in American football, soccer, track athletics, basketball and boxing confirm that sport can act as an avenue for social mobility for a very small minority of ethnic youngsters. Nevertheless, because they perpetuate stereotypical assumptions regarding ethnic youngsters' 'natural' suitability for, or predispositions towards, some sports over others, PE teachers (and coaches) are said to limit the opportunities for youngsters from these groups to develop general sporting skills (Coakley, 2004). This is particularly true among youngsters from ethnic minorities for whom sport is not so significant a cultural practice. Their limited childhood opportunities for play and sporting experiences result in a restricted vocabulary of basic motor and sporting skills (Fleming, 1991). Consequently, their opportunities for developing the relevant skills are restricted to PE lessons (Fleming, 1991) where any perceived deficiencies merely serve to reinforce stereotypical assumptions regarding ethnic youngsters' (in)abilities. In this manner, PE teachers' assumptions about young people from particular ethnic minorities are said to impact quite profoundly upon their future sports participation.

As the proportion of South Asians and East African Asians in the UK population has grown since the 1970s, so too have tensions between youngsters from Asian ethnic groups and PE teachers. While the issue for teachers has not been how to incorporate black youngsters into sport but, rather, how to incorporate them into the rest of education, the reverse has been true for South Asian youngsters, in general, and Muslims, in particular. At the heart of the problematic relations between PE teachers in the UK and South Asian ethnic pupils lies the issue of cultural conflict and, in particular, the tension between what are supposedly British or Western values and those of Islam. Requiring pupils from ethnic minority groups to adopt sports and activities historically and traditionally associated with white, middle-class young men and women has, almost inevitably, led to disengagement and alienation among some ethnic groups – most notably South Asians Muslims and, to a lesser extent, African-Caribbeans. The next section rehearses some of the issues that surfaced in PE as a consequence of these conflicts of culture and PE teachers' attempts to resolve them.

The 'issue' of ethnicity in PE

In the USA, in the latter decades of the twentieth century, PE teachers increasingly confronted with, for example, African-American pupils who favoured some sports (such as basketball), sometimes to the exclusion of other sports, inevitably viewed them as not only disinterested and uncooperative but as lacking the necessary skills for those other sports; in other words, lacking competence rather than merely lacking motivation (Harrison and Belcher, 2006). Consequently, PE teachers in the USA seem to hold low expectations of ethnic minority pupils' likely achievements in PE generally while, at the same time, hold high expectations of their performances in specific sports (Harrison and Belcher, 2006).

Similarly, the response of PE teachers in the UK in the 1970s and 1980s (especially in inner-city schools) to finding themselves increasingly 'confronted with an unfamiliar "client" group ... inevitably seen as disturbing the status quo' (Fleming, 1994: 161) was to treat them as a problem (Benn and Dagkas, 2006; Carroll and Hollinshead, 1993) to be overcome or endured. While ethnic pupils took the view that their PE teachers were being racist and grossly unfair, the teachers themselves claimed that, far from being racist, they were simply upholding the traditions of PE and, in so doing, treating all groups equitably. As if to compound the problem, PE teachers argued that 'giving way' to religious beliefs would amount to a form of positive discrimination likely to be seen as grossly unfair by other groups, while, in the process, making the teachers' job more difficult in the future.

Areas of 'conflict' between PE teachers and ethnic minority pupils in the UK have increasingly revolved around South Asian – especially Pakistani and Bangladeshi – youngsters. Many conflicts have centred upon issues related to appropriate clothing, religious festivals such as Ramadan and extra-curricular PE and, within these, matters of dress, swimming, diet, fasting and parental attitudes towards sport and out-of-school activities. In the following extract from his research, Carroll (1998b: 325–6) provides a summary of the conflicts and dilemmas inherent in what he referred to as the cultural 'clash' between PE teachers and South Asian pupils:

> The teachers were trying to maintain many of the traditional values in PE, such as changing into suitable PE kit, showering after lessons, developing ability and offering extra-curricular activities, and making a full effort all the time. Not fully understanding the Muslim and South Asian culture, they had expected the Bangladeshi and Pakistani children to conform to their value system. It was in fact a simple integrationist policy. After all, they had met resistance before from many white English working class children and the pupils had been made to conform. As the number of ethnic minority children grew this policy brought increasing pupil embarrassment, anger and hostility and eventual conflict.

At the heart of much of the ongoing tension between South Asian pupils and PE lies a clash between PE traditions and Islamic culture. Dagkas and Benn (2006) found, for example, that while the Greek and British Muslim girls and young women in their study (in their early and late teenage years respectively) held positive views towards PE, their participation in extra-curricular PE was nevertheless restricted by their consciousness of Islamic requirements – more so among the British than the Greek young women.

Some of the issues resulting from the tension between the conventions of PE and Islam have implications for both sexes, such as the demands for high levels of physical activity in PE during periods when the physical condition of Muslim youngsters is weakened as a consequence of the requirements of the festival of Ramadan for fasting in daylight hours. Other orthodox PE practices have ramifications for girls, in particular. Over the past decade or more, increasing numbers of researchers have turned their attention to Muslim communities concentrating on young Muslim women, in particular. It seems that among young British Muslim women, religious consciousness grows during adolescence and, as Islamic identity strengthens, new and greater tensions arise in various areas of their lives but especially as regards PE and sport (Dagkas and Benn, 2006). Studies have tended to focus upon the constraints that can affect young Muslim women's participation in PE and sport and 'how these are related to Islam' (Kay, 2007). The conventional games kit (including short skirts or knickers and T-shirts) and expectations regarding changing and showering, for example, tend to be a problem for all girls regardless of ethnicity (see Chapter 8). However, this is exacerbated in the case of Muslim youngsters because such requirements conflict with the need for modesty of dress on the part of girls and the requirement that arms and legs be covered. Student teachers in Benn's (1996a: 10) research recollected surviving the conflict between their religious obligations and the demands of PE using a variety of 'coping strategies' which included 'managing to cover their legs by wearing longer games skirts and socks; missing PE or feigning sickness to avoid showers; and rushing into the toilet to get changed'.

Despite their initial inclination to resist altering their 'traditional' practices, PE teachers have felt compelled to amend their policies and practices to meet the constraints posed by religiosity in particular. These constraints range from pupils being reluctant to participate to parents withdrawing their children from PE. So, over the course of the last 20 years or so, a shift has taken place in PE teachers' practices, if not necessarily their attitudes, towards Muslim pupils' engagement with PE (Carroll, 1998b). The NCPE in England and Wales requires PE teachers to accommodate religious and cultural requirements and this, as well as the hard-learned lessons of several decades of teaching increasing numbers of South Asian Muslim pupils, has impacted upon the practice of PE. Examples of the ways in which PE teachers have adapted their practices to cater for Muslim youngsters in particular include:

- more single-sex activities
- a relaxation of dress codes (allowing the wearing of tracksuit trousers and shalwars and secured hijabs)
- the introduction of less strenuous activities such as table tennis during Ramadan and less provocative dances
- making showering optional
- allowing greater individual privacy in changing and showering arrangements where possible and incorporating such arrangements in new sports buildings
- amending expectations towards vigorous physical exertion
- the incorporation of greater choice of activities among older pupils (Benn, 1996a; Benn and Dagkas, 2006; Carroll, 1998b; Dagkas and Benn, 2006).

Despite such adaptations, the Loughborough Partnership (2005) have reported 'mixed evidence' that School Sports Partnerships have been successful in targeting specific groups such as girls and young women and black and ethnic minorities in schools where these categories of pupils comprised the majority, or a substantial minority, of the school population.

Before concluding this chapter, it is worth reflecting on research related to patterns of sports participation among minority ethnic groups, because the evidence flags up a number of issues regarding the relationship between PE and sport, as far as ethnic minorities are concerned.

ETHNICITY AND SPORT

Although Sport England's (2000b: 37) national survey reported 'relatively low levels of sports participation among ethnic minority groups', the gap in participation rates between ethnic groups is not as considerable as might be expected. The overall *frequent* participation rate among ethnic minority groups in 1999/2000 was 40 per cent compared with a national average of 46 per cent. Nevertheless, there is 'considerable variation in the levels of participation between different ethnic groups, between men and women and between different sports' (Sport England, 2000b: 37). Indeed, in recent years, the 'gulf in participation' between white adults and ethnic minority groups in England appears to have grown (Sport England, 2005: 4): in 2002, '44 percent of white adults participated in at least one activity (excluding walking) compared to 35 percent of adults from an ethnic minority group' (Sport England, 2005: 4).

Despite the evident differences, the Sport England (2000b) survey confirmed the findings from other, much smaller-scale studies (see, for example, Verma and Darby, 1994) to the effect that the picture of participation among ethnic groups is more complex than common-sense, stereotypical generalizations suggest. Even though they 'tend to congregate in their own districts, teams, clubs and ... groups' (Roberts, 1999: 217), many ethnic minorities are by no means under-represented in what Roberts (1999: 217) refers to as 'most "normal" forms of British leisure'. This is particularly true for Chinese and African-Caribbean males (Verma and Darby, 1994). It is less true for young Asian Muslims. In broad terms, Sport England's (2000b) findings confirmed Verma and Darby's smaller-scale research in the mid-1990s in which Chinese and White British adults were the most active sports participants and Pakistani and Bangladeshi the least. Among the minority ethnic groups, the Sport England (2000b) survey found that, when walking is excluded, Black African (60 per cent) and Black 'Other' (80 per cent) males have higher frequent or regular participation rates than the national average, with Black Caribbean (45 per cent) Bangladeshi (46 per cent) and Pakistani (42 per cent) males less likely to participate in sport than men generally.

With regard to school-age youngsters, the North-West Development Agency's (NWDA) (2005) study of Year 9 pupils in the north-west of England found youngsters from 'Asian' communities less likely to participate in sport than any other group. This was particularly so in relation to extra-curricular sport (67 per cent compared with 73 per cent for white people) and sports club membership (51 per cent and 62 per cent respectively) among the 13–14 year-olds in the study. The picture is similar in the USA, where Trost (2006) points to studies indicating that white children reported higher levels of sports participation than African-American or Hispanic children.

The overall participation rates also camouflage substantial discrepancies between males and females. The rates for ethnic minority males in Sport England's survey were 49 per cent compared with the national average for men of 54 per cent and for ethnic minority females 32 per cent compared with the national average for women of 39 per cent (Sport England, 2000b). The survey highlighted significant differences between men and women within particular ethnic groups and between different sports and studies in the UK (see, for example, Carroll, 1993; Sport England, 2000b; Verma and Darby, 1994) and the USA (Trost, 2006) reveal how, overall, adult males from each ethnic group participate in sport more than females. In Sport England's (2000b) survey, the gap in frequent participation between men and women was more marked in some ethnic groups than others. The gap between

Bangladeshi, Black African and Pakistani men and women was 27, 26 and 20 percentage points respectively; especially important because these groups are among the lowest participants in general. Although the difference in levels of participation between men and women in the Black Other ethnic group was especially wide, at 35 percentage points, this group had relatively high participation rates in general (Sport England, 2000b). In Verma and Darby's (1994) research, variations between ethnic groups were minimal as far as males' involvement with sport in their leisure time was concerned. Among females, however, there was far greater variety: only African and East African Asian women indicated sport as their first choice leisure activity. Similarly, in Carroll's (1993) study, 40–50 per cent of Bangladeshi/Pakistani/African women were not involved in physical activity compared with 33 per cent of Indian, 25 per cent of Caribbean and 20 per cent of White British women.

In terms of the kinds of sports minority ethnic groups undertake in both the UK and the USA, there are substantial differences. African-Caribbeans, for example, are hugely over-represented and Asians under-represented in athletics and soccer in England. Athletics and basketball are deemed more appropriate for African-American and African-Caribbean males in the USA, with activities such as golf and hockey seen as more appropriate for European-Americans (Harrison and Belcher, 2006). In England, ethnic minorities' levels of participation in walking are significantly below those for the population as a whole. At one extreme, 19 per cent of Bangladeshis take long walks regularly compared with 44 per cent of the population as a whole (Sport England, 2000b). Similarly, ethnic minorities – and all black groups and Pakistani and Bangladeshi women, in particular – are far less likely to take part in swimming and cycling than is the population as a whole. Irrespective of ethnic group, football, snooker and pool were the preserve of males in Sport England's (2000b) survey, while keep-fit, aerobics and dancing were the province of females. For males, football regularly tends to be the major team game overall, in England, irrespective of ethnicity and is particularly popular among 'black' males. Interestingly, participation in football among South Asians is around the national average and, in the case of Pakistani men, above the average. While by no means the preserve of one particular ethnic groups, cricket, badminton and basketball were particularly popular among Asian, Chinese, African-Caribbean and 'black' males respectively (Sport England, 2000b). As if to illustrate the complexity of patterns of participation, and the attendant danger of turning empirical trends into stereotypes, pool and snooker tend to have a reasonable following among some ethnic minority female groups (Sport England, 2000b; Verma and Darby, 1994). Similarly, many activities are relatively more popular with females in particular ethnic minority groups than the population overall. Basketball, for example, was more popular with Black Caribbean and Black African females, cricket with Pakistani women, and weight training with black females. Keep-fit/aerobics/yoga was by far the most popular activity after walking among all women except Bangladeshis.

Despite the complexity and diversity of patterns of participation, sex and ethnicity combine to greatly affect participation in sport. To be female and a Muslim, Hindu or Sikh from any of the South Asian groups – Bangladeshi, Pakistani and Indian – is likely to result in a lower participation rate in sport. However, change may well be occurring in the rates and forms of participation among female Muslims and, where this is so, it appears to be being driven by increased involvement in 'lifestyle activities' (see Chapter 7). Dagkas and Benn (2006: 33), for example, observe that Greek Muslim young women in their study were more likely to participate at weekends and 'preferred a more relaxed way of exercising, for example visiting local fitness clubs or playing informal games with their friends'.

Patterns of participation highlight, above all, the significance of religiosity for sports participation. The more emphasis is placed upon religion among particular ethnic groups, the lower the levels and rates of participation in sport tend to be (Verma and Darby, 1994). White British and Chinese Christians and non-believers participated more than Muslims, Hindus and Sikhs. This is also true elsewhere: in Germany, for example, 'immigrants from Islamic cultures' are 'among those least active in sports' (Pfister and Reeg, 2006: 11).

There is also a gender dimension to the significance of religiosity for sports participation similar to that found in PE. Although participation among women (but, interestingly, not the desire to participate) decreased as importance placed on religion increased, the same was not true for men. It seems that being a young Muslim woman and participating in sport challenges the boundaries of their ethnic identities (Benn, 2005), because it draws attention to women behaving in an unfeminine manner when sport is not viewed as an expression of respectable femininity (Walseth, 2006).

When added together, ethnicity and gender are a particularly potent mix in relation to participation in sport as well as PE. This is exacerbated when configured with other social dynamics, such as social class and disability (see Chapters 9 and 11). Burgess (2007) for example, observes that young people with a disability from ethnic minorities are least likely to be engaged in sport. While the significance of social class on levels of participation among ethnic minorities is relatively under-explored, the correlation between low levels of participation and the disproportionate over-representation among the lower socio-economic groups of South Asians suggests that it is entirely plausible that social class is an important explanatory variable. Indeed, as indicated in Chapter 9, the interactive effects of ethnicity and social class is evident in the form of black males' prominence in sports such as football, boxing and athletics.

In their study of participation in Germany, Pfister and Reeg (2006: 11) observed that religion, social class and ethnic cultures generally seem to 'combine to form an insurmountable obstacle, frequently making sporting activities impossible for the parents as well as the children'. This is unsurprising given that a feature of the increasingly culturally diverse countries of the western world is the large socio-economic inequalities experienced by minority ethnic groups.

CONCLUSION

Although differences remain in the levels and forms of participation in PE and sport among young people, Roberts (1999) notes a blurring, in recent decades, of not only class and gender but also ethnic differences in the kinds of sports and physical activities participated in, as well as the variety within and between all these groups. In this regard, British Muslim young women in Dagkas and Benn's (2006) study suggested that life has become more free (in sporting as well as other cultural arenas) for younger generations.

Nevertheless, differences between ethnic groups' involvement in PE and sport remain. Depending on their degree of assimilation into British culture and religiosity, South Asian youngsters' involvement in PE tends to be differentially affected by Islamic guidance on issues like dress and the degree of segregation between the sexes (Benn, 1996a). For girls and devout Muslims, PE is frequently perceived as threatening individuals' 'ability to live their lives as practising Muslims' (Benn, 1996b: 5).

The shortage of teachers from ethnic minority groups in British state schools entering and staying in the teaching profession in Britain (Benn, 1996a; Benn and Dagkas, 2006) and the USA (Harrison and Belcher, 2006) may well exacerbate the tension between minority pupils and their PE teachers. It has been amply demonstrated that newly qualified or beginning teachers think and act in terms of their own sporting and school PE experiences (see Chapter 12) and, given that they are an almost entirely White group, PE teachers in the Western world are unlikely to be prepared for teaching minority ethnic pupils especially in those, typically inner-city, schools where they constitute the majority of pupils (Ennis, 1995).

While ethnicity heightens or exacerbates gender differences, it seems that 'changes in family life and educational experiences place Muslim young women in the vanguard of changing South Asian ethnic identities in Britain' (Kay, 2005: 99). There may, then, be grounds for optimism regarding the levels of participation of Muslim youngsters in PE and sport, especially to the extent that more girls in particular stay on in education for longer. Nevertheless, in England and Wales, the potentially positive impact (on their sporting participation) of ethnic minority girls remaining in education may well be undermined by the development of faith schools. In addition, their increasing involvement in education may not lead to improved access or retention of Muslim women in teaching PE and sport, because of the incompatibility of their requirements for same-sex tuition and the compulsory mixed-sex nature of teacher training (Benn and Dagkas, 2006).

This chapter began by asking whether the differences in the degrees of engagement with PE and sport between and within ethnic groups are simply expressions of differences in cultural perspectives on PE and sport, or whether, in one form or another, they are expressions of individual or structural and institutional racism? In reality, the 'ethnic penalty' (Platt, 2005) that youngsters from some minority groups experience is a consequence of a configuration of all these. In other words, the relatively lower levels of engagement with, and alienation from, PE (and sport) of some youngsters is explainable in terms of:

- structural effects in terms of differences between ethnic groups in relation to education, health and fitness, income and so forth. Those minority groups who value education, for example, tend to place a low premium on PE and sport for their children. In this regard, Muslim young women in Dagkas and Benn's (2006: 33) studies indicated that participation in extra-curricular PE and sport would be problematic 'if it interfered with "academic progress"'. Similarly, South Asian Muslims tend to be disproportionately over-represented in the lower social classes and they, in turn, are the least likely to be involved in sport
- structural effects in the form of institutionalized ethnocentrism embedded in the history of PE – in the form of conventional PE programmes (in terms of the particular sporting activities that dominate curricula) and practices (such as specific teaching and changing arrangements, and facilities) – that amount to ethnocentric PE processes (Carroll, 1998b)
- discrimination on the part of teachers in the form of the ideological perspectives of PE teachers regarding, for example, the abilities and predispositions of particular ethnic groups and the nature and purposes of PE
- discrimination on the part of pupils that discourage engagement by fellow pupils from particular ethnic groups.

When set alongside the varying culturally specific claims on youngsters from, for example, their families and the inevitable differences in the perspectives on PE and sport of particular ethnic youngsters, it is debatable which of these factors is most influential among particular ethnic groups and in particular schools and PE settings. What is not debatable, however, is that differences in engagement with PE continue to exist and that while White British, Chinese and, to a lesser extent, African-Caribbeans are likely to engage with conventional PE programmes, South Asian Muslims are far less likely to do so. Neither is it debatable that in many countries (such as Britain, the USA and Canada) African-Caribbean (Solomon and Tarc, 2003) and South Asian Muslim pupils have developed a 'vibrant' culture of resistance not only to PE but also, in some cases, to schooling.

RECOMMENDED READING

Benn, T. (2005) 'Race and physical education, sport and dance', in K. Green and K. Hardman (eds), *Physical Education: Essential Issues*. London: Sage. pp.197–219.
Sport England (2000b) *Sports Participation and Ethnicity in England: National Survey 1999/2000. Headline Findings*. London: Sport England.
Verma, G.K. and Darby, D.S. (1994) *Winners and Losers: Ethnic Minorities in Sport and Recreation*. London: Falmer Press.

NOTE

1 It is important to recognize that what, from a Eurocentric perspective, constitutes a restriction on equal opportunities, in Islamic cultural traditions, Muslims view as a positive moral code to guide their community (Carroll, 1998b).

Disability, Special Educational Needs and Physical Education

11

The promotion of 'equal opportunities' in educational policy in recent decades has led to a shift in the education of youngsters with disabilities away from segregation in 'special schools' and towards their 'inclusion' in 'mainstream' (or 'regular', as they are known in the USA) schools. Consequently, the proportion of young people with disabilities educated in mainstream schools in developed countries has increased considerably in recent years (Fitzgerald, 2006).

This chapter examines key aspects of the 'inclusion' of young people with disabilities in mainstream PE. It explores the rationale, implementation and efficacy of 'mainstreaming', including the difficulties PE teachers report with inclusion, and the sports and physical activities young people with disabilities participate in both in and out of school. First, however, it is necessary to say something about disability itself as well as its corollary, special educational needs (SEN), as well as associated terms such as 'integration' and 'inclusion'.

DEFINING DISABILITY, SPECIAL EDUCATIONAL NEEDS AND INCLUSION

Disability and Special Educational Needs

Changes in policy orientation towards 'inclusion' have reflected a re-conceptualization of disability away from the hitherto sharp distinction between two groups of seemingly homogenous pupils – the (physically and mentally) handicapped (as they were often referred to) and the non-handicapped – and towards the recognition of a wider range of disabilities and abilities. The rigid categories of handicap that had previously formed the basis for the provision of special educational *services* (such as special schools) were gradually replaced by more nuanced categories of disability or impairment and the identification of special educational *needs* (SEN) among youngsters.

The label 'SEN' tends to be used to refer to limitations in (young) people's capacity to participate in and benefit from education as a consequence of enduring physical, cognitive, sensory, communicative or behavioural difficulties or any other condition which is said to require particular pedagogic responses (Meegan and MacPhail, 2006; Smith, 2004). The corresponding 'statements' of SEN are supposed to identify children's individual educational needs – for which some kind of special educational provision should be made – and typically result in what are sometimes referred to as Individual Educational Plans. Nevertheless, youngsters identified as having SEN are by no means a homogenous group. They include not only those with disabilities of one kind or another but also young people said to have a 'learning difficulty' because they experience significantly greater difficulty in learning than the majority of children of the same age.

The incorporation of physical and mental disability, alongside other learning difficulties (since the late 1970s [DES, 1978]) in the overall concept of SEN represents not only a reorientation of educational policy but also a major change away from so-called 'medical models' of disability towards a 'social model' (see Tregaskis, 2002). It does not, however, necessarily reflect a shift in the attitudes and practices of teachers. The continued pre-eminence of medicalized conceptions of disability in the beliefs and practices of PE make it necessary to say a little more about these models of disability.

Medical and social models of disability The successful application of science, in general, and medicine, in particular, to combating illness and disease over the last few hundred years has led to the dominance of scientific models of health and illness. The corresponding privileging of medical diagnoses and prognoses resulted in what became known as the 'medical model' of disability (Barnes et al., 1999). Consequently, those medical and educational experts (such as doctors and educational psychologists) charged with the diagnosis of, and prescription for, 'disability' tended to focus on young people's particular mental or physical impairments in the medical terms associated with dis/functionality. Such diagnoses invariably ignored wider social processes (of stigmatization, for example) and the general socially constructed physical (for example, sports facilities without disabled access) and cultural (such as sports and games that, in unmodified form, are inaccessible to youngsters with disabilities) barriers to participation in wider, supposedly 'able-bodied', societies.

People working in PE and sport have internalized many of the dominant conceptions of disability (as fundamentally anatomical or biological) of the kind associated with medical models. As a consequence, the commonplace perception of people with disabilities – as disabled as people – has become normalized among PE teachers who often focus upon children's deficiencies: in effect, what they can and cannot do.

In response to what were (and, in many cases, continue to be) seen as the individualistic and decontextualized – and, correspondingly, partial and inhibiting (Meegan and MacPhail, 2006) – views of individuals with disabilies manifest in medical models of disability, an alternative 'social model' emerged in the latter decades of the twentieth century to challenge the 'personal tragedy view of disability' (Fitzgerald, 2006: 756). From this perspective, disability, like race and gender, came to be seen as a social construct rather than a biological or medical category. Social models or explanations express a view of people with disabilities as constrained by situations that, in their effects, disable (and, therefore, oppress) them – not as an unavoidable consequence of their disability, as such, but rather because of the ways in which people and institutions respond or, more often, do not respond to them and their needs (Oliver, 1996). In practice, their engagement with various institutions (such as education and sport) is mediated by a wide variety of socially constructed restrictions – which often go hand in hand with impoverishment – such as inaccessible public transport and venues and stigmatizing, discriminatory attitudes.

Because PE emphasizes physical performance and the acquisition and development of physical skills, a lack of these marks out youngsters (whether disabled or not) as inferior. In its effects, therefore, PE is a process within which teachers (and fellow pupils) are prone to stigmatize young people with SEN, because physical educationalists are primarily concerned with the development of masculine, mesomorphic and able-bodied (in the sense of being both physically competent and unimpaired) young people. In other words, a normative paradigm prevails in PE (Fitzgerald, 2005) that corresponds to what is often referred to as 'ableism' or discrimination on the basis of perceived ability or lack of it.

A consequence of the shift towards viewing disability as socially constructed has been a preference for the term 'SEN' over 'disability' but also calls for much greater inclusion of youngsters with SEN in mainstream education. What has occurred, in practice, however has not always met with the approval of those favouring inclusion.

Integration, inclusion and mainstreaming

Debate surrounding the inclusion of young people with SEN in 'regular' or mainstream education has tended to revolve around two main themes: the meaning and significance of the terms 'integration' and 'inclusion' and the fundamental assumptions underpinning mainstreaming policies.

The most popular terms in existence to describe the incorporation of young people with SEN in mainstream schools are 'integration' and 'inclusion'. Although these terms are often used interchangeably, it has become conventional to view inclusion as indicative of a good deal more than merely integration – or incorporation. In the USA, for example, inclusion is considered to involve programmes, of which PE is one, 'that educate students with and without disabilities together' (Hodge et al., 2004: 395). However, this merely implies the physical incorporation of pupils with SEN into existing, mixed-ability lessons, which have neither been adapted nor planned deliberately in order to involve youngsters with SEN in a genuinely equitable manner. Consequently, adapting conventional PE lessons in order to simply incorporate youngsters with SEN is often derided as mere integration and, thus, a form of tokenism which neither results in substantive changes to PE nor their genuine inclusion (Barton, 1993). But this is not unusual. Teachers tend to hold particular and differing perspectives on what constitutes inclusion (Smith, 2004) and while some can and do distinguish between integration and inclusion, very many evidently cannot and do not.

Despite the prominence of mainstreaming policies, there are those that contest the notion of inclusion itself and what they view as proselytizing on the basis of misguided and ideological premises:

> Many people believe it to be obvious that one should 'include' as much as one can; that is to say, while they may concede some inevitable instances of exclusion, selection or differential treatment in schools ... their belief is that the less differentiation or discrimination between students on any grounds, the better. (Barrow, 2000: 305)

It is far from self-evident, however, that inclusion is inherently a good thing in either a moral or an educational sense. Both Barrow (2000) and Wilson (2000) argue that the idea that it is undesirable to differentiate or discriminate within education is not only unfair and iniquitous, but also contradicts many practices that educationalists implicitly accept and, indeed, carry out on a daily basis when and where they consider there to be good (educational) reasons for doing so. Physical and sporting ability are, for example, crucial variables in relation to participation in PE and sport and PE teachers typically differentiate within classes between individuals and groups with differing physical characteristics (for example, in relation to height) and sporting abilities. Indeed, it would be deemed undesirable – on grounds of either safety or maximizing learning and achievement, for example – to ignore such differences. On a larger scale, schools in England and Wales, for example, deem it desirable to discriminate in favour of particular pupils when identifying those deemed 'gifted and talented' or, in the case of Specialist Sports Colleges, selecting a proportion of their pupil intake on the basis of sporting ability. The real issue, it seems, is not the extent of integration into mainstream schools and PE lessons but, rather, which differences to recognize and which to overlook (Penney, 2002), and that, Wilson (2000) and Barrow (2000) suggest, remains an unresolved issue.

Despite ongoing debate regarding the nature and purposes of inclusion, the bulk of research into mainstreaming has focused upon its implementation.

IMPLEMENTATION

In many countries within Europe, such as Italy, young people with disabilities are legally entitled to 'full integration' (Stocchino et al., 2007) or, rather, inclusion in mainstream schooling, while, in the USA, there is a relatively long-standing requirement for teachers to teach students with disabilities – including those with severe to profound physical and cognitive disabilities (Ladenson, 2005) – in their 'regular' classes to the maximum appropriate (Meegan and MacPhail, 2006). In England and Wales, the first detailed and all-embracing statement regarding inclusion of pupils with SEN in PE came in the NCPE 2000 (Smith, 2004). The NCPE 2000 (DfEE/QCA, 1999) established the expectation that teachers would design and deliver PE curricula in relation to several principles intended to bring about equal opportunities in and through PE. Vickerman et al. (2003) summarized these as entitlement (to access learning and assessment in the PE curriculum); accessibility (placing responsibility on teachers to devise doable, relevant and challenging lessons); integration (educating SEN and non-SEN pupils alongside each other and together while responding to their diverse learning needs); and integrity (the expectation that teachers would demonstrate a commitment to the goals of mainstreaming). Unlike the 'zero-reject' policy of the USA, the NCPE in England and Wales has, since its inception, featured explicit recognition that implementation would, of necessity, 'see children in different schools experiencing a different range of activities, taught in different ways' (Penney, 2002: 110) due to the difficulties teachers would inevitably experience in 'fully integrating children with (SEN and disabilities) into all aspects of a physical education programme' (DES/WO, 1991: 36). 'Traditional' team games, rather than more individualized pursuits (such as dance, swimming and Outdoor and Adventurous Activities [OAA]), are activities in which it was assumed that teachers would experience particular difficulty in including pupils with SEN and disabilities (DES/WO, 1991: 36). And, in practice, this has been the case even though it remains a contentious issue whether or not such difficulties – and 'safety' concerns – are real or merely a ready-made justification for PE teachers to avoid the demands of inclusion.

Overall, the practice or implementation of mainstreaming has tended to be at variance with the principles of inclusion. For many commentators, it has been a long way short of ideal. There are a number of reasons for this. Ferri and Connor (2005) point to resistance on the part of teachers in the USA to school desegregation and the inclusion of students with disabilities in general education. Although PE teachers in the USA in Hodge et al.'s (2004) study, appeared ideologically committed to the notion of inclusion (viewing inclusion as a 'good' thing in principle), many pointed to what they saw as the often insurmountable practical difficulties of teaching students with disabilities. These difficulties were said to include the nature of PE provision and resources; behavioural difficulties (and the attendant teaching styles and class management issues); assessment; lack of support (for example, from their schools and from learning support assistants [LSAs]), especially with large classes; and inadequate training and preparation (for example, inadequate initial teacher training [ITT]/physical education teacher education (PETE) or continuing professional development). It is worth saying something about each of these in turn.

PE provision and resources

Time Time allocation is a common measure of PE provision (see Chapter 3) and primary and secondary pupils with disabilities[1] in England appear particularly disadvantaged in this regard when compared with their able-bodied counterparts (Sport England, 2001b). In 2000, 20 per cent of 6–16-year-olds (consisting of 16 per cent of primary-aged and 24 per cent of secondary-aged pupils) with disabilities in England were receiving the recommended two hours or more of timetabled PE, compared with 33 per cent of the general school population (16 per cent of primary-aged and 48 per cent of secondary-aged pupils). Almost two-thirds (65 per cent) of primary- and secondary-aged youngsters with a disability were receiving less than one and a half hours – compared with 40 per cent of all young people – while almost half (47 per cent compared with 18 per cent) received less than an hour. Reductions in time allocations for PE were particularly pronounced among primary-aged youngsters, with 53 per cent, compared with 41 per cent of secondary pupils, receiving less than an hour of PE each week. Similar percentages of primary-aged youngsters with and without disability (16 per cent) received two hours or more PE each week in 1999. These latter figures suggest that time allocation in primary schools in England has as much to do with a broader set of issues faced by primary schools than simply inclusion.

The amount of curriculum time allocated to PE in mainstream schools has increased substantially since 1999, with the greatest progress towards that threshold having been made in the primary sector. It is likely, therefore, that the gap in time allocated to PE between the general school population and disabled youngsters will have grown since the turn of the twenty-first century. Indeed, the Loughborough Partnership (2005) reported a more marked decline in the mean curriculum time for pupils with a self-reported disability, in the 22 schools in its study, than their able-bodied counterparts: 'the proportion of schools achieving the 2 hour threshold for pupils with a self-reported disability is between 5% and 7% lower than that for girls and boys in years 7 to 9' (2005: 26). The Partnership noted, however, that the gap closed in Years 10 and 11 moving 'in favour of pupils with a self-reported disability in years 12 and 13' (2005: 26). This may be explainable in terms of the decrease in PE time overall in the later secondary school years.

When moving beyond the simple matter of time allocated to PE towards examining the proportion of active (in the sense of physical involvement and energy expenditure) or productive (in the sense of learning opportunities) time within PE lessons, research in the USA suggests that pupils with disabilities typically accrue less active learning time in PE compared with their able-bodied counterparts (Van Der Mars, 2006). In the UK, Brittain (2004) found that the physical and social barriers to participation in mainstream schools often resulted in decreased activity levels and social isolation as a result of diminished opportunities to participate in organized and competitive sport in particular. More recently, Burgess's (2007) study explored the extent to which wheelchair-using pupils were offered opportunities to participate in sport and exercise in PE lessons and found 'a strong association between being the only person in the class who is a wheelchair user, being asked to sit and watch, or do physiotherapy instead of participating and having no specialized sport equipment' (2007: 38).

Rates of participation The *Young People with a Disability and Sport* (Sport England, 2001b) survey revealed that the majority of school-age youngsters with disabilities participated in sport both in and out of school lessons.[2] Sport England found that the overall rate of participation and the frequency of participation reported was lower than for young people in general. While overall participation among young people with disability was low in all settings (in and out of school), it was particularly low among primary-aged youngsters. Unsurprisingly, perhaps, the higher the number of disabilities young people had the less likely they were not only to participate in sport frequently but to participate at all.

In the Sport England (2001b) survey, 10 per cent of youngsters with a disability did not participate even 'occasionally' (at least once) in any sport or physical activity in school lessons in 2000 and over one-third (36 per cent) did not participate frequently (compared with 1 and 17 per cent respectively of able-bodied youngsters in 1999[3] [Sport England, 2003a]). In her study of

100 teenage (11–19-year-old) pupils who used wheelchairs, Burgess (2007) found that 30 per cent were excluded from PE. If Burgess's study of wheelchair users is indicative of the experiences of disabled youngsters, generally, it seems that the fewer youngsters with disabilities there are in a school the less likely they are to be included in PE. The third (30 per cent) of pupils who reported being the only wheelchair user in their school were the most likely to be excluded: 70 per cent of this group were not included in PE lessons. While almost two-thirds (58 per cent) of the pupils in Burgess's (2007) study were among a group of two to five pupils that used wheelchairs in their school, only 13 per cent of the sample had another wheelchair user in their PE lessons.

Frequency of participation and range of activities undertaken in NCPE
Where pupils with SEN are included in mainstream PE, many do not experience the same breadth, nor often the same kinds, of activities (Morley et al., 2005; Smith and Thomas, 2005). Among the secondary-school age group in Sport England's (2001b) survey, the average number of sports undertaken by youngsters with a disability either at least once (six) or frequently (two) within school, by both boys and girls, was lower than the averages for the overall population of young people (eight and four respectively). While the average bouts of frequent participation among youngsters with a disability was consistent for both boys and girls, it was lower for the younger age groups than secondary-aged pupils. Indeed, over a third of disabled youngsters had not taken part in any sport frequently during school time (consisting of slightly more secondary- than primary-aged youngsters, but similar numbers of boys and girls) and over three-quarters (78 per cent) did less than four sports frequently. The average number of sports undertaken decreased as the number of disabilities increased (Sport England, 2001b). Less than one-in-ten (8 per cent of male and 9 per cent of female) pupils with a disability undertook seven or more sports and activities frequently in PE lessons and almost half those with seven or more disabilities frequently undertook no sport at all (Sport England, 2001b).

The types of sports and physical activities in which young males and females with disabilities took part frequently in school lessons in England in 2000 consisted, like their able-bodied counterparts, of an amalgam of team games and 'lifestyle' or recreational activities, with the balance tilted in favour of the latter (see Chapter 7). The top five sports undertaken frequently in school PE by youngsters with a disability were:

- swimming (38 per cent:[4] comprising 41 and 38 per cent primary-aged boys and girls respectively and 37 and 36 per cent secondary-aged boys and girls)
- 'other games skills' (24 per cent: 34 and 37 per cent primary-aged boys and

girls, respectively, and 14 and 21 per cent secondary-aged boys and girls)
- gymnastics (21 per cent: 27 and 28 per cent primary-aged boys and girls, respectively, and 16 and 21 per cent secondary-aged boys and girls)
- football – the only team game present in the top five activities – (14 per cent: 15 and 5 per cent primary-aged boys and girls, respectively, and 26 and 8 per cent secondary-aged boys and girls)
- athletics (11 per cent: 8 and 10 per cent primary-aged boys and girls, respectively, and 11 and 13 per cent secondary-aged boys and girls). (Sport England, 2001b)

The range of activities young people with disabilities experience through PE is a salient issue, not least because of the difficulties PE teachers report, not only in teaching SEN pupils in general, but also in fully integrating them into all aspects of PE in its conventional form (Fitzgerald, 2006; Hodge et al., 2004; Morley et al., 2005; Smith, 2004; Stocchino et al., 2007). Consequently, relatively smaller proportions of youngsters with SEN participate in the team games that constitute the core of 'traditional' PE curricula. The top five 'games' undertaken frequently by 6–16-year-old youngsters in school lessons in 2000, for example, were:

- football (14 per cent)
- rounders (11 per cent)
- basketball (6 per cent)
- cricket (5 per cent)
- hockey (5 per cent). (Sport England, 2001b)

Physical education teachers, it seems, view individualized activities (such as swimming, gymnastics and dance) as more conducive to the inclusion of pupils with SEN and often acknowledge that these pupils are frequently excluded from or take a limited part in those activities that make up the core of curricular (and extra-curricular) PE – team games (Morley et al., 2005). The result is that pupils with SEN are more likely to be included in those PE activities in which the skills are of the 'closed' variety and the youngsters are more able to control the intensity and duration and, therefore, the physical demands of those movements than they are in more 'open' and, therefore, complex, competitive and physically-demanding team sports (Smith and Green, 2004). The Sport England (2001b: 14) survey identified swimming and horse-riding as 'important sports for young people with a disability'. In the Sport England survey, 37 per cent of young people with a disability had undertaken swimming frequently during school time (compared with 30 per cent of the general 6–16 school population) and 6 per cent (compared with 1 per cent) horse-riding. Nevertheless, Fitzgerald and Jobling's (2004) small-scale study pointed to the popularity in PE lessons not only of these activities but also basketball, in particular, among young people with disabilities.

Physical education teachers often justify the marginalization or exclusion of youngsters with disabilities in terms of the difficulties they face constructing meaningful lessons for those pupils whose disabilities put them at a substantial disadvantage in particular activities, such as team games. The problem of *what* to deliver (in terms of content) to classes which include SEN youngsters is compounded in teachers' eyes by the question of *how* best to deliver it in a manner that does not disadvantage either the able-bodied or SEN pupils. In this regard, Stocchino et al.'s (2007) study of 79 11–12-year-olds in five secondary schools in Cagliari (Italy) concluded that suitable adaptations to PE lessons can increase the participation levels of pupils with a mild intellectual disability without reducing the involvement of pupils without a disability. Nevertheless, several small-scale studies in the USA (Hodge et al., 2004) and England (Smith and Green, 2004) report PE teachers' perceptions of feeling constrained towards adopting a utilitarian stance, in the interests of the majority of their pupils, by sacrificing the interests of the handful of pupils with SEN because the teachers claim to be distracted from their main purpose by the difficulties 'caused' by the presence of SEN pupils. A key aspect of what PE teachers view as their necessarily pragmatic approaches to inclusive PE is the issue of safety. Hodge et al. (2004) suggest that teachers in the USA often appear preoccupied with safety issues while 25 per cent of pupils in Burgess's (2007) study in England claimed that safety was often given as a reason to exclude them, as wheelchair users, from involvement in PE and sport at school.

It seems that in very many schools, PE teachers tend to focus on how the child with SEN can be made to fit into the lesson rather than the other way around (Brittain, 2004; Thomas and Green, 1994). Teachers are primarily concerned with integration rather than inclusion. In practical terms, PE teachers appear to take sufficiency as their benchmark; that is, they seek to make the minimum of changes to their original lessons in order to enable participation by SEN pupils, albeit in a restricted form. This tendency towards minimal disruption of existing PE practices compounds the constraints (and attendant pressures) upon PE teachers to ensure that they deliver the requisite NCPE material and '[B]ecause teachers feel under pressure to move on to the next stage of PE activities, the progress of pupils with SEN is often inhibited because repetition and consolidation of skills are frequently neglected' (OFSTED, 2005a: 19).

The specific nature of a pupil's difficulty (coupled with any additional teaching support they may receive) can be fundamental in determining what activities they are able or allowed to participate in. Nonetheless, the degree of emphasis upon 'performance' and 'skills' in lessons can ultimately be the factor that precludes many SEN pupils from participating fully with their peers in mainstream PE (Stocchino et al., 2007). The outcome is that youngsters with disabilities do not experience as broad a range of activities as able-bodied pupils, with games and athletics likely to be less available to them (Smith, 2004). Sometimes, PE provision is set against SEN pupils' particular educational or health needs. Forty per cent of the school-age wheelchair users in Burgess's (2007) study, for example, reported that physiotherapy was only available to them as a substitute for their PE lessons.

Resources Resources and, in particular, PE and sporting equipment, is an important issue in relation to pupils with SEN. The Office for Standards in Education (2005a: 19) claim that half the SSCs in England and Wales 'offer good support for pupils with SEN'. However, they add that in order to 'meet these pupils' needs more effectively the schools often provide a broader range of equipment'. To some extent the provision of a breadth of equipment (such as brightly coloured bats and audible balls for pupils with visual impairment) may be being met by organizations such as the YST (see Chapter 2) (Thomas and Smith, 2008). Burgess (2007) reported that the size of the secondary schools they attended made little difference to the experience of pupils using wheelchairs. While the 13 per cent of those who had another wheelchair user in their group were most likely to be at a school that had specialized sports equipment for PE, 60 per cent of the sample as a whole reported their schools to have no such equipment. It seems that the fewer wheelchair users there are in a school, the more likely it is that their experiences of PE will be unsatisfactory. Burgess (2007) suggests that, despite the fact that an increasing number of UK pupils that use wheelchairs want to attend mainstream schools, when they are there very many find that they 'may have no opportunity in school to engage in sport with another student that is a wheelchair user' (2007: 42).

Behavioural difficulties

Teaching styles and class management In order to facilitate the inclusion of pupils with SEN into mainstream education, teachers are expected to employ differentiated teaching styles or strategies (see Chapter 12) and provide suitable challenges for all pupils, regardless of how diverse their needs and capabilities are. The chief pedagogic concern of PE teachers when teaching SEN pupils is one of control. In this regard, PE teachers in the USA consider it especially difficult to include pupils with severe or multiple disabilities (in which sensory and physical disability is combined with learning disability) (Hodge et al., 2004) and those with severe emotional and behavioural disabilities (EBD) in particular (Van Der Mars, 2006). Research in the UK, North America and Norway suggests that where pupils fail to make progress in PE classes because they have a motor learning difficulty – including developmental coordination disorder, dyspraxia or developmental clumsiness – this tends to compound social and behavioural difficulties (Mannisto et al., 2006).

There may, however, be a gender dimension to perceptions of difficulty among teachers. Meegan and MacPhail (2006) found that, in Ireland, female PE teachers displayed more positive attitudes towards teaching youngsters with specific learning disabilities and those who were moderately severe mentally impaired than did male teachers.

Assessment

One aspect of PE within which PE teachers experience particular difficulty implementing inclusion is assessment. The NCPE 2000 for England and Wales introduced an eight-level scale of descriptions of pupil performance against which teachers are required to assess all pupils, including those with SEN. Ironically, the prescriptive nature of these statements seems to have exacerbated uncertainty among PE teachers in secondary schools regarding what they perceive as their inability to make accurate assessments of pupils with SEN. Teachers in Smith and Green's (2004) small-scale study, for example, suggested that many of their SEN pupils were unable to meet the assessment criteria as set out in the NCPE, because the criteria for achievement involved being able to perform activities at a level many of the pupils were unable to attain.

Although assessment criteria have been supplemented in England and Wales with a set of performance descriptions intended as a more adequate representation of SEN pupils' needs, these are 'not always well known or used in secondary schools' (OFSTED, 2003: 17). In addition, it remains the responsibility of PE teachers to adapt activities and skills included in the NCPE to suit the needs of their SEN pupils on the basis of whatever guidance is available from various disability sport organizations (Thomas and Smith, 2008).

Support

In England and Wales, there are two main groups of people (beyond teachers themselves) whose role it is to facilitate the inclusion of pupils with SEN in mainstream schooling by supporting teachers and pupils alike: Special Educational Needs Co-ordinators (SENCOs) – teachers with responsibility for the implementation of policies related to children with SEN – and Learning Support Assistants (LSAs) – whose job it is to accompany particular SEN pupils and provide assistance to both the pupil and the teacher in any given classroom setting.

A common complaint from PE teachers is the alleged dearth of support from these two groups but especially LSAs (Burgess, 2007; Hodge et al., 2004). More specifically, PE teachers express concern at the lack of support from LSAs (as well as the relatively poor quality of what support there is) – compared with other, ostensibly more academic, subjects such as English, mathematics and science – and point to what they view as the need for more active involvement from the (SEN pupil) 'helpers'. As far as PE teachers are concerned, one of the functions of LSAs is assisting them in ensuring the safety of SEN pupils in their PE classes; especially where PE classes include pupils with EBD and severe learning difficulties as well as wheelchair users. Despite the issue of safety, it seems that, in practice, by supporting the ostensibly less able SEN pupils, the presence of LSAs allows PE teachers to concentrate upon what they deem to be the main focus of their roles: teaching the able-bodied pupils.

The apparent lack of general support PE teachers point to is, perhaps, unsurprising given that, in general, SENCOs are said to be overwhelmed by the operational aspects of their roles (Cole, 2005) and removed from the day-to-day difficulties encountered by PE teachers. In addition, LSAs have little by way of specialist knowledge or preparation for the potentially demanding roles they are required to carry out by teachers in the PE setting.

Training and preparation

It is frequently observed that teachers, generally, and PE teachers, in particular, feel inadequately prepared for the demands of mainstreaming and inclusion (Avramidis and Norwich, 2002; Hodge et al., 2004). The Office for Standards in Education (2003: 24) observes that teachers often feel that they are 'being asked to teach children with significant learning needs and manage difficult situations' without sufficient or appropriate training. Teachers' perceptions of their inadequate knowledge base are corroborated by the SEN pupils themselves. Many of the youngsters in Burgess's (2007: 39) study, for example, complained 'about the complete absence of knowledge among school staff of sports undertaken by wheelchair users'. The teenagers themselves, commented upon the need for better training of teachers and more links with expertise outside schools. The problems caused by a lack of knowledge (regarding SEN and inclusion) from the outset on the part of prospective teachers are exacerbated by a lack of appropriate training. In Ireland, training in SEN within PE teacher training is usually restricted to one, relatively short course (Meegan and MacPhail, 2006).

The brevity of any preparation for inclusion that teachers encounter on ITT courses appears to be compounded by the focus of much training upon abstract and general aspects of inclusion rather than the more practical and specifically subject (PE)-related realities of the process. In practice, much of what PE teachers actually learn about inclusion is acquired 'on the job' – that is, in the form of occupational socialization (see Chapter 12) – from their colleagues in schools (Morley et al., 2005; Vickerman, 2002).

Consideration of the important issues surrounding the implementation of inclusion leads, inevitably, to one outstanding issue, namely, the efficacy or otherwise of mainstreaming.

EFFICACY

The transference of pupils from special to mainstream schools, and thus mainstream PE, has not only been gradual, it has also been partial and incomplete. It has been partial in that it has typically been those pupils with less severe difficulties who have been educated in mainstream schools, while those with more severe difficulties have tended to remain in the special school sector.

The issue of whether those children with SEN who are included in mainstream education benefit from the experience or would be better catered for in special schools has been a matter of animated debate in the UK since the 1970s (Brittain, 2004). Nonetheless, the introduction of the policy of mainstreaming or inclusion has led to the closure of many special schools in Britain over the last decade. During the 1970s, proponents of mainstreaming, as it became known, often argued a similar case to that underpinning developments such as co-educational PE and comprehensive schooling; namely, that the beneficial by-products of these processes would include challenging some of the stereotypical assumptions about youngsters with disabilities and a corresponding breaching of the kinds of barriers to inclusion that special schools, it was argued, simply perpetuated. However, research findings that point to SEN policy as tantamount to integration rather than inclusion have merely fanned the flames of debate regarding the efficacy of mainstreaming. In practice, mainstreaming often appears tantamount to 'segregated inclusion' where students with and without disabilities coexist separately from one another within the same PE classes (Hodge et al., 2004).

Subsequently, it has been suggested that not only have the needs of pupils with disabilities been sacrificed at the altar of 'inclusion' but also that mainstreaming has merely served to perpetuate, even exacerbate, stigma attached to SEN. Similarly, it has been suggested that the special school system may better serve the interests of young people with SEN. Despite the fact that PE has tended to be marginalized in special schools because special school teachers have tended not to receive any instruction in PE (Fitzgerald, 2006), Brittain (2004: 83) claims that 'not everybody who has been through the special school system feels that it has or would have let them down' in relation to PE and sport. Similarly, in terms of their more general education, young people with physical disabilities who attended special schools in Curtin and Clarke's (2005) study reported positive experiences, whereas those who attended a mainstream school held mixed views about their education.

In exploring the efficacy of inclusion and mainstreaming it is instructive to consider the levels and forms of sports participation, beyond school, among young people with a disability, and compare and contrast these with participation in school PE.

DISABILITY AND SPORT

In England, the differences in participation in sport in school is mirrored in the differences out of school where approximately half the number of young people with a disability (40 per cent) took part in 1999 compared with the general population of young people (79 per cent) (Sport England, 2001b). Similarly, just over a third (37 per cent) of children and young people with a disability had taken part in sport during lunch breaks on school days compared with two-thirds (67 per cent) of the overall population of youngsters, while half (47 per cent) had participated in sport at the weekend compared with three-quarters (74 per cent) of the overall school population.

The Sport England (2001b) study revealed that approximately one in six (15 per cent: 17 per cent of boys and 14 per cent of girls) 6–16-year-olds with a disability did no sport or physical activity out of school in the previous year. More recently, Burgess's (2007) small-scale survey of 11–19-year-olds reported 27 per cent of wheelchair users did no sport at all, either in or out of school. By contrast, virtually all (98 per cent) primary- and secondary-aged youngsters in the study participated at least once in out-of-school lessons in 1999 (Sport England, 2003a).

The picture regarding the average number of sports undertaken by youngsters with a disability was similar out of school to in school. The average number of sports played frequently out of school, for example, was a good deal less than half (1.7) the number played frequently by children and young people generally (4.5) (Sport England, 2001b). As with in-school participation, it was generally the case that the greater the number of disabilities (or the more complex the disability), the lower the average number of sports participated in either at all or frequently out of school by young people (Sport England, 2001b).

The types of sports and physical activities in which young males and females with disabilities frequently took part in out-of-school lessons in England in 2000 consisted, like the general school population, of an amalgam of team games and 'lifestyle' or recreational activities, albeit with the balance tilted firmly in favour of the latter. The top five sports undertaken frequently were:

- swimming (35 per cent: comprising 40 and 36 per cent primary-aged boys and girls respectively and 34 and 32 per cent secondary-aged boys and girls)
- football (18 per cent: 26 and 9 per cent primary-aged boys and girls respectively and 29 and 9 per cent secondary-aged boys and girls)
- cycling (16 per cent: 20 and 17 per cent primary-aged boys and girls respectively and 17 and 12 per cent secondary-aged boys and girls)
- 'other game skills' (12 per cent: 19 and 18 per cent primary-aged boys and girls respectively and 7 and 9 per cent secondary-aged boys and girls)
- walking (12 per cent: 11 and 13 per cent primary-aged boys and girls respectively and 11 and 13 per cent secondary-aged boys and girls). (Sport England, 2001b)

The Sport England (2001b) survey revealed secondary-age youngsters to be involved in similar sports out of school as in PE lessons. The activities in which 11–16-year-olds with disabilities participated frequently, for example, were similar for males and females: swimming (34 per cent and 32 per cent, respectively), football (29 and 9 per cent), cycling (17 and 12 per cent), walking (11 and 13 per cent) and 'other games skills' (7 and 9 per cent) (Sport England, 2001b). Approximately three-quarters (74 per cent of boys, 70 per cent of girls) did one or more of 21 different sports undertaken by the sample, of which basketball and swimming were the most popular. Fitzgerald and Jobling's (2004) study confirmed swimming as disabled youngsters' favourite free-time activity.

As is the case with young people generally, the activity profiles of many youngsters with SEN are increasingly likely to include 'lifestyle activities' and more conventional sport, including team games such as football and basketball. Indeed, the top five 'games' undertaken frequently out of school by youngsters with disabilities (football [18 per cent]; skittles or tenpin bowling [5 per cent]; rounders [4 per cent]; cricket [4 per cent]; basketball [4 per cent] [Sport England, 2001b]) all feature in the top 10 sports and physical activities undertaken frequently by the general school population.

More individualized activities tend to play a large part in the participatory profiles of those youngsters with disabilities engaged in sport both in and out-of-school lessons. However, whereas in school this is often because youngsters with disabilities have little choice, out of school (that is, in their leisure) it is more an expression of their preferences. As with young people's sport, in general, however, it would be an oversimplification to assume that the popularity of individualized activities such as swimming means that youngsters with disabilities are avoiding sports and games. Basketball, for example, is very popular among wheelchair users (Burgess, 2007) as are disability-specific activities such as boccia.

Despite the popularity of sport, Thomas and Smith (forthcoming) point out the relatively weak provision of leisure-sport opportunities for young people with disabilities, beyond formally organized sports clubs and national governing bodies of sport. Against this, and despite the limited opportunities in school PE, as far as wheelchair users in Burgess's (2007: 38) study were concerned, 'the situation in the community was a good deal better' than in schools. Nevertheless, young people with SEN readily identify 'barriers' to participation for those in their situation. These barriers include:

- lack of money/high costs
- lack of or problems with transport
- dependence on other people (especially family)
- the inaccessibility of sports facilities and equipment[5]
- lack of adequate and knowledgeable coaching
- negative attitudes of those without disability.
  (Blauwet, 2007; Sport England, 2001b)

Some of these (such as money, transport and facilities) are, of course, often identified as barriers to participation among the general population. Nonetheless, their effects appear more pronounced and pervasive among disabled groups than among the rest of the population. The manner in which many of these barriers – cost (or lack of money), lack of transport and dependence on other people, for example – are not only strongly correlated but also seemingly insurmountable becomes apparent when one considers that over half (53 per cent) of those youngsters surveyed in Sport England's (2001b) study were living in rented accommodation and approximately one-third (30 per cent) were from one-parent families.

CONCLUSION

Many countries in the developed world have policy commitments to the inclusion of youngsters with SEN in mainstream schools and PE lessons. In

England and Wales, the NCPE ostensibly guarantees an entitlement to all children to a 'broad and balanced' PE curriculum. Nevertheless, the process of inclusion has been far from straightforward and is far from complete.

There continues to be a good deal of debate regarding exactly what youngsters with SEN are supposed to be included in, in the name of PE, and how that inclusion is best facilitated. Is it, for example, all activity areas in the *same* ways (often impossible), or all activity areas in *similar* (or as close as possible) ways, or all activity areas in their *adapted* versions (wheelchair basketball being an obvious example) – where the latter two are distinguishable? Put another way, do young people with SEN require different *kinds* of curricula and teaching styles to those without such 'needs'? Or is it simply a matter of degree: the extension and refinement of core activities and teaching styles? If so, the issue of SEN appears to be simply one facet of a wider, more general question related to the various teaching styles said to be suited to the whole pupil population with their supposedly differing learning styles and abilities (see Chapter 12).

It is also debatable what the consequences for inclusion are likely to be – the unforeseen and unintended consequences as well as those intended – especially for the youngsters with SEN. Although PE teachers talk of providing 'as much opportunity as possible' for all pupils, in providing SEN pupils with the 'same opportunities' as their able-bodied peers, they have tended to exacerbate rather than diminish inequity by, in effect, requiring SEN pupils to 'fit into' the existing PE curriculum. In other words, pupils tend to be integrated (in the sense of merely being present) in PE lessons even if they are not included (in the sense of taking a full and active part). At one level, the inclusion of pupils with SEN in mainstream PE can be viewed as providing similar pedagogical challenges (in terms, for example, of setting appropriate and worthwhile tasks) for teachers as other diverse or specialist groups, such as so-called 'gifted and talented' pupils. The differences, however, lie in the far more central place of the latter in PE teachers' perceptions of the nature and purposes of PE compared to the former. Physical education teachers appear to view pupils with SEN as 'outsiders' to the established PE curriculum and their 'traditional' practices. In this regard, PE teachers' approaches to inclusion seem to parallel their treatment of particular (usually South Asian) ethnic minority pupils and some girls; namely, as 'problem' groups to be reconciled to conventional PE rather than requiring a re-evaluation of 'traditional' PE forms. It is unsurprising, therefore, that young disabled people participate less in PE and in a narrower range of activities when they do so (Sport England, 2001b). Overall, their experiences of PE tend to reinforce their sense of marginalization rather than inclusion, emphasizing their lack of particular attributes and inability to perform particular skills (Fitzgerald and Jobling, 2004).

Many PE teachers not only lack full awareness of their legal obligations towards SEN pupils, they also tend to view mainstreaming as one more unde-sirable and unsatisfactory burden upon them as teachers, requiring modified activities, modified equipment and modified and differing goals for PE (from individual lessons through to PE curricula as a whole). As a result PE teachers tend to view pupils with disabilities negatively (Meegan and MacPhail, 2006).

Inclusion and SEN is an interesting example of the problems associated with unclear – some would argue, contradictory – policy goals that result in outcomes associated with the implementation of a policy that (a) were not intended, and (b) may make matters worse rather than better for the groups concerned – pupils with SEN. In this regard, the achievement of a degree of inclusion may militate against the achievement of other goals – such as com-bating the particularly sharp rise in obesity among wheelchair groups by reducing their levels of involvement in PE in comparison with that achieved in special schools. In marketized education systems, policies of inclusion do not easily complement those that, for example, promote competition between schools while, at the same time, making schools accountable for their own finite budgets and promoting 'excellence' as well as the identification and promotion of the so-called 'gifted and talented' (see Chapter 2).

Legal entitlement to equitable treatment for pupils with SEN and corre-sponding policies of mainstreaming constrain PE teachers in many countries to confront the inclusion of a heterogeneous group on the basis of little or no suitable training or ongoing professional development at a time when a host of other policy initiatives have been introduced (such as those that focus on sports performance) that are not necessarily compatible with the principle of inclusion. For example, mainstreaming encompasses those deemed to be 'gifted and talented' and who are equally 'entitled' to make the most of them-selves. When implemented alongside other policies – such as those aimed at privileging a group that is already advantaged by the process of PE, namely talented sports performers among the school population – there is a real pos-sibility that policies of inclusion in mainstream PE might exacerbate feelings of difference and detachment among youngsters with disabilities. Indeed, as Wilson (2000) points out, we simply cannot avoid the likelihood that some people will feel inferior or superior to others in some way or other. It is not only that education has always tended to encourage this; contemporary PE appears actively to celebrate the differences.

RECOMMENDED READING

Fitzgerald, H. (2006) 'Disability and physical education', in D. Kirk, D. Macdonald and M. O'Sullivan (eds), *The Handbook of Physical Education*. London: Sage. pp.752–66.

Sport England (2001b) *Young People with a Disability and Sport*. London: Sport England.

Thomas, N. and Smith, A. (2008) *Disability, Sport and Society: An Introduction*. London: Routledge.

NOTES

1 Sport England's (2001b) survey uses the term 'disability' (incorporating learning difficulties) in its report. Therefore, when referring to Sport England data, 'disability' will be the preferred term, elsewhere the term 'disability' will be subsumed by the concept of SEN.

2 When examining these figures it needs to be borne in mind that the Sport England (2001b) study defined in-school sport as that undertaken within school lessons (and, almost exclusively, PE). Participation out-of-school lessons, however, includes not only break and lunch times but also extra-curricular PE as well as leisure time generally.

3 The figures for 'occasionally' (at least once) and frequently in the past 12 months remained identical or virtually so in 2002, at 1 per cent and 18 per cent respectively (Sport England, 2003a).

4 Where percentages do not sum up to 100 per cent this is due to the various ways in which Sport England have processed the data for presentation, such as rounding figures up or down.

5 The popularity of swimming among wheelchair users is ironic given that it is one of the activities that they are most likely to be excluded from while at primary school because of the inaccessibility of transport, pools and changing rooms (Burgess, 2007).

Teaching Physical Education

12

Central to teaching are the teachers themselves. As well as reflecting upon teaching PE, this chapter explores the processes of becoming and being a specialist PE teacher of the kind typically found in secondary schools – for it is they who form the vast majority of teachers of PE and whose model of PE tends to influence, directly or indirectly, what happens at primary school level. It is important to note that the background and experience of secondary PE teachers tends to be substantially different to the vast majority of primary teachers, very many of whom would have received little or no specific training in PE. Virtually all primary school teachers are generalists – in the sense that they teach all or many subjects to their pupils, irrespective of their academic specialism(s) – even though some will have overall responsibility for planning and developing the curriculum, and its delivery, for particular subject areas (such as PE). Consequently, despite the fact that they will be bound to teach PE to their pupils, the vast majority of primary teachers will have little or no expertise in the subject. Indeed, they are likely to have very different backgrounds compared with secondary PE teachers, in terms of their socialization into (or, more likely, away from), and subsequent experiences of, PE and sport.

First, the chapter explores the process of becoming a PE teacher. It examines the ways in which background and experiences influence not only their reasons for becoming PE teachers, but also their practices as PE teachers: in terms of the activities they are inclined to teach, the teaching styles they adopt, and their tendency towards engagement with profesional reflection and development. The chapter then focuses upon the main features of the process of teaching itself – typically referred to as the pedagogy of PE – before concluding with a brief overview of the contextual aspects of PE teaching.

BECOMING AND BEING A TEACHER OF PHYSICAL EDUCATION

The socialization of teachers

Much has been written about PE teachers' values and beliefs (see, for example, Lortie, 1975; Tsangaridou, 2006a) – in other words, their 'philosophies' or ideologies (Green, 2003) – and this has been used to make sense of the blend of conservative or innovative (Curtner-Smith and Meek, 2000; Ennis and Chen, 1995) teaching strategies and styles they employ. But how do these values and beliefs emerge and develop? How do teachers internalize the attitudes, behaviours and customs that make up the subculture(s) of PE teaching? How, in other words, do particular attitudes and practices become part and parcel of PE teachers' personalities or habituses – their 'second nature'?

Lawson (1986) has outlined what he sees as the three types of socialization that teachers experience:

- *acculturation* (childhood and adolescent sporting and PE experiences and the predispositions these are said to engender)
- *professional socialization* (the teacher-training process of initiating trainees into the 'official' requirements of teaching PE and associated notions of exemplary or 'good' and 'effective' practice)
- *occupational socialization* (the attitudes and behaviours learnt 'on the job' in the company of fellow PE teachers and pupils, for example).

It is worth saying something about each of these in turn, as well as an additional aspect of professional socialization in the form of Continuing Professional Development (CPD).

Acculturation: habituses and beliefs Valuing sport is a pervasive and enduring influence on PE teachers (Dewar and Lawson, 1984; O'Bryant et al., 2000). Their biographies and, in particular, their early and profound emotional attachments to and identification with sport, tends to lead prospective PE teachers to develop particular orientatons towards sport generally and PE in particular (Green, 2003). Evidence suggests that both male and female teacher trainees have been attracted to careers in teaching PE precisely because it provides them with an opportunity to continue their association with sport (Evans and Williams, 1989).

Evans and Williams (1989) and Mawer (1996) highlight what they view as the second most common reason for entering the PE profession after 'love of sport'; namely, the positive influences their PE teachers had on them during young people's own school lives. Prospective PE teachers typically had positive sporting experiences and their PE teachers and coaches provided influential role models for them. In effect, 'their experiences in sports during schooling influenced their understanding of what it means to be a physical education teacher' (Tsangaridou, 2006a: 492). However, the same cannot be said for many primary school teachers whose characteristically negative attitudes towards PE (Hopper, 2005) have often been shaped in reaction to their own experiences of PE and PE teachers.

Their early childhood experiences of PE and sport constitute an 'anticipatory phase' of occupational socialization (Dewar and Lawson, 1984; O'Bryant et al., 2000) and act, in effect, to socialize future teachers into particular values and beliefs (Chen and Ennis, 1996) regarding the nature and purposes of PE (Behets and Vergauwen, 2006; Placek et al., 1995). A 'love of sport' is influential at the outset of PE teaching careers – in terms of teachers' original orientation or 'subjective warrant' (Lawson, 1983a) – and continues to be so regardless of age or gender. Therefore, PE teachers' early experiences tend to have 'a long-lasting impact on school programs' (Placek et al., 1995: 247) and provide the basis for an enduring sport-oriented ideology that withstands, to a large extent, the onslaught of competing ideologies.

Consequently, PE teachers are inclined towards replicating (because they feel more comfortable with) 'traditional' approaches to 'traditional' curricula. This is why the sport- and games-oriented PE programme associated with so-called 'traditional' PE has an element of self-replication built into it and has become self-fulfilling – PE teaching is a largely self-selecting and self-replicating process. In this regard, PE teachers frequently act as carriers of a de facto PE curriculum in the sense that it is possible to identify, within and across national boundaries, a relatively orthodox or conventional PE curriculum consisting largely of those activities which student teachers have themselves been taught and which revolve around sport and games. To this extent, 'unplanned and unrecognized' standard or national PE curricula (Placek et al., 1995: 256) exist not only in the USA but everywhere where PE teachers are recruited – as they almost invariably are – from sportspeople.

Prospective PE teachers are generally comfortable with the more traditional games and sports-based curriculum models with custodial orientations, with which they themselves grew up. If each new generation of teachers emulates the PE which they have themselves experienced then they are likely to deduce – from their experience 'on the receiving end' – that the nature and purposes of PE (what the subject *should* be about) are to be found, generally, in sport and, in particular, in team games. So, by the time many teachers reach the training stage they have become accustomed to associating PE primarily with 'sport in schools'.

The professional socialization of teachers through Physical Education Initial Teacher Training (PEITT) The process by which people in occupations learn to become members of their 'profession' – by acquiring shared values and knowledge – is referred to as professional socialization. Professional socialization involves the informal as well as formal processes by which prospective teachers are initiated into their 'trade'. Throughout the developed world, the vast majority of PE teachers nowadays are graduates of Sports Science (or its equivalent, such as Human Movement Studies and Kinesiology) and have subsequently completed a one-year post-graduate PEITT programme which gives them what, in England and Wales, is referred to as 'Qualified Teacher Status' (QTS).

This 'emergence of a graduate profession armed (supposedly) with a greater breadth and depth of theoretical knowledge' (McNamee, 2005: 5) has been one of the most significant changes in PE worldwide in recent decades. Nevertheless, McNamee (2005) harbours several reservations about the widely assumed benefits of this development. First, he questions whether or not a graduate profession does, in fact, have a broader and deeper theoretical grasp of its subject than previous generations of PE teachers who did not obtain a specialist degree and who, from the outset, simply trained to be teachers. Second, McNamee questions whether having this subject-specific expertise (in sport) leads to better teaching and learning in PE. The graduatization of teacher education and the dramatic growth in popularity of Sports Science degree programmes has resulted (or so it is frequently claimed by existing PE teachers) in newly qualified teachers lacking both the personal expertise in various sporting activities as well as the teaching and coaching expertise that would enable them to select practical tasks, sequence them logically, offer insightful teaching points to pupils and provide suitable demonstrations with sufficent confidence (Sloan, 2007; Training and Development Agency, 2006). Although many trainee teachers from sporting backgrounds possess expertise in games and sport (Capel and Katene, 2000), they are frequently described as less well prepared to teach PE – in its practical form – than those trained two decades or more ago (Houlihan and Green, 2006). Concern with subject expertise is particularly acute in relation to primary PE because the time allocated to the training of primary school teachers in PE has significantly declined (Caledcott et al., 2006a, 2006b) and this has led to primary school teachers having 'inadequate subject knowledge' (Waring et al., 2007: 27).

Whatever the veracity of claims about a decline in sporting competence among new generations of PE teachers, there is a tendency to overemphasize the impact of professional training on prospective teachers. Physical Education Initial Teacher Training appears to have little impact on the largely established beliefs of would-be PE teachers and only limited – largely indirect

– impact upon their practices (Capel, 2005; Evans et al., 1996; Placek et al., 1995). Student teachers seldom, if ever, question their background and its influence on PE. This is said, by those engaged with initial teacher training in PE, to be one of the reasons that student teachers tend to be fundamentally unresponsive, during their training, to attempts to encourage them to reflect critically upon various aspects of the subject: from teaching styles through to the nature and purposes of PE (Capel, 2007).

Indeed, teacher training tends to confirm rather than challenge student teachers' beliefs about PE (Capel, 2005; Curtner-Smith, 2001). Behets and Vergauwen (2006: 407) prefer to explain 'The historical ineffectiveness of teacher education' in terms of 'the disjointedness of program goals and curricula'. However, it may have more to do with the deep-seated nature of prospective PE teachers' sporting habituses in conjunction with the immediacy and significance of their experiences 'in the field'; that is, in schools. This is made more likely by the fact that a large proportion of time during training is 'devoted to enabling teachers to "deliver" the curriculum' (Hallam and Ireson, 1999: 83) and nowhere more so than in PE. Although the extended school placements, characteristic of teacher training in England and Wales in particular, may have improved trainees' preparedness to teach PE (Stidder and Hayes, 2006), this may have more to do with introducing them to the realities of teaching and the preferred pedagogic practices of their mentors than enabling delivery of the ideal-type PE lessons experienced in the higher education training institution. Understandably, 'practice' is perceived by trainees as significantly more influential than theorizing. Consequently, the aspect of PEITT that has the most substantial impact on PE teachers' views and behaviours is, unsurprisingly, teaching *practice* where student teachers learn to adopt a 'pedagogy of necessity' (Tinning, 1988).

The emphasis upon teaching practice in training teachers has been reinforced by a major development in teacher training in Britain and the USA in recent years – the introduction of school- (as opposed to university-) based ITT. The requirement for schools taking on greater responsibility for teacher training has brought with it an increase in the time given to 'teaching practice' and the introduction of 'mentoring'.

In Britain, mentoring typically occurs in the training of PE teachers, while elsewhere it is part of the induction of newly qualified teachers. In principle, mentoring involves the guidance of student teachers by 'wise' tutors (who might function as both trainers and counsellors). In practice, mentors are often established teachers who (by virtue, of teaching within 'successful' PE departments) are taken to embody 'good practice'. In its formal sense, mentoring consists of the twin functions of peer assistance and peer review (Stroot and Ko, 2006). Mentoring involves advice and guidance on not only content and teaching (styles) but also on the broader and more philosophical dimensions of PE, such as the aims and purposes of the subject. In practice, however, mentors see themselves as guiding teacher trainees in three main aspects of PE: the content of lessons, the management and delivery of lessons, and more general reflection on their teaching. In effect, mentors see themselves primarily as having a *practical* role – passing on to student teachers practical advice about the day-to-day demands of teaching PE, focused upon 'the immediate, practical issues of subject-specific teaching and classroom management and control' (Booth, 1993: 194).

Perhaps unsurprisingly – given trainee teachers' inevitable concerns with the day-to-day realities of teaching and accumulating school-based practical experience of teaching (Tinning, 2006) – mentors appear to have greater impact upon the teaching behaviours and attitudes of trainees than their training programmes (Behets and Vergauwen, 2006). Conseqently, mentors and fellow teachers play a more substantial part in the socialization of trainee teachers than their university tutors, especially where the mentors are older, more established and more 'set in their ways'. In light of what is known about the significance of proximity for role-modelling, it is hardly surprising that trainee PE teachers tend to be more influenced by their mentors and colleagues on teaching practice. Mentors and other PE teachers are not only in greater proximity to the trainee teacher on a daily basis, they are also inevitably seen as more realistic representations of what the trainee aspires to become. Student teachers' perceived need to emulate what their mentors do means that custom and practice tend to be reinforced rather than challenged.

The move towards school-centred and school-based teacher training – well-established in Britain and growing rapidly in the US – is also associated with the development of 'competencies'. In recent years, many countries have begun to follow the lead of the UK and the USA in adopting a behaviouristic approach to teacher education, resulting in the identification of competencies for teachers – specific teaching skills deemed to constitute effective teaching 'performed at a pre-specified level of mastery' (Tinning, 2006: 371). Teacher trainees are now required to audit their experiences and expertise prior to commencing their teacher training programme, with a view to identifying what action they need to take to enable them to meet the professional standards for QTS and in order to develop professional 'competencies' (Stidder and Hayes, 2006) during their 'blocks' of school experience or 'teaching practice'.

With the exception of 'teaching practice', the negligible impact of professional socialization – in the form of PEITT – on the ideologies and preferred practices of prospective PE teachers has been described by Evans et al. (1996: 169) as leaving their views and practices 'neither shaken nor stirred by training'. In other words, trainee teachers tend to make short-term situational adjustments to the immediate demands of their training courses in order to achieve their primary goal of qualifying as a teacher.

In practical terms, however, teacher training appears to make no difference; that is, the difference between teachers with varying 'philosophies' is unlikely to be explainable in terms of their training. Prospective PE teachers assimilate what they are taught on PEITT courses through the prism of their own (typically sport-oriented) presuppositions and preoccupations. What PE teachers think, as well as the behaviours they are inclined towards, are best explained in terms of a blend of more deeply-seated values, beliefs and attitudes, and the context in which they operate. In particular, what tends to make a substantive difference to practice are differences in people's *circumstances*; in other words the constraints arising within particular school settings (Green, 2003).

Overall, in the same way that the significance of academic debate about the nature and purposes of PE is frequently exaggerated, so too is the (negligible) impact of professional socialization in the form of PEITT. Recruits to PE teaching who share a common background – typically consisting of sport and games – may have great difficulty envisaging alternative curriculum models for the subject. Since so few recruits have experience in models other than that of 'traditional' PE (with its emphasis on sport and games), few may accept that such alternatives can exist except in the minds of textbook writers and teacher educators. Evans's research illustrates the ways in which teacher training in England and Wales merely serves to reinforce the already existing values and beliefs of new teachers.

Lawson (1983a) coined the term 'subjective warrant' to refer to the various ways in which 'a person's perception of the requirements of and benefits of work in a given profession weighed against self-assessments of aspiration and competence'. One form of subjective warrant, he suggested, is a 'coaching orientation'; that is, the desire to coach school sport and school teams, in particular. Many PE teachers, it seems, view 'teaching as a career contingency for coaching' (Tsangaridou, 2006a: 492). The other prominent form of subjective warrant is, according to Lawson, a 'teaching orientation', wherein the teacher's main concern is with teaching curricular PE (Curtner-Smith, 2001). Although such a distinction expresses a false dichotomy, Green's (2003) study added weight to the view that not only do trainee PE teachers with a strong sporting ideology tend to focus on coaching sports, some teachers also act as coaches outside their work as teachers. Indeed, in the USA, 'teachers are often hired because of their ability to coach a sport rather than their teaching prowess' (Curtner-Smith et al., 2007: 133). While Tsangaridou (2006a) explores the tensions that many PE teachers experience in managing their dual roles of teacher and coach, Green (2003) argues that, in fact, PE teachers tend not to clearly distinguish between these roles, either in theory or in practice.

Professional (or occupational) socialization and reproduction 'on the job'
Like all knowledge, PE teachers' knowledge of their subject is social; that is,
it is acquired from other people, sometimes casually (for example, through
playing sport) and sometimes deliberately (through mentoring, for example).
The socially constructed nature of PE teachers' 'philosophies' and practices
is, of course, a process and as such does not cease on completion of teacher
training. Newcomers to the PE 'profession' are frequently obliged to adapt
their behaviours – and subsequently their views – upon joining their new
colleagues, departments and schools, since all the surrounding positions are
still occupied by the same teachers as before and they generally want things
to carry on as before. The workplace, especially early-on in teachers' careers,
is important in supporting or restricting their practices (Capel, 2005;
Lawson, 1983a, 1983b) as they find themselves constrained not only by the
dominant values and beliefs of their colleagues, departments and schools,
but also by practical matters to do with facilities and equipment. This helps
explain why the impact of teacher education tends to be 'washed out'
relatively soon after teachers begin teaching 'properly' (Stroot and Ko, 2006).
Teachers only tend to move away from their preferred teaching styles and
practices when they are constrained to do so by their circumstances (Green,
2003) and return to their earlier, preferred methods as soon as they can
(Stroot and Ko, 2006).

Time spent 'on the job' is likely to lead to longer-term changes in PE
teachers' habituses for two main reasons: first, the significance of everyday
teaching (or 'field') experiences for their views on the nature and purposes of
the subject and, second, the sheer duration of this experience. Not only will
context tend to have profound significance for PE teachers' practices, it will
impact upon their 'philosophies' and lead to reinforcement, adaptation or
change in their views and practices. When the working situation changes,
teachers' behaviours tend to change. Constraints on practice matter more
than theory in determining what teachers do and how they do it. PE teachers
respond to the immediate pressures of the job in terms of dealing with the
constraints of the day-to-day practice of teaching. Solving practical problems
(Fejgin, 1995) is a form of 'on-the-job' training in the craft of teaching. Those
on teaching practice or newly qualified as teachers often experience a marked
disjuncture between what is taught in teacher training and what is actually
practised in the gym or on the sports field. It is perhaps unsurprising, then,
that the most common response upon entering the work place is a 'custodial
stance' (Tsangaridou, 2006a) in which teachers accept, and rarely question,
the ways things *are*, thereby reinforcing the status quo: 'The new teacher ...
learns, accepts and implements ... the customary strategies' (Stroot and Ko,
2006: 427). As newcomers, they are once again junior members of staff keen
to fit in with, and become established among, their colleagues.

It is important to recognize that what teachers do in practice is not nec-essarily the best ways of teaching – either in their own minds or in terms of ideal-type models of 'good practice'. Rather, they are often the 'best on offer' (Evans and Davies, 1986) in the context of the constraints of orthodox depart-mental practice, staffing constraints, available resources and pupils. The 'styles' of teaching that emerge and develop in the context of such constraints come to be so deeply embedded in teachers' behaviours that they become part of their habituses and are viewed as inevitable, irrespective of whether or not they are deemed desirable, let alone examples of 'good practice' (Evans and Davies, 1986). Hence, teachers' reluctance or inability to embrace change wholesale and the, perhaps inevitable, 'slippage' between policy and practice. Consequently, conservatism often appears an inherent feature of PE (Evans and Davies, 1986).

Nevertheless, because the new arrivals are never completely identical to their predecessors and their adjustment is never total, what happens in the name of PE is bound to change over time. There is, inevitably, a degree of change alongside continuity. Acting as a dragnet to change is (a) the involve-ment of the established teachers in the selection of the new ones, and (b) their tendency to 'co-opt' teachers like themselves to teach what they already have in place on the curriculum. Indeed, because established groups of PE teach-ers have a tendency to close ranks when confronted with new policies or new teachers, differences between old and new often tend to be exaggerated and the outsiders perceived and portrayed as not only different but in some ways inferior. This certainly appears to be the case with regard to graduate PE teachers with Sports Science backgrounds. One common consequence of this process is that newcomers are constrained to adopt an 'if you can't beat them, join them' mentality and they, in turn, close ranks.

Thus, occupational socialization as a process is characterized by consec-utive generations of PE teachers absorbing newcomers into what amount to very similar PE department networks. Consequently, and despite incremental changes, there remains a large degree of continuity as PE departments repro-duce and regenerate themselves. It is the tendency towards self-replication that enables the dominant ideologies in PE to become self-replicating, as the common-sense ways of defining PE (evident in teachers' discourse [Penny and Evans, 1999]) serve to constrain teachers towards particular ideologies of PE. The manner in which PE teachers joke, for example, about physically unco-ordinated pupils, criticize national sporting performance in 'traditional' team games, and gossip and ridicule overweight pupils serves as a form of social coercion upon teachers which leads to 'self-coercion'. Nevertheless, the net-works individuals and groups of people belong to often change over time. In the same way that individual PE teachers' sporting participation styles may change as they grow older (for example, from team to individual sports) with correlative changes in their perceptions of appropriate PE content, the networks of generations of PE teachers may change and the involvement of recent generations holding Sports Science degrees and public qualifications in PE (see Chapter 5) may be an example.

It is often external constraint that leads to changes in the individual and group habituses of PE teachers, departments and organizational networks. Recent developments in England and Wales – linking secondary schools with each other and their feeder primary schools (see Chapter 2) – have meant that many PE departments and teachers have been expected to take on an increasingly diverse range of roles, such as Director of Sport and School Sport Coordinator (O'Donovan and Kay, 2005). Similarly, and despite increasing resources for schools (and PE, in particular), teachers find themselves in a period characterized by excessive workloads, poor pupil behaviour, public criticism and a lack of autonomy (Armour and Yelling, 2004). The teaching of any subject, but particularly one as emotionally resonant as PE, is inevitably influenced by the 'prevailing social and economic circumstances' and related 'attitudes towards education and beliefs about learning and teaching' (Hallam and Ireson, 1999: 68). In recent decades politicians and policy-makers have demonstrated increased interest in both pedagogy and PE (see Chapter 2). Despite their many public rhetorical commitments to 'letting teachers teach', successive governments have found ways of making their prescriptions for good practice clear; prescriptions which have a tendency towards oversimplification and 'folk pedagogy' (Watkins and Mortimer, 1999).

Professional socialization through CPD According to Armour (2006: 203), pedagogical research to date has tended to focus upon the 'relatively brief process' of PEITT and eschewed teachers' education and training throughout the rest of their careers. In light of the fact that over a 35-year teaching career a single teacher could teach approximately 30,000 lessons and up to 100,000 pupils, Armour (2006: 204) is concerned not only with the apparent dearth of CPD but also its quality: 'historically', she observes, 'professional development programmes have had ambitious aspirations that have not been realised'. Citing Ward and O'Sullivan (1998) Armour (2006) suggests that teachers' failure to engage in ongoing training is likely to result in professional isolation and lead to pedagogic reductionism.

Professional and political interest in CPD (see, for example, DfEE, 2000, 2001; *Journal of Teaching Physical Education*, 2006) – defined in broad terms as 'all types of professional learning undertaken by teachers beyond the initial point of training' (Craft, 1996: 6, cited in Armour and Yelling, 2004: 96) – has grown substantially around the world (Bechtel and O'Sullivan, 2006) and in England and Wales (Armour, 2005), in particular, over the past decade or so.

Improving the quantity and quality of CPD is viewed as a means of dealing with a number of issues in education generally and PE in particular. Continuing Professional Development, it is claimed, should involve teachers coming to appreciate how 'high-quality'[1] PE and school sport can be used as a tool for raising educational standards and improving schools as a whole, particularly in terms of attendance, behaviour management and pupil attainment (Armour, 2005; DfES/DCMS, 2003). The policy is underpinned by 'the assumption that more [and more closely regulated] CPD, properly structured and funded, will ensure that standards [of teaching and then pupil learning] will rise' (Armour and Yelling, 2004: 97). There is an expectation not only that the impact of initiatives such as CPD will be monitored and evaluated but that, in the process, causal links between CPD and pupil learning will be identified and measured (Armour and Duncombe, 2004).

All this begs the question, what constitutes useful or effective CPD, not only in general terms but specifically in PE? Armour's work explores the effectiveness of PE-CPD and 'the ways in which experienced PE teachers learn throughout their careers' (Armour and Yelling, 2004: 96). She points to 'the high value … teachers placed on learning together and from each other' (Armour, 2005: 22). This should not surprise us given what we know about the efficacy and primacy of 'occupational socialization'. Indeed, it is easy to overlook the fact that CPD – in the sense of socialization into the teaching profession – goes on all the time; it is a career-long process (Lawson, 1983b). It is simply not always planned or even, for that matter, something teachers are conscious of. Indeed, it is often informal rather than formal. In effect, it is occupational socialization in the sense that PE teachers inevitably acquire 'knowledge' from those around them (Stroot and Ko, 2006) while 'on the job'. In other words, CPD – in the broader sense corresponding to ongoing 'training' – takes the form of informal or formal constraints that result from being profoundly interdependent with groups of colleagues in particular settings on a regular basis, often for many years.

It is, then, unsurprising that CPD tends to be less about their personal and professional development in any profoundly reflexive sense of the term and more about teachers resolving what, for themselves at least, are the more pressing practical issues and problems. This is why teachers have tended to view CPD with some scepticism (Armour and Yelling, 2004) and as merely 'going on a course' (Armour and Yelling, 2007): they want immediate, practical benefits and tend to view CPD as tantamount to short courses of the in-service training variety (Keay, 2007). It is also why, traditionally, 'PE teachers have engaged in comparatively little CPD' (Armour and Yelling, 2004: 103): Bechtel and O'Sullivan (2006) note that many PE teachers in the USA do not perceive CPD as beneficial to their development or practice. Where PE teachers do engage with CPD it is no accident that they have tended to focus upon three things: traditional content knowledge (for example, improving sporting expertise via governing body awards), new content knowledge (in order to deliver examinations in PE) and career development (such as preparing for future head of department roles).

An increasingly important dimension to PE teachers' collective, 'we' identities is the professional status of their occupation.

PROFESSIONALIZATION AND PHYSICAL EDUCATION

The term 'profession' is usually used to denote a type of occupation accorded high status and a high degree of control over its work, and the term 'professional' is often taken to connote 'expertise and probity' (Gabe et al., 2004: 163). In short, 'professionalization' is the process by which an occupational grouping (such as physical educationalists or even sports scientists) lays claim to such characteristics. There tend to be several key features of occupational groupings which are viewed as professions: long formal training, a high degree of autonomy and self-regulation, and correspondingly high status. Of particular concern to those claiming professional status is their freedom to exercise judgement through discretionary powers (Frowe, 2005).

Occupational groups who position themselves at 'the nodes where numerous links converge' (de Swaan, 2001: 19) are likely to be perceived as fulfilling the needs of others (for example, in relation to the health of the nation or national sporting success) and to be in a relatively sufficient position of power – as 'purveyors of specialized knowledge … to those who believe they need such knowledge' (de Swaan, 2001: 37) – to become recognized as a 'profession'. Physical education has historically been characterized by relatively low and marginal academic status at all levels of the educational system, and this has been an ongoing concern for PE teachers and PE academics (Fitzclarence and Tinning, 1990). In recent times, physical educationalists – particularly academicians – have appeared preoccupied with establishing themselves as a profession and have become increasingly aware of the need to occupy a central position in one or more networks (for example, health promotion, school examinations and sports performance). Consequently, the bases for claims to professional status among physical educationalists have tended to revolve around claims to 'scientific' expertise in health promotion, the personal and social development of young people and the identification and nurturing of elite sporting talent.

So much for becoming a PE teacher and establishing PE as a profession, what about the science or art of teaching itself?

THE SCIENCE, ART AND CRAFT OF TEACHING

Pedagogy

A seldom clearly defined and frequently contested term (Watkins and Mortimer, 1999), 'pedagogy' tends to find employment as a catch-all term for the 'science', 'art' or even 'craft' of teaching; that is, what we come to know and understand about the process of teaching via empirical research, reflection and theorizing. Watkins and Mortimer (1999: 3) define pedagogy as 'any conscious activity by one person designed to enhance learning in another'. This very general definition allows for such varied activities as hinting, encouraging, guiding, instructing, informing, narrating, lecturing, demonstrating, exercising, testing, examining, criticizing, drilling and so on, and is redolent of Oakeshott's (1972) definition of teaching itself; that is, anything (morally acceptable) that enables something (of worth) intended by a teacher to be learned, understood and remembered by the learner. The concept of pedagogy seems, however, to connote something more than this. It implies a technical and scientific understanding of the process of teaching. This is what Clark (2005: 289) seems to have in mind when he says that 'teaching today is treated as a technology – an applied social science'.

The knowledge base of teaching has, as with knowledge over time, simultaneously become more differentiated and more integrated (Watkins and Mortimore, 1999). Thus, pedagogy encompasses such diverse aspects as teaching and learning styles, subject and lesson content, and the organization of lessons as well as the grouping of pupils therein. These are, of course, interdependent dimensions of teaching. In PE, for example, the skill and ability levels of pupils and the numbers of pupils in a class tend to have a substantial impact upon the delivery of lessons and, in particular, the teaching style(s) employed. Recognition that the content of what is taught influences how it is taught is one thing, but what exactly is the relationship between pedagogy and the curriculum? The relationship between content and teaching is perhaps best illustrated via one area of pedagogical research that has developed substantially over the last two decades; namely, teaching styles.

Teaching styles[2]

It is widely accepted, in academic circles, that *how* young people are taught is as important as *what* – in terms of content – is taught (see, for example, Capel, 2005). Although there is a National Curriculum for England and Wales that prescribes the latter, it does not prescribe the former. Implicit, however, is the suggestion that a variety of teaching strategies (or styles) should be utilized (Mawer, 1993).

Teaching strategies, approaches or styles have been the subject of study in PE for 30 years or more. Research on PE teaching has tended to focus on teaching behaviours and classroom experiences of pupils with a view to discerning the most effective teaching 'styles'. In general terms, concern with styles can be traced back to debates surrounding 'authoritarian' and 'democratic' approaches to leadership and teaching during the inter- and post-war years. These were often euphemisms for what were implicitly viewed as 'good' and 'bad' approaches to teaching (Watkins and Mortimore, 1999). This crude dichotomy gave way to attempts to establish a continuum between formal and informal poles, of the kind that continue to underpin discussions about the teaching of PE. Since the publication in the USA of Mosston's (1966) *Teaching Physical Education*, the use of a range of teaching styles has increasingly been advocated in PE literature internationally and has become a leitmotif of the training of PE teachers. The spectrum represents a continuum of (11) supposedly identifiable teaching styles (Mosston and Ashworth, 2002) – ranging from direct, formal, teacher-centred to indirect, informal, student-centred approaches – that tend to be grouped in a variety of ways in relation to the tendency for decision-making within PE lessons to be dominated by the teacher at one end of the continuum or by pupils at the other. Thus, at one end of the spectrum, lies the most teacher-centred style, referred to as the 'command' style, where the teacher makes virtually all the decisions. At the other end is what is known as the 'self-teaching' style whereby learners are centrally involved in decision-making about the learning process, if not the content: as Byra (2006) puts it, the 'how' and 'why' if not the 'what'.

It is suggested that the different styles of teaching PE not only vary in their purpose but are appropriate depending upon the diversity of students' needs, the context in which teaching is taking place and the particular content and aims of the lesson (for example, safety considerations, skill development, personal and social development, and health promotion) (Byra, 2006). Many academic physical educationalists, including the PE advisory and inspection service, OFSTED – promote the view that 'good teachers' utilize a range and variety of approaches or models of teaching to 'cater for differences in pupils' abilities, attainment, needs and ages' (Capel, 2005: 112).

Despite debates surrounding the appropriateness or otherwise of particular teaching styles, it is worth remembering that for very many teachers – newly qualified and relatively inexperienced teachers, in particular – control is the first priority and pupil learning comes a long way second (Ireson et al., 1999). In addition, pupil compliance tends to be seen by many teachers as a necessary prerequisite for effective teaching. In PE, the more 'traditional', teacher-led, 'command' or teacher-centred teaching styles are held to be most effective in helping teachers control and manage the classroom (Curtner-Smith et al., 2001) and to facilitate the teaching of physical and sporting skills

(Salvara et al, 2006). Therefore, 'teacher-centred instructional styles continue to be the most commonly observed approaches to teaching in physical education classes in the 2000s' (Byra, 2006: 450). This is especially the case with what are perceived as more problematic classes. Secondary school teachers in general in the UK tend, for example, when teaching lower-ability grouped classes, to provide structured work with more opportunities for rehearsal and repetition, fewer opportunities for discussion or self-direction and less feedback to pupils (Hallam and Ireson, 2005); in effect, they employ a more traditional, direct style of teaching to match a perceived need for student control (Cothran et al., 2005).

Traditional teacher-centred teaching styles continue to dominate the practice of PE teachers despite the emphasis on 'pupil-centred' approaches in the NCPE and innovations such as sport education and model-based teaching (Kirk, 2005; Morgan et al., 2005). Indeed, internationally, 'reproduction styles' are 'much more commonly used and viewed more positively than the production styles, regardless of the country' (Cothran et al., 2005: 199). It seems that many PE teachers' abiding concern with developing their pupils' sporting skills and performance encourages them to employ direct teaching styles (Capel, 2005; Curtner-Smith, 1999). That said, while PE teachers, in general, use more formal than informal teaching approaches, there is a gender dimension to teaching PE. Male and female PE teachers tend to favour particular content (Waddington et al., 1998) and particular teaching strategies or styles (Capel, 2005; Harris and Penney, 2002). While both men and women utilize guided discovery approaches, male PE teachers have a predilection for more direct, didactic strategies and women have a greater tendency to utilize problem-solving approaches (Capel, 2005). To some extent this is likely to be a product of their own socialization into PE and sport. Teachers who have participated in 'traditional' sport at a high level appear to be more likely to hold a conservative orientation towards the content and teaching styles of 'traditional' PE (Lawson, 1986). By contrast, teachers who have participated in non-traditional sports and other types of physical activity are 'more likely to have an innovative orientation towards physical education' (Capel, 2005: 117).

Of the six activity areas in the NCPE in England and Wales, the more formal, teacher-centred styles are typically associated with the teaching of games and athletic activities, and those areas that involve profound safety issues (for example, swimming and outdoor and adventurous activities). The more informal (pupil-centred) styles, on the other hand, tend to be reserved for the two 'areas' that lend themselves to greater degrees of independence and discovery: namely, dance and (educational) gymnastics (Evans et al., 1996) – particularly when female teachers teach girls. This tendency is reinforced by the long-standing tradition of pupil-centred 'guided discovery' in these areas. The more pupil-centred, 'productive' teaching styles are said to be particularly useful in those lessons that require pupils to think for themselves.

The presence of a mandatory curriculum (such as the National Curriculum in England and Wales), along with the mandatory assessments that tend to accompany it, has profound consequences for teaching styles. The requirements for ongoing assessment of pupils' achievement, for example, constrains teachers towards more didactic teaching methods. Overall, PE teachers' predispositions towards utilizing teacher-centred approaches tend to be reinforced by a variety of internal and external pressures. Government concern with teacher effectiveness, in particular, tends to focus teachers' attention on pupil achievement in tasks where there are measurable outcomes (Hallam and Ireson, 1999) and this tends to lead to more centralized and standardized organization and sequencing of the curriculum and its content. The discourse of 'effective teaching' (Hallam and Ireson, 1999: 75) also serves to constrain teachers towards outcomes and thus towards more directed teaching styles. Thus, the employment of appropriate and effective teaching styles is one aspect of a broader political and academic focus upon 'good' and 'effective' teaching and 'high-quality PE'.

'Good' teaching and 'high-quality PE'

Nowhere is the desire to make policy and practice more 'evidence-based' – and, as a corollary, research into the various facets of education more 'scientific' and less ideological – more apparent than in education. Many educationalists advocate the scientific investigation of 'the causes of "effective" teaching' (Clark, 2005: 289) and this is particularly pertinent in relation to government policy towards 'high-quality PE'.

The terms 'quality PE' and 'good teaching' are sufficiently commonplace in the discourse surrounding PE (see, for example, DfES/DCMS, 2003; DfES/DCMS, 2004; OFSTED, 2005a; World Summit on Physical Education, 1999) to suggest that there is widespread consensus regarding both what these terms mean and their suitability as ideal types. But this is far from true. What constitutes a 'good' PE teacher and 'high-quality' PE teaching is not clear in the policy documents and related strategies. The supposed characteristics of 'good' or 'high-quality' PE teachers and teaching have to be interpreted from lengthy lists of 'outcomes' and features of 'provision' (DfES/DCMS, 2004: 1). Indeed, there is very little in these documents that any contemporary PE teacher might plausibly dissent from or might not simply assume to be part and parcel of what is expected of PE teachers. 'High-quality [PE] teachers' are, among other things, committed and enthusiastic individuals who provide positive role models, listen to their pupils and improve their own subject expertise (DfES/DCMS, 2004: 16).

Similarly, the 'basic principles' (DfES/DCMS, 2004: 1) describe how 'high-quality PE' enables all young people to take part in and enjoy PE and sport, whilst improving their abilities and promoting health. The stated 'outcomes' include developing 'young people who ... are *committed* to PE and sport ... understand that PE and sport are an important part of a *healthy, active lifestyle* ... have the skills ... they need ... [and] enjoy PE, school and community sport' (p.3; emphases in the original). There is, in short, much (in idealistic terms) about the end product but little or nothing (in practical terms) about the process by which 'high quality PE' might be achieved. In effect, government publications on 'high-quality PE and sport' (DfES/DCMS, 2004) read more like a 'call to arms' than guides to good practice.

We have to look elsewhere for descriptions of what are perceived as 'good' or 'effective' teachers. And it becomes clear that more than subject expertise is seen as necessary. On the basis of his study, Mawer (1995: 4) suggested that, in addition to being skilled at sport and knowledgeable about their subject, 'the most frequently mentioned attributes and personality characteristics of a good PE teacher were considered to be: enthusiasm, sense of humour, approachability, patience and the ability to be a good communicator and organizer'. Similarly, according to Hare (1993), the attributes deemed admirable for the 'good teacher', in general, include a number of qualities of character beyond 'excellence' in subject knowledge such as humility, courage, impartiality, open-mindedness, empathy and enthusiasm. It seems almost impossible to say which of the above are necessary and which are sufficient characteristics of the 'good teacher', not least because education involves a relationship in which one person (the pupil) tends to be highly dependent upon the other (the teacher). This is the reason why many take the view that teachers should have personal and moral as well technical 'skills'.

In this vein, it has been conventionally assumed over the last quarter of a century or so – at least in academic rhetoric – that a good teacher is one who, rather than being a mere technician (Behets and Vergauwen, 2006), regularly reflects upon his or her philosophy and practice.

The 'reflective practitioner'

Since the early 1990s, one of the major developments in teacher education has been the rise to prominence of the notion of 'reflective practice' (Capel, 2005; Tinning, 2006) Reflective practice is said to come in three broad forms ranging from a weak to a strong sense of the term. The weakest sense is also the most frequently used sense of the term, in which reflection is viewed 'as a utilitarian mechanism for improving the execution of teaching skills' (Williams,

1993: 137). In this sense, reflection is purely instrumental insofar as it is intended to help teachers replicate practices that both experience and empirical research have suggested are effective (Capel, 2005; Williams, 1993, 1998; Zwozdiak-Myers, 2006): it 'involves the identification of a number of specific strategies which are seen to be central to "good teaching"' (Williams, 1993: 138). Somewhere towards the halfway point on the continuum of reflexivity is 'reflection as a form of deliberation among competing views of teaching' (Williams, 1993: 139). 'A teacher', for example, 'who is able to use a variety of styles is more likely to be able to select the most effective for a specific learning activity' (1993: 139). The strongest sense of the term interprets reflexivity as 'the reconstruction of oneself as a teacher, with an expectation that teachers will become more aware of the cultural milieu in which they operate' (1993: 140). This, for Williams (1993), would necessarily involve teachers reviewing and reconstructing their taken-for-granted assumptions about teaching, PE and education itself.

Populating PE with reflective practitioners remains an avowed goal of PEITT and CPD in PE. However, achieving the strongest sense of reflexivity seems an unlikely prospect and a naive aspiration given that most mentors encourage reflection upon day-to-day practice and seldom encourage student teachers to contemplate broader, philosophical concerns. Indeed, the very practice of being a PE teacher militates against any inclination to reflect. Opportunities are seldom available[3] for teachers to analyse and reflect upon their teaching (Tsangaridou, 2006a). Indeed, the trend evident in many countries in recent decades, towards more centralized, and therefore tighter, control over education generally and the training of teachers in particular, has reinforced the focus upon practically based skills and 'competencies'.

The claim that the strong sense of reflective practice matters because it is contiguous with practice, does not stand up to scrutiny. The view that reflection on PE affects how PE is taught is neither true for teachers or academics – it is to misunderstand the nature of PE as it is practised. Physical education teachers tend not to take a 'reflexive attitude' towards either their subject or their practices (Evans and Davies, 1986). Physical education teachers' 'philosophies' and practices have far more to do with their predispositions or habituses and the contexts in which they teach.

THE CONTEXT OF TEACHING

In moving towards a conclusion to this chapter, it is worth reminding ourselves just how constrained teachers are by their contexts. At a national level, constraint takes the form of national curricula, the funding arrangments for schools, school denomination, national examination systems and the advent of measurements of performance (such as the ubiquitous 'league tables'). At a local level, constraint is manifest in the denomination of the school, the catchment area (in the USA, retention rates after five years' teaching run at approximately 50 per cent but rates of attrition tend to be higher for those teaching in impoverished schools [Stroot and Ko, 2006]), the traditions of the school, governing body and headteacher ideologies, available resources, timetabling and policies towards the organization and grouping of students and class sizes, subject departments and their inherited characteristics and so on. Viewed in such contexts, the 'professional' autonomy of teachers was perhaps never as great as was commonly believed and appears to have diminished further with growing political interest and intervention (Fitz et al., 2006; Gorard et al., 2003; Mortimer, 1999; Penney and Evans, 1999).

CONCLUSION

This chapter has summarized some of the important processes and issues in teaching PE. The main focus has been on the process of becoming and being a PE teacher, including personal and professional socialization. It has explored the 'science' or pedagogy of PE and, in particular, teaching styles and the much vaunted ideal of the reflective practitioner. It seems that teachers view PE as a practical subject and teaching as a technical process. The socialization of PE teachers into sport and PE, helps us begin to understand why there is a tendency towards conservatism among PE teachers, which manifests itself in the passing on of skills-oriented and sport-dominated curricula. Teacher trainees and 'beginning' teachers are intuitively oriented towards 'reproducing and preserving the physical education they have experienced' (Placek et al., 1995: 248), and their experiences tend to reinforce this.

The longer they remain in the occupation, and the longer they remain at a particular school, the more conservative in their 'philosophies' and practices PE teachers are likely to become. Hence the tendency for PE to reflect a good deal of continuity alongside some degree of change. But PE is a process – it develops, inevitably. Because (1) newly qualified teachers are never completely identical to their predecessors and their slight differences (for example, in the sports they have experience of and in their academic background), and (2) changes in context (teaching in different schools, taking on new roles and implementing new legislation, for example) constrain teachers to change their practices (and their beliefs), PE is almost bound to develop, albeit incrementally, over time.

RECOMMENDED READING

Capel, S. (2005) 'Teachers, teaching and pedgagogy in physical education', in K. Green and K. Hardman (eds), *Physical Education: Essential Issues*. London: Sage. pp.111–27.

Tsangaridou, N. (2006a) 'Teachers' beliefs', in D. Kirk, D. Macdonald and M. O'Sullivan (eds), *The Handbook of Physical Education*. London: Sage. pp.486–501.

Tsangaridou, N. (2006b) 'Teachers' knowledge', in D. Kirk, D. Macdonald and M. O'Sullivan (eds), *The Handbook of Physical Education*. London: Sage. pp.502–15.

NOTES

1 The phrase 'quality PE' is increasingly prominent in PE even though attempts to establish its contours, where they exist, tend to be relatively brief, superficial and question-begging. According to the World Summit on Physical Education (1999), 'quality PE' is defined as 'the most effective and inclusive means of providing all children ... with the skills, attitudes, knowledge and understanding for lifelong participation in physical activity and sport'. But this begs the question what kinds of PE are the most effective and inclusive in achieving these purposes?

2 There is some confusion surrounding terminology with regard to teaching strategies and styles. Teaching strategies are often referred to as the planned episodes of teaching that are intended to bring about particular outcomes with particular individuals and groups, and thereby meet particular lesson objectives (Capel, 2005). Strategies involve decisions about how to organize lessons, what material to teach and how to teach it (Mawer, 1993). Teaching styles, by contrast, are generally understood to encompass the cluster of skills and strategies that a teacher uses, often habitually (Capel, 2005). Put another way, 'when a teacher begins to use a consistent set of teaching tactics, this is then considered to be their "teaching style"' (Mawer, 1993: 5). For the sake of simplicity, teaching styles is used as a generic term in this chapter.

3 However, in England and Wales in recent years, teachers (including trainees) have been 'guaranteed' a proportion of their teaching time for 'planning, preparation and assessment'. This allows for the possibility of reflective practice by building time into teachers' workloads. It is an open question, however, the extent to which such reflection as occurs is in anything other than the weakest sense or, for that matter, the extent to which schools meet this obligation.

Conclusion

Perhaps the most obvious way to conclude a book entitled *Understanding Physical Education* would be to reflect upon the preceding chapters as a basis for returning, full circle, to reconsider the nature and purposes of PE. To do so, however, may simply serve as a reminder that, as Telama (2002: ix) put it, 'the gap between what we say we want to do and what we are doing in practice has been and still is the main problem in physical education'. Rather than return (directly, at least) to the ideologically loaded question 'What *ought* to happen to PE?', it might be more interesting to speculate upon the likely future of the subject assuming the direction of recent policies and developments were to continue. This is, of course, a risky venture and will inevitably generate a number of hostages to fortune. It may be worthwhile, nonetheless, if only as a heuristic device to reflect upon the content of the book thus far and to return, indirectly, to the supposed nature and purposes of PE.

In an attempt to anticipate the consequences of trends and developments in PE, the remainder of the conclusion is structured around several processes which have been prominent themes in the book thus far and which may point the way to a major change in PE in many countries. The first of these processes – the 'sportization of PE' – has long been a feature of the subject.

THE SPORTIZATION OF PE

The term 'sportization' is employed as shorthand for a process by which sport becomes more and more prominent in not only the justification for but, more especially, the practice of PE. In extreme form, it represents the transformation of PE into school sport; in other words, a transformation from something nominally focused upon education to something essentially focused on sport (in both leisure or recreational and high-performance forms) and to which educational outcomes are purely incidental.

An initial phase of sportization within PE can be traced back to the emergence and development of games in the Victorian public schools (Kirk, 1992; 1998). A second phase took the form of the establishment of games, and sport generally, alongside gymnastic-type activities as the two staples of secondary school PE in the second half of the twentieth century. Recent developments suggest a third phase of sportization may be under way, one which finds expression in the increasing emphasis on school sport in government policies and, in England and Wales at least, in the increasing prevalence of the term 'school sport' alongside PE in the title of the subject. While the place of PE in school curricula may have been 'secured' (in terms of its place on the curriculum and time allocated to it) in some countries (Belgium and Holland and some Eastern European countries, for example) (Fisher, 2003) there is a trend towards treating PE as synonymous with school sport in many countries. This development hints at the possibility that PE – in the guise of school sport – might increasingly be driven towards the margins of school curricula (as an extra-curricular or even extra-school subject, for example) along the lines of either the American model of after-school, inter-school sporting competition or the European model of club-based sports participation; or even a combination of the two in the shape of the 'sports academies' that have emerged recently in Flanders (see Chapter 4). Indeed, in recent years a number of countries, such as Sweden, and some regions of Germany, have considered 'locating physical education outside the main school curriculum, delivered essentially in local sports centres', while in some parts of Australia 'curriculum physical education has been franchised out to external agencies in the interests of cost effectiveness' (Fisher, 2003: 141).

The preconditions for the process of sportization to result in a transformation of PE into school sport can be identified in several recent developments:

- The marketization of education in many countries and the associated demands for value for money from, and reduced expenditure towards, education. At the secondary level in England and Wales, for example, general educational policy aimed at loosening state control of schools has created educational markets in which competitive sport has become a marketing tool for schools. The economic and symbolic value of extra-curricular sport and inter-school sporting competition has long been recognized in the USA (see Chapter 4) and the marketization of education constrains PE departments to 'sell themselves' to their pupils and parents and, in so doing, their schools.
- The increased investment in, and greater policy emphasis on, school *sport* (see Chapter 2) which has made school sport a source of power for

external agencies such as governing bodies of sport and sports development agencies (for example, the YST in England). The often vocal demands of the representatives of (elite) sport and sporting organizations continue to 'drive' the policy agenda towards PE and school sport in many countries (Fisher, 2003).

- The range and utility of resources for PE (in the form of both people and equipment) made available to schools by sports organizations – the wealthier ones, in particular – and which tend to be received appreciatively by teachers (in primary schools especially) (see Chapters 2 and 3).

- The associated and increasing tendency for schools to turn for support towards adults other than teachers (AOTTs) – especially in the form of sports coaches and SDOs – to deliver aspects of curricular and extra-curricular PE (see Chapter 3). The wealthier, more established sports governing bodies (such as rugby union and football[1]) possess an abundance of coaches or development officers and are best able to fund an extensive supply of personnel and equipment to assist the delivery of PE. Although this may facilitate opportunities for participation (in primary schools in particular) and for the improvement through coaching of talented youngsters, the representatives of these sporting bodies tend to have sporting rather than educational priorities and tend to prefer working with and developing the more able youngsters.

- The high costs of maintaining sports facilities in schools may exacerbate the trend in policy to encourage schools to forge stronger links with sports clubs that, incidentally, can afford newer and more elaborate facilities (see Chapter 3).

- The likelihood that government and sporting agencies' funds will increasingly be diverted towards talent identification and nurturing, particularly in the lead-up to global sporting events (such as the Olympic Games or soccer World Cup) and especially in countries hosting such events.

- The fact that 'the bulk of the population of most countries and almost all politicians would be hard pressed to differentiate' (Fisher, 2003: 141) between PE and sport in schools – as, indeed, would PE teachers (see Chapter 1) – and are more likely to support rather than resist the sportization of PE.

Despite claims regarding the sportization of PE, it is important to note that the conceptual distinction between PE and school sport represents something of a false dichotomy. The former has almost always incorporated a good deal of the latter, while the latter is almost invariably perceived by its advocates as incorporating educational outcomes whether intentionally or otherwise. The significance of sportization may, therefore, be a matter of degree. In other words, the extent to which the process involves a shift towards one end of a continuum: towards a polarized version of sport in schools – consisting almost exclusively of sporting (predominantly team) games in the form of intra- and inter-school competition with a focus on the development of sporting skills and fitness for sporting performance at the expense of the other elements (such as HRE) that constitute conventional or ideal-type forms of PE.

For some physical educationalists, one of the features of anything worthy of the label 'physical education' would be HRE, and concern with PE as a vehicle for health promotion has rivalled sport for occupancy of the ideological high ground of the subject in recent decades.

THE HEALTHIZATION OF PE

Although this term jars on the ear it does allow for consistency by conceptualizing the relationship between health promotion and PE as a process, thereby underlining the claim that the orientation of PE towards health promotion may wax and wane. The first phase of the healthization of PE occurred around the turn of the twentieth century with the emergence and development of physical training in the nascent elementary schools (Kirk, 1992a). Whether emphasis upon physical fitness in the service of sports performance in the decades following the introduction of compulsory secondary schooling after the Second World War can reasonably be said to constitute a second phase, the emphasis upon exercise as a vehicle for health promotion in the last two decades of the twentieth century represents a significant reinvigoration of health-related exercise as a justification for PE. Nowhere is this better illustrated than in the re-badging of PE as Health and Physical Education in Australia.

Whether or not, the current context is likely to lead to a strengthening or diminution of the place of HRE in PE is difficult to anticipate. On the one hand, the conditions appear favourable for the growth of a health dimension to PE (see Chapter 6), in the form of:

- the increasing prevalence of physical and mental health illnesses for which more exercise is thought to be a, if not the, main antidote
- the fact that sport and PE offer a relatively cheap and easy policy 'solution' for governments and a ready-made justification for the existence of PE
- the likelihood that schools will continue to be viewed by governments as a suitable setting for health promotion via early intervention
- the existence of a vibrant lobby for PE as a vehicle for health promotion in PEITT and academe as well as among governments and the medical profession

• succesive generations of PE teachers with an ideological and, to some extent, practical grounding in HRE.

On the other hand, the future of a health orientation to PE (and HRE itself) may be uncertain for the following reasons. Claims by PE teachers to a central role in promoting health are likely to provide a substantial hostage to fortune. Hitherto, physical educationalists have been able to respond to criticisms that their subject appeared unable to combat under-exercising and, by extension, obesity by pointing out that it had never been given a realistic chance (in the form of the resources) to carry out such a mission. Substantial sums of money have been allocated to PE in recent years (in the UK, in particular), in the expectation that it would result in changes in levels of physical activity and, consequently, an improvement in the prevalence of overweight and obesity. However, such grand expectations may return to haunt the PE profession when it becomes evident to all concerned that no matter how much money is 'invested' in PE and school sport, PE may be powerless to provide a silver bullet solution to a problem that is more complex in its origins.

Overall, the healthization of PE appears set to remain the least transformative of the three major processes. While HRE has become more central to justifications for the subject, this has not been reflected in the practice of PE to the extent that might have been expected. Although HRE has become established as a de facto 'activity area' in its own right in a number of countries, this does not appear to represent a substantial shift towards a pre-eminence of HRE at the expense of sport and games in mainstream PE curricula – quite the reverse, in fact. Nevertheless, HRE is one aspect of a process that does appear to be changing the practice of PE: that of academicization.

THE ACADEMICIZATION OF PE

Physical educationalists have long sought to provide theoretical and practical justifications for their subject in ways that have, in effect, treated PE as a vehicle for other, seemingly more laudable and educationally valid, goals than merely playing sport. In recent decades a genuinely academic justification for PE has become available (see Chapter 5). The rapid growth of academic qualifications in PE has enabled physical educationalists to present theirs as a more authentically academic subject than up to now: one that not only satisfies the epistemological requirements of the dominant liberal conception of education but also provides very tangible benefits for schools in terms of an additional and popular examination subject. The preconditions for a continuation of the process of academicization appear visible in several recent developments, including:

- the economic and status value, and corresponding marketing appeal, of examinable PE (in the form, for example, of GCSE and A level PE/Sport in England and Wales)
- the corresponding demands (in some schools) for PE to make a contribution to academic success at a time when there is growing political pressure on schools to 'free up curriculum time for supposedly more important subjects' (Fisher, 2003: 141) such as mathematics, national languages and literature, science and vocational subjects
- the desire on the part of physical educationalists at all levels for professional status and the apparent potential for the academic version of the subject to provide this
- the increasing numbers of qualified PE teachers who are predisposed towards an academic variant of PE having themselves (1) undertaken some form of PE or sport-related qualification while at school and, (2) studied sports science (or its equivalent) at university
- the potential of examinable PE as a power resource for PE teachers within their schools.

Although the twin processes of sportization and academicization appear set to dominate PE in the near future, they seem somewhat paradoxical. This apparent paradox may not, however, be irreconcilable. A number of interested groups within the PE network in England and Wales (for example, OFSTED, a number of academics, headteachers and many PE teachers themselves) appear happy to endorse both processes and both appear to be gathering pace.

WHAT FUTURE FOR PE?

Whether or not the above processes are likely, in configuration, to result in major, long-term or more subtle, even transitory, changes to PE – or even cancel each other out – is impossible to say. Currently, PE continues to be relatively established on school curricula in many countries and PE teachers retain a large measure of professional autonomy and control over curricular and extra-curricular PE. Nevertheless, viewed on a continuum from stability through fragmentation to transformation, PE is evidently becoming more fragmented and unstable.

The upshot of a configuration of the twin processes of sportization and academicization could well be that the term 'physical *education*' becomes increasingly associated with, and reserved for, examinable (and especially academic) forms of the subject, while 'traditional' PE – re-branded as 'school sport' – is moved to the margins of the curriculum (that is, to extra-curricular PE and sports clubs). In academic form, PE might be available only to pupils in the later years of secondary schooling as a vocational and/or academic subject offering qualifications that point pupils towards employment opportunities (in the growing fields of leisure sport and health and exercise) or further study (in related fields, such as Sport and Exercise Sciences).

Ironically, and despite the potential for enhanced professional status that appears inherent in examinable PE, the success of examinations in PE in configuration with the emphasis on links between PE and external sporting agencies may bring about a realignment between PE and external agencies (such as sports governing bodies) as a consequence of the tilting of the power-balance away from the former and towards the latter. The networks that PE teachers are involved in are becoming ever more complex, and policies aimed at encouraging AOTTs to become involved with curricular and extra-curricular activities threaten the status of PE and the autonomy of PE teachers. Their increasing dependence upon and integration with SDOs and sports coaches points to the possibility of status convergence between PE teachers and these occupational groups. Indeed, the steady influx of 'unqualified' outsiders such as coaches and SDOs alongside the increased division of specialized labour in PE (between examination and practical roles among PE teachers and between PE teachers themselves and AOTTs) is set to reinforce the likelihood that PE teachers will one day oversee an examinable subject while SDOs and coaches are left to train youngsters in particular sports. This might, in turn, be expected to lead to a preference for the recruitment of PE teachers with coaching specialisms and coaching orientations (in a manner similar to the present situation in the USA). It might even lead to the recruitment of coaches rather than qualified teachers (similar to the situation that currently exists in many private schools in the UK) as the sole or main deliverers of school sport. What would amount to a *de-professionalization* of PE as such would likely be exaggerated by the following current trends:

- the normalization of the involvement of sports coaches and SDOs in PE
- the widespread acceptance among physical educationalists that PE and sport, are to all intents and purposes, synonymous (see Chapter 1). Jones (2006: 7) observes that, 'some scholars,[2] while acknowledging that both activities are sometimes driven by distinct goals, consider that the line of demarcation between teaching and coaching is not so obvious or, indeed, necessary'
- developments including the increasing significance of assessment in

education and the growth of public examinations in PE and expectations regarding the development of youngsters with sporting talent and links with sports clubs and the growth in provision of coaching awards for teachers.

It is perfectly feasible that these developments will reinforce, not to say exaggerate the well-established tendencies among PE teachers to (1) rely upon formal, command-style teaching strategies redolent of and common-place among sports coaches, and (2) utilize CPD opportunities to resolve pressing practical issues, such as the delivery of examinable PE or the need for specific coaching-oriented courses and qualifications (rather than the more personal and professional development programmes that academics, at least, might favour) thereby preparing themselves for one of two distinct roles – teaching academic PE or coaching sport.

The consequences of the continued sportization and academicization of PE for pupils are equally difficult to second guess, not least because of the relative independence of young people's sporting and leisure lives from PE (see Chapters 7 and 8). Evans and Davies (1986) observed that PE makes both friends and enemies of young people, it both inspires and enables and alienates and dissuades pupils; and sometimes both at the same time! Some aspects of the aforementioned processes hold out the promise of enhancing the wide sporting repertoires that appear an important aspect of lifelong participation in sport and physical activity. Nevertheless, to the extent that we are witnessing a separation of PE and school sport – with the former revolving around examinations and HRE and the latter consisting solely of sport – the potential contribution of PE to youngsters' sporting participation is likely to remain under-explored. Nonetheless, there are no grounds for thinking that class, gender and ethnicity will cease to be anything other than the most significant of determinants of participation and success in PE and sport, because of the continued significance of cultural and social capital irrespective of economic developments. Boys' and girls' involvement in PE and sport may well continue, by degrees, to converge as girls' participation in leisure sport and PE increase, albeit to an optimal level: with both girls and boys there are always likely to be out-of-reach groups. Even though girls are likely to participate in increasing numbers – including in activities once associated with boys, such as football, basketball, cricket and some outdoor pursuits – the constraints caused by the relative incompatibility of sport generally and some sports in particular with many girls' perceptions of preferred femininity (as well as some boys' perceptions of masculinity) will very probably continue to delimit levels and forms of participation. Women's and ethnic minorities' perceptions of some places and some facilities as unconducive even prohibitive to their participation will undoubtedly continue to restrict the involvement of all but the most independent. That said, increasing numbers of young women (especially from the expanding middle classes) are, indeed, beginning to lead the kinds of leisure lives once associated with young males.

One thing seems certain in the short term: as its borders become more contested, PE is likely to lose some of the coherence it may once have possessed for PE teachers and pupils alike. Indeed, the more the power differentials between more established (such as PE teachers) and less established (sport coaches, for example) occupational groupings with an interest in PE diminish, the more the course of PE is likely to become not merely uncertain, but also beyond the control of any single individual or group. Nevertheless, the portents of a future with PE teachers in the classroom, sports coaches and development officers on the field and in the sports hall and fitness instructors in the gym are there for all to see. Whether that is a good or bad thing depends entirely upon one's ideological position regarding the nature and purposes of PE.

NOTES

1 There are very many more football coaches in the UK than any other sport.
2 Also, Green (2003) would add, as PE teachers themselves.

References

Alderson, J. and Crutchley, D. (1990) 'Physical education and the national curriculum', in N. Armstrong (ed.), *New Directions in Physical Education 1*. Champaign, IL: Human Kinetics. pp. 37–62.

Alexander, K., Taggart, A. and Thorpe, S. (1996) 'A spring in their steps? Possibilities for professional renewal through sports education in Australian schools', *Sport, Education and Society*, 1(1): 23–46.

Alley, T.R. and Hicks, C.M. (2005) 'Peer attitudes towards adolescent participants in male- and female-oriented sports', *Adolescence*, 40: 273–80.

All Party Parliamentary Group (APPG) (2005) The All Party Parliamentary Group on Obesity. Spring 2005 Newsletter.

Amade-Escot, C. (1997) 'Selection criteria for physical education teachers in France from 1947 to 1989', *European Physical Education Review*, 3(1): 49–57.

American College of Sports Medicine (ACSM) (2000) *ACSM's Guidelines for Exercise Testing and Prescription* (6th edn). Baltimore: Williams and Wilkins.

Armour, K. (2005) 'Professional foul', *PE & Sport Today*, 17: 21–3.

Armour, K. (2006) 'Physical education teachers as career-long learners: a compelling research agenda', *Physical Education and Sport Pedagogy*, 11(3): 203–7.

Armour, K. and Duncombe, R. (2004) 'Teachers' continuing professional development in primary physical education: lessons from present and past to inform the future', *Physical Education and Sport Pedagogy*, 9(1): 3–21.

Armour, K. and Yelling, M.R. (2004) 'Continuing professional development for experienced physical education teachers: towards effective provision', *Sport, Education and Society*, 9(1): 95–114.

Armour, K.M. and Yelling, M. (2007) 'Effective professional development for physical education teachers: the role of informal, collaborative learning', *Journal of Teaching in Physical Education*, 26(2): 177–200.

Armstrong, N. (1991) 'Children's physical activity patterns: the implications for physical education', in N. Armstrong and A. Sparkes (eds), *Issues in Physical Education*. Champaign, IL: Human Kinetics. pp. 9–10.

Armstrong, N. and McManus, A. (1994) 'Children's fitness and physical activity – a challenge for physical education', *British Journal of Physical Education*, 25(1): 20–6.

Armstrong, N. and Welsman, A. (1997) *Young People and Physical Activity*. Oxford: Oxford University Press.

Arnold, P. (1992) 'Sport as a valued human practice: a basis for the consideration of some moral issues in sport', *Journal of Philosophy of Education*, 26(2): 237–55.

Arnold, P.J. (1997) *Sport, Ethics and Education*. London: Cassell.

Aspin, D. (1976) '"Knowing how" and "knowing that" and physical education', *Journal of Philosophy of Sport*, 3: 97–117.

Avramidis, E. and Norwich, B. (2002) 'Teachers' attitudes towards integration/inclusion: a review of the literature', *European Journal of Special Needs Education*, 17(2): 129–47.

Azzarito, L. and Solomon, M.A. (2005) 'A reconceptualization of physical education: the intersection of gender/race/social class', *Sport, Education and Society*, 10(1): 25–47.

Balding, J. (2001) *Young People in 2001*. Exeter: Schools Health Education Unit.

Baldwin, T. and Halpin, T. (2004) 'Schools ordered to double hours of sport for pupils', *The Times*, Thursday 25 November: 1.

Barnes, C., Mercer, G. and Shakespeare, T. (1999) *Exploring Disability: A Sociological Introduction*. Cambridge: Polity Press.

Barrow, R. (1983) *The Philosophy of Schooling*. 2nd edn. Brighton: Harvester. (1st edn, 1968).

Barrow, R. (2000) '"Include me out": a response to John Wilson', *European Journal of Special Needs Education*, 15(3): 305–7.

Barton, L. (1993) 'Disability, empowerment and physical education', in J. Evans (ed.), *Equality, Education and Physical Education*. London: Falmer Press. pp. 43–54.

Bass, D. and Cale, L. (1999) 'Promoting physical activity through the extra-curricular programme', *European Journal of Physical Education*, 4(1): 45–64.

BBC News, UK edition (2005a) 'Number of playing fields goes up', http://news.bbc.co.uk/1/hi/education/4707903.stm, accessed 1 August 2005.

BBC News, UK edition (2005b) 'Almost 45 percent of sports fields "lost"', http://news.bbc.co.uk/1/hi/uk/4733801.stm, accessed 1 August 2005.

Bechtel, P.A. and O'Sullivan, M. (2006) 'Effective professional development – what we now know', *Journal of Teaching in Physical Education*, 25(4): 363–78.

Behets, D. and Vergauwen, L. (2006) 'Learning to teach in the field', in D.

Kirk, D. Macdonald and M. O'Sullivan (eds), *The Handbook of Physical Education*. London: Sage. pp. 407–24.

Benn, T. (1996a) 'Female, Muslim and training to be a primary school teacher – experiences of physical education in one college', *British Journal of Physical Education*, 27(1): 8–12.

Benn, T. (1996b) 'Muslim women and physical education in initial teacher training', *Sport, Education and Society*, 1(1): 5–21.

Benn, T. (2005) 'Race and physical education, sport and dance', in K. Green and K. Hardman (eds), *Physical Education: Essential Issues*. London: Sage. pp. 197–219.

Benn, T. and Dagkas, S. (2006) 'Incompatible? Compulsory mixed-sex physical education initial teacher training (PEITT) and the inclusion of Muslim women: a case-study on seeking solutions', *European Physical Education Review*, 12(2): 181–200.

Bernstein, B. (1975) *Class, Codes and Control. Towards a Theory of Educational Transmission*. London: Routledge and Kegan Paul.

Berthoud, R. (2000) 'Family formation in multi-cultural Britain: three patterns of diversity', working paper, Institute for Social and Economic Research, University of Essex, Colchester.

Biddle, S. (1989) '"Innovation without change" and the ideology of individualism: a reply to Sparkes', *British Journal of Physical Education*, 20(2): 64-6.

Biddle, S. (2003) 'The 2000 national consensus: how far have we come?' *BASES World*, December: 8.

Biddle, S. (2006) 'Researching the psycho-social outcomes of youth sport', paper presented at Researching Youth Sport: Diverse Pespectives', Institute of Youth Sport/Institute of Sport Policy Conference, Loughborough University, 20 September.

Biddle, S., Coalter, F., O'Donovan, T., MacBeth, J., Nevill, M. and Whitehead, S. (2005) *Increasing Demand for Sport and Physical Activity by Girls*. SportScotland Research Report No. 100. Institute for Youth Sport (IYT)/Institute for Sport Research (ISR). Edinburgh: SportScotland.

Bissix, G., Kruisselbrink, D., Carlsson, L., MacIntyre, P. and Hatcher, T. (2005) 'Active lifestyle, physical recreation and health outcomes of youth in two contrasting Nova Scotian communities', in K. Hylton, J. Long and A. Flintoff (eds), *Evaluating Sport and Active Leisure for Young People*. Eastbourne: Leisure Studies Association Publication. pp. 141–55.

Blackshaw, T. and Long, J. (2005) 'What's the big idea? A critical exploration of the concept of social capital and its incorporation into leisure policy discourse', *Leisure Studies*, 24(3): 239–58

Blauwet, C. (2007) 'Promoting the health and human rights of individuals with a disability through the Paralympic movement', in C. Higgs and Y. Vanlandewijck (eds), *Sport for Persons with a Disability*. Berlin: ICCSPE. pp. 21–34.

Bloodworth, A. and McNamee, M. (2007) 'Conceptions of well-being in psychology and exercise psychology research: a philosophical critique', *Health Care Analysis*, forthcoming.

Bloyce, D. (2007) Personal communication.

Bloyce, D. and Smith, A. (forthcoming) *Sport Development and Policy in Society*. London: Routledge.

Booth, M. (1993) 'The effectiveness and role of the mentor in school: the students' view', *Cambridge Journal of Education*, 23(2): 185–97.

Boreham, C. and Riddoch, C. (2001) 'The physical activity, fitness and health of children', *Journal of Sports Sciences*, 19: 915–29.

Boseley, S. (2004) '15-year study links fast food to obesity'. *The Guardian*, 31 December: 6.

Bouchard, C. (ed.) (2000) *Physical Activity and Obesity*. Champaign, IL: Human Kinetics.

Bouchard, C. (2004) 'Foreword', in P. Oja and J. Borms (eds), *Health Enhancing Physical Activity*. Oxford: Meyer and Meyer Verlag. pp.15–16.

Bourdieu, P. (1984) *Distinction: A Social Critique of the Judgement of Taste*. London, Routledge.

Braddock, J.H., Sokol-Katz, J., Greene, A. and Basinger-Fleishman, L. (2005) 'Uneven playing fields: state variations in boys' and girls' access to and participation in high school interscholastic sports', *Sociological Spectrum*, 25(2): 231–50.

Bramham, P. (2003) 'Boys, masculinity and PE', *Sport, Education and Society*, 8(1): 57–71.

Brettschneider, W.-D. (1992) 'Adolescents, leisure, sport and lifestyle', in T. Williams, L. Almond and A. Sparkes (eds), *Sport: Moving Towards Excellence. Proceedings of the AISEP World Convention*. London: Spon. pp. 536–50.

Brettschneider, W.-D. and Sack, H.G. (1996) 'Germany', in P. De Knop, L.-M. Engstrom, B. Skirstad and M.R. Weiss (eds), *Worldwide Trends in Youth Sport*. Champaign, IL: Human Kinetics. pp. 139–51.

Brittain, I. (2004) 'The role of schools in constructing self-perceptions of sport and physical education in relation to people with disabilities', *Sport, Education and Society*, 9(1): 75–94.

Broadfoot, P. and Black, P. (2004) 'Redefining assessment? The first 10 years of assessment in education', *Assessment in Education*, 11(1): 7–26.

Brodersen, N.H., Steptoe, A., Boniface, D.R. and Wardle, J. (2007) 'Trends in physical activity and sedentary behaviour in adolescence: ethnic and socioeconomic differences', *British Journal of Sports Medicine*, 41(3): 140–4.

Brook, V. (1993) 'The resurgence of external examining in Britain: a historical review', *British Journal of Educational Studies*, 41(1): 59–72.

Buisman, A. and Lucassen, J.M.H. (1996) 'The Netherlands', in P. De Knop, L.-M. Engstrom, B. Skirstad and M.R. Weiss (eds), *Worldwide Trends in Youth Sport*. Champaign, IL: Human Kinetics. pp. 152–69.

Burgess, E. (2007) 'Participation in sport', in C. Higgs and Y. Vanlandewijck (eds), *Sport for Persons with a Disability*. Berlin: ICCSPE. pp. 35–44.

Burke, J. (2006) 'Muslim anger: the real story', *The Observer*, 20 August: 16–17.

Bynner, J., Elias, P., McKnight, A., Pan, H. and Peirre, G. (2002) *Young People's Changing Routes to Independence*. London: Joseph Rowntree Foundation.

Byra, M. (2006) 'Teaching styles and inclusive pedagogies', in D. Kirk, D. Macdonald and M. O'Sullivan (eds), *The Handbook of Physical Education*. London: Sage. pp. 449–66.

Caldecott, S., Warburton, P. and Waring, M. (2006a) 'A survey of the time devoted to the preparation of primary and junior school trainee teachers to teach physical education (part one)', *British Journal of Teaching Physical Education*, 37(1): 45–8.

Caldecott, S., Warburton, P. and Waring, M. (2006b) 'A survey of the time devoted to the preparation of primary and junior school trainee teachers to teach physical education (part two)', *Physical Education Matters*, 1(1): 45–8.

Cale, L. (2000) 'Physical activity promotion in secondary schools', *European Physical Education Review*, 6(1): 71–90.

Capel, S. (1996) 'Physical education and sport: how can they work together to "raise the game" in schools?' *Pedagogy in Practice*, 2(1): 31–44.

Capel, S. (2005) 'Teachers, teaching and pedgagogy in physical education', in K. Green and K. Hardman (eds), *Physical Education: Essential Issues*. London: Sage. pp. 111–27.

Capel, S. (2007) Personal communication.

Capel, S. and Katene, W. (2000) 'Secondary PGCE PE students' perceptions of their subject knowledge', *European Physical Education Review*, 6(1): 46–70.

Carr, D. (1979) 'Aims of physical education', *Physical Education Review*, 2(2): 91–100.

Carr, D. (1997) 'Physical education and value diversity: a response to Andrew Reid', *European Physical Education Review*, 3(2): 195–205.

Carroll, B. (1991) 'Examinations and assessment in physical education', in N. Armstrong (ed.), *New Directions in Physical Education*. Vol.1. Champaign, IL: Human Kinetics. pp. 137–60.

Carroll, B. (1993) 'Factors influencing ethnic minority groups' participation in sport', *Physical Education Review*, 16(1): 55–66.

Carroll, B. (1994) *Assessment in Physical Education Review: A Teacher's Guide to the Issues*. London: Falmer Press.

Carroll, B. (1998a) 'The emergence and growth of examinations in physical education', in K. Green and K. Hardman (eds), *Physical Education: A*

Reader. Aachen: Meyer and Meyer Verlag. pp. 335–52

Carroll, B. (1998b) 'Multicultural education and equal opportunities in physical education', in K. Green and K. Hardman (eds), *Physical Education: A Reader*. Aachen: Meyer and Meyer Verlag. pp. 314–32.

Carroll, B. and Hollinshead, G. (1993) 'Ethnicity and conflict in physical education', *British Educational Research Journal*, 19(1): 59–76.

Cashmore, E. (1982) *Black Sportsmen*. London: Routledge and Kegan Paul.

Cashmore, E. (1990) *Making Sense of Sport*. London: Routledge.

Catford, J. (2003) 'Promoting healthy weight – the new environmental frontier', *Health Promotion International*, 18(1): 1–4.

Central Council for Physical Recreation (CCPR) (1960) *Sport and the Community*. London: CCPR.

Central Council for Physical Recreation (CCPR) (2001) *Charter for Physical Education and School Sport*. London: CCPR.

Chen, A. and Ennis, C.D. (1996) 'Teaching value-laden curricula in physical education', *Journal of Teaching in Physical Education*, 15: 338–54.

Clark, C. (2005) 'The structure of educational research', *British Educational Research Journal*, 31(3): 289–308.

Clarke, G. (2006) 'Sexuality and physical education', in D. Kirk, D. Macdonald and M. O'Sullivan (eds), *The Handbook of Physical Education*. London: Sage. pp. 723–39.

Coakley, J.J. (2004) *Sport in Society. Issues and Controversies* (8th edn). New York: McGraw-Hill. (1 edn, 1978.)

Coakley, J. and White, A. (1999) 'Making decisions: how young people become involved and stay involved in sports', in J. Coakley and P. Donnelly (eds), *Inside Sports*. London: Routledge. pp. 77–85.

Coalter, F. (1996) 'Trends in sports participation', paper presented at the Institute for Leisure and Amenity Management annual conference, Birmingham.

Coalter, F. (1999) 'Sport and recreation in the United Kingdom: Flow with the flow or buck the trends', *Managing Leisure*, 4(1): 24–39.

Coalter, F. (2004) 'Future sports or future challenges to sport?' in Sport England (ed.), *Driving Up Participation: The Challenge for Sport*. London: SportEngland. pp. 79–86.

Coalter, F. (2005) 'Sport, social inclusion and crime reduction', in G.E. Faulkner and A.H. Taylor (eds), *Exercise, Health and Mental Health. Emerging Relationships*. Abingdon: Routledge. pp. 190–209.

Coalter, F. (2006a) 'Sport-in-development: monitoring and evaluation: accountability or development?', paper presented at Researching Youth Sport: Diverse Perspectives, Institute of Youth Sport/Institute of Sport Policy Conference, Loughborough University, 20 September.

Coalter, F. (2006b) 'Sports development: measurement and evaluation', keynote lecture, 2nd Sport Cheshire Research Seminar, University of Chester, 11 October.

Coalter, F., Allison, M. and Taylor, J. (2000) *The Role of Sport in Regenerating Deprived Urban Areas*. Edinburgh: Scottish Executive Central Research Unit.

Coalter, F., Dowers, S. and Baxter, M.J. (1995) 'The impact of social class and education on sports participation: some evidence from the General Household Survey', in K. Roberts (ed.), *Leisure and Social Stratification*. Eastbourne: Leisure Studies Association Publications No. 53. pp. 59–73.

Cockburn, C. and Clarke, G. (2002) '"Everybody's looking at you!": girls negotiating the "femininity deficit" they incur in physical education', *Women's Studies International Forum*, 25(6): 651–65.

Cohen, L., Perales, D.P. and Steadman, C. (2005) 'The O word: why the focus on obesity is harmful to community health', *Californian Journal of Health Promotion*, 3(3): 154–61.

Cole, B.A. (2005) 'Mission impossible? Special educational needs, inclusion and the re-conceptualization of the role of the SENCO in England and Wales', *European Journal of Special Needs Education*, 20(3): 287–307.

Collier, C. (2006) 'Models and curricula of physical education teacher education', in D. Kirk, D. Macdonald and M. O'Sullivan (eds), *The Handbook of Physical Education*. London: Sage. pp. 386–406.

Collins, M. (2003) 'Social exclusion from sport and leisure', in B. Houlihan (ed.), *Sport and Society: A Student Introduction*. London: Sage. pp. 67–88.

Collins, M., with Kay, T. (2003) *Sport and Social Exclusion*. London: Routledge.

Colquhoun, D. (1991) 'Health-based physical education: the ideology of healthism and victim-blaming', *Physical Education Review*, 14(1): 5–13.

Connolly, P. (2006) 'The effects of social class and ethnicity on gender differences in GCSE attainment: a secondary analysis of the youth cohort study of England and Wales, 1997–2001', *British Educational Research Journal*, 32(1): 3–22.

Cothran, D.J., Kulinna, P.H., Banville, D., Choi, E., Amade-Escot, C., MacPhail, A., Macdonald, D., Richard. J.-F., Sarmento, P. and Kirk, D. (2005) 'A cross-cultural investigation of the use of teaching styles', *Research Quarterly for Exercise and Sport*, 76(2): 193–201.

Cox, L., Coleman, L. and Roker, D. (2005) *Understanding Participation in Sport: What Determines Sports Participation Among 15–19 Year Old Women?* London: Sport England/Trust for the Study of Adolescence.

Csikszentmihalyi, M. (1990) *Flow: The Psychology of Optimal Experience*. New York: Harper and Row.

Curtin, M. and Clarke, G. (2005) 'Listening to young people with physical disabilities' experiences', *International Journal of Disability, Development and Education*, 52(3): 195–214.

Curtner-Smith, M. (2001) 'The occupational socialization of a first-year physical education teacher with a teaching orientation', *Sport, Education and Society*, 6(1): 81–105.

Curtner-Smith, M.D. (1999) 'The more things change the more they stay the same: factors influencing teachers' interpretations and delivery of National Curriculum Physical Education', *Sport, Education and Society*, 4(1): 75–97.

Curtner-Smith, M.D. and Meek, G.A. (2000) 'Teachers' value orientations and their compatibility with the National Curriculum for Physical Education', *European Physical Education Review*, 6(1): 27–45.

Curtner-Smith, M.D., Sofo, S., Choiunard, J. and Wallace, S.J. (2007) 'Health-promoting physical activity and extra-curricular sport', *European Physical Education Review*, 13(2): 131–44.

Curtner-Smith, M.D., Todorovich, R.J., McCaughtry, N.A. and Lacon, S.A. (2001) 'Urban teachers' use of productive and reproductive teaching styles within the confines of the National Curriculum for Physical Education', *European Physical Education Review*, 7(2): 177–90.

Dagkas, S. and Benn, T. (2006) 'Young Muslim women's experiences of Islam and physical education in Greece and Britain: a comparative study', *Sport, Education and Society*, 11(1): 21–38.

Daley, A. (2002) 'Extra-curricular physical activities and physical self-perceptions in British 14–15-year-old male and female adolescents', *European Physical Education Review*, 8(1): 37–49.

De Knop, P. and De Martelaer, K. (2001) 'Quantitative and qualitative evaluation of youth sport in Flanders and the Netherlands: a case study', *Sport, Education and Society*, 6(1): 35–51.

De Knop, P., Skirstad, B., Engstrom, L.-M., Theebom, M. and Wittock, H. (1996a), 'Sport in a changing society', in P. De Knop, L.-M. Engstrom, B. Skirstad and M.R. Weiss (eds), *Worldwide Trends in Youth Sport*. Champaign, IL: Human Kinetics. pp. 8–14.

De Knop, P., Vanreusel, B., Theebom, M. and Wittock, H. (1996b) 'Belgium', in P. De Knop, L.-M. Engstrom, B. Skirstad and M.R. Weiss (eds), *Worldwide Trends in Youth Sport*. Champaign, IL: Human Kinetics. pp. 88–100.

De Martelaer, K. and Theebom, M. (2006) 'Physical education and youth sport', in D. Kirk, D. Macdonald and M. O'Sullivan (eds), *The Handbook of Physical Education*. London: Sage. pp. 652–64.

De Swaan, A. (2001) *Human Societies: An Introduction*. Trs. B. Jackson. Cambridge: Polity Press.

Department for Culture, Media and Sport (DCMS) (2000) *A Sporting Future for All*. London: DCMS.

Department for Culture, Media and Sport (DCMS)/Department for Education and Skills (DfES) (2005) *The Results of the 2004/05 School Sport Survey*. London: DCMS/DfES.

Department for Culture, Media and Sport (DCMS)/Department for Education and Skills (DfES) (2006) *The Results of the 2005/06 School Sport Survey*. London: DCMS/DfES.

Department for Culture, Media and Sport (DCMS)/Strategy Unit (2002) *Game Plan: A Strategy for Delivering Government's Sport and Physical Activity Objectives*. London: DCMS/Strategy Unit.

Department for Education and Employment (DfEE) (2000) *Professional Development: Support for Learning and Teaching*. Nottingham: DfEE.

Department for Education and Employment (DfEE) (2001) *Learning and Teaching: A Strategy for Professional Development*. Nottingham: DfEE.

Department for Education and Employment (DfEE) (2003a) *GCE/VCE, A/AS Examination Results for Young People in England, 2001/02* Accessed August, 2003 www.dfee.gov.uk/statistics.

Department for Education and Employment (DfEE) (2003b) *National Curriculum Assessments for Key Stage 3 (Revised), GCSE/GNCQ Examination Results (August, 2003) and Associated Value Added Measures for Young People in 2001/02*. www.dfee.gov.uk/statistics.

Department for Education and Employment (DfEE) and Qualifications and Curriculum Authority (QCA) (1999) *The National Curriculum for England: Physical Education*. London: DfEE/QCA.

Department for Education and Skills (DfES) (2004a) *GCSE Results of 15-year-olds in All Educational Establishments, by the End of 2002/2003, Subject and Grade*. www.dfes.gov.uk/rsgateway/DB/SFR/s000442/tab009.shtml.

Department for Education and Skills (DfES) (2004b) *GCE A level Examination Results of All Students in All Schools and Colleges by Subject and Grade in 2002/03*. www.dfes.gov.uk/rsgateway/DB/SFR/s000441/tab007a.shtml.

Department for Education and Skills (DfES)/Department for Culture, Media and Sport (DCMS) (2002) *Learning Through PE and Sport. A Guide to the Physical Education, School Sport and Club Links Strategy*. London: DfES.

Department for Education and Skills (DfES)/Department for Culture, Media and Sport (DCMS) (2003) *Learning Through PE and Sport. A Guide to the PESSCL Strategy*. London: DfES.

Department for Education and Skills (DfES)/Department for Culture, Media and Sport (DCMS) (2003) *Learning Through PE and Sport. A Guide to the Physical Education, School Sport and Club Links Strategy*. London: DfES.

Department for Education and Skills (DfES)/Department for Culture, Media and Sport (DCMS) (2004) *High Quality PE and Sport for Young People. A Guide to Recognising and Achieving High Quality PE and Sport in Schools and Clubs*. London: DfES.

Department of Education and Science (DES) (1978) *Special Educational Needs: Report of the Committee of Enquiry into the Education of Handicapped Children and Young People (The Warnock Report)*. London: HMSO.

Department of Education and Science (DES) (1991) *Physical Education for Ages 5 to 16*. London: DES.

Department of Education and Science/Welsh Office (DES/WO) (1991) *Physical Education for Ages 5 to 16. Proposals of the Secretary of State for Education and the Secretary of State for Wales*. London: DES/WO.

Department of Health (2004) (DoH) *Choosing Health: Making Healthy Choices Easier*. London: DoH.

Department of Health (2005) (DoH) *Choosing Health. Obesity Bulletin Issue 1*. London: DoH.

Department of National Heritage (DNH) (1995) *Sport: Raising the Game*. London: DNH.

Department of National Heritage (DNH) (1996) *Sport: Raising the Game: One Year On*. London: HMSO.

LondonDewar, A.M. and Lawson, H.A. (1984) 'The subjective warrant and recruitment into physical education', *QUEST*, 30(1): 15–25.

Diamond, I. (2007) 'Mosaic society', in J. Clarke (ed.), *Britain Today 2007*. Swindon: Economic and Social Research Council. pp. 91–3.

Dodds, P. (2006) 'Physical education teacher education (PE/TE) policy', in D. Kirk, D. Macdonald and M. O'Sullivan (eds) *The Handbook of Physical Education*. London: Sage. pp. 540–61.

Dohnt, H. K. and Tiggerman, M. (2005) 'Peer influences on body dissatisfaction and dieting awareness in young girls', *British Journal of Developmental Psychology*, 23(1): 103–16.

Doll-Tepper, G. (2005) 'The UK in the world of physical education', *British Journal of Teaching Physical Education*, 36(1): 41–3.

Dollman, J., Boshoff, K. and Dodd, G. (2006) 'The relationship between curriculum time for physical education and literacy and numeracy standards in South Australian primary schools', *European Physical Education Review*, 12(2): 151–63.

Dollman, J., Norton, K. and Norton, L. (2005) 'Evidence for secular trends in children's physical activity behaviour', *British Journal of Sports Medicine*, 39(12): 892–7.

Donnelly, P. (1996) 'Approaches to social inequality in the sociology of sport', *QUEST*, 48: 221–42.

Dopson, S. and Waddington, I. (1996) 'Managing social change: a process sociological change to understanding change within the National Health Service', *Sociology of Health and Illness*, 18: 525–50.

Dore, R.P. (1997) The *Diploma Disease: Education, Qualification and Development* (2nd edn). London: Allen and Unwin. (lst edn, 1976).

Dunning, E. (1999) *Sport Matters: Sociological Studies of Sport, Violence and Civilization*. London: Routledge.

Dunning, E. and Waddington, I. (2003) 'Sport as a drug and drugs in sport:

some explanatory comments', *International Review for the Sociology of Sport*, 38(3): 351–68.

Dyson, B. (2006) 'Students' perspectives of physical education', in D. Kirk, D. Macdonald and M. O'Sullivan (eds), *The Handbook of Physical Education*. London: Sage. pp. 326–46.

Easton, L. (2003) 'School sport coordinator programme 2003', *British Journal of Teaching in Physical Education*, 34(4): 21–2.

Egger, K. (2001) 'Qualität des Sportunterricht', *Mobile*, pp. 1–7.

Eggleston, J. (1990) 'School examinations – some sociological issues', in T. Horton (ed.), *Assessment Debates*. Buckingham: Open University Press. pp. 57–67.

Elias, N. (1978) *What is Sociology?* London: Hutchinson.

Elias, N. (1994) *The Civilizing Process*. Oxford: Basil Blackwell.

Ennis, C.D. (1995) 'Teachers' responses to non-compliant students: the realities and consequences of a negotiated curriculum', *Teacher and Teacher Education*, 11: 445–60.

Ennis, C.D. (1999) 'Creating a culturally relevant curriculum for disengaged girls', *Sport, Education and Society*, 4(1): 31–49.

Ennis, C.D. and Chen, A. (1995) 'Teachers' value orientations in urban and rural school settings', *Research Quarterly for Exercise and Sport*, 66: 41–50.

Evans, J. (1989) 'Swinging from the crossbar: equality and opportunity in the physical education curriculum', *British Journal of Physical Education*, 20(2): 84–7.

Evans, J. (1992) 'A short paper about people, power and educational reform. Authority and representation in ethnographic research. Subjectivity, ideology and educational reform: the case of physical education', in A.C. Sparkes (ed.), *Research in Physical Education and Sport: Exploring Alternative Visions*. London: The Falmer Press. pp. 231–47.

Evans, J. (2004) 'Making a difference: education and "ability" in physical education', *European Physical Education Review*, 10(1): 95–108.

Evans, J. and Davies, B. (1986) 'Sociology, schooling and physical education', in J. Evans (ed.), Physical Education, Sport and Schooling: Studies in the Sociology of Physical Education. London: Falmer Press. pp. 11–37.

Evans, J. and Davies, B. (2006a) 'The sociology of physical education', in D. Kirk, D. Macdonald and M. O'Sullivan (eds), *The Handbook of Physical Education*. London: Sage. pp. 109–22.

Evans, J. and Davies, B. (2006b) 'Social class and physical education', in D. Kirk, D. Macdonald and M. O'Sullivan (eds), *The Handbook of Physical Education*. London: Sage. pp. 796–808.

Evans, J. and Davies, B. (2006c) 'The poverty of theory: class configurations in the discourse of Physical Education and Health', paper presented to the Physical Education Special Interest Group, British Educational Research Conference, University of Warwick, 6–9 September.

Evans, J. and Williams, T. (1989) 'Moving up and getting out: the classed and gendered opportunities of physical education teachers', in T. Templin and P. Schempp (eds), *Socialization into Physical Education: Learning to Teach*. Indianapolis, IN: Benchmark Press. pp. 235–51.

Evans, J., Castle, F., Cooper, D., Glatter, R. and Woods, P.A. (2005) 'Collaboration: the big new idea for school improvement?' *Journal of Educational Policy*, 20(2): 223–36.

Evans, J., Davies, B. and Penney, D. (1996) 'Teachers, teaching and the social construction of gender relations', *Sport, Education and Society*, 1(2): 165–83.

Evans, J., Penney, D. and Bryant, A. (1993) 'Improving the quality of physical education? The Education Reform Act 1988 and physical education in England and Wales', *Quest*, 45: 321–38.

Farrell, L. and Shields, M.A. (2002) 'Investigating the economic and demographic determinants of sporting participation in England', *Journal of the Royal Statistical Society*, 165: 335–48.

Fejgin, N. (1995) 'The academicization of physical education teacher training: a discourse analysis case study', *International Review for the Sociology of Sport*, 30(2): 179–90.

Ferri, B.A. and Connor, D.J. (2005) 'Tool of exclusion: race, disability and (re)segregated education', *Teachers College Record*, 107(3): 453–74.

Field, J. (2003) *Social Capital*. London: Routledge.

Fisher, A., Reilly, J.J., Kelly, L.A., Montgomery, C., Williamson, A., Paton, J.Y. and Grant, S. (2005) 'Fundamental movement skills and habitual physical activity in young children', *Medicine and Science in Sports and Exercise*, 37(4): 684–8.

Fisher, K. (2002) 'Chewing the fat: the story time diaries tell about physical activity in the United Kingdom', *Working Papers of the Institute for Social and Economic Research, Paper 2002–13*. Colchester: University of Essex.

Fisher, R. (2003) 'Physical education in Europe: policy into practice', in K. Hardman (ed.), *Physical Education: Deconstruction and Reconstruction – Issues and Directions*. Schorndorf: Verlag Karl Hofmann. pp. 137–52.

Fitz, J., Davies, B. and Evans, J. (2006) *Educational Policy and Social Reproduction*. London: Routledge.

Fitzclarence L. and Tinning, R. (1990) 'Challenging hegemonic physical education: contextualizing physical education as an examinable subject', in D. Kirk and R. Tinning (eds), *Physical Education, Curriculum and Culture: Critical Issues in the Contemporary Crisis*. London: Falmer Press. pp. 169–92

Fitzgerald, H. (2006) 'Disability and physical education', in D. Kirk, D. Macdonald and M. O'Sullivan (eds), *The Handbook of Physical Education*. London: Sage. pp. 752–66.

Fitzgerald, H. and Jobling, A. (2004) 'Student-centred research. Working with Disabled students', in J. Wright, D. Macdonald and L. Burrows (eds)

Critical Enquiry and Problem-Solving in Physical Education. London: Routledge. pp. 74–92.

Fleming, S. (1991) 'Sport, schooling and Asian male youth culture', in G. Jarvie (ed.), *Sport, Racism and Ethnicity.* London: Falmer Press. pp. 30–57.

Fleming, S. (1994) 'Sport and South Asian youth: the perils of 'false universalism' and stereotyping', *Leisure Studies*, 13(3): 159–77.

Fletcher, S. (1984) *Women First: The Female Tradition in English Physical Education, 1880–1980.* London: Athlone.

Flintoff, A. and Scraton, S. (2001) 'Stepping into active leisure? Young women's perceptions of active lifestyles and their experiences of school physical education', *Sport, Education and Society*, 6(1): 5–21.

Flintoff, A. and Scraton, S. (2005) 'Gender and physical education', in K. Green and K. Hardman (eds), *Physical Education: Essential Issues.* London: Sage. pp. 161–79.

Flintoff, A. and Scraton, S. (2006) 'Girls and physical education', in D. Kirk, D. Macdonald and M. O'Sullivan (eds), *The Handbook of Physical Education.* London: Sage. pp. 767–83.

Flintoff, A., Long, J. and Hylton, K. (2005) 'Editors' introduction. Youth sport and active leisure: theory, policy and practice', in A. Flintoff, J. Long and K. Hylton (eds), *Youth, Sport and Active Leisure: Theory, Policy and Participation.* Eastbourne: Leisure Studies Association. Publication No. 87. pp. v–x.

Foster, C., Hillsdon, M., Cavill, N., Allender, S and Cowburn, G. (2005) *Understanding Participation in Sport – A Systematic Review.* London: Sport England.

Fox, K. (2003) 'Physical activity, psychological well-being and mental health: from evidence to practice', *BASES World*, December: 8.

Fox, K. and Rickards, L. (2004) *Sport and Leisure: Results from the 2002 General Household Survey.* London: The Stationery Office.

Frew, M. and McGillivray, D. (2005) 'Health clubs and body politics: aesthetics and the quest for physical capital', *Leisure Studies*, 24(2): 161–75.

Frowe, I. (2005) 'Professional trust', *British Journal of Educational Studies*, 53(1): 34–53.

Furlong, A. and Cartmel, F. (2007) *Young People and Social Change: New Perspectives.* Maidenhead: Open University Press. (1st edn. 1997).

Furlong, A., Campbell, R. and Roberts, K. (1990) 'The effects of post-16 experiences and social class on the leisure patterns of young adults', *Leisure Studies*, 9(3): 213–24.

Gabe, J., Bury, M. and Elston, M.A. (2004) *Key Concepts in Medical Sociology.* London: Sage.

Gard, M. (2006) 'More art than science? Boys, masculinities and physical education research', in D. Kirk, D. Macdonald and M. O'Sullivan (eds), *The Handbook of Physical Education.* London: Sage. pp. 784–95.

Gard, M. and Wright, J. (2005) *The Obesity Epidemic: Science, Morality and Ideology*. London: Routledge.

George, L. and Kirk, D. (1988) 'The limits of change in physical education: ideologies, teachers and the experience of physical activity', in J. Evans (ed.), *Teachers, Teaching and Control in Physical Education*. Lewes: Falmer Press. pp. 145–55.

Gorard, S. (2005) 'Academies as the "future of schooling": is this an evidence-based policy?', *Journal of Educational Policy*, 20(3): 369–77.

Gorard, S., Taylor, C. and Fitz, J. (2003) *Schools, Markets and Choice Policies*. London: RoutledgeFalmer.

Gorely, T., Holroyd, R. and Kirk, D. (2003) 'Muscularity, the habitus and social construction of gender: towards a gender-relevant physical education', *British Journal of Sociology of Education*, 24(4): 429–48.

Goudas, M. and Biddle, S. (1993) 'Pupil perceptions of enjoyment in physical education', *Physical Education Review*, 16(2): 145–50.

Graef, R., Csikszentmihalyi, M. and McManama-Giannino, S.M. (1983) 'Measuring intrinsic motivation in everyday life', *Leisure Studies*, 2(2): 155–68.

Greater Manchester Sports Partnership (2001) *Greater Manchester 2001 Year 9 Participation Survey*. Manchester: Greater Manchester Sports Partnership.

Green, E., Hebron, S. and Woodward, D. (1990) *Women's Leisure, What Leisure?* London: Macmillan.

Green, K. (2000a) 'Extra-curricular physical education in England and Wales: a sociological perspective on a sporting bias', *European Journal of Physical Education*, 5(2): 178–207.

Green, K. (2000b) 'Exploring the everyday "philosophies" of physical education teachers from a sociological perspective', *Sport, Education and Society*, 5(2): 109–29.

Green, K. (2001) 'Examinations in physical education: a sociological perspective on a "new orthodoxy"', *British Journal of Sociology of Education*, 22(1): 51–74.

Green, K. (2003) *Physical Education Teachers on Physical Education: A Sociological Study of Philosophies and Ideologies*. Chester: Chester Academic Press.

Green, K. and Scraton, S. (1998) 'Gender, co-education and schooling: a brief review', in K. Green and K. Hardman (eds), *Physical Education: A Reader*. Aachen: Meyer and Meyer Verlag. pp. 272–90.

Green, K., Smith, A. and Roberts, K. (2005) 'Young people and lifelong participation in sport and physical activity: a sociological perspective on contemporary physical education programmes in England and Wales', *Leisure Studies*, 24(1): 27–43.

Green, N. (2002) 'A level physical education', *British Journal of Teaching Physical Education*, 33(3): 34.

Greenwell, L. (2005) 'Assessment: teacher-friendly statements and what is Level 4 anyway?', *Sportsteacher*: 35–7.

Gruneau, R. (2006) '"Amateurism" as a sociological problem: Some reflections inspired by Eric Dunning', *Sport in Society*, 9(4): 559–82.

Gunn, S. (2005) 'Translating Bourdieu: cultural capital and the English middle-class in historical perspective', *British Journal of Sociology*, 56(1): 49–64.

Hallam, S. and Ireson, J. (1999) 'Pedagogy in the secondary school', in P. Mortimer (ed.), *Understanding Pedagogy and its Impact on Learning*. London: Sage. pp. 68–97.

Hallam, S. and Ireson, J. (2005) 'Secondary school teachers' pedagogic practices when teaching mixed and structured ability classes', *Research Papers in Education*, 20(1): 3–24.

Hardman, K. (1998) 'To be or not to be? The present and future of school physical education in international context', in K. Green and K. Hardman (eds), *Physical Education: A Reader*. Aachen: Meyer and Meyer Verlag. pp. 353–82.

Hardman, K. (2007) Personal communication. 6 February.

Hardman, K. and Marshall, J.J. (2000) 'The state and status of physical education in schools in international context', *European Physical Education Review*, 6(3): 203–29.

Hardman, K. and Marshall, J. (2005) 'Physical education in schools in European context: charter principles, promises and implementation realities', in K. Green and K. Hardman (eds), *Physical Education: Essential Issues*. London: Sage. pp. 39–64.

Hare, W. (1993) *What Makes a Good Teacher: Reflections on Some Characteristics Central to the Educational Enterprise*. London: Althouse Press.

Hargreaves, J. (1994) *Sporting Females*. London: Routledge.

Harrington, M. (2006) 'Sporting and leisure as contexts for fathering in Australian families', *Leisure Studies*, 25(2): 165–83.

Harris, J. (1994a) 'Physical education in the National Curriculum: is there enough time to be effective?', *British Journal of Physical Education*, 25(4): 36–41.

Harris, J. (2005) 'Health-related exercise and physical education', in K. Green and K. Hardman (eds), *Physical Education: Essential Issues*. London: Sage. pp. 78–97.

Harris, J. and Cale, L. (2006) 'A review of children's fitness testing', *European Physical Education Review*, 12(2): 201–25.

Harris, J. and Penney, D. (2000) 'Gender issues in health-related exercise', *European Physical Education Review*, 6(3): 249–73.

Harris, J. and Penney, D. (2002) 'Gender, health and physical education', in D. Penney (ed.), *Gender and Physical Education: Contemporary Issues and Future Directions*. London: Routledge. pp. 123–45.

Harrison Jr, L. and Belcher, D. (2006) 'Race and ethnicity in physical education', in D. Kirk, D. Macdonald and M. O'Sullivan (eds), *The Handbook of Physical Education*. London: Sage. pp. 740–51.

Hay, P.J. (2006) 'Assessment for learning in physical education', in D. Kirk, D. Macdonald and M. O'Sullivan (eds), *The Handbook of Physical Education*. London: Sage. pp. 312–25.

Heinemann, K. (2005) 'Sport and the welfare state in Europe', *European Journal of Sport Science*, 5(4): 181–8.

Hendry, L., Kloep, M., Espnes, G.A., Ingebrigsten, J.E., Glendenning, A. and Wood, S. (2002) 'Leisure transitions – a rural perspective', *Leisure Studies*, 21(1): 1–14.

Hendry, L.B. (1986) 'Changing schools in a changing society: The role of physical education', in J. Evans (ed.), *Physical Education, Sport and Schooling: Studies in the Sociology of Physical Education*. Basingstoke: Falmer Press. pp. 41–70.

Hendry, L.B., Shucksmith, J., Love, J.G. and Glendenning, A. (1993) *Young People's Leisure and Lifestyles*. London: Routledge.

Hirst, P. (1974) *Knowledge and the Curriculum*. London: Routledge and Kegan Paul.

Hirst, P. (1994) 'From forms of knowledge to forms of practice', keynote address at Working Together for Physical Education, the National Conference for Physical Education, Sport and Dance, Loughborough University, 9 July.

Hirst, P. and Peters, R.S. (1970) *The Logic of Education*. London: Routledge and Kegan Paul.

Hodge, S.R., Ammah, J.O.A., Casebolt, C., Lamaster, K. and O'Sullivan, M. (2004) 'High school general physical education teachers' behaviors and beliefs associated with inclusion', *Sport, Education and Society*, 9(3). 395–419.

Hopper, B. (2005) 'Confronting one's own demons: exploring the needs of non-specialist Primary Initial Teacher Trainees in Physical Education', *British Journal of Teaching Physical Education*, 36(1): 6–10.

Houlihan, B. (1991) *The Government and Politics of Sport*. London: Routledge.

Houlihan, B. (2000) 'Sporting excellence, schools and sport development', *European Physical Education Review*, 6(2): 171–94.

Houlihan, B. (2002) 'Political involvement in sport, physical education and recreation', in A. Laker (ed.), *The Sociology of Sport and Physical Education: An Introductory Reader*. Abingdon: RoutledgeFalmer. pp. 190–210.

Houlihan, B. (2003) 'Politics, power, policy and sport', in B. Houlihan (ed.), *Sport and Society: A Student Introduction*. London: Sage. pp. 28–48.

Houlihan, B. (2005) 'Public sector sport policy: developing a framework for analysis', *International Review for the Sociology of Sport*, 40(2): 163–85.

Houlihan, B. and Green, M. (2006) 'The changing status of school sport and physical education: explaining policy change', *Sport, Education and Society*, 11(1): 73–92.

Houlihan, B. and White, A. (2002) *The Politics of Sports Development: Development of Sport or Development through Sport?* London: Routledge.

Humberstone, B. (2002) 'Femininity, masculinity and difference: what's wrong with a sarong?', in A. Laker (ed.), *The Sociology of Sport and Physical Education: An Introductory Reader*. Abingdon: RoutledgeFalmer. pp. 58–78.

Hunter, L. (2006) 'Research into elementary physical education programs', in D. Kirk, D. Macdonald and M. O'Sullivan (eds), *The Handbook of Physical Education*. London: Sage. pp. 580–95.

Hunter, P. (1995) *Community Use of Sports Facilities*. London: Office of Population, Censuses and Surveys.

Iacovou, M. and Berthoud, R. (2001) *Young People's Lives: A Map of Europe*. Colchester: University of Essex Institute for Social and Economic Research.

Ireson, J., Mortimore, P. and Hallam, S. (1999) 'The common strands of pedagogy and their implications', in P. Mortimer (ed.), *Understanding Pedagogy and its Impact on Learning*. London: Sage. pp. 212–32.

Jarvie, G. (ed.) (1991) *Sport, Racism and Ethnicity*. London: Falmer Press.

Jarvie, G. (2006) *Sport, Culture and Society: An Introduction*. Abingdon: Routledge.

Johns, D.P. (2005) 'Recontextualizing and delivering the biomedical model as a physical education curriculum', *Sport, Education and Society*, 10(1): 69–84.

Johnson, M. (2000) 'Perceptions of barriers to healthy physical activity among Asian communities', *Sport, Education and Society*, 5(1): 51–70.

Joint Council for Qualifications (2006) www.jcq.org.uk/attachments/published/256/ A-level, accessed 2 April 2007.

Jones, R. (2006) 'How can educational concepts inform sports teaching?', in R.L. Jones (ed.), *The Sports Coach as Educator. Re-conceptualisng Sports Coaching*. Abingdon: Routledge. pp. 3–13.

Jones, R. and Cheetham, R. (2001) 'Physical education in the National Curriculum: its purpose and meaning for final year secondary school students', *European Journal of Physical Education*, 6(2): 81–100.

Journal of Teaching in Physical Education (2006) *Professional Development in Urban Schools*. Champaign, IL: Human Kinetics.

Kay, T. (2005) 'The voice of the family: influences on Muslim girls' responses to sport', in A. Flintoff, J. Long and K. Hylton (eds), *Youth, Sport and Active Leisure: Theory, Policy and Participation*. Eastbourne: Leisure Studies Association. Publication No. 87. pp. 91–114.

Kay, T. (2006) 'Editorial. Fathering through leisure', *Leisure Studies*, 25(2): 125–31.

Kay, T. (2007) Personal communication.

Kay, W. (2003) 'Physical education, R.I.P?', *British Journal of Teaching Physical Education*, 34(4): 6–10.

Keay, J. (2007) 'Learning from other teachers: gender influences', *European Physical Education Review*, 13(2): 209–27.

Kew, F. (1997) *Sport: Social Problems and Issues*. Oxford: Butterworth-Heinemann.

Kilminster, R. (1998) *The Sociological Revolution: From the Enlightenment to the Global Age*. London: Routledge.

Kirk, D. (1992) *Defining Physical Education. The Social Construction of a School Subject in Post-War Britain*. London: Falmer Press.

Kirk, D. (1998) *Schooling Bodies. School Practice and Public Discourse, 1880–1950*. London: Leicester University Press.

Kirk, D. (2002a) 'Quality physical education, partnerships and multiple agendas: a response to Karel J. van Deventer', paper presented to the Commonwealth International Sport Conference, Manchester University, 19 July.

Kirk, D. (2004) 'Towards a critical history of the body, identity and health: corporeal power and school practice', in J. Evans, B. Davies and J. Wright (eds), *Body Knowledge and Control: Studies in the Sociology of Physical Education and Health*. London: Routledge. pp. 52–67.

Kirk, D. (2005) 'Model-based teaching and assessment in physical education: the tactical games model', in K. Green and K. Hardman (eds), *Physical Education: Essential Issues*. London: Sage. pp. 128–42.

Klomsten, A.T., Marsh, H.W. and Skaalvik, E.M. (2005) 'Adolescents' perceptions of masculine and feminine values in sport and physical education: a study of gender differences', *Sex Roles*, 52(9–10): 625–36.

Koska, P. (2005) 'Sport: The road to health?', in T. Holkkala, P. Hakkareinen and S. Laine (eds), *Beyond Health Literacy: Youth Cultures, Prevention and Policy*. Helsinki: Finnish Youth Research Society. pp. 295–337.

Ladenson, R.F. (2005) 'The zero-reject policy in special education: a moral analysis', *Theory and Research in Education*, 3(3): 273–98.

Lake, J. (2001) 'Young people's conceptions of sport, physical education and exercise: implications for physical education and the promotion of health-related exercise', *European Physical Education Review*, 7(1): 80–91.

Laker, A. (1996a) 'The aims of physical education within the revised national curriculum: lip service to the affective?', *Pedagogy in Practice*, 2(1): 24–30.

Laker, A. (1996b) 'Learning to teach through the physical as well as of the physical', *British Journal of Physical Education*, 27(3): 18–22.

Lang, T. (2006) 'Can health be a driver of the food supply chain?', Haygarth Public Lecture for Cheshire, University of Chester, 2 November.

Lapchick, R. (1986) *Fractured Focus*. Lexington, MA: Heath.

Lapchick, R.E. (1989) 'For the true believer', in D.S. Eizen (ed.), *Sport in*

Contemporary Society. New York: St. Martin's Press. pp. 17–23.

Laws, C. and Fisher, D. (1999) 'Pupils' interpretations of physical education', in C.A. Hardy and M. Mawer (eds), *Learning and Teaching in Physical Education*. London: Falmer Press. pp. 23–37.

Lawson, H.A. (1983a) 'Toward a model of teacher socialization in physical education: the subjective warrant, recruitment, and teacher education', *Journal of Teaching in Physical Education*, 2(3): 3–16.

Lawson, H.A. (1983b) 'Toward a model of teacher socialization in physical education: entry into schools, teachers' role orientations, and longevity in teaching', *Journal of Teaching in Physical Education*, 3(1): 3–15.

Lawson, H.A. (1986) 'Occupational socialization and the design of teacher education programs', *Journal of Teaching Physical Education*, 5(1): 107–16.

Leaman, O. (1984) *Sit on the Sidelines and Watch the Boys Play: Sex Differentiation in Physical Education*. York: Longman for Schools Council.

Lirgg, C. (2006) 'Social psychology and physical education', in D. Kirk, D. Macdonald and M. O'Sullivan (eds), *The Handbook of Physical Education*. London: Sage. pp. 141–62.

Littlefield, R., Green, B., Forsyth, S. and Sharp, B. (2003) 'Physical education in Scottish schools – a national case study', *European Journal of Physical Education*, 8(2): 211–27.

Lortie, D. (1975) *Schoolteacher: A Sociological Study*. Chicago, IL: University of Chicago Press.

Loughborough Partnership (2005) *School Sport Partnerships: Annual Monitoring and Evaluation Report*. Loughborough: Institute Youth Sport/Loughborough University.

Lowrey, J. and Kay, T. (2005) 'Doing sport, doing inclusion: an analysis of provider and participant perceptions of targeted sport provision for young Muslims', in A. Flintoff, J. Long and K. Hylton (eds), *Youth, Sport and Active Leisure: Theory, Policy and Participation*. Eastbourne: Leisure Studies Association. pp. 73–90.

Macdonald, D. (2006) 'Physical education curriculum', in D. Kirk, D. Macdonald and M. O'Sullivan (eds), *The Handbook of Physical Education*. London: Sage. pp. 563–64.

Macdonald, D. and Brooker, R. (1999) 'Assessment issues in a performance-based subject: a case study of physical education', in P. Murphy (ed.), *Learners, Learning and Assessment*. London: Paul Chapman Publishing. pp. 171–90.

Macdonald, D., Kirk, D. and Braiuka, S. (1999) 'The social construction of the physical activity field at the school/university interface', *European Physical Education Review*, 5(1): 31–51.

Macdonald, D., Rodger, S., Abbott, R., Ziviani, J. and Jones, J. (2005) '"I could do with a pair of wings": perspectives on physical activity, bodies and health from young Australian children', *Sport, Education and Society*, 10(2): 195–209.

Macdonald, D., Rodger, S., Ziviani, J., Jenkins, D., Batch, J. and Jones, J. (2004) 'Physical activity as a dimension of family life for lower primary school children', *Sport, Education and Society*, 9(3): 307–25.

MacKreth, K. (1998) 'Developments in "A" level physical education', *British Journal of Physical Education*, 29(4): 16–17.

MacPhail, A., Kirk, D. and Eley, D. (2003) 'Listening to young people's voices: youth sports leaders' advice on facilitating participation in sport', *European Physical Education Review*, 9(1): 57–73.

Mannisto, J-P., Cantell, M., Huovinen, T., Kooistra, L. and Larkin, D. (2006) 'A school-based movement programme for children with motor learning difficulty', *European Physical Education Review*, 12(3): 271–85.

Marshall, S.J., Biddle, S.J.H., Sallis, J.F., McKenzie, T.L. and Conway, T. (2002) 'Clustering of sedentary behaviors and physical activity among youth: a cross-national study', *Pediatric Exercise Science*, 14: 401–17.

Martino, W.. and Pallotta-Chiarolli, M. (2003) *So What's a Boy?* Maidenhead: Open University Press.

Mason, V. (1995a) *Young People and Sport: A National Survey, 1994.* London: Office of Population and Census Surveys.

Mason, V. (1995b) *Young People and Sport in England, 1994: The Views of Teachers and Children.* London: The Sports Council.

Mawer, M. (1993) 'Teaching styles, teaching strategies and instructional formats in physical education: Total teaching or ideology', *British Journal of Physical Education*, 24 (1): 5–9.

Mawer, M. (1995) *The Effective Teaching of Physical Education.* London: Longman.

McConachie-Smith, J. (1996) 'Physical education at Key Stage 4', in N. Armstrong (ed.), *New Directions in Physical Education: Change and Innovation.* London: Cassell. pp. 82–93.

McDonald, I. (2003) 'Class, inequality and the body in physical education', in S. Hayes and G. Stidder (eds), *Equity and Inclusion in Physical Education and Sport.* London, Routledge. pp. 169–83.

McDonald, R. and Scott-Samuel, A. (2004) 'Missed opportunities? Wanless and the white paper', *Public Health News*, 21 May.

McNamee, M. (1988) 'Health-related fitness and physical education', *British Journal of Physical Education*, 19(2): 83–84.

McNamee, M. (1998) 'Philosophy and physical education: analysis, epistemology and axiology', *European Physical Education Review*, 4(2): 75–91.

McNamee, M. (2005) 'The nature and values of physical education', in K. Green and K. Hardman (eds), *Physical Education: Essential Issues.* London: Sage. pp. 1–20.

Meece, J.L., Anderman, E.M. and Anderman, L.H. (2006) 'Classroom goal structure, student motivation and academic achievement', *Annual Review of Psychology*, 57: 487–504.

Meegan, S. and MacPhail, A. (2006) 'Irish physical educators' attitudes toward teaching students with special educational needs', *European Physical Education Review*, 12(1): 75–97.

Meighan, R., with Siraj-Blatchford, I. (2003) *A Sociology of Educating* (4th edn). London: Continuum. (1st edn. 1981).

Mennell, S. (1998) *Norbert Elias: An Introduction*. Dublin: University College Dublin Press.

Mirza, M., Senthilkumaran, A. and Ja'far, Z. (2007) *Living Apart Together: British Muslims and the Paradox of Multiculturalism*. London: Policy Exchange.

Moran, A.P. (2004) *Sport and Exercise Psychology: A Critical Introduction*. London: Routledge.

Morgan, K., Kingston, K. and Sproule, J. (2005) 'Effects of different teaching styles on the teacher behaviours that influence motivational climate and pupils' motivation in physical education', *European Physical Education Review*, 11(3): 257–85.

Morley, D., Bailey, R. Tan, J. and Cooke, B. (2005) 'Inclusive physical education: teachers' views of including pupils with Special Educational Needs and/or disabilities', *European Physical Education Review*, 11(1): 84–107.

Mortimer, P. (1999) 'Preface', in P. Mortimer (ed.), *Understanding Pedagogy and Its Impact on Learning*. London: Sage. pp. vii–viii.

Mosston, M. (1966) *Teaching Physical Education*. Columbus. OH: Charles E. Merrill.

Mosston, M. and Ashworth, S. (2002) *Teaching Physical Education*. (5th edn). New York: Benjamin Cummings.

Murphy, P. (1998) 'Reflections on the policy process', *M.Sc. in the Sociology of Sport and Sports Management*, Module 4, Unit 7, Part 15. Leicester: Centre for Research into Sport and Society. pp. 85–104.

Murphy, P. (2007) Personal communication. 1 February.

Murphy, P. and Waddington, I. (1998) 'Sport for all: some public health policy issues and problems', *Critical Public Health*, 8: 193–205.

Nagel, C. (2006) 'Immigrants can "belong" while maintaining their own culture', *The Edge*. November: 25.

National Audit Office. (2001) *Tackling Obesity in England*. London: National Audit Office.

Naul, R. (2003) 'European concepts of physical education', in K. Hardman (ed.), *Physical Education: Deconstruction and Reconstruction -- Issues and Directions*. Schorndorf: Verlag Karl Hofmann. pp. 35–53.

North-West Development Agency (NWDA) (2005) *Participation in Sport, the*

Arts, Physical and Creative Activities in England's Northwest. Executive Summary. Manchester: Knight, Kavanagh and Page.

O'Bryant, C., O'Sullivan, M. and Raudetsky, J. (2000) 'Socialization of prospective physical education teachers: the story of new blood', *Sport, Education and Society,* 5(2): 177–93.

O'Donovan, T. (2003) 'Negotiating popularity: an ethnographic exploration of social motivation in physical education', paper presented at the British Educational Research Association, University of Edinburgh, 12 September.

O'Donovan, T. and Kay, T. (2005) 'Focus on "Girls in Sport" ', *British Journal of Teaching Physical Education,* 36 (1): 29–31.

O'Donovan, T. and Kay, T. (2006) *Girls in Sport. Monitoring and Evaluation: Final Report.* Loughborough University: Institute of Youth Sport/Youth Sport Trust.

O'Hear, A. (1981) *Education, Society and Human Nature: An Introduction to the Philosophy of Education.* London: Routledge and Kegan Paul.

O'Sullivan, S. (2002) 'The physical activity of children: a study of 1,602 Irish schoolchildren aged 11–12 years', *Irish Medical Journal,* 95(3): 78–81.

Oakeshott, M. (1972) 'Education: the engagement and its frustration', in R.F. Dearden, P.H. Hirst and R.S. Peters (eds), *Education and the Development of Reason.* London: Routledge and Kegan Paul. pp. 19–49.

Odhams, H. (2007) Personal communication.

Office for Standards in Education (OFSTED) (1998) *Secondary Education 1993–97: The Curriculum.* www.opengov.gov.uk.

Office for Standards in Education (OFSTED) (2001) *Secondary Subject Reports 1999/2000: Physical Education.* London: OFSTED.

Office for Standards in Education (OFSTED) (2002) *Secondary Subject Reports 2000/01: Physical Education.* HMI 38. London: OFSTED.

Office for Standards in Education (OFSTED) (2003) *Good Assessment Practice in Physical Education.* HMI 1481. London: OFSTED Publications Centre.

Office for Standards in Education (OFSTED) (2005a) *Specialist Schools: A Second Evaluation.* HMI 2362, February. London: OFSTED Publications Centre.

Office for Standards in Education (OFSTED) (2005b) *The Physical Education, School Sport and Club Links Strategy.* HMI 2397, July. London: OFSTED Publications Centre.

Oliver, M. (1996) *Understanding Disability: From Theory to Practice.* Basingstoke: Macmillan.

Parry. J. (1988) 'Physical education, justification and the National Curriculum', *Physical Education Review,* 11(2): 106–18.

Parry, J. (1998) 'Reid on knowledge and justification in physical education', *European Physical Education Review,* 4(2): 70–4.

Penney, D. (2002) 'Equality, equity and inclusion in physical education and sport', in A. Laker (ed.), *The Sociology of Sport and Physical Education: An Introductory Reader*. Abingdon: RoutledgeFalmer. pp. 110–28.

Penney, D. (2006) 'Curriculum construction and change', in D. Kirk, D. Macdonald and M. O'Sullivan (eds), *The Handbook of Physical Education*. London: Sage. pp. 565–79.

Penney, D. and Evans, J. (1998) 'Dictating the play: government direction in physical education and sport policy development in England and Wales', in K. Green and K. Hardman (eds), *Physical Education: A Reader*. Aachen: Meyer and Meyer Verlag. pp. 84–101.

Penney, D. and Evans, J. (1999) *Politics, Policy and Practice in Physical Education*. London: F.N. Spon/Routledge.

Penney, D. and Evans, J. (2002) 'Talking gender', in D. Penney (ed.), *Gender and Physical Education: Contemporary Issues and Future Directions*. London: Routledge. pp. 13–23.

Penney, D. and Evans, J. (2005) 'Policy, power and politics in physical education', in K. Green and K. Hardman (eds), *Physical Education: Essential Issues*. London: Sage. pp. 21–38.

Penney, D. and Harris, J. (1997) 'Extra-curricular physical education: more of the same for the more able', *Sport, Education and Society*, 2(1): 41–54.

Penney, D., Clarke, C. and Kinchin, G. (2002) 'Developing physical education as a "connective specialism": is sport education the answer?' *Sport and Society*, 7(1): 55–64.

Peters, R.S. (1966) *Ethics and Education*. London: Allen and Unwin.

Pfister, G. and Reeg, A.-M. (2006) 'Fitness as "social heritage": a study of elementary school pupils in Berlin', *European Physical Education Review*, 12(1): 5–29.

Pidd, H. (2004) 'Go figure'. *Guardian 2*, 31 December, pp. 2–5.

Placek, J., Dodds, P., Doolittle, S., Portman, P., Ratliffe, T. and Pinkham, K. (1995) 'Teaching recruits' physical education backgrounds and beliefs about purposes for their subject matter', *Journal of Teaching in Physical Education*. 14(3): 246–61.

Platt, L. (2005) 'New destinations? Assessing the post-migration social mobility of minority ethnic groups in England and Wales', *Social Policy and Administration*, 39 (6): 697–721.

Puig, N. (1996) 'Spain', in P. De Knop, L.-M. Engström, B. Skirstad and M.R. Weiss (eds), *Worldwide Trends in Youth Sport*. Champaign, IL: Human Kinetics. pp. 245–59.

Puska, P. (2004) 'Foreword', in P. Oja and J. Borms (eds), *Health Enhancing Physical Activity*. Aachen: Meyer and Meyer Verlag. pp. 17–19.

Putnam, R.D. (2000) *Bowling Alone: The Collapse and Revival of American Community*. New York: Simon and Schuster/Touchstone.

Qualifications and Curriculum Authority (QCA) (2001) 'Physical education and school sport project', www.qca.org.uk/ca/subjects/pe/pess.asp accessed 3 April 2001.

Qualifications and Curriculum Authority (2005) *PE Update (Autumn)*. London: Qualifications and Curriculum Authority.

Qualifications and Curriculum Authority (QCA) (2005a) 'The future of PE', *PE Update*, Spring. London: QCA.

Qualifications and Curriculum Authority (QCA) (2005b) 'The state of play with PESS', *PE Update*, Autumn. London: QCA.

Qualifications and Curriculum Authority (QCA) (2006) *Programmes of Study: Physical Education. Draft 26/5/06*. London: QCA.

Qualifications and Curriculum Authority and the Department for Education and Employment (QCA and DfEE) (1999a) *The Review of the National Curriculum in England: The Secretary of State's Proposals*. London: Qualifications and Curriculum Authority.

Reid, A. (1996a) 'Knowledge, practice and theory in physical education', *European Physical Education Review*, 2(2): 94–104.

Reid, A. (1996b) 'The concept of physical education in current curriculum and assessment policy in Scotland', *European Physical Education Review*, 2(1): 7–18.

Reid, A. (1997) 'Value pluralism and physical education', *European Physical Education Review*, 3(1): 6–20.

Renton, A. (2006) 'The rot starts here', *Observer Food Monthly*, May. London: The *Observer*.

Rich, E.J., Holroyd, R. and Evans, J., (2004) 'Hungry to be Noticed. Young Women, Anorexia and Schooling', in *Body Knowledge and Control. Studies in the Sociology of Physical Education and Health*, Evans, J., Davies, B. and Wright, J. (eds). London: Routledge. pp. 173–91.

Riddoch, C. and Boreham, C. (1995) 'The health-related physical activity of children', *Sports Medicine*, 19(2): 86–102.

Roberts, K. (1995) 'School children and sport', in L. Lawrence, E. Murdoch and S. Parker (eds), *Professional and Development Issues in Leisure, Sport and Education*. Brighton: Leisure Studies Association. pp. 337–48.

Roberts, K. (1996a) 'Young people, schools, sport and government policy', *Sport, Education and Society*, 1(1): 47–57.

Roberts, K. (1996b) 'Youth cultures and sport: the success of school and community sport provisions in Britain', *European Physical Education Review*, 2(2): 105–15.

Roberts, K. (1997) 'Same activities, different meanings: British youth cultures in the 1990s', *Leisure Studies*, 16(1): 1–15.

Roberts, K. (1999) *Leisure in Contemporary Society*. Wallingford: CABI.

Roberts, K. (2001) *Class in Modern Britain*. Basingstoke, Palgrave.

Roberts, K. (2005) 'The Athenian dream in leisure studies', *Leisure Issues*, 7(1): 2–13.

Roberts, K. (2006) *Leisure in Contemporary Society*. Wallingford: CABI. (1st edn, 1999.)

Roberts, K. and Brodie, D. (1992) *Inner-City Sport: Who Plays and What Are the Benefits?* Culemborg: Giordano Bruno.

Roberts, K., Fagan, C., Boutenko, I. and Razlogov, K. (2001) 'Economic polarization, leisure practices and policies, and the quality of life: a study in post-communist Moscow', *Leisure Studies*, 20(3): 161–72.

Rowe, N. (2005) 'Foreword', in C. Foster, M. Hillsdon, N. Cavill, S. Allender and G. Cowburn (2005) *Understanding Participation in Sport – A Systematic Review*. London: Sport England. p. 2.

Rowland, T. (2002) 'Declining cardiorespiratory fitness in youth: fact or supposition?', *Pediatric Exercise Science*, 14(1): 1–8.

Royal College of Physicians, Royal College of Paediatrics and Child Health, Faculty of Public Health (2004) *Storing up Problems: The Medical Case for a Slimmer Nation. Report of a Working Party*. London: Royal College of Physicians.

Sage, G. (1980) 'Parental influence and socialization into sport for male and female intercollegiate athletes', *Journal of Sport and Social Issues*, 4(2): 1–13.

Salter, M. (2005) 'Applying the Key Stage 3 National Strategy to examination theory lessons in physical education', *British Journal of Teaching Physical Education*, 36(1): 23–7.

Salvara, M.I., Jess, M., Abbott, A. and Bognar, J. (2006) 'A preliminary study to investigate the influence of different teaching styles on pupils' goal orientations in physical education', *European Physical Education Review*, 12(1): 51–74.

Sandford, R. and Rich, E. (2006) 'Learners and popular culture', in D. Kirk, D. Macdonald and M. O'Sullivan (eds), *The Handbook of Physical Education*. London: Sage. pp. 275–91.

Scheerder, J., Taks, M., Vanreusel, B. and Renson, R. (2005a) 'Social changes in youth sport partnership styles: the case of Flanders (Belgium)', *Sport, Education and Society*, 10(3): 321–41.

Scheerder, J., Vanreusel, B., Taks, M. and Renson, R. (2005b) 'Social stratification patterns in adolescents' active sports participation behaviour: a time trend analysis 1969–1999', *European Physical Education Review*, 11(1): 5–27.

Scheerder, J., Vanreusel, B. and Taks, M. (2005c) 'Stratification patterns of active sport involvement among adults: social change and persistence', *International Review for the Sociology of Sport*, 40(2): 139–62.

Schenker, S. (2005) 'Tackling the obesity epidemic', *PE and Sport Today*, 17: 10–11.

Schizzerotto, A. and Lucchini, M. (2002) *Transitions to Adulthood during the Twentieth Century: A Comparison of Great Britain, Italy and Sweden*. EPAG Working Paper 2002-36. Colchester: University of Essex.

Schools Health Education Unit (SHEU) (2006) *Young People into 2006*. Exeter: SHEU.

Scraton, S. (1992) *Shaping Up to Womanhood. Gender and Girls' Physical Education*. Buckingham: Open University Press.

Scraton, S. (1993) 'Equality, coeducation and physical education in secondary schooling', in J. Evans (ed.), *Equality, Education and Physical Education*. Lewes: Falmer Press. pp. 139–53.

Seefeld, V., Malina, R. M. and Clark, M A. (2002) 'Factors affecting levels of physical activity in adults', *Sports Medicine*, 32(3): 143–68.

Shaw, I., Newton, D.P., Aitkin, M. and Darnell, R. (2003) 'Do OFSTED inspections of secondary school make a difference to GCSE results?', *British Educational Research Journal*, 29(1): 63–75.

Shildrick, T. (2006) 'Youth culture, subculture and the importance of neighbourhood', *Young: Nordic Journal of Youth Research*, 14(1): 61–74.

Shilling, C. (1998) 'The body, schooling and social inequalities: physical capital and the politics of physical education', in K. Green and K. Hardman (eds), *Physical Education: A Reader*. Aachen: Meyer and Meyer Verlag. pp. 243–71.

Shilling, C. (2005) 'Culture, the "sick role" and the consumption of health', in T. Hoikkala, P. Hakkareinen and S. Laine (eds), *Beyond Health Literacy: Youth Cultures, Prevention and Policy*. Helsinki: Finnish Youth Research Society. pp. 25–41.

Siedentop, D. (1994) *Sport Education*. Champaign, IL: Human Kinetics.

Sigman, A. (2007) 'Visual voodoo: the biological impact of watching TV', *Biologist*, 54(1): 12–17.

Sisjord, M.-K. and Skirstad, B. (1996) 'Norway', in P. De Knop, L.-M. Engstrom, B. Skirstad and M.R. Weiss (eds), *Worldwide Trends in Youth Sport*. Champaign, IL: Human Kinetics. pp. 170–83.

Skelton, C. (2000) 'A passion for football: dominant masculinities and primary schooling', *Sport, Education and Society*, 5(1): 5–18.

Skille, E.A. and Waddington, I. (2006) 'Alternative sport programmes and social inclusion in Norway', *European Physical Education Review*, 12(3): 251–70.

Sloan, S. (2007) 'An investigation into the perceived level of personal subject knowledge and competence of a group of pre-service physical education teachers towards the teaching of secondary school gymnastics', *European Physical Education Review*, 13(1): 57–80.

Small, G. and Nash, C. (2005) 'The impact of School Sport Co-ordinators in Dundee: a case study', in K. Hylton, J. Long and A. Flintoff (eds), *Evaluating Sport and Active Leisure for Young People*. Eastbourne: Leisure Studies Association. pp. 93–107.

Smith, A. (2004) 'The inclusion of pupils with special educational needs in secondary physical education', *Physical Education and Sport Pedagogy*, 9(1): 37–54.

Smith, A. (2006) 'Young people, sport and leisure: a sociological study of youth lifestyles'. PhD thesis, University of Liverpool, Liverpool.

Smith, A. and Green, K. (2004) 'Including pupils with special educational needs in secondary school physical education: a sociological analysis of teachers' views', *British Journal of Sociology of Education*, 25(5): 593–607.

Smith, A. and Parr, M. (2007) 'Young people's views on the nature and purposes of physical education: a sociological analysis', *Sport, Education and Society*, 12(1): 37–58.

Smith, L. (2006) 'Absent voices', *Society Guardian*, 6 September pp. 1–2.

Solomon, R.P. and Tarc, A.M. (2003) 'The subversion of antiracism: missed education of African-Caribbean students in Britain, the USA and Canada', *Caribbean Journal of Education*, 25(1): 1–24.

Sparkes, A. (1989) 'Health-related fitness: an example of innovation without change', *British Journal of Physical Education*, 20(2): 60–4.

Sport Cheshire (2002) *Cheshire: 2002 Year 9 Participation Survey*. Chester: Sport Cheshire.

Sport England (2000a) *Young People and Sport National Survey 1999*. London: Sport England.

Sport England (2000b) *Sports Participation and Ethnicity in England. National Survey 1999/2000. Headline Findings*. London: Sport England.

Sport England (2001) *Young People and Sport in England 1999. A Survey of Young People and PE Teachers*. London: Sport England.

Sport England (2001b) *Young People with a Disability and Sport*. London: Sport England.

Sport England (2003a) *Young People and Sport in England. Trends in Participation 1994–2002*. London: Sport England.

Sport England (2003b) *Young People and Sport in England, 2002: A Survey of Young People and PE Teachers*. London: Sport England.

Sport England (2005) *Participation in Sport in Great Britain: Trends 1987 to 2002*. London: Sport England.

Sport England (2006) *Understanding Participation in Sport: What Determines Sports Participation Among 15–19 Year Old Women*. London: Sport England.

Sport England/UK Sport (2001) *General Household Survey: Participation in Sport – Past Trends and Future Prospects*. London: Sport England/UK Sport.

Sports Coach UK (2004) *Sport Coaching in the UK. Final Report*. London: Sports Coach UK.

Sports Council for Wales (SCW) (1995) *The Pattern of Play. Physical Education in Welsh Schools: 1990 to 1994*. Cardiff: SCW.

Sports Council for Wales (SCW) (2000) *A Strategy for Welsh Sport: Young People First*. Cardiff: SCW.

Sports Council for Wales (SCW) (2001) *Widening the Net? Young People's Participation in Sport 1999/2000*. Cardiff: SCW.

Sports Council for Wales (SCW) (2002) *Swimming Against the Tide? Physical Education and Sports Provision in Secondary Schools in Wales*. Cardiff: SCW.

Sports Council for Wales (SCW) (2003a) *Secondary School Aged Children's Participation in Sport in 2001*. Cardiff: SCW.

Sports Council for Wales (SCW) (2003b) *Young People's Participation Year 2001 Data: Research and Evaluation Section*. Cardiff: SCW.

Sports Council for Wales (SCW) (2006) *Active Young People. Sports Update No. 58*. Cardiff: SCW.

Sportsteacher (2005a) 'Big Lottery funding for sport continues', *Sportsteacher*: 4.

Sportsteacher (2005b) 'PE is pupils' favourite subject', *Sportsteacher*: 9. Summer.

Spurlock, M. (2004) *Super Size Me*. DVD/Video. Tartan.

Stevinson, C. (2003) 'How can specific populations benefit?' *BASES World*, December: 11–12.

Stewart, D. (2005) 'President's diary', *British Journal of Teaching Physical Education*, 36(1): 32–3.

Stidder, G. (2001a) 'Curriculum innovation in physical education at Key Stage 4: a review of GCSE results in one English secondary school', *Bulletin of Physical Education*, 37(1): 25–46.

Stidder, G. and Hayes, S. (2006) 'A longitudinal study of physical education teachers' experiences on school placements in the south-east of England (1994–2004), *European Physical Education Review*, 12(2): 313–33.

Stidder, G. and Wallis, J. (2003) 'Future directions for physical education at Key Stage four and Post-16: some critical questions', *British Journal of Teaching Physical Education*, 34(4): 41–7.

Stocchino, G., Selis, A., Guicciardi, M. and Mereu, F. (2007) 'Full integration in Italian school during physical education and sports activities', in C. Higgs and Y. Vanlandewijck (eds), *Sport for Persons with a Disability*. Berlin: ICCSPE. pp. 105–26.

Stroot, S.A. (2002) 'Socialization and participation in sport', in A. Laker (ed.), *The Sociology of Sport and Physical Education: An Introductory Reader*. Abingdon: RoutledgeFalmer. pp. 129–47.

Stroot, S.A. and Ko, B. (2006) 'Induction of beginning physical educators into the school setting', in D. Kirk, D. Macdonald and M. O'Sullivan (eds), *The Handbook of Physical Education*. London: Sage. pp. 425–48.

Talbot, M. (1995) 'The politics of sport and physical education', in S. Fleming, M. Talbot and A. Tomlinson (eds), *Policy and Politics in Sport, Physical Education and Leisure: Themes and Issues*. Brighton: LSA. pp. 3–26.

Taplin, L. (2005) Editor's comments, *British Journal of Teaching Physical Education*, 36(1): p. 3.

Telama, R. (2002) 'Foreword', in M. Mosston. and S. Ashworth (eds), *Teaching*

Physical Education. New York: Benjamin Cummings. pp. ix–x.

Telama, R., Laakso, L. and Yang, X. (1994) 'Physical activity and participation in sports of young people in Finland', *Scandinavian Journal of Medicine and Science in Sport*, 4(1): 65–74.

Telama, R., Naul, R., Nupponen, H., Rychtecky, A. and Vuolle, P. (2002) *Physical Fitness, Sporting Lifestyles and Olympic Ideals: Cross-Cultural Studies on Youth and Sport in Europe*. Schorndorf: Verlag Karl Hofmann.

Telama, R., Nupponen, H. and Pieron, M. (2005) 'Physical activity among young people in the context of lifestyle', *European Physical Education Review*, 11(2): 115–37.

Thomas, N. and Green, K. (1994) 'Physical education teacher education and the 'special needs' of youngsters with disabilities – the need to confront PETE's attitude problem', *British Journal of Physical Education*. 25(4): 26–30.

Thomas, N. and Smith, A. (forthcoming) *Disability, Sport and Society: An Introduction*. London: Routledge.

Thomas, N.-E., Cooper, S.-M., Williams, S.P., Baker, J.S. and Davies, B. (2005) Coronary heart disease risk factors in young people of differing socio-economic status, *European Physical Education Review*, 11(2): 169–83.

Thorburn, M. and Collins, D. (2006) 'The effects of an integrated curriculum model on student learning and attainment', *European Physical Education Review*, 12(1): 31–50.

Thorpe, R. (1996) 'Physical education: beyond the curriculum', in N. Armstrong (ed.), *New Directions in Physical Education: Change and Innovation*. London: Cassell Education. pp. 145–56.

Tinning, R. (1988) 'Student teaching and the pedagogy of neccessity', *Journal of Teaching in Physical Education*, 7: 82–9.

Tinning, R. (1991) 'Problem-setting and ideology in health-based physical education: an Australian perspective', *Physical Education Review*, 14(1): 40–9.

Tinning, R. (2006) 'Theoretical orientations in physical education teacher education', in D. Kirk, D. Macdonald and M. O'Sullivan (eds) *The Handbook of Physical Education*. London: Sage. pp. 369–85.

Training and Development Agency (TDA) (2006) *Handbook of Guidance*. London: TDA.

Tregaskis, C. (2002) 'Social model theory: the story so far ...', *Disability and Society*, 17(4): 457–70.

Trost, S.G. (2006) 'Public health and physical education', in D. Kirk, D. Macdonald and M. O'Sullivan (eds), *The Handbook of Physical Education*. London: Sage. pp. 163–87.

Trowler, P., with Riley, M. (1984) *Topics in Sociology*. London: University Tutorial Press.

Tsangaridou, N. (2006a) 'Teachers' beliefs', in D. Kirk, D. Macdonald and M. O'Sullivan (eds), *The Handbook of Physical Education*. London: Sage. pp. 486–501.

Tsangaridou, N. (2006b) 'Teachers' knowledge', in D. Kirk, D. Macdonald and M. O'Sullivan (eds), *The Handbook of Physical Education*. London: Sage. pp. 502–15.

UK Sport/Sport England (2001) *Participation in Sport, Past Trends and Future Prospects*. London: Sport England.

US Department of Health and Human Services (USDHHS) (2000) *Healthy People 2010: Understanding and Improving Health*. Washington, DC: U.S. Government Printing Office.

US Department of Education (2002) *Public Law 107–110: The No Child Left Behind Act of 2001*. Washington: US Department of Education.

Van Der Mars, H. (2006) 'Time and learning in physical education', in D. Kirk, D. Macdonald and M. O'Sullivan (eds), *The Handbook of Physical Education*. London: Sage. pp. 191–213.

Verma, G.K., and Darby, D.S. (1994) *Winners and Losers: Ethnic Minorities in Sport and Recreation*. London: Falmer Press.

Vertovec, S. (2007) 'New ethnic communities: from multi-culturalism to super-diversity', in J. Clarke (ed.), *Britain Today 2007*. Swindon: Economic and Social Research Council. p. 94.

Vescio, J., Wilde, K. and Crosswhite, J. (2005) 'Profiling sport role models to enhance initiatives for adolescent girls in physical education and sport', *European Physical Education Review*, 11(2): 153–70.

Vickerman, P. (2002) 'Perspectives on the training of physical education teachers for the inclusion of children with special education need. Is there an official line view?' *The Bulletin of Physical Education*. 38(2): 79–98.

Vickerman, P., Hayes, S. and Whetherly, A. (2003) 'Special Educational Needs and National Curriculum Physical Education', in S. Hayes and G. Stidder (eds), *Equity and Inclusion in Physical Education and Sport*. London: Routledge. pp. 47–64.

Vulliamy, E. (2002). '"Super-sized" teenagers sue McDonald's', The *Observer*, 24 November.

Waddington, I. (2000) *Sport, Health and Drugs: A Critical Sociological Perspective*. London: Routledge.

Waddington, I., Malcom, D. and Cobb, J. (1998) 'Gender stereotyping and physical education', *European Physical Education Review*, 4(1): 34–46.

Waddington, I., Malcolm, D. and Green, K. (1997) 'Sport, health and physical education: a reconsideration', *European Physical Education Review*, 3(2): 165–82.

Wallace, C. and Kovatcheva, S. (1998) *Youth in Society*. London: Macmillan.

Wallhead, T.L. and Buckworth, J. (2004) 'The role of physical education in the promotion of youth physical activity', *QUEST*, 56: 285–301.

Walseth, K. (2006) 'Young Muslim women and sport: the impact of identity work', *Leisure Studies*, 25(1): 75–94.

Walseth, K. and Fasting, K. (2003) 'Islam's view on physical activity and sport: Egyptian women interpreting Islam', *International Review for the Sociology of Sport*, 38: 45–60.

Wang, C.K.J. and Liu, W.C. (2007) 'Promoting enjoyment in girls' physical education: the impact of goals, beliefs, and self-determination', *European Physical Education Review*, 13(2): 145–64.

Wanless, D. (2004) *Securing Good Health for the Whole Population: Final Report*. London: Department of Health.

Warikoo, N. (2005) 'Gender and ethnic identity among second-generation Indo-Caribbeans', *Ethnic and Racial Studies*, 28(5): 803–31.

Waring, M., Warburton, P. and Coy, M. (2007) 'Observation of children's physical activity levels in primary schools: is the school an ideal setting for meeting government activity targets?', *European Physical Education Review*, 13(1): 25–40.

Watkins, C. and Mortimer, P. (1999) 'Pedagogy: what do we know?' in P. Mortimer (ed.), *Understanding Pedagogy and its Impact on Learning*. London: Sage. pp. 1–19.

Welk, G.J., Eisenmann, J.C. and Dollman, J. (2006) 'Health-related physical activity in children and adolescents: a bio-behavioral perspective', in D. Kirk, D. Macdonald and M. O'Sullivan (eds), *The Handbook of Physical Education*. London: Sage. pp. 665–84.

White, J. (2006) *Intelligence, Destiny and Education: The Ideological Roots of Intelligence Testing*. London: Routledge.

Whitehead, M. (2001) 'Physical literacy – opening the debate', *British Journal of Teaching Physical Education*, 32(1): 6–8.

Whitehead, M. (2006) 'Physical literacy and physical education: conceptual mapping', *Physical Education Matters*, 1(1): 6–9.

Whitson, D. (1990) 'Sport in the social construction of masculinity', in M.A. Messner and D.F. Sabo (eds), *Sport, Men and the Gender Order: Critical Feminist Perspectives*. Champaign, IL: Human Kinetics. pp. 19–29.

Whyte, G. (2006) 'Exercise is BAD for you …', *Sport and Exercise Scientist*, 10 (December): 14.

Williams, A. (1989) 'Girls and boys come out to play (but mainly boys) – gender and physical education', in A. Williams (ed.), *Issues in Physical Education for the Primary Years*. London: Falmer Press. pp. 145–59.

Williams, A. (1993) 'The reflective physical education teacher: implications for Initial Teacher Education'. *Physical Education Review*, 16(2): 137–44.

Williams, A. (1998) 'The reflective physical education teacher: implications for Initial Teacher Education', in K. Green and K. Hardman (eds), *Physical Education: A Reader*. Aachen: Meyer and Meyer Verlag. pp. 204–16.

Williams, A., Bedward, J. and Woodhouse, J. (2000) 'An inclusive National Curriculum? The experience of adolescent girls', *European Journal of Physical Education*, 5(1): 4–18.

Wilson, J. (2000) 'Doing justice to inclusion', *European Journal of Special Needs Education*, 15(3): 297–304.

Wilson, T.C. (2002) 'The paradox of social class and sports involvement', *International Review for the Sociology of Sport*, 37(1): 5–16.

Winsley, R. and Armstrong, N. (2005) 'Physical activity, physical fitness, health and young people', in K. Green and K. Hardman (eds), *Physical Education: Essential Issues*. London: Sage. pp. 65–77.

World Health Organization (WHO) (2002) *World Health Report 2002: Reducing Risk – Promoting Healthy Life*. Geneva: WHO.

World Summit on Physical Education (1999) *The Berlin Agenda for Action for Government Ministers*. Berlin: ICSSPE.

Wray, R. (2006) 'Surfing booms as TV watching stalls', *Guardian*, 29 November, p. 26.

Wright, J. (1999) 'Changing gendered practice in physical education: working with teachers', *European Physical Education Review*, 5(3): 181–98.

Wu, Y. (2006) 'Editorial: overweight and obesity in China', *British Medical Journal*, 333: 362–3.

Wyn, J., Tyler, D. and Willis, E. (2002) 'Researching the post-1970 generation: reflections on the life-patterns study of Australian youth', paper presented at 15th World Congress of the International Sociological Association, Brisbane, 7–13 July.

Yates, L., Butterfield, S., Brown, S. and Baudelot, C. (1997) 'Review symposium: education, assessment and society: a sociological analysis', *British Journal of Sociology of Education*, 18(3): 435–39.

Youth Sport Trust (YST) (2000) *Towards Girl-Friendly Physical Education. Girls in Sport Partnership Project Final Report*. Loughborough: YST.

Zeijl, E., du Bois Reymond, M. and and te Poel, Y. (2001) 'Young adolescents' leisure patterns', *Loisir and Societe*, 24(2): 379–402.

Zwozdiak-Myers, J. (2006) 'The reflective practitioner', in S. Capel, P. Breckon and J. O'Neill (eds), *A Practical Guide to Teaching Physical Education in the Secondary School*. Abingdon: Routledge. pp. 18–27.

Index

Added to a page number 't' denotes a table and 'n' denotes notes.

abseiling 67
academic curriculum model 9–10
academic success, middle-class lifestyle 163
Academic/Active Learning Time in Physical Education (ALT-PE) research 51
academization of PE 88–9, 90–1, 92, 95n, 231–2, 233, 234
accountability 80–1
acculturation 208–9
achievement 79, 80
active learning, disabled youngsters 193
activity choice (option PE) 37, 50, 123
adherence to sport 129–32, 135
adipose tissue 108
adults
    other than teachers (AOTT) 50, 72, 75, 229, 233
    physical activity, fitness and health 109
    social class and participation 159–60
Advanced (A) Level PE/Sport 81
    comparison of grades (2006) 85t
    segregation between vocational qualifications and 88
    standards of attainment 84–6
    total entries for (1990–2006) 82t
    widespread expansion and acceptance of 82, 93

aerobic fitness 109
aerobics 140, 142, 160
aesthetic activities 10
African-Americans 107, 167, 172, 176–7, 178
African-Caribbeans 107, 167, 176–7, 181, 182
age, and participation 128
alcohol consumption, young people 103–4
alienation, resistance of gender stereotypes 146
ALT-PE see Academic/Active Learning Time in Physical Education
American football 177
analytical-philosophical perspective 8–11, 13–14, 15
angling 154, 160
anti-intellectualism 18
anxiety 99
AOTT see adults other than teachers
archery 55
Asians 107, 177, 181, 182
    see also South Asians
aspirational model, efficacy expectancy 132
assessment 79–81, 93, 198, 222
'assessment for learning' 79
Association for Physical Education (AfPE) 22n, 28
athletics 55, 57, 69, 73, 140, 142, 182, 183, 195
attainment 84–6, 158

Attainment Targets (NCPE) 34
attitudes to sports and physical activities
 59
Australia
  academization of PE 95n
  anti-intellectualism 18
  centrality of health to PE 96
  curriculum for PE 60
  lifestyle activities 120
  sex and extra-curricular PE 67
  sport participation 162
  time spent on PE 51–2

badminton 55, 57, 76, 120, 121, 123, 140,
 182
ball sports 121
Bangladeshis 169, 171, 175–6, 178, 181,
 182
'barriers' to participation 153, 203
baseball 56, 58, 69
basketball 55, 56, 58, 69, 70, 71, 73, 120,
 121, 140, 142, 148, 160, 177, 182,
 195, 196, 202, 203
behaviour change, evidence-based model
 132, 133
behavioural difficulties, mainstreaming
 and inclusion 197–8
behaviouristic approach, teacher
 education 212
Belgium 118–19, 120, 126, 160
Black Africans 181, 182
Black Other ethnic groups 181, 182
black students, sedentary behaviours 107
boccia 55, 203
bodies of knowledge 9
body
  class, sport and PE 157
  sexualization of female 146
body mass index 107–8
bowls 55
boxing 160, 177, 183
boys
  ego-oriented dispositions 130
  valuing of activity choice 123
  see also gender
'break' from schooling, PE as 20
British Association of Advisers and
 Lecturers in Physical Education
 (BAALPE) 22n

British Olympic Association 24
bureaucracy 87

canoeing 55
cardiovascular risk, waist-hip ratio 108
Central Council for Physical Recreation
 21, 24
centres of excellence 33
changeability, young people's leisure
 activities 131
cheerleading 55
China 97, 104
Chinese 67, 172, 181, 182
choice biographies 132
Choosing Health (DoH) 96
circus skills 55
class management, mainstreaming and
 inclusion 197–8
class sizes, pressure on teaching
 resources 50
climbing 67, 69
clothing, conflicts between teachers and
 pupils 178
club-based sport 126, 228
co-educational PE 147–9
coaches 50, 235n
coaching orientation 213
coaching support 37
Coaching for Teachers 51
collaboration, calls for 40
'command' style of teaching 220
Community Use of Sports Facilities 47
competence 129–30, 149
competencies 212
competition, academization of PE 92
competitive sports 57, 58, 67, 68, 71, 74,
 119, 120, 140, 144
competitiveness, policy networks 28
contact sports 140, 148
continuing professional development
 (CPD) 216–18, 224
coping strategies, religion and demands
 of PE 179
couch potatoes 139
Council of Europe 53
cricket 55, 56, 57, 69, 120, 121, 182, 195,
 202
cross-country 56, 69, 70
cultural capital 155–6

cultural clash, teachers and pupils 177, 178–9
curling 55
curriculum
    externally-driven change 60
    games-based 123
    impact of examinations upon 87–8
    number and range of activities 54–6
    replication of traditional 209
    the state of sport 56–8
    see also academic curriculum model; National Curriculum for Physical Education
cycling 55, 76, 119, 120, 121, 160, 182, 202
Czech Republic 118–19

dance 55, 56, 57, 69, 70, 71, 140, 142, 144, 147, 173, 191, 195, 221
DCMS *see* Department of Culture, Media and Sports
debates 204
decentralized control 40
democratization of leisure 164
Denmark 120, 123, 171
Department of Culture, Media and Sports (DCMS) 24, 28, 31–2, 34
Department for Education and Skills (DfES) 24, 32, 34
Department of Health (DoH) 24
Department of National Heritage (DNH) 35
depression 99
deprofessionalization 233
DfES *see* Department for Education and Skills
diabetes 108
didactic teaching styles 222
diet and health 103–4, 157–8
disability and SEN 189–91
    contradictory policy goals 205
    defining 187–9
    mainstreaming *see* mainstreaming
    participation in extra-curricular PE 67
    sport 201–3
    teachers lack of awareness of legal obligations 204–5
discourses, policy ideology 30
discrimination, engagement in sport 185
disengagement 135

diversity
    among ethnic groups 169–72
    in family formation 174
    participation, youth sport 119, 122, 130–1
DNH *see* Department of National Heritage
DoH *see* Department of Health
dominance hierarchy, PE classes 148–9
drop-out, sport and physical activity 128, 131, 133, 158
dual-use sports centres 48–9
Duke of Edinburgh Award 81

Eastern Europe 49
economic deprivation, and health 158
economic inequality, leisure inequality 165
education
    and health 112
    marketization of 40, 47–8, 60, 92–3, 228
    social class and participation 158–9
    see also physical education
Education Act (1944) 22n
Education Reform Act (1988) 29, 34
educational attainment, and social class 158
educational nature/worth
    physical education 16
    practical knowledge 11–12
educational sociologists 13
educationally worthwhile knowledge 8–9
efficacy expectancy 132
ego-oriented dispositions 129, 130
elite sport, tension between mass participation and 40
embarrassment 146
End of Key Stage Statements 34
end-of-term/year reports 78–9
energy consumption, weight-gain 103
England
    balance of power in school sport 28
    expectations of PE 25
    extra-curricular PE 68, 69, 71
    gender and participation 139, 141
    investment in PE 46
    time allocation, PE 59
enjoyment 20, 129–30

Estonia 118–19, 120
ethnic minorities
  diversity and integration among
    169–72
  lower levels of physical activity 106–7
  and participation 71, 234–5
  terminology 169
  youthful make-up 172
ethnic penality 185
ethnicity 167–86
  key dimensions 172–6
  obesity 107
  and PE 176–80
    extra-curricular 67
    gender, social class and sport 163–4
  and race 168–72
  sport participation 180–4
Europe
  extra-curricular provision 62–3
  gender and participation 139
  lifestyle activities 119–20
  sedentary lives of children 97–8
  time devoted to PE 51
  youth sport 118–19, 122, 126
  see also individual countries
evidence-based model, behaviour change
    132, 133
examinable PE 82–94
  the case for 89–90
  growth and development of 82–3
  issues in 83–9
  making sense of 90–3
examinations 28, 81, 87–8
  see also Advanced (A) Level; General
    Certificate of Secondary Education
exercise
  health promotion 99, 104
  social networks 125
  see also health-related exercise
expectations
  policy networks 25
  pupil achievement 80
extra-curricular PE 62–77
  cultural clash, teachers and pupils
    177, 178–9
  defined 62
  empirical information 62
  explaining 73–4
  gender and participation 141

gender-stereotyping 75
  greater support for 37
  levels of participation 64–7
  non-specialist teachers 50
  outside agencies 72
  provision 63–4
  School Sport Partnerships 72–3
  social class and participation 161
  sporting bias 71, 72
  types of sport on offer 68–72
*Extra-curricular physical education: more
    of the same for the more able?* 68
extrinsic rewards 129

facilities
  Muslim participation 173–4
  provision 46–9, 58–9
  rebuilding 37
  youth sport 127–8
family, and ethnicity 174–6
fast food, and obesity 103
femininity 138, 144, 149–51, 183
fencing 160
Finland 118–19, 120, 126
firearms sports 160
fitness
  decline in 98
  physical activity and adult health 109
  psychosocial outcomes 99
  testing 108–9
  see also keep fit
Flanders 63, 71, 126, 162
'flow' 129
football 56, 57, 67, 69, 73, 120, 121, 140,
    142, 148, 151, 154, 182, 183, 195, 202
see also soccer
Football Association (FA) 24, 28
football coaches 235n
formative assessment 79, 81
France 120
friends, impact on participation 125–6,
    132, 134

Game Plan 161
games 37, 228
games kit 179
games skills 194–5
gender 137–53
  and activity 105

ethnicity and participation 181–2, 183
health-related exercise (HRE) 101
and PE
    co-educational 147–9
    examinable 83–4, 86
    extra-curricular 67, 69, 70–1
    motivation and competence 149
    nature of provision 143–4
    participation 138–43, 234
    self image 145–7
    social class, ethnicity, sport
        163–4
    social dynamics 151–2
    socialization 149–51
sex and 138
stereotypes 75, 139, 145, 146, 150
teaching styles 221
see also boys; girls; male teachers;
    women
General Certificate of Secondary
    Education, PE/Sport 81
comparison of grades (2006) 86t
as compulsory subject 94n
segregation between vocational
    qualifications and 88
standards of attainment 84–6
total entries (1990–2006) 82t
widespread expansion and acceptance
    82, 93
Germany
    co-educational PE 149
    lifestyle activities 119, 120
    Muslims 171
    participation 118–19, 140–1, 184
    popularity of traditional sports 123
    sports club membership 160
    time spent on PE 51
'gifted and talented' pupils 41, 58, 205
girls
    involvement in male-dominated
        activities 121
    Muslim 174–6
    participation in sport 56
    task-oriented dispositions 130
    see also gender; sex
Girls in Sport 139, 142, 144
'global crisis of PE' 60
goal orientations 129
goalball 55

gold standard 84
golf 55, 121, 140, 160, 182
'good' teachers 220
'good' teaching 222–3
government
    policy *see* policy
    quangos 24, 28, 77n
    White Papers 30
grade inflation 84
grammar schools 22n
Greece 71, 148
guided discovery 221
gym 69, 76
gymnastics 55, 57, 69, 70, 140, 142, 147,
    195, 221

handball 55
head teachers 28, 92, 94
health
    economic deprivation 158
    key contributors to 102–7
    limits to education 112
    limits to individualism 110–11
    limits to PE 113–14
    limits to sport 112–13
    major problems 96–8
    physical activity and sport as solution
        18, 20, 36, 99–102
    physical capital 157–8
    psychological 98–9
health-related exercise (HRE) 100–1
    growing strength of lobby 37
    limits of science 107–10
    in practice 101–2
    social class 158
healthism 110–11
healthization of PE 230–1
Healthy People 2010 96
heart conditions 108
hierarchical/linear model, policy
    implementation 25
Hindus 169, 170, 171, 173
Hispanic 168–9
hockey 55, 56, 57, 69, 70, 121, 142, 144,
    182, 195
horse-riding 195
host-immigrant thesis 170
HRE *see* health-related exercises
Hungary 118–19

hunting 160

ice hockey 148
ice-skating 76
ideology, policy and 29–30, 36
inactivity 98, 105, 158
inclusion 189–91
    debates 204
    individualized activities 195
    support for 198–9
independence 125
individualism, and health 110–11
individualization 125, 126
indoor facilities 47, 127
'informing the mind' 16
Inner-City Sport 99–100
instability, young people's leisure
        activities 131
insulin resistance 108
integration
    among ethnic groups 169–72
    disability and SEN 189–91
intellectual dimension, of sport 10
intellectual knowledge 17, 22n
inter-scholastic sport 58
inter-school competitive sport 57
internal fat 108
International Council for Sports Science
        and Physical Education (ICSSPE)
        53
intra-school competitive sport 57
intrinsic motivation 149
intrinsic rewards 129
investment, in PE 46
Islam 173, 179
Italy 120

jogging 119–20, 140, 142
Junior Sports Leaders Award (JSLA) 81
junk food 103

kabbadi 55
karate 160
keep fit (fitness) 55, 73, 76, 142
Key Stages 34
kick-boxing 142
knowledge
    educationally worthwhile 8–9
    see also intellectual knowledge;

practical knowledge; propositional
    knowledge

'leadership' awards 81
learning environments 129
Learning Support Assistants (LSAs) 199
legislation, and participation 142, 148
leisure
    activities 125–6, 131, 142, 154
    democratization of 164
    economic inequality 165
    renaissance 128
liberal-analytical tradition 8–11, 13–14, 15
lifelong participation 128–32, 133
lifestyle activities 73, 119–20, 121, 122,
        123, 142, 144, 183, 194, 202
'lifestyle' diseases 37, 99
Link Teachers 38, 51
Living for Sport 59, 118
locations (class), and involvement in
        sport 157
'locked-in' to sport 130, 133
Loughborough Partnership survey 50,
        53, 54, 55, 57, 73, 180, 193
'love of sport' 209

mainstreaming 189–91
    efficacy 200–1
    implementation 191–200, 205
male dominance, 'open' sporting settings
        148–9
male teachers, skill/sport-oriented extra-
        curricular PE 74
manual workers, participation in sport
        159–60
marketization of education 40, 47–8, 60,
        92–3, 228
martial arts 55, 121
masculinity 138, 144, 147, 149–51
mass participation 37, 40
measurement
    fitness 108–9
    overweight and obesity 107–8
medical model of disability 188–9
mental ill health 98–9
mentoring 211–12
mid-adolescence 134
middle classes 154, 157–8, 160, 161,
        162–3, 164, 165

mixed race 169–70
mixed-sex PE 147–9
moral education 10
moral responsibility, towards health 111
motivation 59, 129–32, 135, 149
motor boating 160
multi-activity PE programmes,
    significance of 122–4
Muslim communities 179
Muslims 67, 170, 171, 172–3, 174–6, 179,
    181, 184, 185

National Curriculum for Physical
    Education (NCPE) 16, 29, 30–1, 42,
    43
    1995 35–6
    2000 36–7, 191
    England and Wales 34–5
    gender and PE 144
    teaching styles 222
National Junior Sport Programme
    (NJSP) 32
National Playing Fields Association 48
netball 55, 57, 67, 69, 70, 73, 121, 140,
    142, 144
Netherlands 118
networks see policy networks; social
    networks
'new condition of youth' 124–7
New Opportunities Fund (NOF) 34
New Zealand 96
NJSP see National Junior Sport
    Programme
No Child Left Behind 50
NOF see New Opportunities Fund
non-specialist teachers 50
North-West Development Agency (2005)
    study 181
Norway 119, 141–2, 148, 151, 161, 171
Norwegian Sports City Programme
    162

obesity 97
    energy consumption 103
    environment 105
    ethnicity 107
    satisfactory measures 107
    science of 110
    socio-economic status 158

see also weight
obesogenic environments 98
occupational groups, policy networks
    24–5
occupational socialization 90, 91, 209,
    214–16, 217
OFSTED 39, 51, 79–80, 91
optimal experiences 129
'option' PE (activity choice) 37, 50, 123
organizations, attempts to influence PE
    28
organized competitive sport 119
orienteering 55
'out of lessons' sport and PE 166n
    see also extra-curricular PE
out-of-school hours' programmes 57
outdoor and adventurous activities
    (OAA) 191
outdoor facilities 47, 48, 59
overweight 107, 108, 158

Pakistanis 169, 171, 175–6, 178, 181, 182
parental behaviours, and participation
    150, 162
part-time jobs, non-participation in
    extra-curricular PE 71
participation
    barriers to 153, 203
    constraints to 71–2
    curricular PE 38–9, 48
    disabled youngsters 193–4
    diversity in 119, 122, 130–1
    education 158–9
    ethnic minorities 180–1
    extra-curricular PE 64–7
    fun and enjoyment as major motive
        129
    gender 56, 138–43
    Islam 173
    significance of friends 125–6, 132, 134
    social class 106–7, 159–63
    youth sport 117–22, 124, 126–7, 133–4
    see also lifelong participation; mass
        participation
partnership
    calls for 40
    see also School Sport Partnerships
partnership development managers 38
pedagogy 219

peer groups, impact on participation 125–6, 132, 134
performance, as measure of school standard 91
personal development, PE and 18, 20
personal and social development, PE as contributory to 18
PESSCL *see* Physical Education, School Sport and Club Links
Peters-Hirst (Petersian) approach 8–11, 13–14, 15
philosophy, terminology 94n
physical activity
  adult fitness and health 109
  aerobic fitness 109
  decline in 97–8
  disabled youngsters 194–7
  health promotion 99–102
  national recommendations/guidelines 98
  psychological well-being 99
physical capital 156–8
physical education
  academization 88–9, 90–1, 92, 95n, 231–2, 233, 234
  assessment 79–81, 93, 198, 222
  disability and SEN 187–205
  ethnicity 167–86
  future for 232–6
  gender 137–53
  health 96–115
  healthization 230–1
  nature and purposes of 7–22, 28
  non-educational justifications 20
  participation *see* participation
  policy 23–44
  preconditions for delivery 46
  professionalization 91–2, 218
  social class 154–65
  sportization 43, 44n, 122, 227–30, 232, 234
  state of 45–61
  teachers *see* teachers
  teaching *see* teaching
  see also examinable PE; extra-curricular PE; quality PE; sport
Physical Education Association of the United Kingdom (PEA-UK) 22n
Physical Education Initial Teacher

Training (PEITT) 210–13, 224
Physical Education, School Sport and Club Links (PESSCL) strategy 37–9, 40–1, 57
physical educationalists 24, 42, 231
physical skills, and sport 157
'planning, performing and evaluation' 34, 36, 226n
playing fields *see* public playing fields; school playing fields
policy 23–44, 132
  basic questions about 23
  blindness of 29
  conflict in implementation 26
  definition 23–4
  goals 24, 39–41, 205
  ideology 29–30, 36
  likely outcomes 41–2
  networks 24–5, 28, 233
  power balances, shifting 27–8, 42
  power relations 26–7, 41–2
  process 25, 26, 30–9
  significance for practitioners 42–4
  as statement of intent 23
pool 182
Position Statement on Physical Education 16
power balances, shifting 27–8, 42
power relations, policy and 26–7, 41–2
practical knowledge 8, 11–12
primary schools
  extra-curricular PE 64, 65, 66, 69, 73
  facilities 47
  gender, PE and sport 56, 140
  links between sports clubs and 57
  National Curriculum 34
  number and range of activities 55
  progress in participation 38
  sport provision 56, 57
  sporting curriculum packages 33
  teachers 38, 49, 50–1
  time allocation, PE 52
professional socialization
  through CPD 216–18
  through PEITT 210–13
professionalization of PE 91–2, 218
Programmes of Study (NCPE) 34
propositional knowledge 8, 11, 22n, 93

psychological health 98–9
public playing fields 48
public sector facilities 127
Public Service Agreement Target, school
    sport 52
pupil choice, significance of 131–2
pupil compliance 220
pupil-centred teaching styles 221–2
pupil-teacher ratios 50
pupils
    cultural clash between teachers and
        178–9
    gifted and talented 41, 58, 205
    middle class youngsters as ideal 163
    PE according to 19–20
    power resources between teachers and
        27–8
    see also boys; girls
push-pull effects, stereotypical
    assumptions 167

qualifications
    PE and sport-related 81
    see also Advanced (A) Level; General
        Certificate of Secondary Education
Qualifications and Curriculum
    Authority (QCA) 7, 21, 51, 79
quality PE 222–3, 226n

race, and ethnicity 168–72
racial stereotypes 167, 176
Ramadan 178, 179
recreational, PE as 20
recreational activities 76, 119, 125–6,
    127, 140, 194
recreationalism/academic dilemma 10
recruitment potential, examinable PE 92
reflective practice 223, 226n
reflective practitioners 223–4
religion
    conflicts between teachers and pupils
        178
    demands of PE 179
    and ethnicity 171, 172–4
    and participation 71, 183
reluctant participants 139
reproduction styles, teaching 221
resources
    class sizes and pressure on 50

mainstreaming and inclusion 197
sportization of PE 229
role models, motivation toward sport
    132
rollerblading 121
rounders 55, 57, 69, 70, 140, 195, 202
rugby 55, 56, 57, 69, 70, 140, 148, 157
running 120, 121, 140

sailing 55, 160
Scandinavia 119
    see also Denmark; Norway; Sweden
school experiences, and social class 158
school playing fields, sale of 48, 59
school sport 52, 228–9
School Sport Alliance 34
School Sport Coordinators (SSCOs) 37,
    38–9, 73
School Sport Partnerships 38–9, 50, 54,
    55, 57, 72–3, 180
    see also Loughborough Partnership
        survey
School Sport Survey (2005–06) 38, 52–3,
    55, 57
schooling 12
schools
    gender and participation 152
    performance as measurement of
        standard 91
    see also primary schools; secondary
        schools
Scotland
    doubling of sugar-intake 103
    extra-curricular PE 65, 69, 73
secondary schools
    curricular PE, time allocation 52–3
    disabled youngsters 194
    extra-curricular PE 63, 64–5, 66, 69,
        70, 73
    facilities 46–7, 48
    gender and participation 56, 140, 141
    National Curriculum 34
    number and range of activities 55
    social class and PE 163
    sports provision 57
    teachers 49
    teaching styles 221
sedentary behaviours/lifestyle 104, 105,
    107

self-consciousness 146, 149
self-determination 131
self-image 145–7
'self-teaching' style 220
SENCOs *see* Special Educational Needs
    Coordinators
sex
    and extra-curricular PE 66–7, 70
    and gender 138
sexualization, female body 146
shame 146
'shared illusion' 22
significant others, desirability of
    examinable PE 90
Sikhs 169, 170, 171
skateboarding 73, 76, 121
skiing 157, 160
skill acquisition 18–19
skittles 202
slippage, implementation of policy 43
snooker 182
soccer 55, 58, 119, 120, 140, 177, 182
see also football
social capital 155
social class 154–65
    cultural dimension 155–6
    defining 154–5
    education 158–9
    examinable PE 84
    gender, ethnicity and sport and PE
        163–4
    health 106–7
    physical dimensions 156–8
    physical education 163
    social dimensions 155
    sport participation 159–63, 183
social dynamics, gender and 151–2
social model of disability 189
social networks 125
socialization
    class-based orientations 157
    gender 147, 149–51
    sports participation 162
    teachers 208–18
    young people 125
socially constructed bodies, young
    people 157
socially constructed nature of PE 13–14,
    214

socially-oriented pursuits 134
socio-economic status *see* social class
softball 55, 58
South Asians 67, 169, 172, 175, 177, 178,
    179, 182, 183
    see also Bangladeshis; Pakistanis
Spain 118, 120
special educational needs *see* disability
    and SEN
Special Educational Needs Coordinators
    (SENCOs) 198–9
specialist coaches 50
specialist schools programme 32–3
Specialist Sport Coordinators 73
Specialist Sports Colleges 32, 33, 37–8,
    44n, 50
Sport: Raising the Game 35–6, 56
Sport for All 123
sport education 15
Sport England 24, 28, 47, 48, 55, 56, 68,
    76, 118, 132, 139, 140, 142, 150,
    166n, 181, 193, 201–2, 206n
sport scientists 107
sporting bias, extra-curricular PE 71, 72
sporting curriculum packages 33
A Sporting Future for All 37
sportization 43, 44n, 122, 227–30, 232,
    234
sport(s)
    continuation in 135
    curricular provision 56–8
    disability and 201–3
    ethnicity and 180–4
    extra-curricular PE 68–72
    facilities *see* facilities
    health promotion 99–102, 112–13
    justifying as valued cultural practice
        14–16
    moral, health and aesthetic education
        10
    number and range of activities 54–6
    performance, played down emphasis
        on 36–7
    social class 159–63
    see also school sport; youth sport
sports academies 63, 73
sports centres 48–9, 59, 127–8
sports clubs 38, 57, 121, 126, 160
Sports Coach UK 50

Sports Council for Wales 64
sports development officers (SDOs) 24, 41, 50, 75, 233
sports literacy 130
SportScotland study 140, 141, 149
Sportsmark/Sportsmark Gold 35–6
sporty types 139
squash 160
standards of attainment, in PE 84–6
stereotypes see gender stereotypes; racial stereotypes
structural effects, alienation from PE 185
subjective warrant 213
sugar intake 103
support, and inclusion 198–9
Sweden 51, 171
swimming 56, 69, 70, 76, 120, 121, 140, 142, 144, 160, 182, 191, 194, 195, 202, 203, 206n
Switzerland 123
syllabi, examinable PE 92–3

table tennis 55, 120
task-oriented dispositions 129, 130
teacher-centred instructional styles 221
teachers
    adaptation of practices for Muslim youngsters 180
    call for two hour curricular PE 53
    claims for efficacy of sport and PE 41
    cultural clash between pupils and 177, 178–9
    disability and SEN 195, 196, 199–200, 204–5
    ethnic minority, shortage of 184
    examinable PE 90
    extra-curricular PE 73–4
    frustrations with administrative demands 80
    gender stereotypes, reinforcement of 145
    PE according to 17–19, 21
    policy networks 24–5, 233
    power balances, shifting 27–8, 42
    power differentials between other parties and 26–7, 41–2
    push-pull effects, stereotypical assumptions 167

significance of policy for 42–4
socialization of 208–18
state of PE in terms of 49–51
see also 'good' teachers; head teachers; Link Teachers; reflective practitioners
teaching
    context of 224–5
    examinable PE 87
    science, art and craft of 219–24
    strategies 226n
    styles 144, 197–8, 219–22, 226n
teaching orientation 213
Teaching Physical Education 220
team games/sports 19, 35, 56, 67, 68, 69, 120, 121, 123, 126, 144, 163, 191, 194
television watching 104, 105
tennis 56, 57, 69, 76, 120, 140, 160
tenpin bowling 121, 140, 142, 202
theoretical knowledge 8, 22n
theoretical PE 85, 87, 88
time allocation
    curricular PE 51–4, 59
    extra-curricular PE 64
    GCSE PE 87–8
    PE, disabled youngsters 192–3
Title IX legislation 142, 148
TOFIs 108
TOP Play/Top Sport 32, 33
'traditional' curricula, replication of 209
'traditional' sports/games 57, 69, 120, 121, 123, 163, 191
trampolining 123
transitions, and drop out 133
transport problems, and participation 67, 71
triathlon 55
two hour curricular PE 53–4

'unadventurous' types 139
unhealthy behaviours, young people 103–4
United Kingdom
    co-educational PE 149
    government policy towards sport 132
    obesity problem 97, 107
    sedentary lives of children 97–8
    youth sport 120
    see also England; Scotland; Wales

United States
  co-educational PE 149
  competitive sports 71
  extra-curricular PE 62, 66, 71
  gender and participation 139
  inclusion 190
  legislation, gender and participation
    142, 148
  mainstreaming 191
  obesity 97, 107
  PE teachers 49–50
  sedentary lives of children 97–8
  social class and sport 160
  state of sport in 57–8
  time spent on PE 52
untapped potential 139
upper classes 160
use-value of examinations 28

valued cultural practice, sport as 14–16
vested interests, policy-makers and
    implementers 24, 29–30
volleyball 55, 56, 58, 123
voluntariness, sport participation 149

waist-hip ratio, cardiovascular risk 108
Wales
  balance of power in school sport 28
  club-based sport 126
  extra-curricular PE 64, 65, 66–7, 68,
    69
  time allocation, PE 59
walking 56, 120, 182, 202
weight
  self-image and PE 146
  see also obesity
weight training 142
weight-lifting 157, 160
Western Europe 126, 161
  see also individual countries
wheelchair users 67, 193, 194, 202, 206n
White Christians 171

White Papers 30
'wide sporting repertoires' 122, 123, 130,
    131
Wolfenden gap 59, 136n
women
  involvement in PE and sport 234–5
  see also young women
working classes 158, 160, 163
workplace socialization 90

young people
  alcohol consumption 103–4
  decline in fitness 98
  inactivity 98
  obesity 97
  psychological health 99
  sedentary leisure 104
  social class and participation in sport
    160–3
  socially constructed bodies 157
  see also mid-adolescence; new
    condition of youth
Young People with a Disability and Sport
    193
Young People and Sport in England 63, 140
young women
  leisure activities 235
  Muslim 174–6
  participation in sport 121, 139–40,
    142, 146
youth cultures, normalization of sport
    124, 133
youth sport 117–36
  facilities 127–8
  lifelong participation 128–32, 133,
    135
  multi-activity PE programmes 122–4
  participation 117–22, 133–4
  team games 120–1
  underlying assumptions in
    commentaries 117
Youth Sport Trust (YST) 28, 32–4, 55, 59